Financial Management and Risk Analysis Strategies for Business Sustainability

Joaquín Enríquez-Díaz
University of A Coruña, Spain

Laura Castro-Santos
University of A Coruña, Spain

Félix Puime-Guillén
University of A Coruña, Spain

IGI Global
PUBLISHER of TIMELY KNOWLEDGE

A volume in the Advances in Finance, Accounting, and Economics (AFAE) Book Series

Published in the United States of America by
IGI Global
Business Science Reference (an imprint of IGI Global)
701 E. Chocolate Avenue
Hershey PA, USA 17033
Tel: 717-533-8845
Fax: 717-533-8661
E-mail: cust@igi-global.com
Web site: http://www.igi-global.com

Library of Congress Cataloging-in-Publication Data

Names: Enríquez-Díaz, Joaquín, 1991- editor. | Castro-Santos, Laura, editor. | Puime-Guillén, Félix, 1963- editor.
Title: Financial management and risk analysis strategies for business sustainability / Joaquín Enríquez-Díaz, Laura Castro-Santos, and Félix Puime-Guillén.
Description: Hershey, PA : Business Science Reference, [2021] | Includes bibliographical references and index. | Summary: "This book proposes a series of practical and theoretical perspectives on how the business world has to evolve to adapt the new situation caused by the undeniable climate change, presenting productive processes and the internal organization of companies with the tools to navigate the costly and complex transition"-- Provided by publisher.
Identifiers: LCCN 2020049321 (print) | LCCN 2020049322 (ebook) | ISBN 9781799876342 (hardcover) | ISBN 9781799876359 (paperback) | ISBN 9781799876366 (ebook)
Subjects: LCSH: Management--Environmental aspects. | Organizational change. | Sustainable development. | Risk management.
Classification: LCC HD30.255 .F556 2021 (print) | LCC HD30.255 (ebook) | DDC 658.15--dc23
LC record available at https://lccn.loc.gov/2020049321
LC ebook record available at https://lccn.loc.gov/2020049322

This book is published in the IGI Global book series Advances in Finance, Accounting, and Economics (AFAE) (ISSN: 2327-5677; eISSN: 2327-5685)

British Cataloguing in Publication Data
A Cataloguing in Publication record for this book is available from the British Library.

For electronic access to this publication, please contact: eresources@igi-global.com.

Advances in Finance, Accounting, and Economics (AFAE) Book Series

Ahmed Driouchi
Al Akhawayn University, Morocco

ISSN:2327-5677
EISSN:2327-5685

Mission

In our changing economic and business environment, it is important to consider the financial changes occurring internationally as well as within individual organizations and business environments. Understanding these changes as well as the factors that influence them is crucial in preparing for our financial future and ensuring economic sustainability and growth.

The **Advances in Finance, Accounting, and Economics (AFAE)** book series aims to publish comprehensive and informative titles in all areas of economics and economic theory, finance, and accounting to assist in advancing the available knowledge and providing for further research development in these dynamic fields.

Coverage

- International Trade
- Economic Policy
- Finance
- Economics of Innovation and Knowledge
- Investments and Derivatives
- Economics of Migration and Spatial Mobility
- E-finance
- Economic Theory
- Economics Geography
- Corporate Finance

IGI Global is currently accepting manuscripts for publication within this series. To submit a proposal for a volume in this series, please contact our Acquisition Editors at Acquisitions@igi-global.com or visit: http://www.igi-global.com/publish/.

The Advances in Finance, Accounting, and Economics (AFAE) Book Series (ISSN 2327-5677) is published by IGI Global, 701 E. Chocolate Avenue, Hershey, PA 17033-1240, USA, www.igi-global.com. This series is composed of titles available for purchase individually; each title is edited to be contextually exclusive from any other title within the series. For pricing and ordering information please visit http://www.igi-global.com/book-series/advances-finance-accounting-economics/73685. Postmaster: Send all address changes to above address.

Titles in this Series

For a list of additional titles in this series, please visit: http://www.igi-global.com/book-series/advances-finance-accounting-economics/73685

Comparative Research on Earnings Management, Corporate Governance, and Economic Value
Elisabete S. Vieira (University of Aveiro, Portugal) Mara Madaleno (University of Aveiro, Portugal) and Graça Azevedo (University of Aveiro, Portugal)
Business Science Reference • © 2021 • 433pp • H/C (ISBN: 9781799875963) • US $215.00

Examining the Intersection of Circular Economy, Forestry, and International Trade
Badri Narayanan Gopalakrishnan (University of Washington, USA) Taranjeet Duggal (Amity University, India) and Tavishi Tewary (Amity University, India)
Business Science Reference • © 2021 • 315pp • H/C (ISBN: 9781799849902) • US $195.00

Influence of FinTech on Management Transformation
Amira Sghari (Faculty of Economics and Management, University of Sfax, Tunisia) and Karim Mezghani (Al Imam Mohammad Ibn Saud Islamic University, Saudi Arabia & University of Sfax, Tunisia)
Business Science Reference • © 2021 • 273pp • H/C (ISBN: 9781799871101) • US $215.00

Handbook of Research on Institutional, Economic, and Social Impacts of Globalization and Liberalization
Yilmaz Bayar (Bandirma Onyedi Eylul University, Turkey)
Information Science Reference • © 2021 • 699pp • H/C (ISBN: 9781799844594) • US $445.00

Bridging Microeconomics and Macroeconomics and the Effects on Economic Development and Growth
Pantelis C. Kostis (National and Kapodistrian University of Athens, Greece)
Business Science Reference • © 2021 • 340pp • H/C (ISBN: 9781799849339) • US $195.00

Machine Learning Applications for Accounting Disclosure and Fraud Detection
Stylianos Papadakis (Hellenic Mediterranean University, Greece) Alexandros Garefalakis (Hellenic Mediterranean University, Greece) Christos Lemonakis (Hellenic Mediterranean University, Greece) Christiana Chimonaki (University of Portsmouth, UK) and Constantin Zopounidis (School of Production Engineering and Management, Technical University of Crete, Greece & Audencia Business School, France)
Business Science Reference • © 2021 • 270pp • H/C (ISBN: 9781799848059) • US $225.00

Corporate Governance and Its Implications on Accounting and Finance
Ahmad Alqatan (University of Portsmouth, UK) Khaled Hussainey (University of Portsmouth, UK) and Hichem Khlif (University of Sfax, Tunisia)
Business Science Reference • © 2021 • 425pp • H/C (ISBN: 9781799848523) • US $195.00

IGI Global
PUBLISHER of TIMELY KNOWLEDGE

701 East Chocolate Avenue, Hershey, PA 17033, USA
Tel: 717-533-8845 x100 • Fax: 717-533-8661
E-Mail: cust@igi-global.com • www.igi-global.com

Editorial Advisory Board

Table of Contents

Section 2
Business Sustainability

Detailed Table of Contents

In this chapter, the VaR of the MSCI emerging market index (MSCI-EMI) developed by Morgan Stanley Capital International (MSCI) is estimated using linear, nonlinear time series and ANN. In this context, the aim of the study is to estimate the VaR exceedance of the MSCI-EMI as a global financial risk indicator compared with traditional time series methods and ANN. In addition, the most effective method on this index is determined by statistical information criteria, and the comparative evaluation of the model selection criteria is carried out. The period of analysis is between December 1987-April 2020 with monthly frequency and VaR exceedance obtained with ARMA-GARCH, TGARCH, EGARCH, GJR, and ANN models. Confidence levels of models, VaR exceedance, and Kupeic statistics are obtained. VaR exceedances are examined through the superior model.

Innovation is an essential aspect for the sustainable development of small and medium-sized enterprises (SMEs). Defining formulas to encourage innovation is therefore crucial. Financial literacy is an area of growing interest in both theory and practice and its relationship with innovation performance has been little studied. This chapter examines the importance of financial literacy for business innovation and the effect that risk-taking has on this relationship. Using a quantitative approach, 309 Spanish SMEs of different sectors are analysed. A mediation analysis shows both a direct and an indirect positive effect on innovation. Thus, this chapter brings insights, developing the existing literature of SMEs. So, it contributes to broaden the scope of the innovation and therefore the sustainable development of these firms. Practical implications are presented for four differentiated areas, which may enhance the sustainable development of SMEs: business management, entrepreneurship, public policies, and university.

Universities are experiencing a transition to sustainable universities, as addressing environmental concerns has become a cornerstone for the governance of higher education institutions. As responsible for the formation of decision-makers and because of its duty with the society, these institutions must be

Preface

The book will propose a series of practical and theoretical perspectives on how the business world has to evolve to adapt the new situation we have reached due to an undeniable climate change that forces us to redefine the productive processes and the internal organization of companies.

We intend with it to provide the instruments and the adequate knowledge that facilitates to the companies this transition so complex and of enormous cost.

The book comprises financial management, risk analysis and business sustainability.

In September 2015, 193 countries committed to 17 Sustainable Development Goals, promoted by the United Nations with a compliance objective by 2030. That is why companies must also consider sustainability as a basic requirement in order to develop their activities.

Therefore, sustainability, is a fact to consider if we want to understand the changes that are coming in the business world and in its different areas of management.

Companies must reorient their business objectives towards sustainable and responsible production with the environment and society. Based on this, companies have to readjust their innovation, finance, human resources, accounting department, etc., in order to meet these new challenges.

In this context of changes, it is important to open the debate and obtain a more thorough knowledge on how companies should change their leaderships strategies, carry out their financial planning as well as analyse the risk of their clients and innovative projects that respect the environment, both from a theoretical and practical perspective.

In this book we intend to answer questions such as: how will the new business leadership be outlined that knows how to combine growth with sustainability? What will be the way to finance new innovative projects? What costs caused by negative externalities with the environment should be taken into account? and, how can we value them?

In this context, we open the participation to collaborators of a wide variety of disciplines, who can provide different perspectives and points of view on how to respond to the new challenges that arise from the need that companies have to focus their development on a sustainable way.

This book can be useful for researchers in the areas of management, human resources, accounting and finance, taxation, environmental economics and some engineering areas. It can also be useful for business managers and investors who have to make business decisions in this new environment of changes caused by the need to redirect management towards a more sustainable world. In addition, young researchers or predoctoral students can use this book in order to have more information on this topic.

The book is composed by two sections:

- **Section 1:** Financial Management and Risk Analysis

- **Section 2:** Business Sustainability

Firstly, Part 1 talks about the importance of financial education towards a sustainable development, the real options for the valuation of an investment project, a comparative analysis of value at risk and a financial literacy and innovation performance in SM
Es.

Then, Section 1 is composed by Chapter 1 to Chapter 4:

- **Ch. 1:** The Role of Financial Education in the Path Towards Sustainable Development: A Practical Experience With Students of Secondary Education
- **Ch. 2:** Real Options for the Valuation of Investment Project: Practical Case
- **Ch. 3:** Comparative Analysis of Value at Risk (VaR) of MSCI-EMI With Traditional Time Series Methods and ANN
- **Ch. 4:** Financial Literacy and Innovation Performance in SMEs: The Mediating Effect of Risk-Taking

Chapter 1 shows that the financial decisions are present in everyone's daily life. However, citizens do not always have sufficient knowledge to understand the consequences of their decisions and the risks taken. The lack of financial literacy can contribute, along with other factors, to making wrong financial decisions. This is why financial education becomes a key element to achieve a more sustainable and egalitarian future. This research presents a practical experience intended to foster financial education among high school students. The experience consisted in providing training workshops about financial topics, specifically adapted to the students' needs. The students' level of financial knowledge was evaluated and also their level of satisfaction with the experience. Results showed a high level of satisfaction and a significant improvement in their level of knowledge. The research also helped to identify the students' socio-demographic characteristics that explain the differences in their level of financial culture and their capacity for improvement.

Chapter 2 analyses the methodology for evaluating investment projects through real options. The limitations of traditional models based on cash flows and the current environment that presents constant changes and high uncertainty have led to a new field of research, real options. The valuation of investment projects carries inherent decision-making, where the best options for the company are analyzed, the real options providing a decision flexibility that classic models do not provide. This chapter contains the most important theoretical framework, where the beginnings of this methodology, the most important types of options and the methodology for their evaluation are discussed, as well as two practical examples for a better understanding of this methodology.

Chapter 3 estimates the VaR of the MSCI Emerging Market Index (MSCI-EMI) index developed by Morgan Stanley Capital International (MSCI) using linear, nonlinear time series and ANN. In this context the aim of the study is to estimate the VaR exceedance of the MSCI-EMI as a global financial risk indicator compared with traditional time series methods and ANN. In addition, the most effective method on this index is determined by statistical information criteria and the comparative evaluation of the model selection criteria is carried out. The period of analysis is between December 1987-April 2020 with monthly frequency and VaR exceedance are obtained with ARMA-GARCH, TGARCH, EGARCH, GJR and ANN models. Confidence levels of models, VaR exceedance and Kupeic statistics are obtained. VaR exceedances are examined through the superior model.

Innovation is an essential aspect for the sustainable development of small and medium-sized enterprises (SMEs). Defining formulas to encourage innovation is therefore crucial. Financial literacy is an area of growing interest in both theory and practice and its relationship with innovation performance has been little studied. Chapter 4 examines the importance of financial literacy for business innovation and the effect that risk-taking has on this relationship. Using a quantitative approach, 309 Spanish SMEs of different sectors are analyzed. A mediation analysis shows both a direct and an indirect positive effect on innovation. Thus, this chapter brings insights, developing the existing literature of SMEs. So, it contributes to broaden the scope of the innovation and therefore the sustainable development of these firms. Practical implications are presented for four differentiated areas, which may enhance the sustainable development of SMEs: business management, entrepreneurship, public policies and university.

Secondly, Part 2 talks about the confluence of sustainability and governance at an university, the evolution and future of the marketing and sustainability, the breaking barriers to promote sustainable development in the wine industry and in the textile industry, the country-level determinants of sustainability reporting in emerging markets, the importance of reviving green with accounting, the European perspective of the circular economy and the importance of the corporate social responsibility.

Therefore, Section 2 is composed by Chapter 5 to Chapter 12.

- **Ch. 5:** The Confluence of Sustainability and Governance at the Universidade da Coruña (Spain): A Case Study
- **Ch. 6:** Evolution and Future of the Marketing and Sustainability Linkage: Towards a Civil Marketing Approach
- **Ch. 7:** Breaking Barriers to Promote Sustainable Development in the Wine Industry: A Theoretical Study on the Role of the Entrepreneurial Ecosystem Approach
- **Ch. 8:** Open Innovation as a Strategy to Sustainably Compete in the Textile Industry
- **Ch. 9:** The Country-Level Determinants of Sustainability Reporting in Emerging Markets
- **Ch. 10:** Advancement of Circular Economy: The European Perspective
- **Ch. 11:** The Corporate Social Responsibility on Capital Market: Myth or Reality?
- **Ch. 12:** Offshore Wind as a Base for a New Sustainable Business

Universities are experiencing a transition to sustainable universities, as addressing environmental concerns has become a cornerstone for the governance of Higher Education institutions. As responsible for the formation of decision-makers and because of its duty with the society, these institutions must be in line with the current society. Chapter 5 deals with the implementation of sustainable procedures and initiatives in a concrete university: the Universidade da Coruña in Spain. Great efforts have been done regarding raising awareness on environmental issues and the implementation of sustainable procedures, even with limited economic resources. As a result, this University is very well positioned in international rankings and has a great potential in the field of sustainable development.

The pairing of sustainability and marketing has been around for several decades and has opened new standards in management and marketing. The main objective of Chapter 6 is trifold. First, to shed some light on the distinctions between sustainability marketing and analogous terms. Second, to review some of the criticisms that have arisen, (i.e., greenwashing or green marketing myopia). Finally, we offer a broader term for the marketing and sustainability link. The chapter will review the evolution of these concepts and present future directions of the sustainability and marketing linkage. Taking as a starting point theory that propose a new relationship between society and companies (civil economy, corporate citizenship) and the new paradigm of marketing (Achrol and Kotler), the authors also put forth a wholesome concept: civic marketing. This concept balances the two objectives expected in a marketing approach: positive business results and customer satisfaction- in a sustainable economy.

The focus on sustainability is one of the different strategies adopted by companies looking for arguments for their differentiation from other competitors. Implementing this concept in the wine industry implies environmental soundness, social equity, and economic feasibility since when pursuing sustainable development, these companies are protecting the identity of their terroirs. Nevertheless, this is not an easy task because companies have to face several potential barriers to the adoption of sustainable practices. Therefore, the objective of Chapter 7 is to introduce the entrepreneurial ecosystem approach (EEA) as an instrument to help to understand and identify the mechanisms to remove the barriers to the adoption of sustainable practices in the wine industry, preparing the ground for a more detailed investigation to assess the effective implementation of the EEA.

Innovation is crucial for business in order to meet consumers' need and stakeholders' expectations. Innovation emerges as a must for all activity sectors, including the textile industry. Change can be an opportunity for organizations that present competitive advantages and new solutions. However, not always changes are directly visible and innovation by nature is impossible to quantify and measure. This intangibility requires tools to help managers monitor the results of their investment. Chapter 8 applies the Innovation Scoring 1.0, a Portuguese tool for companies to self-evaluate in what concerns innovation, efficiency and profitability improvement. It is structured in three main parts: literature review, case study and conclusions. The study showed that company may improve its results through open innovation, being leadership and organizational culture determinants in the process.

Chapter 9 examines the role of the institutional environment in the adoption of GRI-based sustainability reporting in emerging markets. Panel data analysis of the relevant data of firms from twenty emerging markets provides evidence that environmental, social, and governance performance, financial structure, and cultural dimensions are the institutional drivers of corporate social responsibility disclosure which was measured by publishing a GRI-based sustainability report. Overall findings of the study show that strategic decisions regarding CSR disclosure of companies are shaped by the institutional context in which they operate.

Chapter 10 provides an overview of the topic circular economy from a European perspective. It focuses on the actual implementation of circular models and processes. Although the European Commission has been trying to address the issue for years and provides many measures, the results of different indicators show a lack of implementation. Therefore, the main challenge of the next stage of development of Circular Economy 4.0 is to develop an inclusive system that involves all relevant stakeholders. This is because only through the efforts of limited groups of stakeholders (e.g., companies), the concept cannot be fully implemented in practice. Instead, the circular economy must become part of the broader culture, way of thinking and acting of all stakeholders involved. This issue represents the main challenges for the next ten-year period in Europe.

The challenges generated by climate change have led to a greater involvement of companies in promoting the principles of sustainable development, one of the tools used being social responsibility programs. International organizations have launched various initiatives or principles to support companies in this complex process of transition to the green economy. Authors focused their analysis on the involvement of stock exchanges in the process of promotion of corporate social responsibility. The objective of Chapter 11 is to identify the main tools used by stock exchanges in order to model the behavior of listed companies. In particular, the activity of the Bucharest Stock Exchange was analyzed. Even if it is an emerging market, the efforts made by this stock exchange and the results obtained can be used as a benchmark by stock exchanges in the region.

The aim of Chapter 12 is to examine the offshore wind as a pillar for a new sustainable business. In this context, the chapter firstly analyses the significance of renewable energies. Secondly, it analyses several types of offshore renewable energies, the state of offshore wind energy in Europe and the projections of offshore wind in the world. Thirdly, it presents an overview of the Levelized Cost Of Energy (LCOE), comparing its value for different energy technologies. Moreover, a new concept, called SCOE is introduced to incorporates society in the LCOE equation. Finally, conclusions talk about the importance of choosing a sustainable way of generating electricity in our future.

This book will have a great impact in the financial management, the risk analysis and the business sustainability of enterprises. Giving them new tools to simplify their transition to a sustainable way of understanding their work and reducing the climate change in order to adequate their activities to the present and future regulation of Governments.

Enterprises must change their business goals to be environmentally friendly in order to coexist with nature and society. This book is a very good starting point of this new way of understanding our future world.

Section 1

Financial Management and Risk Analysis

Chapter 1
The Role of Financial Education in the Path Towards Sustainable Development:
A Practical Experience With Students of Secondary Education

Raquel González Castro
University of A Coruña, Spain

Joaquín Enríquez-Diaz
https://orcid.org/0000-0001-8711-0795
University of A Coruña, Spain

Begoña Alvarez García
https://orcid.org/0000-0001-7918-3986
University of A Coruña, Spain

ABSTRACT

Financial decisions are present in everyone's daily life. However, citizens do not always have sufficient knowledge to understand the consequences of their decisions and the risks taken. The lack of financial literacy can contribute, along with other factors, to making wrong financial decisions. This is why financial education becomes a key element to achieve a more sustainable and egalitarian future. This research presents a practical experience intended to foster financial education among high school students. The experience consisted in providing training workshops about financial topics, specifically adapted to the students' needs. The students' level of financial knowledge was evaluated and also their level of satisfaction with the experience. Results showed a high level of satisfaction and a significant improvement in their level of knowledge. The research also helped to identify the students' socio-demographic characteristics that explain the differences in their level of financial culture and their capacity for improvement.

DOI: 10.4018/978-1-7998-7634-2.ch001

INTRODUCTION

All citizens at some point in their life have to make decisions related to economic and financial issues, such as opening a bank account, requesting a debit or credit card from a bank, buying a house and financing it with a mortgage loan, etc. However, sometimes citizens do not have the necessary knowledge to make these decisions, so they do not understand the risks that they are being taken and the consequences of their decisions (e.g. Cardaci, 2018).

This lack of knowledge is a serious problem from the individuals' point of view, because it can have a very negative impact on the management of personal finances, but also from the macroeconomic point of view, because it can jeopardize the financial system and the global economy as the global financial crisis of 2007 revealed.

This situation also affects young people. At present they have to face various challenges that did not exist in the past such as the increasing complexity of the financial products or the fast development of the financial market in a context in which the contact among customers and markets is becoming more direct. Likewise, youngsters are holders of financial products (such as a bank account), they make payments from their mobile phones, and they buy products from the internet, which implies the use of credit cards. This means that young people come into contact with financial products and make financial decisions from a very early age. Therefore, it is important that financial education begins at school, as early as possible, to prepare young people for adult life (OECD, 2005; Comisión de las Comunidades Europeas, 2007; Ibrahim et al., 2010; Lusardi et al., 2010; OECD, 2014; Ministerio de Educación, Cultura y Deporte, 2017)

Financial education has been defined by the Organization for Economic Co-operation and Development (OECD) as "*... the process by which financial consumers improve their understanding of financial products, concepts and risks and, through information, instruction and/or objective advice, develop the skills and confidence to become more aware of financial risks and opportunities, to make informed choices, to know where to go for help, and to take other effective actions to improve their financial well-being*" (OECD, 2005).

The main objective of financial education is that citizens become able to make informed decisions in financial matters. This means that citizens understand the financial products available on the market and are aware of the consequences associated with them. Consequently, financial education becomes a tool of empowerment for citizens that allows them to enhance individual well-being and improve the welfare of the society (e.g. Jappelli & Padula, 2013 Grohmann et al., 2018). This is why financial education is seen as a key element to achieve a more sustainable and egalitarian future or, in other words, it is a tool to achieve sustainable development.

The concept of sustainable development became known with the publication in 1987 of the report *Our Common Future*, also called the *Brundtland Report* (Rivera Hernández et al., 2017, López et al., 2018). In this report the sustainable development was presented as the development that "*...meets the needs of the present generation without compromising the ability of future generations to meet their own needs*" (WCED, 1987). Hence, it is a concept that refers to a certain balance between economic growth, environmental care, and social welfare.

Over the years, this concept has spread to all areas of society and has become more popular, although the decisive boost came in the year 2015 when world leaders adopted a set of 17 global goals for sustainable development that aim to eradicate poverty, protect the environment, and ensure prosperity for all.

These objectives are a call for action by all countries and constitute the sustainable development agenda for the coming years.

Financial education contributes to achieving several of these 17 sustainable development goals (SDG), in particular the SDG 4 "Quality education", the SDG 5 "Gender equality", the SDG 8 "Decent work and economic growth", the SDG 10 "Reduced inequalities", the SDG 12 "Responsible consumption and production", and the SDG 17 "Partnerships for the goals". For all these reasons, financial education has become a priority for governments, regulatory agencies, and international institutions. It is also a topic of particular interest to scholars (e.g. Hastings & Tejeda-Ashton, 2008; Lusardi & Tufano, 2015; Elan, 2011; Bayar et al., 2017; Grohmann et al., 2018) and institutions that are trying to develop training initiatives in financial education.

In this regard, this chapter presents a practical training experience intended to promote financial education among high school students. The experience consisted in providing training workshops about financial topics, specifically adapted to the students' needs. The objective of this experience was twofold. On the one hand, improving the level of financial education of the students. On the other hand, identifying the socio-demographic characteristics of the students that are related to their level of financial knowledge.

To do this, the chapter is structured as follows. The *Background* section refers to the implications that a lack of financial education may have on individuals' financial decisions and shows some socio-demographic characteristics/factors that are related to the individuals' level of financial education. The section entitled *Main Focus of the Chapter* shows the training workshops that were designed to improve the level of financial education of a group of high school students and the stages followed in their implementation. The students' level of financial knowledge was evaluated before and after taking part in the training workshops in order to know to what extent the training had a positive impact on their learning. Additionally, the level of satisfaction of the students with the training workshops was evaluated. The section entitled *Solutions and recommendations* shows some useful ideas to try to make financial education reach young people all over the Spanish country and not just those in a particular high school. Finally, the *Conclusion* section refers to the advantages that could arise from improving the level of financial education in the country as a whole.

BACKGROUND

There are many models, which began with the contributions of Modigliani and Brumberg (1954) and Friedman (1957), that explore consumers' behavior by relying on the premise that consumers are rational and have unlimited information. This means that consumers won't spend all their capital when they are making profits but, on the contrary, they will save for those moments when income decreases, ensuring their capacity to pay for their consumption at every time. Therefore, consumers would follow optimal saving and consumption patterns throughout their lives.

However, these models may only be fulfilled in practice if individuals have the ability to perform complex calculations and, at the same time, have the knowledge and experience necessary to access the financial markets (Lusardi & Mitchell, 2016). Unfortunately this does not always happen in real life. In fact, many scholars have shown that in reality there is a lack of financial literacy that may have serious implications on individuals' financial decisions (e.g. Chen & Volpe, 1998; Lusardi et al., 2010; Ibrahim et al., 2010). People with a low level of financial literacy seem to be more likely to have debt problems than the others (Lusardi & Tufano, 2015). Likewise, those people find it more difficult to take advantage of the markets and financial products. For example, they are less likely to invest in the stock market (Van Rooi et al., 2007), choose investment funds with the lowest fees (Hastings & Tejeda-Ashton 2008), accumulate wealth and manage it effectively (e.g. Hilgert et al., 2003; Stango & Zinman 2007), or take out a pension plan (e.g. Lusardi & Mitchell 2007, 2011, 2017).

The level of financial knowledge of people can be improved with appropriate training, although it should not be forgotten that it is directly related to their socio-demographic characteristics. Thus, authors such as Delavande et al. (2008), Lusardi and Tufano (2009, 2015), Lusardi et al. (2010), Agnew and Harrison (2015), and Lusardi and Mitchell (2017) show that men have a higher level of financial literacy than women. Hsu (2011) claims that these differences may be the result of racial and cultural issues, so there could be different degrees of gender bias in the level of financial literacy. These gender differences are probably due to the division of domestic tasks, because the domestic finances are normally the responsibility of men.

Another important socio-demographic characteristic for young people is the parents' educational level. Thus, Lusardi et al. (2010) contend that there is a relationship between the students' level of financial literacy and the educational level of their parents, which is fundamentally due to the fact that parents are one of the main sources of information to acquire this type of knowledge. According to Lusardi et al. (2010), students' whose parents do not have either higher education or sophisticated financial products (such as stocks or a pension scheme) are much less likely to know concepts (such as risk diversification) which are essential to make decisions about saving and investing. In this regard, Mancebón et al. (2018) claim that family has a dual impact. On the one hand, the level of education of the mother has a positive impact on the children' mathematical abilities. On the other hand, the professional status of the father has a positive impact on the children' financial abilities. Mancebón et al. (2018) also contend that financial skills depend on mathematical skills.

There are also differences between people who live in the city and those who live in rural areas. As Agnew and Harrison (2015) point out, this happens because social interactions in the workplace or in the community are paths to acquire financial knowledge and these social interactions are more likely to occur in more populated areas.

Regarding the age, some scholars claim that there is a lower level of knowledge among the youth, due to lack of experience, and among people over the age of 60, due to the constant innovation in financial products (e.g. Elan, 2011).

In view of the above, it is important to take into account the socio-demographic characteristics of the students who have participated in the training experience presented in this chapter.

MAIN FOCUS OF THE CHAPTER

Financial education is a potent tool to empower people, whatever their age, because it enables them to make informed decisions with confidence and knowledge. This knowledge helps them to manage their personal finances, but it has also positive effects on markets. In fact, if consumers are better informed and have skills to make economic and financial decisions by themselves, they are going to change their behavior towards a more responsible consumption. Likewise, consumers will be much more demanding, with, in turn, will lead to more quality, competitiveness, and innovation in the financial system. This change will give people more confidence and will help them to develop more sustainable entrepreneurial projects and initiatives.

Given the key role of financial education to empower people, it is important to develop initiatives that help improve their financial knowledge and, in the case of young people, it would be advisable to train them from an early age. In this regard, this chapter presents a practical training experience intended to improve the financial literacy of a group of high school students. To do this, a first survey was carried out in order to evaluate their initial level of knowledge and, subsequently, training materials (adapted to their needs) and training workshops were designed. After training, two more surveys were carried out to 1) know the level of knowledge acquired by the students and 2) know their level of satisfaction with the experience. Additionally, the relation between the socio-demographic characteristics of students and their level of knowledge was examined. In light of these considerations, the main objectives of this chapter are:

1. Evaluating the level of financial literacy of a group of 116 high school students.
2. Training these students according to their initial level of financial knowledge.
3. Assessing whether their degree of knowledge improved after the training.
4. Assessing their level of satisfaction with the training experience.
5. Detecting the factors that lead to significant differences in the students' level of knowledge.

On the basis of the above, this research was structured in four stages that will be explained in detail below.

Stage 1. Selecting the Collaborating Entity and Students

The first step taken in this research was to select a high school interested in collaborating in the challenge of improving the financial education of its students. The High School *Concepción Arenal* in Ferrol (Spain) was chosen for several reasons: it is a big school that has a large number of students (908 students were enrolled in the academic year 2019-2020) and it receives students with different socio-demographic profiles in spite of being located in the center of the city. The second step was to choose the specific students who would participate in the training workshops. The total sample was made up of 116 participants, aged between 15 and 18 years. Table 1 shows the characteristics of the sample.

Table 1. Sample characteristics

Sample Characteristics		Students (%)
Gender	Men	43.10%
	Women	56.90%
Place of residence	Country	22.81%
	City	77.19%
Academic year	Year 11th of Secondary School	38.79%
	Year 12th of Secondary School	61.21%

Source: Prepared by the authors

Stage 2. Identifying the Needs

In order to identify the students' needs data was collected from students through a paper survey during the first work session at the High School *Concepción Arenal.* This survey was useful to know the starting point in terms of financial knowledge and understand the students' needs. At the beginning of the session, each student was assigned a unique numerical code that they would keep in all sessions to ensure the anonymity. This code was written in the survey that every student had to answer. The survey was structured into two blocks: a socio-demographic block and a block related to economic and financial knowledge.

Socio-demographic Block

The first part of the survey was designed to collect socio-demographic data in order to get to know the students better. Some of the questions asked were related to the students' environment, such as the mark obtained in mathematics in the previous year, the language used at home (because in Ferrol students can speak Spanish or Galician), the level of education of their parents, the profession of their parents, if students live in the city or in the country, if they have their own computer or tablet, if they have a bank card, if they consider that economy is important in their daily life, etc. There were several types of questions: closed-answer questions, dichotomous questions (yes/no), and questions measured by a Likert scale of 1-5. Collecting the socio-demographic characteristics of students was very important to know them and identify the key variables that might explain (in the statistical analysis) the differences in the level of knowledge.

Block Related to Economic and Financial Knowledge

Several questions were asked in the second block in order to: 1) know the students' initial level of economic and financial knowledge and 2) detect the training needs to design the training workshops. The second block included 20 questions, in each one of them students had to choose a valid answer from four possible options. All questions include the option "I don't know" to avoid blank answers and identify the cases not answered because of the lack of knowledge. The questions raised were related to several important topics of financial education, such as savings, investment, risk, and payment methods, among others. Here is the content of the questions:

- Question 1. It was related to the legality of paying with a bill knowing that it is false. Students were required to identify whether or not this is a crime.
- Question 2. This question was related to the savings capacity of two people that applied two different savings patterns over time and students had to identify the concept of compound interest.
- Question 3. This question was related to secure transactions on internet. Students had to identify secure websites to do online purchases.
- Question 4. In this question students had to identify among several options which one was the more liquid asset.
- Question 5. This question was related to the bodies of the banking system that offer help when a consumer has a problem with a bank.
- Question 6. This question was related to the concept of financial income. Students had to apply very basic knowledge of financial laws, namely simple and/or compound capitalization, to respond to this question.
- Question 7. This question was related to the concepts of investment and financial risk.
- Question 8. This question was related to the payment methods. Students were asked about the differences between credit cards, debit cards, and department store credit cards.
- Question 9. This question was related to several methods of payment and student had to identify a bank draft.
- Question 10. This question was related to the concept of financial solvency. Students had information on the expenses, incomes and savings of several families and they had to determine which family had the best financial solvency.
- Question 11. This question was related to the concept of financial risk. Students had to distinguish between saving and investing and understand the relation of these actions with the concept of risk.
- Question 12. This question was related to the concepts of interest and inflation. Students had to determine the purchasing power of an individual by taking into account the effect that inflation and the interest rate have on this purchasing power.
- Question 13. This question was related to the types of currency.
- Question 14. This question was related to the students' capacity to do simple calculations in their daily lives and save money on their purchases. They had to choose the option that allowed them to save more money.
- Question 15. This question was related to the fraud on internet. Students were asked about the precautions that individuals should take if they receive an email from a bank asking for personal data but they are not sure if the sender is really a bank or it is a fraud.
- Question 16. This question was related to security in transactions and currency exchange.
- Question 17. This question was related to basic concepts that appear on an invoice.
- Question 18. This question was related to the concepts of banking commissions as well as those of the overdraft. Students should respond on the possible consequences of an overdraft in a bank account.
- Question 19. This question was related to the concept of risk diversification. Students were asked about the relationship between diversification and the evolution of the total risk supported by investors.
- Question 20. This question was related to the basic concepts that appear in a payroll.

Stage 3. Giving Economic and Financial Training

Training began at this stage, which was develop during the second session at the High School *Concepción Arenal.* The high school educational needs that were expressed by its management team during the first meeting and the data obtained from the initial survey were taken into account to design the training workshops. After identifying the most important topics to be addressed, a dynamic presentation was prepared. This presentation included practical and daily examples with a dual purpose: facilitate the understanding of financial concepts and, most importantly, show students that all of them appear in the everyday life of any person, even in their lives. With these examples, students became aware that financial education is a subject of concern to everyone (not only adults). Students' participation was encouraged at all times, so that they could openly expose what they knew about a topic and it was also a way to maintain their attention during every session.

Table 2. Content of the training activity

Economic and Financial Agenda Developed
Family Budget
The importance of saving
Savings vs. Investments
Investments and Risk
Risk diversification
Inflation
Spanish banking system
Currencies in the European Union
Security elements of a banknote
Cash Flow
Payment methods
Secure transactions over the internet and use of cards
Elements of an invoice
Interpretation of a payroll

Source: Prepared by the authors

Stage 4. Exploring Data From Students

This stage was developed during the third and last session at the High School *Concepción Arenal.* At the beginning of the session the training agenda continued and once completed, the survey on economic and financial concepts was carried out again. The survey included the same questions asked in the initial session and every student had the same numerical code. On this occasion the application *Plickers* was used for collecting data from students. In addition, students were asked to fill a new survey intended to know their degree of satisfaction with the training experience.

Initial Results (Before Taking Part in the Training Workshops)

The Stata version 15.1 program was used to process the data. An analysis of the results obtained was carried out to identify the concepts that seem to be more difficult and the possible significant differences according to the socio-demographic characteristics shown in Table 3.

Table 3. Distribution of the socio-demographic characteristics

Characteristics	Students (%)	
Gender	Men	42
	Women	56
Place of residence	City	77
	Country	23
Father's educational level	The father has university studies	23
	The father does not have university studies	77
Mother's educational level	The mother has university studies	33
	The father does not have university studies	67
Mathematics Level	Mark in mathematics < 8	85
	Mark in mathematics ≥ 8	15
Language level	Mark in language < 8	82
	Mark in language ≥ 8	18
Holding of banking products	Do not have a bank account	27
	Have a bank account	73
	Do not have a bank card	62
	Have a bank card	37
Purchasing power	The family do not have a high-income level	69
	The family have a high-income level	31

Source: Prepared by the authors

Table 4 shows the students' answers before participating in the training workshops.

It should be noted that only 19% of the students answered question 2 correctly. In this question, two different savings patterns (and related to different periods) were presented and students had to identify which one would generate a higher final amount by using a compound interest rate. Only 41% of the students correctly answered question 8 (related to payment methods), so it was found that students had problems to distinguish between debit and credit cards. 41% of students correctly answered to question 12 (related to the concepts of interest rate and inflation), so it became clear that there were problems to identify the effects of inflation on the raise or declining of the purchasing power. Regarding question 18, only 38% of the students answered correctly. In this question they were asked about overdrafts in a bank account. This question had two correct answers (the correct answer was "*c*" that said "*a and b are correct*") but it is striking that 34% of the participants marked the answer "*e*" that said "*I don't know*". Therefore it seems to indicate that many students did not know the concept of bank overdraft. Likewise, almost half of the students (48%) answered correctly to question 19 related to the positive effect that diversifying has on investor risk. In this case, more than half of students were unfamiliar with the relationship between diversification and risk.

Regarding the answers related to the socio-demographic questions, the results indicate several interesting outcomes.

Table 4. Correct answers to questions 1 to 20 and average of correct answers

Global Results	Q1	Q2	Q3	Q4	Q5	Q6	Q7	Q8	Q9	Q10	Q11	Q12	Q13	Q14	Q15	Q16	Q17	Q18	Q19	Q20	Average
% Correct initial survey answers	92%	19%	78%	66%	53%	72%	87%	41%	76%	74%	64%	41%	93%	74%	87%	75%	69%	38%	48%	72%	**66%**
Results According to the Socio-Demographic Variables																					
Men	94%	16%	84%	68%	50%	74%	92%	44%	68%	68%	64%	40%	88%	68%	86%	64%	68%	44%	46%	78%	**65%**
Women	91%	21%	74%	65%	55%	70%	82%	38%	82%	77%	64%	41%	95%	77%	86%	82%	70%	33%	48%	67%	**66%**
City	85%	8%	73%	65%	46%	73%	85%	19%	77%	81%	42%	27%	92%	58%	88%	65%	62%	31%	42%	62%	**59%**
Country	95%	23%	80%	68%	56%	72%	88%	47%	76%	73%	70%	45%	93%	78%	86%	78%	73%	39%	49%	75%	**68%**
The father has university studies	92%	12%	92%	72%	48%	76%	92%	20%	76%	88%	68%	40%	96%	80%	92%	72%	60%	52%	48%	76%	**68%**
The father does not have university studies	93%	21%	76%	64%	52%	71%	84%	44%	75%	68%	63%	39%	91%	70%	84%	75%	72%	36%	47%	70%	**65%**
The mother has university studies	92%	16%	89%	73%	54%	76%	95%	91%	76%	76%	59%	46%	95%	89%	95%	70%	73%	33%	54%	78%	**72%**
The mother does not have university studies	93%	20%	73%	65%	55%	72%	84%	43%	77%	72%	65%	40%	92%	68%	97%	79%	68%	49%	47%	69%	**66%**
Mark in mathematics < 8	91%	19%	79%	64%	48%	70%	84%	39%	74%	71%	62%	33%	92%	71%	85%	71%	66%	39%	43%	69%	**63%**
Mark in mathematics ≥ 8	100%	18%	76%	82%	76%	82%	100%	47%	88%	88%	76%	82%	94%	88%	94%	94%	88%	29%	71%	88%	**78%**
Mark in language < 8	92%	19%	77%	64%	48%	71%	85%	45%	76%	73%	62%	38%	91%	72%	85%	71%	65%	37%	41%	68%	**64%**
Mark in language ≥ 8	95%	19%	86%	76%	76%	76%	90%	19%	76%	76%	71%	52%	100%	81%	90%	90%	86%	43%	76%	86%	**73%**
Do not have a bank account	87%	19%	71%	55%	48%	68%	84%	29%	68%	74%	61%	32%	94%	77%	81%	81%	52%	29%	39%	65%	**61%**
Have a bank account	94%	19%	81%	71%	54%	73%	87%	45%	79%	73%	65%	44%	92%	75%	88%	72%	75%	41%	51%	74%	**68%**
Do not have a bank card	92%	18%	77%	68%	56%	73%	86%	36%	77%	74%	63%	40%	95%	77%	85%	79%	70%	38%	86%	73%	**68%**
Have a bank card	93%	21%	81%	63%	47%	72%	86%	49%	74%	72%	65%	42%	88%	67%	88%	65%	67%	37%	42%	72%	**65%**
The family do not have a high-income level	91%	21%	78%	68%	53%	71%	86%	44%	76%	74%	59%	43%	91%	76%	84%	76%	70%	38%	51%	75%	**66%**
The family have a high-income level	94%	14%	81%	64%	53%	72%	86%	33%	75%	72%	75%	36%	94%	67%	92%	69%	67%	39%	39%	64%	**64%**

Source: Prepared by the authors

The first socio-demographic variable is gender and, as it can be seen in Table 4, the percentage of correct answers for men and women is very similar. There were not significant differences. Therefore, this variable does not seem to have a determining influence on the level of financial knowledge. Hence, this research does not confirm the hypotheses (shown in the background section) held by several scholars that claim that men have a higher degree of knowledge than women. This result may be due to the fact that our sample is made up of young people between 15 and 18 years old that have hardly had contact with financial products or faced the economic challenges that are inherent to adult life (such as paying a rent, applying for a mortgage, planning the family budget, etc.). So far, they have received the same type of academic education, therefore gender in the younger population does not seem to be a factor that determines the level of knowledge, which reinforces the idea that other factors, such as racial and cultural issues associated with gender, may result in different degrees of gender bias in financial literacy.

Regarding the differences that may be explained by the place of residence (country vs. city), it should be noted that students who live in the city have a higher percentage of correct answers in all the questions. The difference in the average is 9%, which seems to indicate that in this case, as shown by Agnew and Harrison (2015), the place of residence can be a determining factor that leads to significant differences. The specific questions where there was greater difference are: question 2 (related to the savings capacity), question 5 (related to the right of consumers to submit a complaint when they have a problem with a bank and the bodies that may offer help to consumers), question 8 (related to the difference between debit and credit cards), question 11 (related to the difference between savings and investments), question 12 (related to the concepts of interest rate and inflation), and question 14 (related to the capacity of doing simple calculations when buying some product). In all of these questions there was a difference of 14%. Agnew and Harrison (2015) claimed in their research that these differences could be explained by the fact that people in the cities are in contact with many sources of information.

Concerning the impact that the educational level of parents has on the financial knowledge, it was found that the students whose parents have university studies have a higher average of correct answers. However, the difference is not very great. The percentage of correct answers in the case of students whose father has university studies is 3% higher than the percentage of those whose mother does not have higher education. In addition, students whose mother has university studies achieve an average of 72% of correct answers, which means that mother's studies are also a factor that can lead to differences. In general, everything suggests, as Mancebón et al. (2018) and Lusardi et al. (2010) claimed, that a higher educational level of parents has a positive impact on the level of economic and financial knowledge of high school students.

Results show that there is a direct relationship between the level of knowledge in mathematics and language and the level of financial knowledge. Students with a mark in mathematics greater than or equal to 8 have an average of 78% correct answers, the percentage of correct answers of students in this group is 15% higher than those of the students with a mark in mathematics lower than 8. Students with greater knowledge in mathematics experienced the greatest difficulties in questions 2 (related to the savings capacity), 8 (related to debit and credit cards), and 19 (related to diversification), which coincide with the questions that seem to be the most difficult in global terms. However, 82% of the students with a mark in mathematics higher than 8 answered correctly to question 12 (related to the concept of inflation), while only the 33% of the total students did it. Similarly, 79% of the student with a mark in mathematics higher than 8 answered correctly to question 19 (related to diversification), while only the 43% of the total students did it. Regarding the marks in language, students with a mark higher than 8 had an average of 73% correct answers, 9 percentage points higher than the average of students with a mark in language lower than 8. In short, these two socio-demographic variables characteristics could lead to significant differences.

Figure 1. Correct answers to questions 1 to 20 and average of correct answers before and after taking part in the training workshops
Source: Prepared by the authors

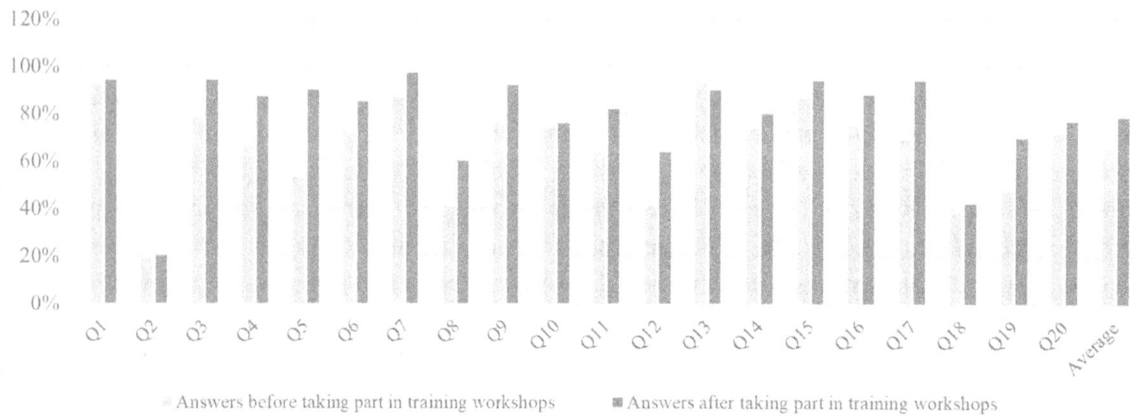

Regarding the real experience that students might have with financial products, two types of financial products were considered, bank accounts and bank cards. It should be noted that the greatest difference was among students who have a bank account and those who do not (7 percentage points). Students who have a bank account got a higher result with a difference of more than 14 percentage points in questions 4 (related to the liquidity of assets), 8 (related to debit and credit cards), 17 (related to invoices), and 19 (related to diversification and risk). Therefore, having some experience with financial products could lead to a significant positive difference. However, it is worth noting that question 18 (about the bank account overdraft) was only correctly answered by 41% of the students who have a bank account, what is indeed worrying because 59% of students who have a bank account are unaware of one of the most important risks associated with this product. The results among students with and without a bank card were very similar, although slightly higher among those who do not have bank cards. It is also quite worrying that 51% of students who have a bank card do not differentiate between credit and debit cards. If they use bank cards without knowing this difference, they could misuse their cards and face a situation in which the balance of their bank account was not enough to meet the drawn down credit.

Finally, results indicate that the income level has not a significant impact on the level of financial knowledge. The answers of students from families with high-income level are very similar to the answers of the other students. In this research the income level was approximated by using proxy variables. The income level of the family was determined with questions about the number of: (1) smart televisions, (2) cars, and (3) musical instruments at home. The high-income level encompasses students who stated that in their home there are: (1) at least two cars, one musical instrument and two or more smart televisions simultaneously or (2) more than 2 cars whatever the number of smart televisions and musical instruments.

Table 5. Average of results by groups

Group	Average of Correct Answers Before the Workshops (%)	Average of Correct Answers After the Workshops (%)	Increase (%)
Year 12th of Secondary School GROUP 1	66	81	22.73
Year 12th of Secondary School GROUP 2	79	81	2.53
Year 12th of Secondary School GROUP 3	59	72	22.03
Year 11th of Secondary School GROUP 1	67	84	25.37
Year 11th of Secondary School GROUP 2	65	73	12.31
Total	**66**	**79**	**19.70**

Source: Prepared by the authors

Results After Taking Part in the Training Workshops

During the last training session given at the High School *Concepción Arenal* students were asked to answer to two new surveys. The first one, was similar to the survey used to know the students' initial level of knowledge (although only the 20 questions of the block related to economic and financial knowledge were included). The survey was used to check for improvement in student responses after taking part in the training workshops. The second one, was a survey intended to evaluate the students' satisfaction with the training experience.

Table 6. Psychometric survey

Questions
1. The objectives of the workshops were achieved 2. The content of the workshops met my training needs 3. The level of depth of the topics covered in the workshops was adequate 4. The role of the coordinator of the workshops was positive 5. The duration of the workshops was adequate to the objectives and contents 6. The methodology used in the workshops was adequate to the objectives and contents 7. The methodology involved active participation 8. Practices, exercises, and assumptions used during the workshops were useful and sufficient 9. The quality and quantity of the material used or offered to me was suitable 10. The resources used (slides, videos, and surveys) were adequate 11. The learning environment was good 12. The schedule and time distribution of the workshops were adequate 13. The lessons learned are useful for my current academic training 14. The lessons learned are useful for my future academic training 15. The lessons learned are useful for my personal training 16. The activity was useful to improve my knowledge, skills and abilities 17. The general evaluation of these workshops is...

Source: Prepared by the authors

Figure 1 shows the differences in the students' answers to the 20 questions of the block related to economic and financial knowledge before and after taking part in the training workshops.

The average of correct responses before taking part in the training workshops was 66%. The average of correct responses after taking part in the training workshops was 79%. This means that the training provided led to an improvement in responses by 13 percentage points (this is an increase of 19.70% from the first survey). The percentage of correct answers to two of the questions in which more difficulties were detected (these are questions 2, 8, 12, 18, and 19), remain unchanged. They were question 2 (related to the savings capacity) and question 18 (related to the bank account overdraft). There were a considerable improvement in the percentage of correct answers in the other questions, including questions 8 (related to debit and credit cards), question 12 (related to the concept of inflation), and question 19 (related to the relationship between diversification and risk). Table 5 shows the average of the results obtained in the different groups of students before and after taking part in the training workshops.

The group with the least variation was the group 2 of the year 12th of secondary school. However, this was the group that obtained the best score in the initial survey. The increase in the percentage of correct answers was notable in the other groups (as shown in table 5). This indicates that the training activity has been useful and that the goal of improving the level of financial literacy of the students of the High School *Concepción Arenal* has been met

In order to know the level of satisfaction of students with the training experience, an additional survey was carried out. It was a psychometric survey measured by a Likert scale of 1-5 that included the questions shown in table 6.

Figure 2 shows the average of the answers to the questions described above.

Figure 2. Average results from the satisfaction survey
Source: Prepared by the authors

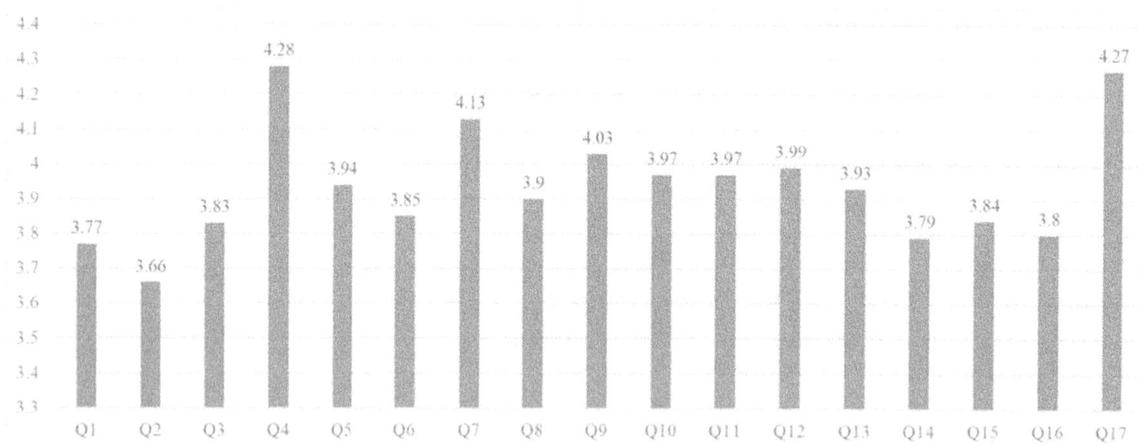

These results show that students valued very positively their active participation in the training workshops (question 7) and the role played by the teacher who taught the activity (question 4) with a score of 4.28 out of 5 points. In contrast, the questions about the content (question 2) and the objectives of the activity (question 1) have a lower evaluation, showing a lower level of satisfaction, though being rather high. The average evaluation of Question 17, which was related to the general satisfaction of the training workshops, was 4.27 out of 5 points, showing that the workshops development was very satisfactory for the students of the High School *Concepción Arenal* in Ferrol (Spain). In addition, this high score means that the training initiative carried out has a positive impact and was very well received by students. The training workshops awakened the students' interest in financial issues and enabled them to become more autonomous to make economic-financial decisions in the future.

However, despite all the positive aspects outlined, this research is just an example of an isolate initiative to foster financial education. Nevertheless, the development of financial education cannot only rely on the good will and determination of some individuals who are committed to improving the financial knowledge and autonomy of young people. It is necessary to act in an organized and global way in order to be successful. In this vein, some recommendations are proposed below.

SOLUTION AND RECOMMENDATIONS

Given the magnitude and importance of financial education in society, it is important to point out that the solution should come from the consensus reached by the various social agents. These agents (including the relevant political and economic authorities and the global educational community, among others) should be involved within a strategic plan perfectly designed to guarantee an effective implementation that reaches a large proportion of students and other segments of the population. Based on this idea, we propose the following recommendations:

- The institutions responsible for drawing up the strategic plan for the development of financial education in Spain are the Bank of Spain and the National Commission for Markets and Securities. For several years now, they are doing a great job through the online financial education platform "Finanzas para todos" [Finance for All]. These institutions are not working on their own, but together with many foundations and institutions that made big efforts to foster financial education. Therefore, we recommend that they continue to develop national plans and strategies for the development of financial education, trying to involve more public and private actors to get more capillarity, especially in view of the current situation of uncertainty that results from the health and economic crisis caused by the COVID-19 pandemic.
- Financial education should be acquired through the academic training provided in schools. Hence, this topic should be included in the curriculum and taught by specialized personnel in the field. This would mean that a high quality education would be provided and it would be the basis of a future in which people would put into practice the acquired knowledge in their daily lives.
- The training should be integrated into a methodology that makes it possible to gradually understand the concepts at the different educational stages, so the content of training would be adapted to each one of the academic courses. The objective of financial education is to enable individuals to make informed decisions. Introducing financial education from an early age is essential for students to become familiar with important concepts in a natural way, be aware that these concepts are part of their daily lives, and understand that they are fundamental to achieving individual well-being in adulthood.
- It is highly recommended to continue developing financial education as part of the lifelong learning process, by adapting the contents to each life stage. Thus, for example, a specific training on "retirement preparation" could be given for elderly people or a training on "the management of a microenterprise" could be given to entrepreneurs and self-employed. The channels responsible

for such training could be very diverse, such as companies, unions, workplaces or associations, among others.

FUTURE RESEARCH DIRECTIONS

As a continuation of this research we would like to study the level of financial education of other groups of population (such as people over 65 years or disadvantaged people) and explore to what extent the financial education might improve their ability to make financial decisions with autonomy and security.

CONCLUSION

This study highlights the importance of financial education for the society as a basic element to achieve social well-being and sustainable economic growth. It is clear that at present time the level of financial knowledge of the population has not yet reached the optimal level necessary to allow people to evaluate by themselves the financial options available and be aware of the risks associated with each one of these options. Likewise, with this research it has become clear that:

- A good level of financial literacy will serve as an engine for sustainable economic growth and for achieving a society in which citizens are able to choose financial products and services adapted to their needs (in line with the SDGs 4, 5, 8, 10, 12, and 17).
- If consumers have more information, they will be more responsible and demanding, driving efficiency in the financial sector. A more efficient, accessible and transparent financial market would attract more people and, therefore, help reduce social inequalities. Beck et al. (2007) argue that a developed financial market would help reduce inequality by 1) raising the country's growth rate, and 2) increasing the income level of the poorest. Therefore, social inequalities would be reduced.
- A financial education equally accessible to all citizens would promote gender equality. On the one hand, financial knowledge allows women to manage domestic economy and make important decisions in monetary matters, which may be translated into a more active role in household negotiations or, in other words, in greater empowerment of women (Bird, 2020). On the other hand, the economic empowerment of women directly favors gender equality. Likewise, the increasing participation of women in the labor market would lead to faster economic growth (OECD 2012). In addition, financial literacy will give women greater confidence to make decisions about savings, investments, or entrepreneurial activities, giving them more opportunities for personal development.

In view of the above, two main ideas emerge from this research

- The national plans and strategies for the development of financial education should continue with the involvement of the maximum possible number of social agents.
- It is still important to develop training initiatives and strategies to promote financial education.

REFERENCES

Agnew, S., & Harrison, N. (2015). Financial literacy and student attitudes to debt: A cross national study examining the influence of gender on personal finance concepts. *Journal of Retailing and Consumer Services*, *25*, 122–129. doi:10.1016/j.jretconser.2015.04.006

Bayar, M. Y., Sezgin, H. F., & Öztürk, O. F. (2017). Impact of Financial Literacy on Personal Savings: A Research on Usak University Staff. *Journal of Knowledge Management, Economics and Information Technology*, *7*(6), 1–19.

Beck, T., Demirgüç-Kunt, A., & Levine, R. (2007). Finance, inequality and the poor. *Journal of Economic Growth*, *12*(1), 27–49. doi:10.100710887-007-9010-6

Bird, M. (2020). *Financial Education, Couple's Communication, and Gender Norms: Explaining the Mixed Effects of Women's Empowerment on Intra-household Bargaining*. Retrieved from https://www.bbvaedufin.com/wp-content/uploads/2020/03/Bird-2019-BBVA-draft-Financial-Education-Couple%E2%80%99s-Communication-and-Gender-Norms-2020.02.16-CLEAN.pdf

Cardaci, A. (2018). Inequality Household Debt and Financial Instability: An agent based perspective. *Journal of Economic Behavior & Organization*, *149*, 434–458. doi:10.1016/j.jebo.2018.01.010

Chen, H., & Volpe, R. P. (1998). An analysis of personal financial literacy among college students. *Financial Services Review*, *7*(2), 107–128. doi:10.1016/S1057-0810(99)80006-7

Comisión de las Comunidades Europeas. (2007). *Comunicación de la Comisión. La Educación Financiera.* 808 final. Retrieved from https://eur-lex.europa.eu/legal-content/ES/TXT/PDF/?uri=CELEX:52007DC0808&from=ES

Delavande, A., Rohwedder, S., & Willis, R. J. (2008, September). *Preparation for retirement, financial literacy and cognitive resources* (Working Paper No.2008-190). Retrieved from https://mrdrc.isr.umich.edu/publications/Papers/pdf/wp190.pdf

Elan, S. (2011). *Financial literacy among retail investors in the United States.* Report prepared by the Federal Research Division, Library of Congress under an Interagency Agreement with the Securities and Exchange Commission, Washington, DC. Retrieved from https://www.loc.gov/rr/frd/pdf-files/Investor_Literacy_Report.pdf

Friedman, M. (2018). *A theory of the consumption function*. Princeton University Press. doi:10.2307/j.ctv39x7zh

Grohmann, A., Klühs, T., & Menkhoff, L. (2018). Does financial literacy improve financial inclusion? Cross country evidence. *World Development*, *111*, 84–96. doi:10.1016/j.worlddev.2018.06.020

Hastings, J. S., & Tejeda-Ashton, L. (2008). *Financial literacy, information, and demand elasticity: Survey and experimental evidence from Mexico* (Working Paper No. w14538). National Bureau of Economic Research. Retrieved from https://www.nber.org/system/files/working_papers/w14538/w14538.pdf

Hilgert, M. A., Hogarth, J. M., & Beverly, S. G. (2003). Household financial management: The connection between knowledge and behavior. *Federal Reserve Bulletin*, *89*, 309–322.

Hsu, J. W. (2016). Aging and strategic learning: The impact of spousal incentives on financial literacy. *The Journal of Human Resources, 51*(4), 1036–1067. doi:10.3368/jhr.51.4.1014-6712R PMID:28148971

Ibrahim, D. I. D., Harun, R., & Isa, Z. M. (2010). A study on financial literacy of Malaysian degree students. *Cross-Cultural Communication, 5*(4), 51–59.

Jappelli, T., & Padula, M. (2013). Investment in Financial Literacy and Saving Decisions. *Journal of Banking & Finance, 37*(8), 2779–2792. doi:10.1016/j.jbankfin.2013.03.019

López, I., Arriaga, A., & Pardo, M. (2018). La dimensión social del concepto de desarrollo sostenible: ¿La eternal olvidada? *Revista Española de Sociología, 27*(1), 25–41. doi:10.22325/fes/res.2018.2

Lusardi, A., & Mitchell, O. (2014). The economic importance of financial literacy: Theory and Evidence. *Journal of Economic Literature, 52*(1), 5–44. doi:10.1257/jel.52.1.5 PMID:28579637

Lusardi, A., & Mitchell, O. S. (2007). Baby Boomer Retirement Security: The Role of Planning, Financial Literacy, and Housing Wealth. *Journal of Monetary Economics, 54*(1), 205–224. doi:10.1016/j.jmoneco.2006.12.001

Lusardi, A., & Mitchell, O. S. (2011). Financial literacy and planning: implications for retirement wellbeing. In A. Lusardi & O. Mitchell (Eds.), *Financial Literacy. Implications for Retirement Security and the Financial Marketplace* (pp. 17–39). Oxford University Press. doi:10.1093/acprof:oso/9780199696819.003.0002

Lusardi, A., & Mitchell, O. S. (2017). How Ordinary Consumers Make Complex Economic Decisions: Financial Literacy and Retirement Readiness. *The Quarterly Journal of Finance, 7*(3), 1–31. doi:10.1142/S2010139217500082

Lusardi, A., Mitchell, O. S., & Curto, V. (2010). Financial literacy among the young. *The Journal of Consumer Affairs, 44*(2), 358–380. doi:10.1111/j.1745-6606.2010.01173.x

Lusardi, A., & Tufano, P. (2009). Teach workers about the perils of debt. *Harvard Business Review, 87*(11), 22–24.

Lusardi, A., & Tufano, P. (2015). Debt literacy, financial experiences, and overindebtedness. *Journal of Pension Economics and Finance, 14*(4), 332–368. doi:10.1017/S1474747215000232

Mancebón, M. J., Ximénez-de-Embún, D. P., Mediavilla, M., & Gómez-Sancho, J. M. (2019). Factors that influence the financial literacy of young Spanish consumers. *International Journal of Consumer Studies, 43*(2), 227–235. doi:10.1111/ijcs.12502

Ministerio de educación, cultura y deporte. (2017). *Pisa 2015. Programa para la evaluación internacional de los alumnos. Competencia financiera.* Informe español. Retrieved from https://www.educacionyfp.gob.es/inee/dam/jcr:e9052910-6614-4cd8-8969-02d20ad42c7e/Competencia%20financiera_Inf%20espa%C3%B1ol.pdf

Modigliani, F., & Brumberg, R. H. (1954). Utility Analysis and the Consumption Function: An Interpretation of Cross-Section Data. In K. K. Kurihara (Ed.), *Post-Keynesian Economics* (pp. 388–436). Rutgers University Press.

OECD. (2005). *Recommendation on principles and good practices for financial education and awareness.* Retrieved from https://www.oecd.org/finance/financial-education/35108560.pdf

OECD. (2012). *Gender Equality in Education, Employment and Entrepreneurship: Final Report to the MCM 2012.* Retrieved from https://www.oecd.org/employment/50423364.pdf

OECD (2014). *PISA 2012 Results: Students and Money: Financial Literacy Skills for the 21st Century (Volume 6).* OECD Publishing. doi:10.1787/9789264208094-en

Rivera-Hernández, J. E., Alcántara-Salinas, G., Blanco-Orozco, N. V., & Houbron, E. P. (2017). ¿Desarrollo sostenible o sustentable? La controversia de un concepto. *Revista Posgrado y Sociedad, 15*(1), 57–67. doi:10.22458/rpys.v15i1.1825

Stango, V., & Zinman, J. (2007). *Fuzzy math and red ink: When the opportunity cost of consumption is not what it seems* (Working Paper). Retrieved from http://legacy.iza.org/en/papers/Zinman12072007.pdf

Van Rooij, M., Lusardi, A., & Alessie, R. (2011). Financial literacy and stock market participation. *Journal of Financial Economics, 101*(2), 449–472. doi:10.1016/j.jfineco.2011.03.006

WCED. (1987). *Report of the World Commission on Environment and Development: Our Common Future.* Retrieved from https://sustainabledevelopment.un.org/content/documents/5987our-common-future.pdf

KEY TERMS AND DEFINITIONS

Financial Decisions: Decisions related to the financial activities that corporations and individuals perform. From the corporate point of view, there are three main types of financial decisions: investment decisions, financing decisions, and dividend decisions. From the individuals' point of view, there are many types of decisions related to the activities performed by individuals to maintain and increase their wealth.

Financial Products: Financial instruments used to formalize an exchange of capitals between two parties. One party needs financing and decide to issue (offer) these instruments to draw funds in exchange for offering a return. The other party has financial resources and decide to offer them by contracting these instruments in exchange for obtaining a return over time.

Personal Finances: It is the process of managing the personal budget over time. Therefore, it means planning and making decisions about financial activities such as saving, investing, spending, income generation, or retirement planning.

Responsible Consumption: It is a manner of consumption that takes into account the basis of sustainable development, that focus on protecting Earth's resources and communities, and improving the quality of life of individuals and the society as a whole.

Chapter 2
Real Options for the Valuation of Investment Projects:
Practical Case

Raisa Pérez-Vas
University of Vigo, Spain

ABSTRACT

The objective of this chapter is to analyze the methodology for evaluating investment projects through real options. The limitations of traditional models based on cash flows and the current environment that presents constant changes and high uncertainty have led to a new field of research, real options. The valuation of investment projects carries inherent decision-making, where the best options for the company are analyzed, the real options providing a decision flexibility that classic models do not provide. This chapter contains the most important theoretical framework, where the beginnings of this methodology, the most important types of options, and the methodology for their evaluation are discussed, as well as two practical examples for a better understanding of this methodology.

INTRODUCTION

Investment decisions are a fundamental aspect for any company, this subject to the constant changes and uncertainties that the markets live today lead to the valuation of investment possibilities having to have an increasingly more dynamic approach than traditional models based in cash flow discounts. This dynamism entails the need for greater flexibility in decision-making, therefore, a sequential or staged assessment is carried out, which allows obtaining more information to carry out another phase in an investment project, that is, traditional valuation models only consider one scenario of action, that is, they do not grant the flexibility to act and evaluate circumstances that were not initially included in the project (Rogers, 2002).

Currently, models based on Net Present Value (NPV) handle the uncertainty inherent in investment projects in a very ineffective way, this is because these models are based on the premise that the deci-

DOI: 10.4018/978-1-7998-7634-2.ch002

sion is "now or never", although Throughout the completion of an investment project there may be the "option" to change or abandon its implementation due to the results that are being obtained.

Therefore, the application of the financial options approach that is used to value financial assets was extrapolated to the valuation of non-financial assets (real assets), which prompted increasing research into new project valuation models, which led to the Real Options Valuation Methodology.

In this chapter it is intended to show the methodology of Real Options through the exposition of the most important elements of the theoretical framework and its application through the realization of practical cases.

BACKGROUND

The beginnings of the real options methodology are based on the article published by Stewart Myers in 1977 where the possibility of using financial option valuation models to value non-financial assets is exposed.

The basic definition of an option is that it is a contract between two parties in which one party has the right (to buy or sell) and the other party the obligation to (sell or buy) a certain financial asset at an exercise price and period determined. This definition was extrapolated to the valuation of investments, where the financial asset is the "option" (expansion, abandonment, exchange ...) that the company wants to carry out and the exercise price its cost.

According to Culík (2016), compared to the passive valuation obtained through traditional valuation models, the real options approach considers two fundamental factors in the valuation: the risk posed by the possible variability of the flows expected cash flow provided by the asset and the flexibility that gives the company the ability to change decisions around the project.

The methodology for valuation of investment projects through real options is based on the valuation models of financial options. The most important models related to the valuation of financial options are the Black-Scholes Model, the Binomial Model proposed by Cox et al. (1979) and the Monte Carlo simulation.

Among the exposed models, the Binomial Model through the decision trees tool is one of the most used models among researchers for the valuation of investment projects, due to its great versatility and adaptation to real assets (Lamothe and Méndez, 2013). Along these lines, Amram and Kulatilaka (2000) argue that the Binomial Option Pricing Model has three important advantages when applied to real options: 1) it is a model that can be applicable to real options, even in real options with a certain complexity; 2) although it is based on the valuation of financial options, it maintains the appearance of the discounted cash flow analysis; 3) a good description of the uncertainty and contingent decisions is made.

Some of the applications carried out include Brandão et al. (2005); Culík (2016); Hernandez et al. (2017); Nunes et al. (2017); Wörsdörfer et al (2017).

OPTIONS TYPES

Option to Defer

The option to defer an investment project grants the right to postpone its completion within a specified time horizon. This allows the company to obtain more information on the evolution of the variables that affect the project.

Like financial options, the company has a right, but not an obligation, to carry out an investment project within a specific time horizon. The exercise price corresponds to the value of the investment at the future time.

The use of this option modality is very interesting when the uncertainty is very high and the cash flows that are postponed or lost due to waiting are very small (Ingersoll and Ross, 1992).

Option to Expand

The expansion or growth option allows the company to make new investments on a project already started. This means that if the various situations affecting the project are favorable, an extension of the project is carried out, but the company will not be obliged to carry it out in the opposite situation. According to Mascareñas (2007) this type of option corresponds to a strategic value. This is because managers have the flexibility to carry out the anticipated growth and expansion phases if market conditions are right.

In analogy with financial options, the growth option allows new investments to be made if conditions are favorable and if the company considers that it will not obtain any advantage or profit, it has the possibility of not carrying out the investment. The exercise price is the value of the investment that the company must make for expansion.

Option to Abandon

The abandonment option provides the company with the possibility of selling or liquidating any asset or capital when market conditions are not adequate, or the project is not proving profitable (Rogers, 2002). In this way, the company will recover a part of the investment (Residual Value) through the sale of certain assets or the company.

The abandonment option in most cases corresponds to an American put option where the exercise price is the value of the liquidation of the assets or the company.

Option to Contract

The option to reduce provides the company the right to reduce the scale of operations of a project because it does not present the expected profitability at the initial moment. With this situation, the company expects a saving in expected costs.

This type of option corresponds to an American put option on the part of the project that can be reduced where the exercise price is the potential saving of costs that can be canceled (Trigeorgis, 1996)

Strategic Option

These types of options are usually used by companies carrying out new projects to evaluate possibilities and strategies that can be used in the future by the company (Ross et al. 2010). Because they allow future alternatives to be analyzed in the event of possible changes in the company, they are a better method than NPV.

Sustainability in Real Options

The application of the real options methodology in the field of sustainability is booming. This circumstance is explained by the fact that sectors such as renewable energies are increasingly important in world economies. Sustainability is represented in three pillars: environment, economy and society (Purvis et al., 2019; Opon & Henry, 2020). Uncertainty is a characteristic closely linked to the real options methodology, and in turn, also to sustainability, according to the study carried out by Jia & Li (2020), uncertainty due to climate change, economic policy and political instability negatively affects the sustainability performance of companies.

Numerous investigations study the methodology of real options in the valuation of companies related to sustainability. Hernandez-Perdomo et al. (2017) carry out a study where they apply the real options to make companies more sustainable. Agaton et al. (2020) analyze Waste-to-energy technologies in Philippines through real options approach under uncertainty. Pringles et al. (2020) applies the real options to determine the value of delaying the investment decision while waiting for better market information that would reduce acquisition costs due to the progress of solar technology. (Aquila et al., 2020) apply the Real Options approach to analyze the economic viability of an investment in a wind power plant with the option of abandoning it throughout the project life cycle.

METHODOLOGY

The valuation of Real Options is based on the financial theory of valuation of financial options, which is why the models used for the valuation of real options are based on the models used in the valuation of financial options. Among the most important are:

- Analytical models, which are usually developed in continuous time and include the Black-Scholes model (1973), as well as the derivations proposed by various authors (Lamothe and Méndez, 2013; Bao et al., 2015)
- Binomial Model proposed by Cox, Ross and Rubinstein (1979).
- Montearlo Simulation (Lamothe and Méndez, 2013; Bao et al., 2015).

Starting from the exposed models, these have been applied to the valuation of investment projects. The Binomial Model through the decision trees tool is one of the most used models among researchers for the valuation of investment projects due to its great versatility and adaptation to real assets (Lamothe and Méndez, 2013). This model has the advantage for the valuation of real options that it presents a better applicability for complex options, such as when there are several sources of uncertainty or volatility changes over time (Loncar et al.2017).

BINOMIAL MODEL

The Binomial Model was developed by Cox, Ross, and Rubinstein in 1979 for the valuation of financial options. The authors of the model considered that the price of the underlying asset at a future point in time, based on the binomial distribution, can take two different prices, one in which the price increases and the other in which the price decreases, with an associated probability of occurrence. Extrapolating this definition to the case of real options, the price of the real asset can be increased or decreased over a period of time.

The model assumes that the price of the underlying asset follows a binomial multiplicative process of discrete periods, therefore, the rate of return of the underlying asset can be defined by two possible values, the first would be u–1 with probability p_u and, the other would be d–1 with probability $p_d = 1 - p_u$. Therefore, if the price of the underlying asset increases, it would take a new value that will be given by uS and, in the case of a drop in value by dS .

The growth and decrease rate are defined by the following expressions:

$$u = e^{\sigma\sqrt{dt}} \tag{1}$$

$$d = e^{-\sigma\sqrt{dt}} = \frac{1}{u} \tag{2}$$

Where: σ = volatility

Binomial Model Applied to Real Options

The Binomial Model through decision trees is the most widely applied and tried model among real options researchers. The use of decision trees lies in the fact that through their use the company can take into consideration possible future decisions that affect the investment project. Therefore, this tool makes it possible to re-evaluate the investment decisions that may affect the project once it has started. Through the foregoing, the company can eradicate prevailing uncertainties around the project, since the company can receive new information in the time horizon in which it is developed, which leads it to modify the course of the project. This allows the company to have a flexibility that allows it, for example, to abandon a project with which, if they continue with it, it will result in high losses.

For the application of the Binomial Model to the valuation of investment projects, it is necessary to define, among others, the following variables:

VP: present value of expected cash flows.

The structure for the valuation of investment projects using real options lies in 4 phases:

1. Estimation of the underlying assets that affect the evolution of cash flows.

In this phase, the variables that constitute the cash flows for the NPV valuation are analyzed and estimated.

2. Investment project estimation without flexibility

Creation of the process of diffusion of the value of the underlying asset. This phase involves the creation of a binomial tree that shows the current value of the expected cash flows (NPV), as well as their respective movements up u and down d, obtaining the results shown in Table 1.

Table 1. Binomial tree of cash flows

VP	$VP_{1,1}=VPu$	$VP_{2,2}=VPu^2$	$VP_{3,3}=VPu^3$	$VP_{4,4}=VPu^4$
	$VP_{0,1}=VPd$	$VP_{1,2}=VPud$	$VP_{2,3}=VPu^2d$	$VP_{3,4}=VPu^3d$
		$VP_{0,2}=VPd^2$	$VP_{1,3}=VPud2$	$VP_{2,4}=VPu^2d^2$
			$VP_{0,3}=VPd^3$	$VP_{1,4}=VPud^3$
				$VP_{0,4}=VPd^4$

3. Investment project estimation with flexibility

The binomial tree is built that collects the value of the investment project with the incorporation of the options. It is representatively shown in Table 2.

Table 2. Binomial tree of project value with options

ROV	$ROV_{1,1}$	$ROV_{2,2}$	$ROV_{3,3}$	$ROV_{4,4}$
	$ROV_{0,1}$	$ROV_{1,2}$	$ROV_{2,3}$	$ROV_{3,4}$
		$ROV_{0,2}$	$ROV_{1,3}$	$ROV_{2,4}$
			$ROV_{0,3}$	$ROV_{1,4}$
				$ROV_{0,4}$

The process that is necessary to carry out to achieve the creation of the structure that makes up the value of the investment project with the incorporation of options consists of two steps. First, the value of the terminal nodes will be calculated, and second, the value of the intermediate nodes will be calculated through the process called backward induction or backward induction.

Step 1: Valuation of the end nodes

The valuation of the nodes will be carried out through a maximization rule in which it is necessary to take into account the type of option being treated.

Step 2: Assessment of intermediate nodes

4. Final evaluation of the project:

Through the ROV calculation, which defines the value of the existing options in an investment project, a complete valuation of an investment project can be carried out. This value will be made up of the NPV (without flexibility) and the value of the options:

$$NPV^{*} = NPV + OPTION\ VALUE \quad (3)$$

The acceptance or not of the realization of an investment project follows the same logic as the traditional NPV, except that with the recalculated NPV, aspects not evaluated so far are being considered. Therefore, an investment project will be accepted when $NPV^{*}>0$.

EXAMPLE CASE (OPTION TO EXPAND)

Company X has to decide the investment of expanding the company through increased production is carried out, which requires investment in new machinery. The required investment amounts to 200,000 euros and the expected cash flows are as shown in Table 3.

Table 3. Free Cash Flow

	1	2	3	4	5	6
FREE CASH FLOW	120.000	122.000	125.000	127.000	128.000	129.000
UPDATED FREE CASH FLOW	114.285´71	110.657´6	107.979´7	104.483´21	100.291´35	96.261´79

The parameters necessary to carry out the valuation of the project through real options are shown in Tables 4 and 5.

Once we have the parameters and the calculation of the NPV is performed, with a value of 633,959'36 euros, the next step is the construction of the binomial tree of cash flows (Table 5):

Where, for example:

633.3959´36 * 1.02244 = 648.188´88

633.959´36 * 0.97804 = 620.042´22

Once the binomial tree relative to cash flows has been calculated, the next step is to build the binomial tree including the expansion option (Table 6).

For the construction of the binomial tree the first step is to calculate the final nodes, where, for example:

741.555´01 = max(742.273´08; 724.273´08 * 1´3 – 200.000)

The next step is the calculation of the intermediates until reaching the zero period, where, for example:

Table 4. Parameters

Variable	Value
(1) Net present value	633.959´36
(2) Strike price (C)	200.000
(3) Expansion factor (E)	1´3
(4) Volatility (σ)	2´22%
(5) Project duration (T)	6 years
(6) Duration of each stage (n)	1
(7) u	1´02244
(8) d	0´97804
(9) p_u	0´77
(10) p_d	0´23
(11) Risk-free rate r_f	1´75%

$$723.425'79 = \max\left(\begin{array}{l} 708.373'3 * 1.3 - 200000; \\ \dfrac{\left(741.555'01 * 0.7777 + 692.822'58 * 0.2222\right)}{\left(1 + 1'25\%\right)^{1}}; 708.373'31 \end{array}\right)$$

The total value of the project including the expansion option is 640,568’62, therefore, it is interesting to carry out the expansion of the company.

Table 5. Evolution of the value of underlying assets (NPV)

0	1	2	3	4	5	6
						724.273,08
					708.373,31	
				692.822,58		692.822,58
			677.613,24		677.613,24	
		662.737,78		662.737,78		662.737,78
	648.188,88		648.188,88		648.188,88	
633.959,36		633.959,36		633.959,36		633.959,36
	620.042,22		620.042,22		620.042,22	
		606.430,60		606.430,60		606.430,60
			593.117,80		593.117,80	
				580.097,24		580.097,24
					567.362,52	
						554.907,37

Table 6. Evolution of the value of the project with expansion option

0	1	2	3	4	5	6
						741.555,01
					723.425,79	
				705.773,51		700.669,36
			688.652,95		683.693,31	
		672.083,13		667.470,62		662.737,78
	656.060,63		651.896,23		648.239,10	
640.568,62		636.887,96		634.057,61		633.959,36
	622.381,15		620.186,36		620.090,26	
		606.618,58		606.524,58		606.430,60
			593.255,68		593.163,75	
				580.187,14		580.097,24
					567.406,49	
						554.907,37

EXAMPLE CASE (OPTION TO ABANDOND)

Company X has the possibility to abandon the project it is carrying out through its liquidation or to continue executing it. The liquidation value is 130,000 euros. The cash flows generated are shown in Table 7.

Table 7. Free Cash Flow

	1	2	3	4	5	6
FREE CASH FLOW	20.000	22.000	22.000	25.000	28.000	29.000
UPDATED FREE CASH FLOW	19.047´62	19.954´65	19.004´43	20.567´56	21.938´73	21.640´25

The parameters necessary to carry out the valuation of the project through real options are:

Once we have the parameters and the calculation of the NPV is carried out, with a value of 122,153’24 euros, the next step is the construction of the binomial tree of cash flows (Table 9).

Once the binomial tree relative to cash flows has been calculated, the next step is to build the binomial tree including the abandon option (Table 10).

The total value of the project taking into account the abandonment option is 130,769’77. In the tree you can see how in the case of a drop in values, when maximizing, in various scenarios it is a better option to liquidate the company for a value of 130,000 euros.

Table 8. Parameters

Variable	Value
(1) Net present value	122.153´24
(2) Residual value	130.000
(4) Volatility (σ)	5´91%
(5) Project duration (T)	6 años
(6) Duration of each stage (n)	1
(7) u	1´0608
(8) d	0´9426
(9) p_u	0´5916
(10) p_d	0´4083
(11) Tasa libre de riesgo r_f	1´75%

FUTURE RESEARCH DIRECTIONS

Future lines of research focus on the application of the real options methodology to assess investment projects from different sectors to analyze whether there are differences in their application and whether the model depending on the sector shows a better acceptance or not. In addition, it will be investigated whether the valuation of this methodology presents better results in sectors that have greater uncertainty.

In addition, this chapter of the book only analyzes the Binomial model, although it would be interesting to discuss other valuation models that have been named and analyze if they offer a better valuation than the Binomial model or not.

Table 9. Evolution of the value of underlying assets (NPV)

0	1	2	3	4	5	6
						174.104,93
					164.119,45	
				154.706,67		154.706,67
			145.833,74		145.833,74	
		137.469,71		137.469,71		137.469,71
	129.585,38		129.585,38		129.585,38	
122.153,24		122.153,24		122.153,24		122.153,24
	115.147,35		115.147,35		115.147,35	
		108.543,28		108.543,28		108.543,28
			102.317,97		102.317,97	
				96.449,71		96.449,71
					90.918,00	
						85.703,56

Table 10. Evolution of the value of the project with abandon option

0	1	2	3	4	5	6
						174.104,93
					164.132,17	
				154.730,65		154.706,67
			146.382,37		145.845,04	
		139.388,37		138.767,29		137.469,71
	134.063,82		133.521,45		132.760,02	
130.769,77		130.452,84		130.007,89		130.000,00
	130.000,00		130.000,00		130.000,00	
		130.000,00		130.000,00		130.000,00
			130.000,00		130.000,00	
				130.000,00		130.000,00
					130.000,00	
						130.000,00

Another line of research lies in the analysis of other types of options that have not been developed in this chapter, in addition to treating the valuation of several options at the same time.

CONCLUSION

This chapter includes a way of evaluating investment projects that is increasingly known in the field of research and also in the business world, the methodology of real options.

The chapter contains the most important theoretical part that encompasses the entire methodology of real options as well as a practical part, where two of the most important types of options, expansion and abandon, are analyzed.

Despite the fact that this methodology is not one of the most used in companies, since, in this sector, traditional models based on cash flows, such as NPV and IRR, are the most used, through The practical examples that have been developed in this chapter are intended to offer a clearer and more concise vision of how to carry out the assessment using this methodology.

ACKNOWLEDGMENT

This research was supported by "Programa de axudas á etapa predoutoral" da Xunta de Galicia (Consellería de Cultura, Educación e Ordenación Universitaria) [ED481A-2018/341].

REFERENCES

Agaton, C. B., Guno, C. S., Villanueva, R. O., & Villanueva, R. O. (2020). Economic analysis of waste-to-energy investment in the Philippines: A real options approach. *Applied Energy*, *275*(May), 115265. doi:10.1016/j.apenergy.2020.115265

Amram, M., & Kulatilaka, N. (2000). Opciones Reales: Evaluación de inversiones en un mundo incierto. *Gestion*.

Aquila, G., de Queiroz, A. R., Balestrassi, P. P., Rotella, P. Junior, Rocha, L. C. S., Pamplona, E. O., & Nakamura, W. T. (2020). Wind energy investments facing uncertainties in the Brazilian electricity spot market: A real options approach. *Sustainable Energy Technologies and Assessments*, *42*(May), 100876. doi:10.1016/j.seta.2020.100876

Bao, C., Bryan, B. A., Connor, J. D., Meyer, W. S., Ostendorf, B., Regan, C. M., & Zhu, Z. (2015). Real options analysis for land use management: Methods, application, and implications for policy. *Journal of Environmental Management*, *161*, 144–152. doi:10.1016/j.jenvman.2015.07.004 PMID:26164637

Black, F., & Scholes, M. (1973). The Pricing of Options and Corporate Liabilities. *Journal of Political Economy*, *81*(3), 637–654. doi:10.1086/260062

Brandão, L. E., Dyer, J. S., & Hahn, W. J. (2005). Using Binomial Decision Trees to Solve Real-Option Valuation Problems. *Decision Analysis*, *2*(2), 69–88. doi:10.1287/deca.1050.0040

Cox, J., Ross, S., & Rubinstein, M. (1979). Option pricing: A simplified approach. *Journal of Financial Economics*, *7*(3), 229–263. doi:10.1016/0304-405X(79)90015-1

Culík, M. (2016). Real options valuation with changing volatility. *Perspectives in Science*, *7*, 10–18. doi:10.1016/j.pisc.2015.11.004

Hernandez, E. A., Mun, J., & Rocco, C. M. (2017). Active management in state-owned energy companies: Integrating a real options approach into multicriteria analysis to make companies sustainable. *Applied Energy*, *195*, 487–502. doi:10.1016/j.apenergy.2017.03.068

Hernandez-Perdomo, E. A., Mun, J., & Rocco, C. M. S. (2017). Active management in state-owned energy companies: Integrating a real options approach into multicriteria analysis to make companies sustainable. *Applied Energy*, *195*, 487–502. doi:10.1016/j.apenergy.2017.03.068

Ingersoll, J. E. Jr, & Ross, S. A. (1992). Waiting to invest: Investment and uncertainty. *The Journal of Business*, *65*(1), 1–29. doi:10.1086/296555

Jia, J., & Li, Z. (2020). Does external uncertainty matter in corporate sustainability performance? *Journal of Corporate Finance*, *65*(July), 101743. doi:10.1016/j.jcorpfin.2020.101743

Lamothe, P., & Méndez, M. (2013). *Opciones Reales: métodos de simulación y valoración*. Ecobook.

Loncar, D., Milovanovic, I., Rakic, B., & Radjenovic, T. (2017). Compound real options valuation of renewable energy projects: The case of a wind farm in Serbia. *Renewable & Sustainable Energy Reviews*, *75*, 354–367. doi:10.1016/j.rser.2016.11.001

Mascareñas, J. (2007). *Opciones reales en la valoración de proyectos de inversión.* Documento de trabajo, Universidad Complutense de Madrid.

Myers, S. (1977). Determinants of Corporate Borrowing. *Journal of Financial Economics, 5*(2), 147–175. doi:10.1016/0304-405X(77)90015-0

Nunes, M., Oliveira, E., Mello, V. E., Áquila, G., Souza, L. C., & Rotela, P. (2017). Oil price volatility: A real option valuation approach in an African oil field. *Journal of Petroleum Science Engineering, 150*, 297–304. doi:10.1016/j.petrol.2016.12.024

Opon, J., & Henry, M. (2020). A multicriteria analytical framework for sustainability evaluation under methodological uncertainties. *Environmental Impact Assessment Review, 83*(April), 106403. doi:10.1016/j.eiar.2020.106403

Pringles, R., Olsina, F., & Penizzotto, F. (2020). Valuation of defer and relocation options in photovoltaic generation investments by a stochastic simulation-based method. *Renewable Energy, 151*, 846–864. doi:10.1016/j.renene.2019.11.082

Purvis, B., Mao, Y., & Robinson, D. (2019). Three pillars of sustainability: In search of conceptual origins. *Sustainability Science, 14*(3), 681–695. doi:10.100711625-018-0627-5

Rogers, J. (2002). *Strategy*. Value and Risk – The Real Options Approach.

Ross, S., Westerfield, R., & Jordan, B. (2010). *Fundamentos de Finanzas Corporativas*. McGraw-Hill.

Trigeorgis, L. (1996). *Real Options: Managerial Flexibility and Strategy in Resource Allocation*. MIT Press.

Wörsdörfer, D., Lier, S., & Crasselt, N. (2017). Real options-based evaluation model for transformable plant designs in the process industry. *Journal of Manufacturing Systems, 42*, 29–43. doi:10.1016/j.jmsy.2016.11.001

ADDITIONAL READING

Ajak, A., & Topal, E. (2015). Real option in action: An example of flexible decision making at a mine operational level. *Resources Policy, 45*, 109–120. doi:10.1016/j.resourpol.2015.04.001

Copeland, T., & Antikarov, V. (2003). *Real options: a practitioner's guide*. Thomson.

González, J. M., Martín, G., & Zamora, C. (2016). Application of real options valuation for analysing the impact of public R&D financing on renewable energy projects: A company's perspective. *Renewable & Sustainable Energy Reviews, 63*, 292–301. doi:10.1016/j.rser.2016.05.073

Hu, Q., & Zhang, A. (2015). Real option analysis of aircraft acquisition: A case study. *Journal of Air Transport Management, 46*, 19–29. doi:10.1016/j.jairtraman.2015.03.010

Kester, W. C. (1984). Today's Options for Tomorrow's Growth. *Harvard Business Review, 62*(2), 153–160.

Myers, S. (1977). - Determinants of Corporate Borrowing. *Journal of Financial Economics*, *5*(2), 147–175. doi:10.1016/0304-405X(77)90015-0

Trigeorgis, L. (1996). *Real Options: Managerial Flexibility and Strategy in Resource Allocation*. MIT Press.

Zhang, M., Zhou, D., & Zhou, P. (2014). A real option model for renewable energy policy evaluation with application to solar PV power generation in China. *Renewable and Sustainable Reviews*, *40*, 944–955. doi:10.1016/j.rser.2014.08.021

KEY TERMS AND DEFINITIONS

Binomial Model: Valuation model based on the binomial distribution where a value can take two different scenarios, one rising and the other falling.

Financial Option: It is a contract where one of the parties has the right but not the obligation to buy (call option) or sell (put option) an asset at a strike at a certain period of the time to the other party.

Investment Project: Possibility of the companies for carry out different investment and possibilities of decision making.

Real Option: Extrapolation of the definition the financial option to non-financial assets.

Uncertainty: Lack of knowledge of the future behavior of an event due to the lack of information on the variables that will affect that event.

Chapter 3
Comparative Analysis of Value at Risk(VaR) of MSCI-EMI With Traditional Time Series Methods and ANN

Emre Çevik
https://orcid.org/0000-0002-2012-9886
Kırklareli University, Turkey

Suzan Kantarcı Savaş
https://orcid.org/0000-0002-1190-6209
Kırklareli University, Turkey

Esin Cumhur Yalçın
https://orcid.org/0000-0002-0457-4971
Kırklareli University, Turkey

ABSTRACT

In this chapter, the VaR of the MSCI emerging market index (MSCI-EMI) developed by Morgan Stanley Capital International (MSCI) is estimated using linear, nonlinear time series and ANN. In this context, the aim of the study is to estimate the VaR exceedance of the MSCI-EMI as a global financial risk indicator compared with traditional time series methods and ANN. In addition, the most effective method on this index is determined by statistical information criteria, and the comparative evaluation of the model selection criteria is carried out. The period of analysis is between December 1987-April 2020 with monthly frequency and VaR exceedance obtained with ARMA-GARCH, TGARCH, EGARCH, GJR, and ANN models. Confidence levels of models, VaR exceedance, and Kupeic statistics are obtained. VaR exceedances are examined through the superior model.

DOI: 10.4018/978-1-7998-7634-2.ch003

INTRODUCTION

Emerging markets (EM) countries are in the process of rapid growth and development. However, the household incomes and capital markets of these countries are less mature than those of developed countries. Although EMs' are characterized by rapid economic growth, their infrastructure and household incomes have failed to catch up with developed countries. The general characteristic of EMs' is that they have a high level of economic development with rapid industrialization. The difference from developed and developing countries is that they are not only primarily based on agriculture, but are also active in infrastructure and industrial growth.

EM countries are growing faster than developed and developing countries. The main reason for this is that the domestic effective demand is lively and foreign direct investment is high. Therefore, they were not significantly affected by the 2008 mortgage crisis. In addition, EMs' have integrated their national financial markets into the international financial network by adopting financial liberalization and de-regulation policies. In summary, EMs' are very active both in the real and financial sectors. For this reason, they serve as the locomotive of the world economy.

EMs', which have become an important market for investors, are markets where financial transactions are intensive and rapidly developing due to a specific risk. As experienced during the Mexican crisis of 1994, especially the rapid outflows of portfolio liabilities can lead EM countries into crisis in a short period of time. It can also be attractive to investors with high growth data. As a result of this situation, a financial crisis in EMs' could spread throughout the world in a short time. Different models are available to predict whether the country is at risk. One of these is the concept of value at risk (VaR). VaR is a method developed for monetary expression of the expected maximum loss over a given time period and at a certain probability level. Different approaches exist in calculating VaR. In addition to econometric models, methods such as computer-based simulation are frequently used in literature to calculate VaR.

In this context, rapidly-developing information technologies and the speed of data transfer and analysis in financial markets are important in evaluating markets. Emerging information technologies also introduce new approaches to data storage and analysis. Artificial intelligence algorithms are also used in economic analysis. Artificial intelligence originated as a concept based on modelling the human system of thought. Artificial intelligence includes different modelling techniques such as expert systems, fuzzy logic, artificial neural networks, deep learning and decision trees. These techniques are used for classification, forecasting and clustering purposes and represent an approach to establishing models. In this context, artificial neural networks (ANN), which are used most frequently among artificial intelligence techniques, in addition to being used in fields such as engineering, biomedical, biostatistics, also contribute reliable analysis in the financial sector. ANN, in particular, are frequently used in financial analysis studies today.

In ANN, it functions as a nonlinear function due to modelling based on the human nervous system. In the ANN approach, the model is established using the training set and the information obtained from the training set is stored throughout the model. This established model is based on optimizing weights among neurons. With the help of the established model, information can be estimated for a new data. This approach can also be used for perception-oriented concepts. They are also used to complete any pattern. One of the major advantages of this approach is that it can work with incomplete information and has the ability to learn on its own.

In this study, "MSCI Emerging Markets Indexes" data calculated by Morgan Stanley Capital International (MSCI) to represent the markets of developing countries was used. Morgan Stanley Capital

International (MSCI) indices were first designed in 1968 as capital international indices to measure the performance of global capital for markets outside the United States. Later, in 1986, international capital indices were acquired by Morgan Stanley and became popular as the MSCI index. By the 1980s, the use of MSCI indices had become very widespread and it was considered among the important reference indices and took its place among the primary indices tracked for markets outside the United States. MSCI indices contribute highly to evaluating investment opportunities, portfolio diversification, and risk distribution in these countries for global investors. MSCI indices offer the opportunity to conduct stock market performance analyses based on regional and selected countries, and to track the performance of stock markets in markets of interest to foreign investors or funds. MSCI indices also produce data such as analyzing and comparing country and industry performances. It is one of the important reference data at the point of which country's Stock Exchange or shares can be invested. Following its acquisition by the Barra company in 2004, MSCI indices began to be tracked as MSCI Barra indices and became a public company structure with an IPO in 2007. MSCI indices, designed in the first place to measure the performance of global capital, are today diversified and developed according to many criteria, such as MSCI USA Index, MSCI EACWI Index, MSCI World Index, MSCI EAFE Index, MSCI Emerging Market Index, MSCI Turkey Index. The MSCI Emerging Markets Index (EMI) was first created based on the market capitalization of 21 countries. Today, the MSCI index consists of 26 countries representing 10 percent of the world's markets. The shares in MSCI EMI cover 85 percent of the listed companies in each country and consist of 1403 components (MSCI, 2020). In summary, the MSCI index is an important indicator for foreign investors to evaluate investment opportunities in other countries, to predict their risks and potential expectations. In the preparation of MSCI indices, the aim is to create country performance indices that are comparable to each other, focusing on the shares of similar companies in each country.

In this chapter, the VaR of the MSCI Emerging Market Index (MSCI-EMI) developed by Morgan Stanley Capital International (MSCI) is estimated using linear, nonlinear time series and ANN. The VaR values are used to search the effects of models on the short and long term predictions. MSCI indices have been used since 1968 to measure global capital performances outside the United States of America. The MSCI-EMI consists of 26 emerging market economies. These countries are Argentina, Brazil, Chile, China, Colombia, Czechia, Egypt, Greece, Hungary, India, Indonesia, Malaysia, Mexico, Pakistan, Peru, Philippines, Poland, Qatar, Russian Federation, Saudi Arabia, South Africa, South Korea, Taiwan, Thailand, Turkey and the United Arab Emirates. With 1,403 constituents, the index covers approximately 85% of the free float-adjusted market capitalization in each country. The aim of the study is to estimate the VaR exceedance of the MSCI-EMI as a global financial risk indicator compared with traditional time series methods and ANN. In this context, the main hypothesis of this study is that the ANN method is more suitable than classical time series methods in determining VaR exceedences. Because the ANN method includes many parametric and non-parametric properties. In addition, the most effective method on this index is determined by statistical information criteria and the comparative evaluation of the model selection criteria is carried out. The period of analysis is between December 1987-April 2020 with monthly frequency and VaR exceedance are obtained with ARMA-GARCH, EGARCH, GJR and ANN models. Confidence levels of models, VaR exceedance and Kupiec statistics are obtained. VaR exceedances are examined through the superior model.

The following sections of the study can be listed as follows: In Chapter 2, a summary of literature is presented. In Chapter 3, methodology information is given. In Chapter 4, the data set and findings are evaluated. In Chapter 5, the findings of the study are discussed. Chapter 6 concludes the research.

BACKGROUND

One of the most commonly used methods in financial risk calculations in literature are VAR models. Researchers adopt various methods to estimate VaR values. In general, studies based on two different approaches as linear and nonlinear methods attract attention. In recent years, ANN has come to the fore in estimating VaR values and its performance has been measured by comparison with other methods.

Chan et al. (2009) proposed a new method for ANN-based VaR models in their study. For the period 02.05.2003-29.12.2006, they calculated the expected return values and volatility with daily data of the Hang Seng Index (HSI) and obtained VaR values by training 500 data points primarily using the rolling-window approach. They also compared the findings with Statistical ANN using ARMA and GARCH from classic time series models. As a result, Statistical ANN showed that the results significantly increased reliability (as measured by P), while maintaining a similar level of accuracy (as measured by MSE) compared to the benchmarking model. However, they stated that the inclusion of external factors in the model as extra explanatory variables could strengthen the model's ability to predict.

Mallikarjuna & Rao (2019) applied ARIMA, SETAR, ANN, SSA and HM models to daily stock market return data of selected indices from developed, emerging, and frontier markets according to MSCI classification for 2018. The findings showed that none of the five models alone could be applied to all markets in the same way. However, the ARIMA and SETAR models performed better in providing more accurate estimates than other models.

Locarek-Junge & Prinzler (1998) presented the Mixture Density Networks approach, one of the ANN approaches, as an alternative to existing VAR models that assume normality in market returns. In the study, daily returns were calculated from September 1985 to August 1994 using daily DEM/USD exchange rate data, using 2000 observation values for training and 250 observations to test model performance (total of 2250 observations). In the light of the findings, it was stated that more complex networks that may be required for multifactor portfolios should be organized and other optimization techniques such as the (Generalized) Expectation Maximization algorithm should be taken into account.

Becker et al. (2020) compared the S&P 500 stock index; MSCI European stock index, Bloomberg, Barclays US Aggregate Bond Index; and USD/Euro daily exchange rates using daily data and the expected shortcoming (EE) and VaR with variables for ARMA and ARMA-GARCH models for the period of 04.01.1999-31.12.2018. In general, the ANN model has been shown to have more favorable results compared to the ARMA-GARCH time series model.

Arimod et al. (2020) investigated whether the ANN approach is suitable for VaR threshold estimation. They stated that well-designed neural networks give favorable results in VaR threshold estimation and will be beneficial for corporate investors.

Halicki & Kwater (2014) suggested that using the WIG20 index for 3-month periods and some macro-economic variables, the ANN approach could be used to make investment decisions in the stock market. They also proposed a set of 12 characteristics of any stock or economic market chosen for ANN to be useful. As a result of the study, they suggested that ANN can be considered an expert system that supports decisions about a quarterly investment period in the stock market.

In their study, Güneri-Tosunoğlu & Keskin-Benli (2012) estimated the MSCI Turkey Index with monthly data for the period 1987-2008. A feed-forward network model consisting of 12 input, 11 hidden, and 1 output neurons was used in the analysis, and as a result, it showed that the predictions obtained with ANN were close to the actual index values.

Walczak (2004) used ANN models in his study for three emerging markets, Singapore, Malaysia and Mexico, and suggested that certain markets are partially dependent on other global markets and that heterogeneous market information should be included in the analysis, and that this would improve neural network prediction performance by up to 12 percent compared to similar homogeneous models. As a result, he advised investors to incorporate heterogeneous market values from both local capital markets and global markets in the neural network working in Emerging Capital Markets into models to achieve optimal forecasting performance.

Bildirici & Ersin (2014) analyzed a family of regime switching neural network augmented volatility models using the daily closing of the Istanbul Stock Index ISE 100, covering the period 07.12.1986-13.12.2010. They evaluated the obtained models with MSE and RMSE error criteria and asymmetric power modeling with fractional integration generalized to Time Lag Recurrent Neural Network architecture and Hybrid Multilayer Perceptron yielded effective results. On the other hand, among the models analyzed, Hybrid-MLP and Recurrent-NN, MS-ARMA FIAPGARCH-HybridMLP and MS-ARMAFIAPGARCH-RNN-based models provided the best prediction performance compared to single-regime GARCH models. In general, it has been proposed that regime-changing models, further enhanced by neural network modeling techniques, can be highly useful in modeling and predicting returns and volatility.

Estimates that also exist in the literature based on time series models are the subject of many studies. Huang et al. (2015) worked with four different models (GARCHM, NA-GARCH, GJR-GARCH, T-GARCH, and AV-GARCH) to find the most suitable model for VAR estimation with MSCI World Index data. According to their results for the period 29.05.2006-06.11.2009, it was stated that on average, GARCH (GARCHM [1,1]), MA-GARCHM (1,1), AR (1) -T-GARCHM (1,1) and ARMA (1,1) -TGARCHM (1,1) performed better than other models in terms of the number of violations.

Fernandez (2005) proposed a time-scale VaR and a time-scale marginal VaR for the period 1990-2004 by proposing the stock of seven Latin American and Asian emerging economies (Brazil, Chile, Mexico, Indonesia, South Korea, Malaysia, and Thailand) indices. As a result of the study, it was stated that countries subject to analysis are more integrated into developed countries, losses in VaR value are greater in the short term, investments in Brazil and Indonesia appear to be risky, while Chile and Malaysia are safer for investments.

Colucci & Brandolini (2011) compared the methods of Historical Simulation and Monte Carlo Filtered Bootstrap, two risk models for predicting VaR. For the period 03.01.2000-22.08.2011, according to VaR 1% and VaR 5% for daily return data of Standard & Poors 500, Topix, Dax, MSCI United Kingdom, MSCI France, Italy ComitGlobale, MSCI Canada, MSCI Emerging Markets and RJ/CRB indices Filtered Bootstrap model gave more effective results than Historical Simulation.

Miletic et al. (2013) used symmetrical GARCH and asymmetric GARCH models with MSCI daily returns on the stock market index for the period 2002-2013 as VAR forecast models to measure the impact of the global financial crisis on the MSCI world stock market index. The performance of VaR was evaluated using the Kupiec test unconditional coverage. Retrospective test results show that the VAR values obtained for the EGARCH model are sufficient at 95% and 99% confidence levels for the pre-crisis period according to the Kupiec test.

Oskay et al. (2017) comparatively analyzed various financial risk models modelling VaR using MSCI index data. As a result of the study, it was found that the forecast performance of the models studied differed according to the confidence level, especially the AVGARCH (2,2) JSU model was superior to the traditional EWMA model when using a 99% confidence level in non-sample estimates, while EWMA performed slightly better for a 95% confidence level.

METHODOLOGY

Value at Risk (VaR)

VaR is a method developed for monetary expression of the expected maximum loss over a certain period of time and at a certain probability level (Jorion, 2001). The most important advantage of the value at risk method is that it can be applied to all types of products traded on the stock exchange. There are various VaR methods developed to calculate market risk. VaR methods can be listed as conventional methods as follows.

- Variance-Covariance Method (parametric method),
- Historical Simulation (non-parametric),
- Monte Carlo Simulations (stochastic simulation)

Variance-Covariance Method (Parametric Method)

In variance-covariance method, while VaR values are calculating, the volatility and correlations of risk factors are firstly determined by using historical data. The variability of risk factors is taken into account through standard deviations, and measures of co-movement are taken into account through correlation coefficients. Based on the assumption of normal distribution, it is possible to calculate the VaR value of portfolio return as a linear function of standard deviations of asset returns. (1) is used to calculate the VaR value using the variance-covariance method in a certain confidence interval under the assumption of normal distribution (Cheng & Hung, 2011):

$$VaR_t = \mu + \hat{\sigma}_t z_\alpha \tag{1}$$

Here, VaR_t refers to the VaR value predicted under the assumption of the normal and student-t distribution of the *t* period; μ refers to the conditional average; $\hat{\sigma}_t$ refers to the conditional standard deviation using GARCH models of the *t* period; and z_α refers to the table value corresponding to the percentage slice of α on the left side of the normal and student-t distribution.

The conditional mean μ in the VaR equation is calculated as in (2) (Chen et al., 2009; Cheng & Hung, 2011).

$$\begin{aligned} r_t &= \mu_t + \varepsilon_t \\ \varepsilon_t &= z_t \sigma_t \\ \mu_t &= \mu(\Omega_{t-1};\theta) \\ \sigma_t^2 &= \sigma^2(\Omega_{t-1};\theta) \end{aligned} \tag{2}$$

r_t refers to the financial rate of return (asset return) in the period *t*; on the other hand, when μt represents the conditional expected return in the t period, σt $_r$epresents the changes in the portfolio or the conditional volatility of changes in the εt. Ω_{t-1} is the information set available at time t-*1*, θ is a finite-dimensional vector of true parameter values, and zt i_s i.i.d. random variable satisfying $E\left(z_t \middle| \Omega_{t-1};\theta\right)=0$ and $Var\left(z_t \middle| \Omega_{t-1};\theta\right)=1$ (Chen et.al., 2009).

Assuming a portfolio (a portfolio of one asset position) containing an asset position of $ 1, VaR can be parametrically defined as in (3):

$$VaR_\alpha^t = \mu_t + q_\alpha \sigma_t \tag{3}$$

where q_α is α quantile of zt

It can be seen that if the level of significant (α) is changed, the value of VaR changes. For example, if the level of confidence is increased, the value of VaR is gone up. Figure 1. can be used to explain this situation.

Figure 1. VaR and Confidence Level
Source: Dowd, 2005

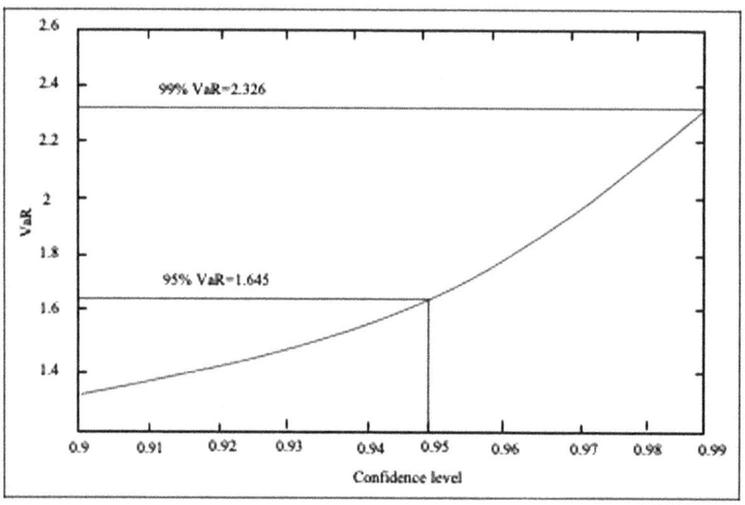

In order to evaluate the ability of the VaR values predicted in the study, the mean square error (MSE), Kupiec statistics, and the *p* value for estimates were calculated. The unconditional coverage test, developed by Kupiec (1995), is widely used to determine whether VaR models adequately estimate the actual risk. In the Kupiec (1995) test with a distribution of 1 degree of freedom, the likelihood ratio is defined in the test statistic (LR) (4).

$$LR = -2Log\left[\left(1-p^*\right)^{n-x}\left(p^*\right)^x\right] + 2Log\left[\left(1-\left[x/n\right]\right)^{n-x}\left(x/n\right)^n\right],\ LR \sim \chi^2(1) \tag{4}$$

In equality (4), *n* gives the sample size, *x* the number of exceedences, *p** the ratio of the number of exceedances to the sample size. In the Kupiec (1995) test, the null hypothesis is expressed as p=p*, and the null hypothesis is rejected if the LR statistic exceeds the critical table value at a certain α level of trust. This shows that the VaR model is not sufficient (Evci & Kandır, 2015).

Historical Simulation Method (Non-parametric Method)

Historical simulation is a nonparametric method and offers a completely different approach to estimate VaR. This method does not require the calculation of volatility, correlation and other parameters and does not require assumptions about the distribution of market risk returns. Instead, in the VaR calculation, the profit or loss that the portfolio may suffer in the

future is calculated by using historical data at market prices and rates. During this calculation, a certain number of historical data sets are selected and changes that have been experienced are applied to the existing portfolio.

Historical simulation, in its simplest form, neglects any temporal dependence between successive market risk changes and should be applied only if the current assumption for market risk returns is reasonable. When applying the Historical simulation method, it is necessary to decide the historical sampling period. Long periods can violate the i.i.d. assumption, and sub-samples can lead to unreliable estimates. Kupiec (1995), VaR estimates are becoming increasingly unreliable for small samples and high values of p (Locarek-Junge & Prinzler, 1998).

Based on criticism of the historical simulation method, although the method does not make any assumptions about the distribution of portfolio returns, calculated VaR estimates yield meaningful results only when historical data with the same distribution is used (Linsmeier & Pearson, 2000).

Monte Carlo Simulations (Stochastic Simulation)

VaR models based on Monte Carlo Simulation require a certain distribution assumption as in the Variance-Covariance method. However, it allows the calculation of VaR for nonlinear loss functions. The basic idea here is to extract a large number of hypothetical observations from the default distribution, apply them to the portfolio loss function, and construct a hypothetical distribution of portfolio losses. In practice, the associated computational burden prohibits the application of this technique to a portfolio with a large number of risk factors (Locarek-Junge & Prinzler, 1998).

Statistical ANN

Artificial neural networks are a computer program that models the human brain and models the brain's learning function. Artificial neural networks use a learning dataset to model the ability of the human brain to process information gained from experience. This modeling tool can adapt to any environment in which it is located. It can work with missing data. Using this modeling technique, it can be decided in an environment of uncertainty. It is a system with fault tolerance. Therefore, it is used in the fields of classification, signal filtering, pattern recognition and optimization artificial neural networks have many advantages. Information is stored throughout the network. They can examine the relationships of patterns and classify them. They can self-train using the training set. One of its most important advantages is that it can work with missing data. It has fault tolerance. In addition to these advantages, there are also disadvantages. Unlike linear models, the behaviour of the network cannot be explained exactly. There are no specific rules for determining parameter values for the network Although it has disadvantages, it is a powerful method in order to solve nonlinear problems in daily life (Jang, 1997; Larose, 2005).

In human body, the nervous system consists of nerve cells. Nerve cells are the smallest units in which the vitality of living things is carried out and spread throughout the body through the central nervous system. The communication system in the brain allows people to communicate through the interaction of nerve cells with each other.

The nervous system structurally consists of four different parts: dendrites, soma, axon and synapse. After the biological nerve cell receives inputs from different sources, it processes the information transmitted by soma. Generally, this data has a non-linear structure. The axon transfers processed input information to the output. Synapses transmit output information from one nerve cell to other nerve cells via the dendrites (Larose, 2005; Özçalışıcı, 2016).

The artificial nervous system takes the nervous system as a model. It has an input, hidden and output layer. Layers come together to form a network system. In order to train the network, it is necessary to have a training set. The information in the training set is first transferred to the input layer. Next, it is necessary to optimize weights in the hidden layer located between the input layer and the output layer. The network is trained to achieve the most optimal weights. Information is called processed. The trained network model is tested using the test set. The model performance is evaluated with measurement criteria (MSE, MAE, etc.) preferred by researchers (Larose, 2005; Yüksel & Akkoç, 2016).

Figure 2. Schematic Representation of the Artificial Neural Network Structure
Source: Yüksel & Akkoç, 2016

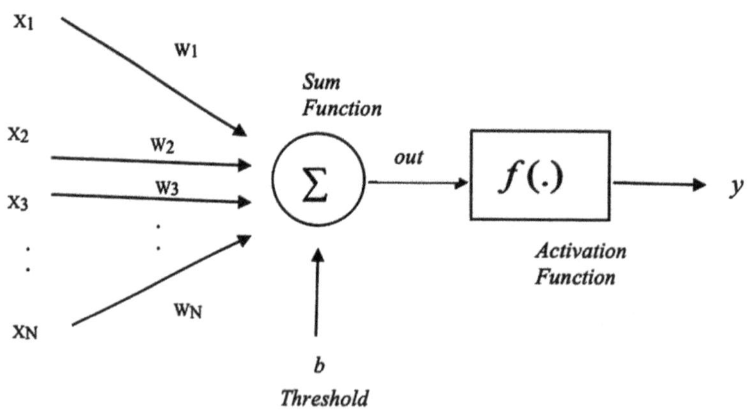

The process of artificial neural networks is given in Figure 2. Artificial neural networks basically need five elements. Basically, five elements can be summarized as inputs, weights, sum function, activation function, and outputs. It is shown with inputs as expressed as x_j in Figure 2. Each of the input values is multiplied by weights called w_j. The threshold value expressed with b is added to the information obtained. The 'net' value is obtained and it is named 'out' in Figure 2. The output value of y is obtained by applying the activation function to 'out'. And this iterative process is repeated until the optimization of weights has been completed. The structure of the neural network depends on learning algorithm. If the learning algorithm is changed, the structure of the networks is changed.

There are many types of artificial neural networks, feed forward neural networks, such as radial basis neural network, convolutional neural network, recurrent neural network, etc. Among these types of artificial neural networks, recurrent neural network is generally preferred to make time series forecasting.

Recurrent Neural Networks

Recurrent neural networks connect nodes form a directed graph in a temporal sequence. It means that it is a recursive artificial neural network. The neurons' connections make a directed cycle. Output relies upon the present inputs. Yet, it also depends on neuron position, which is in previous iteration. Recurrent neural networks came from feedforward networks. They can use their internal memory in order to deal with variable length sequences of inputs. It means that recurrent structures use their output as input in the next process. Recurrent networks have a memory. The reason for adding memory to a network is that the input set that comes in a certain order has a meaning for the output. In recurrent structures, the result is extracted not only based on the current input, but also on other inputs.

Figure 3. Schematic Representation of the Recurrent Neural Network Structure
Source: Sehovac & Grolinger, 2020

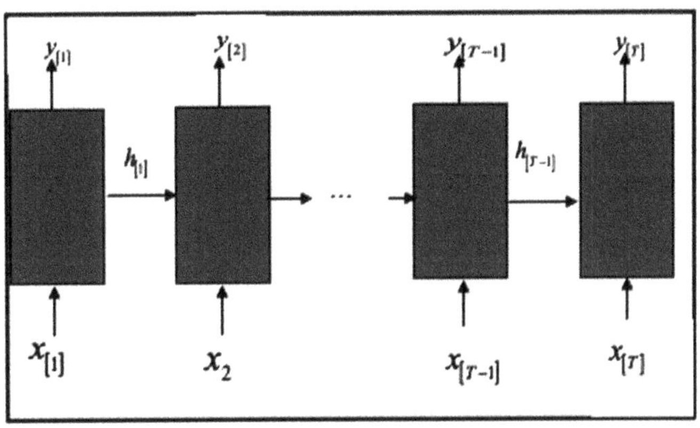

It is seen in the figure, the input data at time t in RNN and hidden layer results from time $t-1$ are the input of the hidden layer at time t. The decision for the input at time $t-1$ also affects the decision to be made at time t. In other words, inputs in these networks generate outputs by combining current and previous information.

Assume that there are units interacting in discrete time directedly and there are weighted connections with weights w_{lm} which are from unit m to unit l. Each unit is activated with $y(t)$ which is updated at each time unit t=1,2,…. (William & Zipser, 1992).

Each unit feeds into other units in the network. There are activations for each unit. One of the activation can be defined as y^l of unit l. Input sum net^l is recalculated in (5) as below:

$$net^l(t) = \sum_m w_{lm} y^m(t-1) \tag{5}$$

And, suppose that function f is a derivative function. $y^l(t)$ is calculated as given in (6):

$$y^l(t) = f(net^t(t)) \tag{6}$$

Recurrent neural network uses sequences. It is aimed to optimize a differentiable objective function E. This objective function is based on the outputs t^k. c_k denotes the error between the output units of the network $t^k(t)$, and the activations y^k (William & Zipser, 1992). It can be defined as below (7):

$$E(t) = \frac{1}{2}\sum_k e_k(t)^2, \; e_k(t) = t^k(t) - y^k(t) \tag{7}$$

And, the error for one of the sequence component at time t is represented with $E(t)$. The sequence component is also named as pattern. It is necessary to calculate E for a data set which consists of all sequences. E is the sum of $E(t)$. An optimization algorithm is selected to optimize E with respect to each weight w_{lm}. It aims to update the weights Δw_{lm}.

$$\Delta w_{lm}(t) = -\alpha \frac{\partial E(t)}{\partial w_{lm}}, \tag{8}$$

where α is called the learning rate.

Long-Short-Term Memory (Lstm) Network

Long-Short-Term Memory (LSTM) network is a type of recurrent neural network. It is designed to solve vanishing gradient problem by Hochreiter & Schmidhuber (1997). *A schematic representation of the LSTM network is given in* Figure 4. There are three blocks seen in Figure 4. These three blocks are called as forget gate, input gate, and output gate, respectively. Forget gate aims to take account the first output and the updated cell state by using the initial network and, the first step of the sequence. There are hidden (output) and cell states. The hidden state at time step t includes the output. The information is transported from the previous time steps to the cell state. Layer pick up the information coming from the cell state. The gates help to the layer in order to control these updates at each time step.

Figure 4. Schematic Representation of the Long-Short-Term Memory Network
Source: Fan et al, 2020

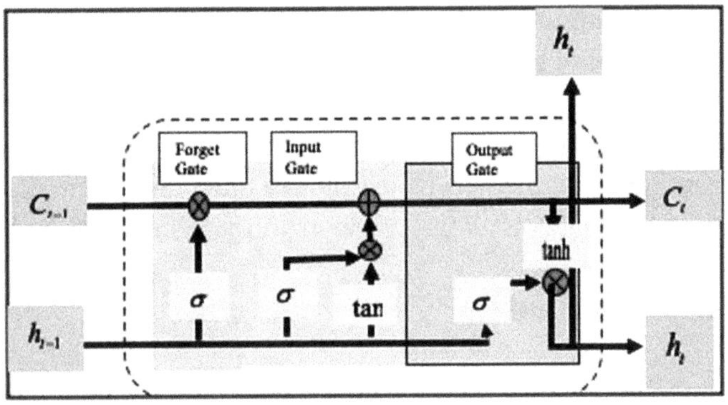

Assume that an input sequence is defined as $x_{[1]},\ldots,x_{[T]}$. It can be thought as time series with C called as *channels*. m_t and c_t denote the output state and cell state at time step t, respectively. The input gate *(i)*, forget gate *(f)*, and output gate *(o)* are defined. And, an output sequence is given as $y_{[1]},\ldots,y_{[T]}$. The equations are given to calculate the network unit activations iteratively from $t = 1$ to T as following:

$$i_{[t]} = \sigma\left(W_{ix}x_{[t]} + W_{im}m_{[t-1]} + W_{ic}c_{[t-1]} + b_i\right) \text{(Input Gate)}$$

$$f_{[t]} = \sigma\left(W_{fx}x_{[t]} + W_{mf}m_{[t-1]} + W_{cf}c_{[t-1]} + b_f\right) \text{(Forget Gate)}$$

$$c_{[t]} = f_t \odot c_{[t-1]} + i_t \odot g\left(W_{cx}x_{[t]} + W_{cm}m_{[t-1]} + b_c\right) \text{(Cell Activation Vectors)}$$

$$o_t = \sigma\left(W_{ox}x_{[t]} + W_{om}m_{[t-1]} + W_{oc}c_{[t]} + b_o\right) \text{(Output Gate)}$$

$$m_{[t]} = o_t \odot h\left(c_{[t]}\right) \text{(Cell Output Activation Vector)}$$

$$y_{[t]} = W_{ym}m_t + b_y$$

Where weight matrices is represented by W. For example, W_{ix} is the matrix of weights from the input gate to the input. The bias vector is shown with b and, b_i means i*th* input gate bias vector. σ shows the *logistic sigmoid function*. Then, g and h implies the cell input and cell output activation functions, respectively. *tanh* is preferred for the cell input and cell output activation function (Sak et al., 2014).

Optimization Algorithm

In artificial neural networks, it is important to minimize the error between actual value and output value. One of the most used methods for optimization of artificial neural networks is gradient descent. There are three gradient descent methods (Batch Gradient Descent, Stochastic Gradient Descent, Mini-Batch Gradient Descent) depending on the size of the data set used in a single iteration. Adaptive moment estimation (adam) is an optimization method which figures out adaptive step for each parameter. This method is computationally efficient. And, it uses little memory (Kingma & Ba, 2014).

Traditional Time Series Methods

Although the GARCH model is a useful method of modeling variance, it has some disadvantages. The biggest disadvantage is that it is a symmetrical model. In other words, the effect of positive and negative shocks on volatility on returns is the same magnitude. However, in the financial time series, it is argued that the effect of the negative shock in volatility and the effect of the positive shock will not be of the same magnitude.

Due to the leverage effect, which is the existence of volatility clusters, the occurrence of volatility continuously over time, the volatility being generally stable and reacting differently to large price increases or decreases, the conditional variance is not symmetrical (Tsay, 2010). Nelson (1991) EGARCH; Glosten et al. (1993) (GJR) and Zakoian (1994) TGARCH models are pioneer models that take into account the asymmetry in conditional variance. For example, the mean equation of the r_t variable for the ARMA (*p, q*) model is in the form of

$$r_t = \mu + \sum_{i=1}^{p} a_i r_{t-p} + \sum_{i=1}^{q} b_i \varepsilon_{t-q} + \varepsilon_t, \quad \varepsilon_t \sim N.i.i.d.\left(0, \sigma_t^2\right) \text{(Mean Equation)}$$

the conditionally changing variance of residuals The ARCH(*m*), GARCH(*m, n*), EGARCH(*m, n*), GJR(*m, n*) and models are as follows:

$$\sigma_t^2 = \alpha_0 + \sum_{i=1}^{m} \alpha_i \varepsilon_{t-i}^2, \quad \alpha_0 > 0, \alpha_i \geq 0 \text{(ARCH)}$$

$$\sigma_t^2 = \alpha_0 + \sum_{i=1}^{m} \alpha_i \varepsilon_{t-i}^2 + \sum_{j=1}^{n} \beta_j \sigma_{t-j}^2, \quad \alpha_0 > 0, \alpha_i \geq 0, \beta_i \geq 0, \sum_{i=1}^{\max(m,n)} \left(\alpha_i + \beta_i\right) < 1 \text{(GARCH)}$$

$$\ln\left(\sigma_t^2\right) = \alpha_0 + \sum_{i=1}^{m} \alpha_i \left|\frac{\varepsilon_{t-i}}{\sigma_{t-i}}\right| + \sum_{i=1}^{n} \beta_i \ln\left(\sigma_{t-i}^2\right) + \sum_{i=1}^{m} \gamma_i \frac{\varepsilon_{t-i}}{\sigma_{t-i}} \text{(EGARCH)}$$

$$\sigma_t^2 = \alpha_0 + \sum_{i=1}^{m} \alpha_i \varepsilon_{t-i}^2 + \sum_{j=1}^{n} \beta_j \sigma_{t-j}^2 + \sum_{i=1}^{m} \gamma_i D_{i,t-i} \varepsilon_{t-i}^2, \qquad \begin{gathered} \alpha_0 > 0, \alpha_i \geq 0, \beta_i \geq 0, \sum_{i=1}^{m} \left(\alpha_i + \gamma_i\right) \geq 1 \\ D_{t-i} = \begin{cases} 1, & for \quad \varepsilon_{t-i} < 0 \\ 0, & for \quad \varepsilon_{t-i} \geq 0 \end{cases} \end{gathered} \qquad \text{(GJR)}$$

Nelson (1991) noted that the EGARCH model corresponds to a Generalized Error Distribution (GED) because it takes into account excessive kurtosis. In the EGARCH model, the γ_i parameter shows the leverage effect. If γ_i is statistically significant, it is concluded that it is an asymmetric model. In practice, the γ_i parameter is expected to be predicted negatively because if the relationship between volatility and return is negative then γ_i will also be negative. (Tsay, 2010; Brooks, 2008). In GJR models, statistically significant estimation of the γ_i parameter again shows that the presence of the leverage effect.

EXPERIMENTAL ANALYSIS

Data

In this study, value at risk of MSCI-EMI with classical time series models and artificial neural networks were investigated. The data set is obtained from the Morgan Stanley website[1] and the data set is between 31 December 1987 and 30 April 2020 and has a monthly frequency.

SOLUTIONS AND RECOMMENDATIONS

The return series of MSCI-EMI has been obtained with

$$r_t^{MSCI-EMI} = \ln\left(MSCI - EMI_t / MSCI - EMI_{t-1}\right).$$

Figure 5 shows the time path graphs of both series. MSCI-EMI reached its highest value in October 2007 and has an increased trend with breaks. According to r_t seen at the bottom panel of Figure 5, it is seen that there is no positive returns that draw attention, but it reached the lowest returns in the periods of August 1998 and October 2008.

Figure 5. MSCI-EMI and Log Return of The Data

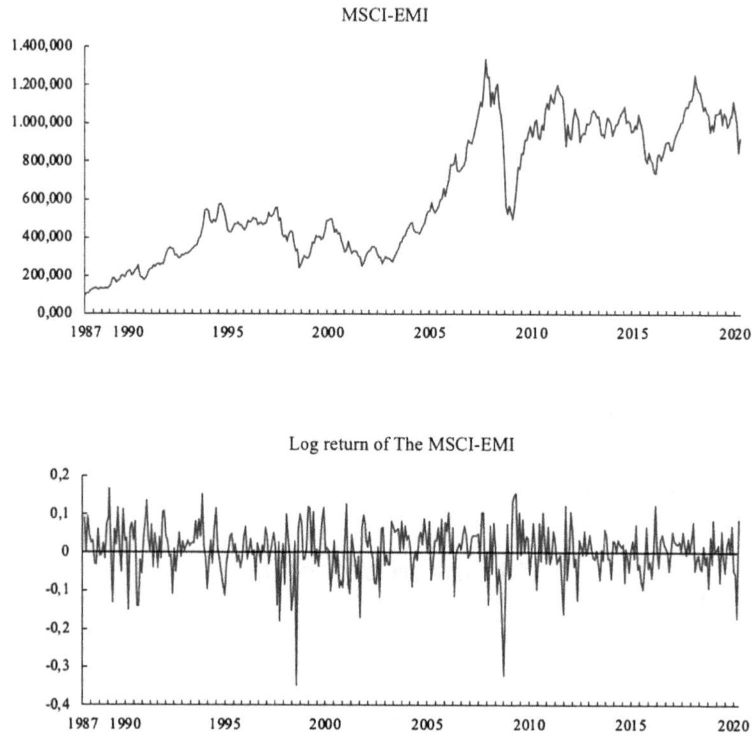

In Table 1, to decide the descriptive statistics and stationarity levels of the return series, Augmented Dickey-Fuller (1979) (ADF), Phillips-Perron (1988) (PP) with unit root tests Kwiatkowski et al. (1992) (KPSS) stationarity test results are included. Average return is 0.6% while std. deviation is 0.003. It was also decided by the Jarque and Bera (1987) (JB) test that the return series was not suited to normal distribution.

Table 1. Descriptive Statistics and Stationary Results of log returns

Mean	0.006	*Range*	0.513
Std. Deviation	0.003	*Maximum*	-0.347
Mean	0.009	*Minimum*	0.166
Kurtosis	3.233	*T*	388
Skewness	-0.962	*Jarque-Bera*	222.419 (0.000)*
Unit Root and Stationary			
	ADF	**PP**	**KPSS**
Test Stat	-16.826	-16.817	0.200
*1% C.V.***	-3.447	-3.447	0.739
5%C.V.	-2.868	-2.868	0.463
10% C.V.	-2.571	-2.571	0.347

*probability values in parenthesis. **critical values obtained from MacKinnon (1996) and Kwiatkowski et al. (1992).

Figure 6. Model Selection Criteria for Mean Equation

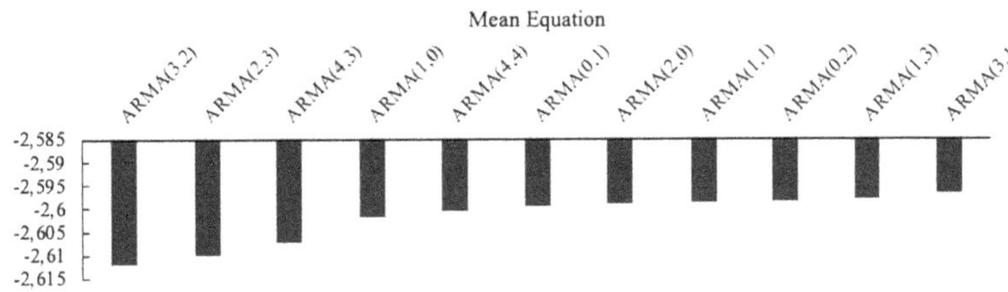

ADF and PP have stated that r_t does not contain a unit root in the level value and is stationary, since the unit root test statistics are more negative than all critical values, and the KPSS test statistic is not greater than all critical values.

Different models were investigated with the Akaike Information Criterion (AIC) in determining the appropriate ARMA (*p,q*) model for the average equation of r_t. As can be seen from Figure 6, the ARMA (3,2) model reached the lowest AIC value. Therefore, the analysis was continued with the model in which the mean equation is ARMA (3,2).

Whether the residuals of the ARMA (3,2) model carry an ARCH effect has been tested by the ARCH-LM test. Test results of whether residuals carry an ARCH effect of up to five delays are included in Table 2. According to these results, it was decided by ARCH-LM test results that the residuals had an ARCH effect at the first, second and third delays. Therefore, the residuals of the ARMA (3,2) model of r_t are not with equal variance. Therefore, it is necessary to determine the appropriate autoregressive conditional heteroskedasticity (ARCH) model to model the variance of residues.

Table 2. ARCH-LM Test Results

	Lag				
	1	**2**	**3**	**4**	**5**
ARCH-LM	5.081	6.119	9.050	9.003	8.988
Prob.	0.024	0.046	0.028	0.061	0.109

Figure 7. Model Selection Criteria for ARCH Type Model

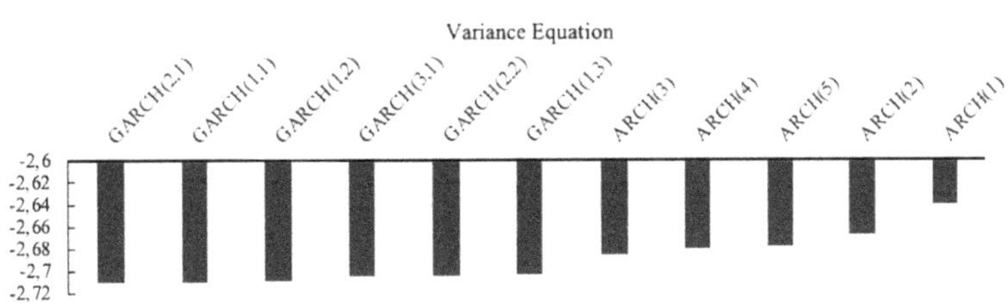

Figure 7 shows the AIC values of different ARCH type models. ARMA (3,2) – GARCH (2,1) model has the lowest AIC value. ARMA (3,2) - GARCH (1,1) model has the lowest Second AIC value.

In the variance equation of the model estimated by ARMA (3,2) - GARCH (2,1), the analysis was continued with ARMA (3,2) - GARCH (1,1), since the $\hat{\varepsilon}^2_{t-2}$ coefficient was statistically insignificant. This is in line with the theory.[2] Therefore, the analyses were continued on the basis of ARMA (3,2) - GARCH (1,1) model.

Table 3. Conditional Variance Models Results

	GARCH(1,1)		EGARCH(1,1)		GJR(1,1)	
	Coefficient	z-stat	Coefficient	z-stat	Coefficient	z-stat
			Mean Equation			
a_0	0.0072	2.1196	0.0050	3.2397	0.0063	1.8200
a_1	1.4218	12.0689	0.1124	2.0057	1.4273	12.0451
a_2	-0.7687	-6.6386	0.9474	55.9365	-0.7729	-6.7326
a_3	-	-	-0.1130	-2.0398	-	-
b_1	-1.2821	-9.4819	-	-	-1.2905	-9.4868
b_2	0.6566	4.7187	-0.9801	-143.9325	0.6616	4.8044
			Variance Equation			
α_0	0.0004	2.4484	-0.9221	-2.2081	0.0004	2.5204
α_1	0.1914	3.6362	0.2771	2.6191	0.1328	1.9840
β_1	0.7396	10.8099	0.8716	12.5763	0.7333	10.3378
γ_1	-	-	-0.0618	-1.0538	0.0869	1.1491
$\bar{R}^2$	0.0225		0.0299		0.0230	
SSR	1.6355		1.6154		1.6347	
LL	531.6230		534.8252		532.1670	
AIC	-2.7131		-2.7264		-2.7107	
SIC	-2.6311		-2.6237		-2.6185	
ARCH-LM	0.4138 (0.5200)		0.5141 (0.4733)		0.7289 (0.3932)	

Table 4. Forecast Comparison of the GARCH and ANN Models

h	1	5	10	20
		ARMA (2,2) - GARCH (1,1)		
MAE	0.113468	0.087000	0.056065	0.049070
RMSE	0.113468	0.097904	0.072472	0.064127
		ANN		
MAE	0.09658	0.0965	0.07679	0.10768
RMSE	0.09490	0.1012	0.08565	0.16253

The conditional heteroskedasticity models estimated for the ARMA (3,2) - GARCH (1,1) model are given in Table 3. When the three models are compared, AIC, SIC and Sum Squared Residual (SSR) values show that the best model is EGARCH (1,1). Adjusted R^2 $\left(\bar{R}^2\right)$ and log-likelihood (LL) values show again that the best model is EGARCH (1,1). However, the estimated coefficient value of γ_i is not statistically significant. The same is true for the GJR (1,1) model. Thus, it has been concluded that there is no leverage effect in the volatility of the r_t variable and that it is symmetric. The most suitable model for MSCI-EMI return series is ARMA (2,2) - GARCH (1,1).

In Table 4, the mean absolute error (MAE) and Root Mean Square Error (RMSE) values of the forecast estimates of the GARCH and ANN models for h=1, 5, 10 and 20 are included. For h=1 (h is the forecast horizon), the ARMA (2,2) – GARCH (1,1) model has greater MAE and RMSE values than ANN, while for h=5,10,20, the predictive performance of the ARMA (2,2) – GARCH (1,1) model is better than ANN. In other words, while MSCI-EMI's ANN gives better results in short-term forecast than conditional heteroskedasticity models, it is the opposite for long-term forecasts.

In this study, 273 of the 388 data were used as training sets when establishing the artificial neural network model. Long-short-term memory network is used to forecast the time series. During training, the number of iterations (epoch) was set to 500 and the learning rate was set to 0.005. Adaptive moment estimation method (adam) is used for the optimization of the weights. 115 data was used as a test data set. The RMSE value of the corresponding model was obtained as 0.0847 and the MAE value as 0.0620.

Table 5 shows VaR exceedences and Kupiec statistics at 1%, 5% and 10% significance levels of both models. First, according to the Kupiec test results, the results of ANN and ARMA (2,2) – GARCH (1,1) models cannot be rejected at 5% VaR. The null hypothesis of the Kupiec test for the ARMA (2,2) – GARCH (1,1) model for 10% VaR cannot be rejected. In the study of VaR exceedences, ARMA (2,2) - GARCH (1,1) and ANN give very different results. The differences between the results obtained from the ARMA (2,2) – GARCH (1,1) model are greater, while the excess numbers of ANN results in all percentile slices are very close to each other. This is because the conditional heteroskedasticity from the ANN model is smaller. In the excess numbers for 5% VaR, the Kupiec statistic is 2.8082 in ARMA (2.2) – GARCH (1,1), while in ANN model 0.6654. The fact that the LR statistic is smaller suggests that the zero hypothesis cannot be strongly rejected. Therefore, accepting VaR for 5% as 23 observations would be the most accurate option.

Table 5. VaR Exceedence Comparison of the GARCH and ANN Model

Model	VaR Exceedence		
	1%	5%	10%
GARCH(1,1)	11	32	42
Kupiec Statistic	6.7930 (0.0091)*	2.8082 (0.0937)	0.13634 (0.7119)
ANN	20	23	26
Kupiec Statistic	34.0420 (0.0000)	0.66540 (0.4146)	5.2467 (0.0220)

*probability value in parenthesis

These results show that ANN method is more effective to estimate VaR exceedance for the log return of the MSCI-EMI. Because of the Kupiec statistics closer to zero in ANN method, it can be said that the real VaR exceedances are 23 times for the analysis period. Thus, as stated in the main hypothesis, it has been concluded that the ANN method is more effective in obtaining VaR exceedances than classical time series models.

FUTURE RESEARCH DIRECTIONS

The current research covers emerging market economies, but in the future, making similar analyses for developed or frontier country groups or on the basis of different indices may contribute to the literature. In addition, VaR values were calculated using a parametric technique in the study. Historical simulation and Monte Carlo simulation, which are nonparametric techniques, can be used to calculate these values.

Different models of the ARCH family from parametric methods (IGARCH, APARCH, FIGARCH, etc.) with also exist estimates can be realized. In addition, since MSCI-EMI is a composite variable, country weights are also different from each other. Therefore, the VaR estimates of the low weight countries included in this index may not reflect the truth. Therefore, countries in the index can be examined separately.

Finally, in the current study, time series estimation was performed using LSMT recurrent network to the MSCI-EMI. In later studies, using a fuzzy logic approach to the corresponding index series, adaptive neural network (Jang et al., 1997) approach to time series estimation can be proposed.

CONCLUSION

Investment markets play a key role in every growing and developing economy, and every investment in the market is aimed at maximizing profit and minimizing the risk involved. A large number of studies have been conducted on market forecasting using technical or fundamental analysis through various software calculation techniques and algorithms.

In this study, it is aimed to make a comparison study on traditional times series and artificial neural networks. On the other hand, the effect of these models on short and long term predictions are searched on MSCI-EMI. Artificial neural networks take their place in the literature as the most widely used machine learning algorithms for investment market forecasting (Nti et al., 2020).

The MSCI-EMI used in the current study is a composite index. The fact that the variable is in this way may not reflect the state of the countries it contains, but it provides information, especially for emerging markets. Emerging market economies are highly susceptible to external shocks such as currency volatility and financial crises. Therefore, investors prefer portfolio investments instead of fixed capital investments in these countries. Like portfolio investments, foreign capital is used as capital in GDP. For this reason, MSCI-EMI provides general information about the effects of external shocks in these countries.

Analysis results show that the predictive performance of the ARMA-GARCH model for MSCI-EMI is better over long periods and ANN is better over short periods. For this reason, ANN may be preferred in investors' short-term yield forecasts. However, it is more appropriate to prefer ARMA-GARCH models for long-term predictions. The varying levels of superiority between models also appear in VaR exceedences. The Kupiec statistic confirms that there are 23 observations for 5% VaR, while the ARMA-GARCH model shows that there are 32 observations. However, the fact that the Kupiec test statistic from ANN is lower than the other model shows that it is more appropriate for MSCI-EMI to have 23 observations at 5% VaR.

When literature is examined, it is possible to reach studies that express that both methods have advantages. There are also studies that suggest that ANN may be the most efficient choice for modeling the future values of emerging markets (Smith, 1993; Trippi, 1995; Güneri Tosunoğlu & Keskin Benli, 2012), and that ANN cannot outperform linear models in return forecasts of developed and emerging markets (Moreno & Olmeda, 2007). As a result of the current study, it can be said that both methods perform well in forecasting when comparing ANN and classical time series models.

REFERENCES

Arimond, A., Borth, D., Hoepner, A. G. F., Klawunn, M., & Weisheit, S. (2020). Neural networks and value at risk. *Michael J. Brennan Irish Finance Working Paper Series, 20*(7). https://ssrn.com/abstract=3591996

Becker, Y. L., Guo, L., & Nurmamatov, O. (2020), Assessing asset tail risk with artificial intelligence: The application of artificial neural network. In Advances in Pacific Basin Business, Economics and Finance (Vol. 8). Emerald Publishing Limited.

Bildirici, M., & Ersin, Ö. (2014). Modeling markov switching ARMA-GARCH neural networks models and an application to forecasting stock returns. *The Scientific World Journal*, 1–21. Advance online publication. doi:10.1155/2014/497941 PMID:24977200

Bollerslev, T. (1986). Generalized autoregressive conditional heteroskedasticity. *Journal of Econometrics, 31*(3), 307–327. doi:10.1016/0304-4076(86)90063-1

Brooks, C. (2008). *Introductory econometrics for finance* (2nd ed.). Cambridge University Press. doi:10.1017/CBO9780511841644

Chen, X., Lai, K. K., & Yen, J. (2009). A statistical neural network approach for value-at-risk analysis. *2009 International Joint Conference on Computational Sciences and Optimization*, 17-21. 10.1109/CSO.2009.350

Cheng, W. H., & Hung, J. C. (2011). Skewness and lep to kurtosis in GARCH-typed VaR estimation of petroleum and metal asset returns. *Journal of Empirical Finance, 18*(1), 160–173. doi:10.1016/j.jempfin.2010.05.004

Kingma & Ba. (2014). *Adam: A method for stochastic optimization.* arXiv preprint arXiv:1412.6980.

Dowd, K. (2005). *Measuring market risk* (2nd ed.). John Wiley & Sons Ltd. doi:10.1002/9781118673485

Colucci, S., & Brandolini, D. (2011). Backtesting value-at-risk: A comparison between filtered bootstrap and historical simulation. SSRN *Electronic Journal, 6*(4), 1-36. doi:10.2139srn.1965377

Dickey, D. A., & Fuller, W. A. (1979). Distribution of the estimators for autoregressive time series with a unit root. *Journal of the American Statistical Association, 74*(366a), 427–431.

Evci, S., & Kandır, S. Y. (2015). Altın piyasasında piyasa riskinin ölçülmesi: Riske maruz değer (VaR) yöntemi ile bir uygulama. *Bankacılar Dergisi*, *26*(92), 5–104.

Fan, H., Jiang, M., Xu, L., Zhu, H., Cheng, J., & Jiang, J. (2020). Comparison of Long Short Term Memory Networks and the Hydrological Model in Runoff Simulation. *Water (Basel)*, *12*(1), 175. doi:10.3390/w12010175

Fernandez, V. P. (2005). The international CAPM and a wavelet-based decomposition of value at risk. *Studies in Nonlinear Dynamics and Econometrics*, *9*(4).

Glosten, L. R., Jagannathan, R., & Runkle, D. E. (1993). On the relation between the expected value and the volatility of the nominal excess return on stocks. *The Journal of Finance*, *48*(5), 1779–1801. doi:10.1111/j.1540-6261.1993.tb05128.x

Güneri Tosunoğlu, N., & Keskin Benli, Y. (2012). Forecasting of Morgan Stanley Capital International Turkey Index with artifcial neural networks. *Ege Academic Review*, *12*(4), 541–547.

Halicki, M., & Kwater, T. (2014). Application of artificial neural network supporting the process of portfolio management in terms of time investment on the Warsaw stock exchange. *MetodyIlościowe w BadaniachEkonomicznych*, *15*(2), 307–316.

Hansen, P. R., & Lunde, A. (2005). A forecast comparison of volatility models: Does anything beat a GARCH (1, 1)? *Journal of Applied Econometrics*, *20*(7), 873–889. doi:10.1002/jae.800

Hau, H., Massa, M., & Peress, J. (2010). Do demand curves for currencies lope down? Evidence from the MSCI global index change. *Review of Financial Studies*, *23*(10), 1681–1717. doi:10.1093/rfs/hhp095

Hochreiter, S., & Schmidhuber, J. (1997). Long short-term memory. *Neural Computation*, *9*(8), 1735–1780. doi:10.1162/neco.1997.9.8.1735 PMID:9377276

Huang, H. C., Su, Y. C., & Tsui, J. T. (2015). Asymmetric GARCH value-at-risk over MSCI in financial crisis. *International Journal of Economicsand Financial Issues*, *5*(2), 390–398.

Jang, J. S. R., Sun, C. T., & Mizutani, E. (1997). *Neuro-fuzzy and soft computing: A computational approach to learning and machine intelligence*. PrinceHall.

Jarque, C. M., & Bera, A. K. (1987). A test for normality of observations and regression residuals. *International Statistical Review/Revue Internationale de Statistique*, 163-172.

Jorion, P. (2001). *Value at risk, the new benchmark for managing financial risk* (2nd ed.). McGraw-Hill.

Kingma, D. P., & Ba, J. (2014). *Adam: A Method for Stochastic Optimization*. arXiv:1412.6980.

Kupiec, P. (1995). Techniques for verifying the accuracy of risk management models. *Journal of Derivatives*, *3*(2), 73–84. doi:10.3905/jod.1995.407942

Kwaitkowski, D., Phillips, P. C. B., Schmidt, P., & Shin, Y. (1992). Testing the null hypothesis of stationarity against the alternative of a unit root. *Journal of Econometrics*, *54*(1-3), 159–178. doi:10.1016/0304-4076(92)90104-Y

Larose, D. T. (2005). *Discovering knowledge in data: An introduction to data mining*. Press, Hoes Lane.

Linsmeier, T. J., & Pearson, N. D. (2000). Value at risk. *Financial Analysts Journal*, *56*(2), 47–67. doi:10.2469/faj.v56.n2.2343

Locarek-Junge, H., & Prinzler, R. (1998). Estimating value-at-risk using neural networks. In C. Weinhardt, H. M. Selhausen, & M. Morlock (Eds.), *Informations systeme in der Finanzwirtschaft*. Springer. doi:10.1007/978-3-642-60327-3_28

MacKinnon, J. G. (1996). Numerical distribution functions for unit root and cointegration tests. *Journal of Applied Econometrics*, *11*(6), 601–618. doi:10.1002/(SICI)1099-1255(199611)11:6<601::AID-JAE417>3.0.CO;2-T

Mallikarjuna, M., & Rao, R. P. (2019). Evaluation of forecasting methods from selected stock market returns. *Financial Innovation*, *5*(1), 40. doi:10.118640854-019-0157-x

Miletic, S., Korenak, B., & Ivanis, I. (2013). Performance of MSCI World Index during the global financial crisis: Value-at-risk approach. *Employment, Education and Entrepreneurship (EEE 2013) Conference Belgrade-Serbia*, 419-436.

Moreno, D., & Olmeda, I. (2007). Is the predictability of emerging and developed stock markets really exploitable? *European Journal of Operational Research*, *182*(1), 436–454. doi:10.1016/j.ejor.2006.07.032

MSCI. (2020). *MSCI Emerging Markets Index*. https://www.msci.com/emerging-markets

Nelson, B. D. (1991). Conditional heteroskedasticity in asset returns: A new approach. *Econometrica*, *59*(2), 347–370. doi:10.2307/2938260

Nti, I. K., Adekoya, A. F., & Weyori, B. A. (2020). A systematic review of fundamental and technical analysis of stock market predictions. *Artificial Intelligence Review*, *53*(4), 3007–3057. doi:10.100710462-019-09754-z

OskayB.LinssenT.Van VlietT.BoumanB.PasmaN. (2017). Advancing financial risk estimates by incorporating GARCH into Value at risk. doi:10.2139srn.3137587

Özçalışıcı, M. (2016). Yapay sinir ağları ile çok aşamalı fiyat tahmini: BIST30 senetleri üzerine bir araştırma. *Dokuz Eylül Üniversitesi İktisadi ve İdari Bilimler Fakültesi Dergisi*, *31*(2), 209–227. doi:10.24988/deuiibf.2016312517

Phillips, P. C., & Perron, P. (1988). Testing for a unit root in time series regression. *Biometrika*, *75*(2), 335–346. doi:10.1093/biomet/75.2.335

Sak, H., Senior, A., & Beaufays, F. (2014). *Long Short-Term Memory Based Recurrent Neural Network Architectures for Large Vocabulary Speech Recognition*. arXiv:1402.1128.

Sehovac, L., & Grolinger, K. (2020). Deep Learning for Load Forecasting: Sequence to Sequence Recurrent Neural Networks with Attention. *IEEE Access: Practical Innovations, Open Solutions*, *8*, 36411–36426. doi:10.1109/ACCESS.2020.2975738

Smith, M. (1993). *Neural networks for statistical modeling*. Van Nostrand Reinhold.

Trippi, R. R. (1995). *Artificial intelligence in finance and investing: state-of-the-art Technologies for securities selection and portfolio management* (1st ed.). McGraw-Hill, Inc.

Tsay, R. (2010). *Analysis of financial time series* (3rd ed.). John Wiley & Sons. doi:10.1002/9780470644560

Uğuz, S. (2019). *Makine öğrenmesi teorik yönleri ve python uygulamaları ile bir yapay zeka ekolü.* Nobel Akademik Yayıncılık Eğitim Danışmanlık Tic. Ltd. Şti. ANKARA.

Walczak, S. (2004). Forecasting emerging market indexes with neural networks. In Neural Networks in Business Forecasting. Idea Group Publishing.

Yılmaz, A. (2020). *Yapay Zeka.* Kodlab Yayın Dağıtım Yazılım ve Eğitim Hizmetleri San. ve Tic. Ltd. Şti.

Yüksel, R., & Akkoç, S. (2016). Altın fiyatlarının yapay siniraăları ile tahmini bir uygulama. *Doğuş Üniversitesi Dergisi, 1*(17), 39–50. doi:10.31671/dogus.2018.41

Zakoian, J. M. (1994). Threshold heteroskedastic models. *Journal of Economic Dynamics & Control, 18*(5), 931–955. doi:10.1016/0165-1889(94)90039-6

ADDITIONAL READING

Aggarwal, C. C. (2018). *Neural Networks and Deep Learning: A Textbook.* Springer. doi:10.1007/978-3-319-94463-0

Bui Quang, P., Klein, T., Nguyen, N. H., & Walther, T. (2018). Value-at-Risk for South-East Asian Stock Markets: Stochastic Volatility vs. GARCH. *Journal of Risk and Financial Management, 11*(2), 18. doi:10.3390/jrfm11020018

Del Brio, E. B., Mora-Valencia, A., & Perote, J. (2014). VaR performance during the subprime and sovereign debt crises: An application to emerging markets. *Emerging Markets Review, 20*, 23–41. doi:10.1016/j.ememar.2014.05.001

Graham, M., Kiviaho, J., & Nikkinen, J. (2012). Integration of 22 emerging stock markets: A three-dimensional analysis. *Global Finance Journal, 23*(1), 34–47. doi:10.1016/j.gfj.2012.01.003

Han, J., & Kamber, M. (2006). *Data Mining: Concepts and Techniques.* Morgan Kaufmann.

Nasreen, S., Naqvi, S. A. A., Tiwari, A. K., Hammoudeh, S., & Shah, S. A. R. (2020). A Wavelet-Based Analysis of the Co-Movement between Sukuk Bonds and Shariah Stock Indices in the GCC Region: Implications for Risk Diversification. *Journal of Risk and Financial Management, 13*(4), 63. doi:10.3390/jrfm13040063

Öztürk, H. (2018). Cointegration Analysis of BIST 30 Index and MSCI Emerging Markets Index: Pre and Post Global Financial Crisis. *Business and Economics Research Journal, 9*(1), 109–121.

KEY TERMS AND DEFINITIONS

Adaptive Moment Estimation (ADAM): Adaptive moment estimation (adam) is a kind of optimization method. It is effective and uses little memory.

Autoregressive Conditional Heteroscedasticity (ARCH): It is a kind of statistical time series model. If the error variance in a time series acts as autoregressive moving average model (ARMA), the model is called as ARCH.

Autoregressive Moving Average Technique (ARMA): It is a type of traditional linear time series modelling technique.

Exponential Autoregressive Conditional Heteroscedasticity (EGARCH): This is another form of GARCH.

Generalized Autoregressive Conditional Heteroscedasticity (GARCH): It is a kind of statistical time series model. If the error variance in a time series acts as autoregressive model (AR), the model is named as GARCH.

Long-Short-Term Memory (LSTM) Network: It is a kind of recurrent neural network technique. LSTM aims to solve vanishing gradient problems.

Recurrent Neural Network (RNN): It is a type of neural network which is used to model sequence or time series data. It has a recursive structure. And, the neural network use previous data to understand future data.

ENDNOTES

1 https://www.msci.com/emerging-markets

2 See for details: Bollerslev (1986), Hansen and Lunde (2005).

Chapter 4
Financial Literacy and Innovation Performance in SMEs:
The Mediating Effect of Risk-Taking

Marta Campos Valenzuela
https://orcid.org/0000-0003-3191-8984
University of Malaga, Spain

Sofía Louise Martínez-Martínez
https://orcid.org/0000-0002-5093-9177
University of Malaga, Spain

Julio Diéguez Soto
https://orcid.org/0000-0001-5116-5604
University of Malaga, Spain

ABSTRACT

Innovation is an essential aspect for the sustainable development of small and medium-sized enterprises (SMEs). Defining formulas to encourage innovation is therefore crucial. Financial literacy is an area of growing interest in both theory and practice and its relationship with innovation performance has been little studied. This chapter examines the importance of financial literacy for business innovation and the effect that risk-taking has on this relationship. Using a quantitative approach, 309 Spanish SMEs of different sectors are analysed. A mediation analysis shows both a direct and an indirect positive effect on innovation. Thus, this chapter brings insights, developing the existing literature of SMEs. So, it contributes to broaden the scope of the innovation and therefore the sustainable development of these firms. Practical implications are presented for four differentiated areas, which may enhance the sustainable development of SMEs: business management, entrepreneurship, public policies, and university.

DOI: 10.4018/978-1-7998-7634-2.ch004

INTRODUCTION

Innovation, understood in the world of economics, reflects a set of works focused on the combination of internal and external resources, transformed into flows of knowledge (e.g. Mangematin and Nesta, 1999). Previous literature on innovation indicates that, in recent years, a systematic and fundamental change in the innovative activities has occurred in small and medium-sized firms (SMEs) (Ripoll and Hervás-Oliver, 2011). The study of financial literacy for these kinds of businesses has been recognized as a topic of great importance, as SMEs are the engine of the economy in many countries (e.g. Fernández Mesa and Alegre, 2015) and financial literacy can guarantee the perpetuation and sustainability of these firms (Starček and Trunk, 2013).

However, in previous literature there is little evidence about the influence of financial literacy on innovation performance (Eniola and Entebang, 2015). Furthermore, a significant gap remains in the understanding of how risk-taking can exert a mediating effect between financial literacy and innovation within the world of SMEs. Therefore, although there are studies that have addressed the influence of financial literacy and risk-taking on innovation, their effect has not been collectively analysed.

On this basis, this chapter aims to provide a better comprehension of the direct influence of financial literacy in the innovation performance of SMEs. Financial literacy plays an essential role in generating product and service innovation (Rauch et al., 2009), given that certain financial behaviours make product and service innovation processes different (De Massis et al., 2015). Second, the authors go beyond the conceptual framework that examines the relation of these two variables by introducing risk-taking as a mediating factor, helping to better understand previous findings on consequences of financial literacy and risk (Thakur and Kannadhasan, 2019). The development of financial literacy enhances individuals' perception of financial knowledge and reduces financial risks (Marques et al., 2015), which in turn may benefit the innovation of products and services (Branson and Zuze, 2012), increasing the sustainability and profitability of the firm (Shen et al., 2016).

In this study, product and service innovation is understood as any improvement in the characteristics or functionalities that allows to reach differentiated performances from other products and services offered by a business (OECD, 2005). Financial literacy refers to the knowledge, behaviours, skills or maturity acquired for adequate and informed financial decision-making (Branson and Zuze, 2012). Finally, risk-taking is considered as the propensity to get involved in risky projects and the capacity to manage their inherent uncertainty.

Based on the above, this chapter seeks to shed light on this topic by addressing the following research questions. How does the level of financial literacy influence the sustainable innovative effort of SMEs? What is the relationship between risk-taking and innovation? Is risk-taking a mediating variable between financial literacy and innovation? To the best of the authors' knowledge, this is the first study analysing the impact of financial literacy in SMEs innovation taking into account the risk propensity of the firms.

To meet these research objectives, information is collected from 309 SMEs from the Spanish context through a survey on expectations, strategic factors and risks affecting the competitiveness of SMEs. The firms are classified by autonomous communities, industry and size. The primary data collected through the survey is complemented with secondary business data, such as R&D expenditure, total assets, leverage and return on assets (ROA), captured from the *Sistema de Análisis de Balances Ibéricos* (SABI) database. The collected data are analyzed through a quantitative approach. A mediation analysis is developed using risk-taking as a mediator variable, studying both the direct and indirect effect of financial literacy on innovation performance.

In such a way, using human capital theory and a new approach in terms of variables definition and sample, this study reinforces the relevance of financial literacy to encourage innovative sustainable practices in SMEs. At the same time, new knowledge is provided demonstrating the importance of risk-taking in this relationship. Financial literacy not only increases innovation performance directly, but also does so by enhancing the risk-taking propensity of decision-makers. SMEs that are more prone to take risks will be more likely to develop innovations. Thus, important contributions are made to the SME literature. The practical implications of the study are also numerous. A greater level of financial literacy may improve management and entrepreneurial decision-making, intensify the definition of public policies in accordance with sustainable innovation strategies and encourage the transfer of research, promoting the creation of SMEs. The knowledge associated with financial literacy may improve risk assessment and foster the creation of both entrepreneurial and intra-entrepreneurial projects that promote the sustainable development of SMEs.

The chapter takes the first step with a brief theoretical review of the relations between financial literacy, risk-taking and innovation performance, followed by the formulation and empirical testing of the hypotheses. Finally, there is a discussion of the theoretical and practical implications of the study and recommendations for future research.

BACKGROUND

The interest of financial literacy in SMEs has been increasing in recent literature. Some authors define it as the knowledge or necessary capacity to run or direct finances and make effective decisions on certain financial matters (Ye and Kulathunga, 2019). According to Hsiao and Tsai (2018), financial literacy can be understood from different aspects. On the one hand, it allows to access to the financial profitability of an investment by understanding the value of money. On the other hand, it refers to the assumptions of risks involved in certain types of investment. Moreover, financial literacy makes managers more skilled to manage risks through distinct strategies, e.g. keeping reserves or diversifying investments. On the contrary, poor financial literacy has been identified as a barrier to the sustainability of SMEs. Thus, Kotz and Smit (2008) conclude that the lack of financial literacy is the main reason for the failure of SMEs. However, by acquiring financial education, people and firms take better advantage of market opportunities, assuming more risks. Likewise, it contributes to the organizational knowledge, fostering a better adaptation to the changes of the business environment and enhancing the obtaining of benefits.

Risk-taking is the disposition of an organization to determine and act without a definite knowledge of possible returns, considering personal, financial and business risks (Dess and lumpkin, 2005). Risk-taking shows the way organizations perceive business chances (Davila et al., 2012) as "valued, treated as essential to innovation and success" (March (1987, p.1408). Likewise, product innovation is often defined as "the introduction of a good or service that is new or significantly improved with respect to its characteristics or intended uses. This includes significant improvements in technical specifications, components and materials, incorporated software, user friendliness or other functional characteristics" (OECD, 2005, p. 48). In this vein, SMEs' managers have to cope with uncertainty linked to innovation actions. Addressing innovation activities imply augments in R&D expenses and larger management considerations, despite the economic performance from these activities is uncertain (Ling et al., 2008). Consequently, this incertitude usually triggers out risk adverse conducts and reduce R&D investments. Yet, the expected high profitability from this type of strategy leads many managers to adopt risky choices, focusing on the potential gains rather than on the potential losses (Ling et al., 2008). In relation to innovation, previous literature has confirmed that executives who develop risky conducts are more likely to achieve better innovation outcomes (Covin and Slevin, 1986). In this sense, the extent to which top managers take risks to promote innovation may be influenced by their financial literacy. This characteristic has been proved to increase the willingness to take risks (Hsiao and Tsai, 2018) and to facilitate risk management and decision-making (Widdowson and Hailwood, 2007).

Drawing on human capital theory, it is asserted that SME's human capital is an essential factor for the business (Zhao and Thompson, 2019) and improves firm innovation (Sung and Choi, 2018). Prior research has confirmed that firms whose employees have higher degrees of general knowledge are more prone to make innovative actions (Calcagno and Monticone, 2015). However, it is important to accent that high levels of general knowledge do not always imply greater financial literacy. Hence, this study maintains that financial literacy, boosting human capital endowment, makes individuals more risk-tolerant and more willing to engage in risky innovation projects.

HYPOTHESES

Financial Literacy - Innovation Performance

The educational background of entrepreneurs often conditions innovation variables (Mihalcova et al., 2020). Consequently, a graduate education level grants more knowledge, know-how and skills, which may be required in innovation markets. Hence, a higher level of education among entrepreneurs and employees in firms, regardless its size, fosters innovation (Knight and Cavusgil, 2004). Some studies have presented comparative findings regarding how access to knowledge, among other elements such as concentrated market structure, uncertain demand, regulation, or financing, has a significant effect on the firm's ability to lead innovation investments to new outputs (Tiwari et al., 2008).

Especially, financial literacy tends to equip owners and managers with the financial knowledge that is necessary to make strategic financial innovative choices (e.g. regarding investments) (Greenspan, 2002). Individuals with a high financial literacy level are expected to have more knowledge about new financial instruments (Boztosun et al., 2017) and are more competent in making decisions about saving and investment (Fluch, 2007), which is likely to impact favourably on innovation outcomes. Conversely, a lack of financial literacy has been associated with poor investment decisions (Bianchi, 2018) and borrowing choices (Stango and Zinman, 2009), such as payday loans (Lusardi and De Bassa Scheresberg, 2013), influencing negatively on innovation performance and sustainable development.

Particularly, components of financial literacy such as up-to-date information, social ability and decision-making, can play an decisive role in understanding SMEs' innovation activity (Branson and Zuze, 2012). Recent empirical work has established that financial managerial attributes usually make easier firm innovation. Individuals with good financial literacy make right financial decisions on innovations (e.g. Hsiao and Tsai, 2018), as they comprehend better how to invest and find the right balance between risk and return. In this regard, the empirical evidence addressing the effect of financial literacy on firm innovation has confirmed a positive relationship between both variables on SMEs (Liu et al., 2020; Tian et al., 2020).

Therefore, it can be understood that individuals with great financial literacy will promote diversified investments and improve the firm's financial decisions. As firm innovation involves making corporate investments, which require a lot of financial resources, financial literacy will impact favourably on firm innovation. Based on this relation the first hypothesis is proposed:

Hypothesis 1. There is a positive relationship between financial literacy and innovation performance.

Financial Literacy - Risk-taking

According to the OECD (2005), financial literacy is a procedure by which users / investors of financial services improve their perception of financial products and services, concepts and risks. Thanks to financial literacy it is possible to make decisions based on sufficient information, know where to seek help and take other effective measures to improve the levels of well-being (Starcek and Trunk, 2013). Therefore, by promoting financial literacy, misunderstanding of financial services could be decreased at the same time as risk awareness and confidence in financial products and services could be raised (Shen et al., 2016). Previous research confirms that people with a high level of financial literacy are far more likely to comprehend risk better (Liu et al., 2020). Thus, by improving risk perceptions and evaluations, they have a greater ability to select innovative risk activities in a context of SMEs. Financially literate individuals are better qualified to choose good financial options (Von Gaudecker, 2015) and obtain profitability from risky investments. Consequently, these people are more predisposed to take risks (Hsiao and Tsai, 2018).

Hence, it is generally expected that people with financial literacy are more aware of financial risks and opportunities and have better competences to determine and handle risk-return trade-offs of investments (Lusardi et al, 2010). Firm's financial literacy enhances both financial knowledge and risk management skills, improving financial management practices and the organizational attitude to financial risks (Eniola and Entebang, 2017). Furthermore, financial literacy provides firms with the knowledge needed to evaluate risks, which may decrease the level of potential losses linked to risky decisions and ease the access to opportunities that lead to high economic performance (Ye and Kulathunga, 2019). Therefore, SMEs with great levels of financial literacy are more likely to adopt strategic risk-taking.

Risk-taking - Innovation Performance

The relationship between risk-taking and innovation performance is particularly successful. Innovative projects are usually accompanied by a certain level of risk and tend to have a long cycle, unpredictable duration and a high probability of failure. Substantial research from diverse fields suggests a close connection between risk-taking and innovation in organizational context (Latham and Braun, 2009; March and Shapira, 1987), and previous studies have highlighted that innovation demands taking risks at all dimensions of the firm (e.g. Zahra, 2005).

Innovation projects are essential for firms to obtain competitive advantages and be successful in the market, but they involve risky decisions and activities, as thinking differently implies a high degree of uncertainty. These high levels of risk justify the need of implementing risk management strategies (Vargas-Hernández, 2011), which can improve the ability to handle successfully all stages of innovation projects (Verbano and Venturini, 2013). Managerial risk-taking entails investing significant resources in activities with a high probability of failure, such as incurring in heavy debt, in the hope of gaining potentially high benefits. This implies that, compared to risk-averse managers, those with higher risk tolerance will be more likely to consider the potential benefits of risky decisions.

Risk-taking has been identified as an important feature for developing SMEs' innovation performance (e.g. García-Granero et al., 2015). From an empirical view, prior studies have found that risk-taking increases the rate of successful innovations (Wang and Poutziouris, 2010). Thus, it can be considered as a method to make the most of innovation even if it is a risky move from SMEs (Lechner and Gudmundsson, 2014).

In summary, the study proposes a mediation model that considers both relationships: on the one hand, that the organization's financial literacy positively affects the risk-taking attitude; and on the other hand, that the risk-taking attitude positively influences innovation performance. In that regard, the following hypotheses reflect a positive mediation:

Hypothesis 2: There is a positive relationship between financial literacy and risk-taking.
Hypothesis 3: Risk-taking positively mediates the relationship between financial literacy and innovation performance.

The theoretical model and hypotheses are pictured in Figure 1.

Figure 1. Theoretical Model

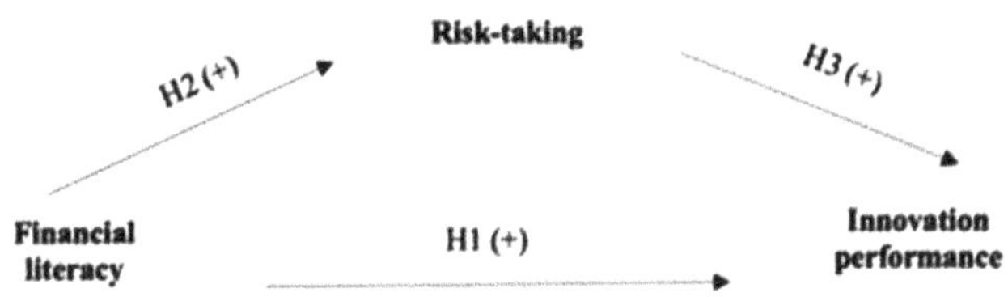

METHODOLOGY

Sample

The data of this study comes from a survey carried out by the Foundation for Strategic Analysis and Development of Small and Medium Enterprises (FAEDPYME), to collect information about economic expectations, strategic factors and risks that affect the competitiveness of the SMEs in Spain. The sample of firms was classified by autonomous communities, activity sector and size. The survey was conducted by telephone and carried out from October to December 2016. The election criteria for the 309 firms was the SABI database of the Bureau van Dijk firm. The sample size was established considering that the maximum error (assumption of greater uncertainty $p = q = 0.5$) in estimating a proportion for the population as a whole was below 3 points percentage with a confidence level of 95%. This procedure assures an objective vision to determine the adequacy of the sample to the objectives of the investigation. However, the tests and statistics carried out throughout the work will have their level of significance based on the data obtained in the survey, according to the statistical techniques used and the level of aggregation established for each case.

The selected 309 SMEs develop their activity in manufacturing, construction, commerce and services sectors (financial, educational, health and public administration services are excluded). The size of the firms was limited, requiring a minimum of 6 workers to ensure the quality of the response issued. Therefore, the sample includes firms with a number of workers between 6 and 249, belonging to the sectors before mentioned. Table 1 shows the sample composition of the study, according to size and industry.

Table 1. Sample distribution and sample error per group

	n	%	Sample Error (95% Confidence)
Industrial sector			
Manufacturing	98	31.6%	9.9%
Construction	90	29.0%	10.3%
Commerce	60	19.4%	12.7%
Services	62	20.0%	12.4%
Size			
Micro	111	35.8%	9.3%
Small	130	41.9%	8.6%
Medium	69	22.3%	11.8%
Total	310	100.0%	5,6%

Source: own elaboration

Measures

Dependent Variable

Product innovation includes any improvement in the technical characteristics or functionalities that allow reaching a differentiated performance from other products offered by a firm. This improvement is achieved through the application of knowledge or technology or through the integration of new materials or components. This consideration of innovation is also extended to the services or timescales associated with such products (OECD, 2005). This study measures the innovation performance through a subjective approach. Specifically, three Likert scale items with 5 options (1-Very unfavourable / 5-Very favourable), show the firm's perception about the evolution of its products and services offered over the last two years, and in comparison with the rest of the firms in the sector (Table 1). This approach has been used in previous studies with samples of similar characteristics (e.g. Diéguez-Soto et al., 2016). Furthermore, it is considered appropriate in SMEs to avoid the underestimation of innovative activity that can result from the use of an objective approach (Hughes, 2001; Kalantaridis and Pheby, 1999).

Independent Variable

The importance of financial literacy for the success of SMEs has been demonstrated (Spinelli, Timmons and Adams, 2011) as it allows optimizing the coverage of the financial needs of the firms through a better choice of resources. Financial literacy includes both the understanding of financial aspects and the application of this knowledge on a personal and professional level (Huston, 2010). This study measures the level of financial literacy in the firm through the degree of agreement with five Likert scale items

(1- Total disagreement / 5-Total agreement). This approach has been employed by previous research in the field (Marriott and Mellett, 1996; Molina-García et al., 2020; Sulaiman, 2016). The items consider not only the importance of financial literacy within the organization, but also its correct application in the decision-making processes at both management and departmental levels (Table 1).

Mediation Variable

Historically, risk-taking has been linked to innovation. Uncertainty is an inherent element of business activity and the risk assumed is directly related to the business profits obtained (Knight, 1921). Thus, innovative activities are conditioned by the fluctuations of the environment and the real and potential risks, so the capacity to manage this uncertainty has a direct influence on business results. Similarly, financial decisions linked to innovation are also related to these risks (Wang et al., 2016). Therefore, it is key to consider a risk-taking variable in order to understand the relationship between existing financial literacy in firms and their innovation performance. In this sense, risk-taking is defined as the degree to which businesses are willing to commit their resources to exploit opportunities or develop strategies with uncertain outcomes that may lead to costly failures (Wiklund and Shepherd, 2005). This variable is measured by means of a Likert scale that reflects the degree of agreement (1-Total disagreement / 5-Total agreement) with three statements about the perception and management of risk (Table 1). These aspects are considered relevant in the literature on SMEs (Brustbauer, 2016) and have been collected in a similar way in previous research on the subject (Fredyna et al. 2019).

Control Variables

Previous studies show the importance of certain variables in business innovation processes, justifying their inclusion in the present study as control variables, in order to obtain results adjusted to reality (Casillas, Moreno and Barbero, 2010). These variables (Table 1) are directly related to the innovation performance. Firstly, R&D expenditure is considered through a Likert scale item (1-Very unfavourable / 5-Very favourable). Many studies understand that this factor is a necessary condition for the development of innovative business activities (Hall, 1996). Secondly, a group of dummy variables is introduced to capture the business sector, differentiating between manufacturing, construction, commerce and services. In this respect, there is evidence that the level and type of innovation differ between sectors (Malerba and Adams, 2014). Third, total assets are introduced as a measure of enterprise size (Lodh, Nandy and Chen, 2014) and some financial variables are added. In particular, leverage, calculated as the ratio of debt to total assets (Diéguez-Soto and López-Delgado, 2019) and corporate profitability, which is included through the return on assets ratio (ROA), measured as EBITDA in relation to total assets (Feng, Morgan and Rego, 2017).

Table 2. Variables measurement

Type of Variable	Variable	Items (Likert Scale 1-5)
Dependent	Innovation performace (IP)	• ip1: The number of new products and services introduced by your firm per year • ip2: The pioneering nature of your firm when introducing new products or services • ip3: The speed of response to the introduction of new products or services by other firms in the sector
Independent	Financial literacy (FL)	• fl1: The firm has updated information on economic and financial sector data • fl2: I am well informed about economic developments and national and international monetary and financial policies • fl3: I am well informed about different financial sources, alternative to bank financing (equity loans, venture capital, MAB, business angels, etc.) • fl4: I am well informed of the financial assets in which to invest excess cash • fl5: The firm's management uses economic and financial information in its decision making
Mediation	Risk-taking (RT)	• rt1: I have a strong propensity for high-risk projects • rt2: I believe that knowing the environment, courageous and far-reaching actions are necessary to achieve the firm's objectives • rt3: When facing decision making under conditions of uncertainty, I normally take a courageous and aggressive stance in order to maximize the probability of exploiting potential opportunities
Control	R&D expenditure	• R&D expenditure for new products or services
	Sector	• Manufacturing, construction, commerce, services
	Total assets	• Total on-balance sheet assets
	Leverage	• Total debt / Total assets
	ROA	• EBITDA / Total assets

Source: own elaboration

Analytical Method

The different analyses of this study, made with Stata/MP 14.0, are explained below. First, the researchers investigated the measurement model for the dependent and independent constructs using the Exploratory Structural Equation Modeling (SEM). This procedure uses both an exploratory and a confirmatory factor analysis - EFA and CFA (Asparouhov and Muthén, 2009), allowing cross-loadings and estimating underlying structures. Once the constructs were defined, a causal mediation analysis (Imai, Keele and Yamamoto, 2010) based on the 3-step Baron and Kenny approach (1986) was conducted. In this study, all variables are continuous and therefore the estimations are done by linear regressions. The mediation effect is equivalent to estimating two regressions. The first one uses the mediator, risk-taking, as independent variable and the second regression estimates the influence of both the mediator and financial literacy, on innovation performance. The uncertainty estimates calculation is based on the quasi-Bayesian Monte Carlo approximation (King, Tomz, and Wittenberg, 2000). The assumption of sequential ignorability (SI) considered for the regressions are tested through a sensitivity analysis (Hicks and Tingley, 2011), a key component of causal mediation that shows the robustness of the result to the violation of the SI assumption. This analysis is based on linear structural equation model (LSEM).

RESULTS

Three constructs are generated with SEM for the latent variables "Financial literacy (FL)", "Risk-taking (RT)" and "Innovation Performance (IP)". A previous exploratory factor analysis showed the dimension of the scale. The orthogonal varimax solution (EFA) presents the following results of the three retained factors using principal components factor: Eigenvalues = 3.930, 2.353, 2.257; Proportions = 0.281, 0.168, 0.161; Extracted variance = 0.610; KMO= 0.846.

Second, a CFA is conducted. All the fitness indexes show favorable results. Regarding the reliability of the scale, the minimum value of 0.7 (Nunnally, 1978) is exceeded by all the coefficients (FL alpha= 0.875; RT alpha= 0.779; IP alpha= 0.766). The covariance between errors is also considered, all the fitness indexes achieve levels of acceptance in the measurement model (Ahmad, Zulkurnain, and Khairushalimi, 2016). The significance of the model is determined by the following values: CFI = 0.963; TLI = 0.951; RMSEA upper bound = 0.076; pclose = 0.154. All the items load significantly in the constructs and the high average variance extracted show small cross-construct loadings (Anderson and Gerbing, 1988), AVE above 0.5 (FL AVE= 0.534; RT AVE = 0.543; IP AVE=0.525), thus, there are no problems with either discriminant or convergent validity (Fornell and Larcker, 1981). These previous values together with the loadings and the values given by the Fornell-Larcker criterion are specified in Table 3.

The aim of the study is to determine both the direct impact of financial literacy on innovation performance and the relationship between these two variables considering the mediation effect of risk-taking. To achieve this purpose, the mediation analysis develops two regressions, considering the dependent, the independent, the mediator and the control variables:

$$Risk\text{-}taking = \beta 0 + \beta 1 Financial\ Literacy + \beta 2 Firm\ size + \beta 3 Leverage$$
$$+ \beta 4 ROA + \beta 5 R\ \&\ D\ Investment + \beta 7 Sector$$

$$Innovation\ performance = \beta 0 + \beta 1 Financial\ Literacy + \beta 2 Risk\text{-}taking$$
$$+ \beta Firm\ size + \beta 4 Leverage + \beta 5 ROA + \beta 6 R\ \&\ D\ Investment + \beta 7 Sector$$

Table 4 shows the results of the regression models (Model 1: impact of financial literacy on risk-taking; Model 2: impact of financial literacy on innovation performance and impact of risk-taking on the previous relation (mediation effect)). The control variables: firm size, leverage, ROA, I+D investment and sector are included in both models. The table provides an answer to whether the data support the hypotheses.

Model 1 reveals that financial literacy is positively related (β= 0.319; p= 0.000) to risk-taking, giving support for hypothesis 2 (There is a positive relationship between financial literacy and innovation performance). Respecting control variables, ROA exert a negative influence on the dependent variable, whereas R&D investment influence positively on risk-taking (β= -0.491; p= 0.04 and β= 0.145; p= 0.000, respectively). The model is highly significant ($p<0.000$) and explains a 24% of the total variance (R^2). It represents a part of the indirect effect of the mediation represented on Table 5.

Table 3. Descriptive statistics, Reliability and validity of measures

PANEL A: Descriptive Statistics and Convergent Validity							
		Mean	**SD**	**λ**	**s.e.*****		
FL – Financial Literacy							
	fl1	3.59	1.27	0.69	0.04	α	0.88
	fl2	3.58	1.19	0.74	0.03	AVE	0.53
	fl3	3.24	1.29	0.75	0.03		
	fl4	3.11	1.32	0.77	0.03		
	fl5	3.68	1.23	0.75	0.03		
	fl6	3.73	1.04	0.67	0.04		
RT – Risk-taking							
	rt1	2.08	1.16	0.69	0.04	α	0.78
	rt2	3.21	1.19	0.77	0.04	AVE	0.54
	rt3	3.03	1.16	0.75	0.04		
IP – Innovation Performance							
	ip1	3.20	1.16	0.68	0.04	α	0.77
	ip2	3.33	1.18	0.80	0.04	AVE	0.53
	ip3	3.09	1.07	0.69	0.04		
One-item control variables		Mean	SD			Mean	SD
	R&D expenditure	2.60	1.24	Leverage		0.54	0.30
	Total assets	5741.15	11080.97	ROA		0.07	0.16
PANEL B: Discriminant Validity							
					FL	**RT**	**IP**
Financial Literacy					*0.73*		
Risk-taking					0.13	*0.73*	
Innovation Performance					0.11	0.20	*0.73*

PANEL A: SD: Standard Deviation; λ: Standardized loadings; s.e.: standard error; α: Cronbach's alpha. AVE: Average Variance Extracted. ***: All the loadings are significant at a p<0.01 level.

PANEL B: Fornell-Larcker criterion: Squared-Root of AVE in diagonal (*cursive*) and factors correlations below the diagonal.

Source: own elaboration

Model 2 reveals the influence of the variables on innovation performance. Both financial literacy (β= 0.130; p= 0.003) and risk-taking (β= 0.340; p= 0.000) have a positive impact on the dependent variable. In this sense, both hypothesis 1 (There is a positive relationship between financial literacy and innovation performance) and 3 (Risk-taking positively mediates the relationship between financial literacy and innovation performance) are supported. The effect of the mediator on innovation performance constitutes the second part of the indirect effect shown on Table 5. Also, there is a higher effect of the control variables comparing with model 1, their effect is more significant on innovation performance than on risk-taking. The effect of ROA is now positive (β= 0.402; p= 0.05), as well as the effect of investment on R&D (β= 0.172; p= 0.000). The sector variables, that were not significant in the first model, have a negative influence on product and service innovation (construction: β= -0.201, p= 0.06;

industry: β= -0.223, p= 0.01; services: β= -0.241, p= 0.01), considering the commerce sector as the reference category. The R^2 of this model is 42,91%, with a level of significance of $p<0.000$. In this sense, the level of significance of both models is sufficient to meet the research objectives. The authors completely agree with the fact that the values for the R^2 are not very high. However, as the final goal of the models is not to "predict" innovation performance, but rather to analyze the "associations" among the variables under study, a low R^2 is acceptable (Field, 2013). In this regard, similar values in the coefficients of determinations, although not very common, could be observed in studies of firm research field (e.g. Asaba and Wada, 2019).

Table 4. Mediation analysis – regression models

Variables	Model 1 (Dependent Variable: Propensity to Take Risk)		Model 2 (Dependent Variable: Product and Service Innovation)	
	Coef.	t	Coef.	t
Main effect				
Financial knowledge	0.319	0.049***	0.131	.044***
Mediator				
Propensity to take risks			0.341	0.051***
Control variables				
Firm size	0.000	0.000	-0.000	0.000
Leverage	0.010	0.126	-0.120	0.105
ROA	-0.491	0.249**	0.402	0.210**
R&D Investment	0.145	0.033***	0.172	0.028***
Construction sector	0.127	0.128	-0.201	0.107*
Industry sector	0.114	0.113	-0.223	.095***
Service sector	0.010	0.113	-0.241	0.095***
R^2	0.240		0.429	
Prob > F	10.71***		22.55***	

* p<0.1; ** p<0.01; *** p<0.001
Source: own elaboration

Table 5. Direct, indirect and total effect on product and service innovation

Effect	Mean	[95% Conf. Interval]	
ACME	0.109	0.0658	0.1559
Direct effect	0.131	0.0451	0.2137
Total effect	0.239	0.1590	0.3322
% Total effect mediated	0.459	0.3272	0.6801

Source: own elaboration

The paths and values of the direct effect of financial literacy on innovation performance (0.131), the indirect effect or ACME (average causal mediation effect) of the treatment variable on the outcome that operates through the mediator, propensity to take risk (0.109; 45.48%), and the total effect of the model (0.239) are presented on Table 5.

Graph 1 shows that there are no concerns regarding confounder bias, for the ACME to be zero the correlation between error terms (rho) should be 0.377. There exists no scale that indicates if this correlation is high or low (Cox et al., 2013). However, these authors reveal that the omitted confounder is less likely to cause a problem in the model the further the curve is from the y-axis when it crosses the x-axis. The product of R^2 measures of sensitivity for the mediator and outcome models is 0.142 for the residual variance, and 0.062 for the total variance.

Figure 2. Average causal mediation effect as a function of degree of violation of sequential ignorability assumption.

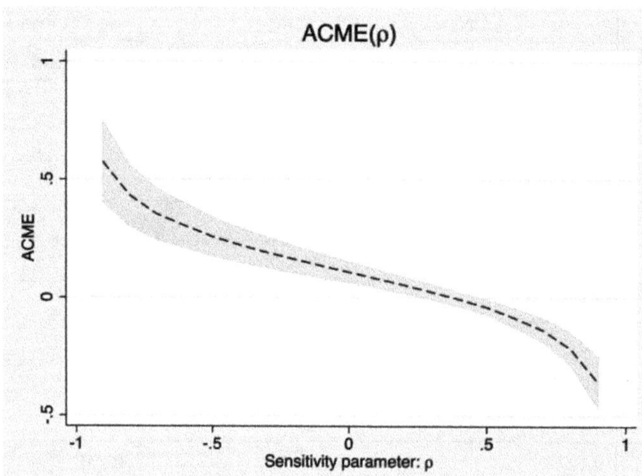

In conclusion, Figure 2 remarks the values of the direct, indirect and total effect of the independent and mediator variable on innovation performance. As it is reflected above, all these effects are positive supporting the three hypothesis presented in the study.

Figure 3. Paths and values of the direct, indirect and total effect of the independent and mediator variable on product and service innovation

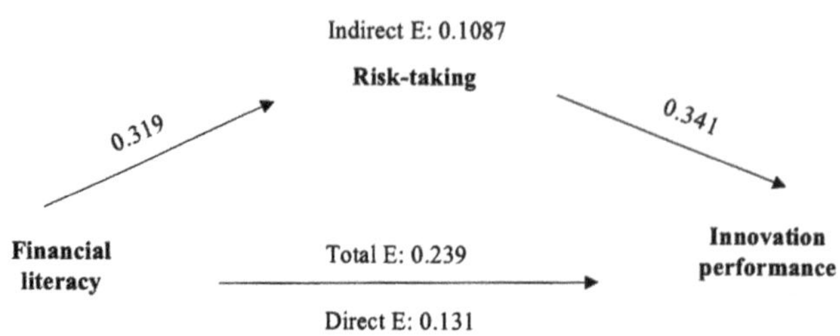

SOLUTIONS AND RECOMMENDATIONS

Theoretical Implications

Financial literacy has been related to innovative business performance and previous literature shows a positive effect on innovation of similar concepts to financial literacy, such as debt literacy, savings literacy or investment literacy (Mwangi and Cheluget, 2018). Yet, specific studies on the relationship between financial literacy and innovation have been scarce (i.e. Eniola and Entebang, 2015) and the focus has been placed on the direct link between these two variables (Branson and Zuze, 2012; Rauch et al., 2009). To cover this gap, the present study analyses the effect of financial literacy on innovation performance, from the point of view of the CEO's knowledge and decision-making, incorporating a third variable as a mediator. Thus, firstly, this chapter makes important contributions to the fields of financial literacy and innovation within the context of SMEs, adding a different perspective in terms of variables definition and sample. To complete the objective of the research, even if the most common way of measuring innovation is through objective data, for example investment in R&D, a subjective measurement of innovation was introduced. This has been possible due to the instrument used for the data collection. The management teams of the firms were asked about the innovation performance through questions that collected their perceptions of the evolution of the products and services offered in the last two years, and in comparison with other firms of the same sector. This approach has been shown to be more suitable for SMEs (Hughes, 2001; Kalantaridis and Pheby, 1999). In relation to the sample used, SMEs is an area that has been little studied and in which further research is enormously needed, given the important role of these firms for the development of world's economy (e.g. Savlovschi and Robu, 2011).

Secondly, this chapter offers a more developed theoretical analysis of the role of risk-taking in the relationship of financial literacy and innovation performance. Previous literature has highlighted the relation between risk-taking and financial literacy (Lusardi et al., 2010; Marques et al., 2015; Thakur and Kannadhasan, 2019). According to these authors, the perception and understanding of risk improves when the level of financial knowledge increases. Thus, manager's financial literacy increases the degree of risk management (Li and Zhou, 2019), which in turn can improve firm performance (Gordon et al., 2009). Likewise, previous literature has analysed the strong link between risk-taking and innovation in SMEs (García-Granero et al., 2015). However, there are no studies that have taken into account the possible existence of a mediating effect of risk-taking in the financial literacy–innovation performance relationship. In this sense, the present research highlights the importance of this mediating effect, which demonstrates that financial literacy increases firm innovation outcomes, not only directly but also by fostering an organizational risk-taking attitude.

Thirdly, it is relevant to add that all of this occurs in a SME context. So, this chapter contributes to better understand what variables influence SMEs. Although SMEs are the potential engine and the backbone of national economies, previous literature shows how innovation performance is studied mostly in listed firms (Moreiras et al., 2019). In this sense, by deepening the understanding of the variables that affect the innovative performance of these firms, the chapter contributes to improve their success and sustainable development in society. In addition, the study also contributes to a better understanding of the relationship of these variables in the economy as a whole.

Finally, innovation performance is an important aspect for SMEs growth and sustainable development (Bausch's et al., 2011). Therefore, the understanding of the use of financial literacy, in terms of innovation performance as the main basis for productivity and success, can also translate into sustainability.

Firms are increasingly choosing to invest in projects that are fully sustainability-oriented, but they must be able to do so. One of the main tools to achieve this goal is knowledge, that is, financial literacy. Regarding the assumption of risk, today's changing world makes firms take increasingly risks to cope with complex situations. Financial literacy will improve the decision-making process and, consequently, the assumption of new challenges to achieve higher profitability (Grable, 2000), which in turn will lead to greater financial sustainability.

Practical Implications

Many practical implications arise from this study and can be grouped into four major blocks: management, entrepreneurship, public policy and university.

Firstly, the management implications refer to the recommendations that can be drawn from this study to improve decision-making by SMEs managers. It has been shown that a greater knowledge of the financial context and the existing financial instruments will reduce uncertainty and favour risk management. Financial literate managers present managerial attributes that support product and service innovation (e.g. Görg and Hanley, 2017) and improve financial decision-making linked to innovation processes such as saving or investment decisions (Greenspan, 2002). Therefore, both the financial literacy of managers and their awareness of the importance of enhancing such knowledge and skills in work teams should be encouraged. Regarding the aforementioned importance of risk-taking for innovation, the development of risk mitigation skills has also been identified as a key for entrepreneurship and innovation (Morris et al., 2003). Thus, the promotion of programmes that develop financial literacy becomes necessary both inside and outside the firm. Internally, this educational commitment would promote innovative intra- and inter-departmental projects in SMEs to achieve competitive advantages in the market (Verbano and Venturini, 2013). Externally, this attitude would favour the creation of entrepreneurial ecosystems that promote innovation (Feldman, Siegel and Wright, 2019).

The entrepreneurial implications are based on the importance of fostering the financial literacy of entrepreneurs, founders of SMEs. This group, through divergent thinking, grants new values to existing resources generating transformations of inputs into innovative outputs. Therefore, historically, entrepreneurs have been understood as people exposed to high levels of uncertainty and risk. Macko and Tyszka (2009, p.470) state that entrepreneurs "are perceived as more risk prone than other people". And according to Wärneryd (1988), these are inherent characteristics of entrepreneurial activity, so risk management is considered a necessary tool for their professional development and the success of the created businesses. Given the positive effect shown in this study between financial literacy and risk-taking, the development of financial knowledge and skills is understood to be crucial for the creation of sustainable SMEs. Moreover, this is reinforced by the direct relationship between financial literacy and innovation. These aspects should also be considered in the formation of entrepreneurial teams, given the importance of entrepreneurial human capital for economic growth and sustainable business innovation.

In terms of public policy implications, the importance of innovation within SMEs for social and economic development makes it necessary to define strategies for its promotion (Szirmai, Naudé, and Goedhuys, 2011). Thus, financial literacy must be understood politically as a strategy to promote innovation in SMEs. This study highlights the importance of financial literacy in achieving this end, advocating the need to increase the focus currently given to this training in the education system. In the same vein, the OECD (2010) highlights the importance of promoting this area of education because of the growing complexity of financial products, services and markets and their inherent risks. Nevertheless, numerous studies indicate that there is a wide range of improvement in this regard, as the degree of global financial literacy remains low, which may constitute an obstacle for SMEs (e.g. OECD, 2014). Therefore, public policies are needed to strengthen financial literacy at all levels of education, in order to improve the skills needed to set up businesses and to design and develop successful sustainable innovative projects within them.

Finally, this study also includes implications for the educational field, especially for higher education institutions such as universities. Firstly, on the basis of the above point, the institution must ensure that the development of financial skills is included in its training plans, in a transversal manner and with special emphasis on economics and business degrees, due to its connection to business creation and management (Hernández, 2015). Secondly, especially in the university context, financial literacy not only brings benefits to the field of teaching but also to the transfer of research results. In this respect, the findings of this study are also applicable to the improvement of university transfer strategies within the framework of the Entrepreneurial University model, which highlights the crucial role of universities in innovation ecosystems (Audretsch, 2009). Collaboration and co-creation between university, government, industry and civil society are key to reach innovation and the sustainable advancement of society (e.g. Trencher et al., 2014). In this sense, the main potential of the university is the generation of qualified entrepreneurial human capital with high competence levels, that promote network creation and foster sustainable innovative environments (Castellacci and Natera, 2013). In this sense, the development of financial competences is essential to improve the sustainable transfer of university research, which in turn leads to the creation of new firms, especially SMEs.

FUTURE RESEARCH DIRECTIONS

The subjective approach used to measure the innovation performance could involve a bias of the interviewee, conditioned by his/her intentions, leadership form or culture. The above could be understood as a possible limitation, even so, this form of measurement is considered appropriate for SMEs to avoid the underestimation of innovative activity (Hughes, 2001; Kalantaridis and Pheby, 1999). In this regard, future studies could consider and combine both subjective and objective financial literacy measurements. The findings of this study may also be conditioned by specific characteristics of the Spanish context. The socioeconomic conditions, the culture, the developed ecosystems and the public policies influence the innovative practices of SMEs, enhancing or constraining them. However, the Spanish context and its conditions are similar to those of other developed economies in the Western world. In this regard, as a possible line of future research, it would be interesting to apply a comparative perspective, replicating the study in other countries with notable cultural and socioeconomic differences.

The research could also be replicated in specific SMEs contexts. In this respect, it would be interesting to explore the existence of differences between family and non-family SMEs or compare firms of different sectors or sizes. Based on the importance of the university as a catalyst for sustainable innovation in society, a replica of this study with focus on academic spinoff firms could also be performed. These businesses are characterized precisely by the high educational levels of their founders and by a great innovative orientation. Finally, future research could also deepen and add value to the subject by using different methodologies, e.g. applying a qualitative perspective that complement the quantitative findings of the present study.

CONCLUSION

In conclusion, this chapter analyses the positive effect of financial literacy on innovation, considering the assumption of risk as a mediating variable. The function that financial literacy plays on SMEs is studied and translated into innovative and sustainable decisions, taking into account the risk involved in making such decisions. In particular, the results show that an increase in the levels of financial literacy is positively associated with the innovation performance of a firm, not only directly, but also indirectly, through increased risk-taking. The security and confidence provided by the financial literacy help to promote innovation performance. Thus, this chapter contributes to shed light on an aspect little studied in the literature, since the variables on which this study is based have not been analysed jointly previously. Likewise, to the best of the authors' knowledge, it is the first time that a mediating effect is introduced in the financial literacy–innovation performance relationship. Both the theoretical and the practical implications of this study, extended to many action areas and fields, contribute to understand some drivers of the SMEs innovative performance and sustainability, namely financial literacy and risk-taking behaviour.

ACKNOWLEDGMENT

The authors gratefully acknowledge the responses received from all the Spanish SMEs that participated in the study. They also acknowledge the collaboration of the Foundation for Strategic Analysis and Development of Small and Medium Enterprises (FAEDPYME) in the development of the data collection process and thank the Cátedra de Viabilidad Empresarial (Universidad de Málaga) for financially supporting one of the authors.

REFERENCES

Ahmad, S., Zulkurnain, N. N. A., & Khairushalimi, F. I. (2016). Assessing the fitness of a measurement model using Confirmatory Factor Analysis (CFA). *International Journal of Innovation and Applied Studies*, *17*(1), 159.

Aksoylu, S., Boztosun, D., Altinişik, F., & Baraz, E. H. (2017). A Baseline Investigation of Financial Literacy Levels: The Case of Kayseri Province. *Journal of Accounting & Finance*, (75).

Anderson, J. C., & Gerbing, D. W. (1988). Structural equation modeling in practice: A review and recommended two-step approach. *Psychological Bulletin*, *103*(3), 411–423. doi:10.1037/0033-2909.103.3.411

Asaba, S., & Wada, T. (2019). The Contact-Hitting R&D Strategy of Family Firms in the Japanese Pharmaceutical Industry. *Family Business Review*.

Asparouhov, T., & Muthén, B. (2009). Exploratory structural equation modeling. *Structural Equation Modeling*, *16*(3), 397–438. doi:10.1080/10705510903008204

Audretsch, D. B. (2009). The entrepreneurial society. *The Journal of Technology Transfer*, *3*(6), 245–254. doi:10.100710961-008-9101-3

Baron, R. M., & Kenny, D. A. (1986). The moderator–mediator variable distinction in social psychological research: Conceptual, strategic, and statistical considerations. *Journal of Personality and Social Psychology*, *51*(6), 1173–1182. doi:10.1037/0022-3514.51.6.1173 PMID:3806354

Bianchi, M. (2018). Financial literacy and portfolio dynamics. *The Journal of Finance*, *73*(2), 831–859. doi:10.1111/jofi.12605

Branson, N., & Zuze, T. L. (2012). Education, the great equaliser: Improving access to quality education. *South African child gauge*, 69–74.

Brustbauer, J. (2016). Enterprise risk management in SMEs: Towards a structural model. *International Small Business Journal*, *34*(1), 70–85. doi:10.1177/0266242614542853

Calcagno, R., & Monticone, C. (2015). Financial literacy and the demand for financial advice. *Journal of Banking & Finance*, *50*, 363–380. doi:10.1016/j.jbankfin.2014.03.013

Casillas, J. C., Moreno, A. M., & Barbero, J. L. (2010). A configurational approach of the relationship between entrepreneurial orientation and growth of family firms. *Family Business Review*, *13*(1), 27–44. doi:10.1177/0894486509345159

Castellacci, F., & Natera, J. M. (2013). The dynamics of national innovation systems: A panel cointegration analysis of the coevolution between innovative capability and absorptive capacity. *Research Policy*, *42*(3), 579–594. doi:10.1016/j.respol.2012.10.006

Covin, J. G., & Slevin, D. P. (1986). The development and testing of an organizational-level entrepreneurship scale. *Frontiers of Entrepreneurship Research*, *1*(3), 628–639.

Cox, M. G., Kisbu-Sakarya, Y., Miočević, M., & MacKinnon, D. P. (2013). Sensitivity plots for confounder bias in the single mediator model. *Evaluation Review*, *37*(5), 405–431. doi:10.1177/0193841X14524576 PMID:24681690

Davila, T., Epstein, M., & Shelton, R. (2012). *Making innovation work: How to manage it, measure it, and profit from it.* FT Press.

De Massis, A., Frattini, F., Pizzurno, E., & Cassia, L. (2015). Product innovation in family versus nonfamily firms: An exploratory analysis. *Journal of Small Business Management*, *53*(1), 1–36. doi:10.1111/jsbm.12068

Dess, G., & Lumpkin, G. T. (2005). Entrepreneurial orientation as a source of innovative strategy. *Innovating Strategy Process, 1*, 3–9.

Diéguez-Soto, J., Duréndez, A., García-Pérez-de-Lema, D., & Ruiz-Palomo, D. (2016). Technological, management, and persistent innovation in small and medium family firms: The influence of professionalism. *Canadian Journal of Administrative Sciences*, *33*(4), 332–346. doi:10.1002/cjas.1404

Diéguez-Soto, J., & López-Delgado, P. (2019). Does Family and Lone Founder Involvement Lead to Similar Indebtedness? *Journal of Small Business Management*, *57*(4), 1531–1558. doi:10.1111/jsbm.12422

Eniola, A. A., & Entebang, H. (2015). Financial literacy and SME firm performance. *International Journal of Research Studies in Management*, *5*(1), 31–43. doi:10.5861/ijrsm.2015.1304

Feldman, M., Siegel, D. S., & Wright, M. (2019). New developments in innovation and entrepreneurial ecosystems. *Industrial and Corporate Change*, *28*(4), 817–826. doi:10.1093/icc/dtz031

Feng, H., Morgan, N. A., & Rego, L. L. (2017). Firm capabilities and growth: The moderating role of market conditions. *Journal of the Academy of Marketing Science*, *45*(1), 76–92. doi:10.100711747-016-0472-y

Field, A. (2013). *Discovering Statistics Using IBM SPSS Statistics* (4th ed.). SAGE Publication Ltd.

Fluch, M. (2007). Selected central banks' economic and financial literacy programs. *Monetary Policy & the Economy Q*, *3*, 85–103.

Fornell, C., & Larcker, D. F. (1981). Evaluating structural equation models with unobservable variables and measurement error. *JMR, Journal of Marketing Research*, *18*(1), 39–50. doi:10.1177/002224378101800104

Fredyna, T., Ruiz-Palomo, D., & Diéguez-Soto, J. (2019). Entrepreneurial orientation and product innovation. The moderating role of family involvement in management. *European Journal of Family Business*, *9*(2), 128–145. doi:10.24310/ejfbejfb.v9i2.5392

García-Granero, A., Llopis, O., Fernández-Mesa, A., & Alegre, J. (2015). Unravelling the link between managerial risk-taking and innovation: The mediating role of a risk-taking climate. *Journal of Business Research*, *68*(5), 1094–1104. doi:10.1016/j.jbusres.2014.10.012

Gordon, L. A., Loeb, M. P., & Tseng, C. Y. (2009). Enterprise risk management and firm performance: A contingency perspective. *Journal of Accounting and Public Policy*, *28*(4), 301–327. doi:10.1016/j.jaccpubpol.2009.06.006

Görg, H., & Hanley, A. (2017). Firms' global engagement and management practices. *Economics Letters*, *155*, 80–83. doi:10.1016/j.econlet.2017.03.026

Grable, J. E. (2000). Financial risk tolerance and additional factors that affect risk taking in everyday money matters. *Journal of Business and Psychology*, *14*(4), 625–630. doi:10.1023/A:1022994314982

Greenspan, A. (2002). Economic volatility. Remarks at a symposium sponsored by the Federal Reserve Bank of Kansas City.

Hall, B. H. (1996). The Private and Social Returns to Research and Development. In B. L. R. Smith & C. E. Barfield (Eds.), *Technology, R&D, and the Economy* (pp. 140–183). Brookings Institution and American Enterprise Institute.

Hernández, M. T. B. (2015). La importancia de la educación financiera y su influencia en los futuros estudiantes de Administración y Dirección de Empresas. *Anuario jurídico y económico escurialense*, *48*, 381–400.

Hicks, R., & Tingley, D. (2011). Causal mediation analysis. *The Stata Journal*, *11*(4), 605–619. doi:10.1177/1536867X1201100407

Hsiao, Y. J., & Tsai, W. C. (2018). Financial literacy and participation in the derivatives markets. *Journal of Banking & Finance*, *88*, 15–29. doi:10.1016/j.jbankfin.2017.11.006

Hughes, A. (2001). Innovation and business performance: Small entrepreneurial firms in the UK and the EU. *New Economy*, *8*(3), 157–163. doi:10.1111/1468-0041.00208

Huston, S. J. (2010). Measuring Financial Literacy. *The Journal of Consumer Affairs*, *44*(2), 296–316. doi:10.1111/j.1745-6606.2010.01170.x

Imai, K., Keele, L., & Yamamoto, T. (2010). Identification, Inference, and Sensitivity Analysis for Causal Mediation Effects. *Statistical Science*, *25*(1), 51–71. doi:10.1214/10-STS321 PMID:20954780

Kalantaridis, C., & Pheby, J. (1999). Processes of Innovation Among Manufacturing SMEs: The Experience of Bedfordshire. *Entrepreneurship and Regional Development*, *11*(1), 57–78. doi:10.1080/089856299283290

King, G., Tomz, M., & Wittenberg, J. (2000). Making the Most of Statistical Analyses: Improving Interpretation and Presentation. *American Journal of Political Science*, *44*(2), 341–355. doi:10.2307/2669316

Knight, F. H. (1921). *Risk, Uncertainty and Profit*. Houghton Mifflin.

Knight, G. A., & Cavusgil, S. T. (2004). Innovation, organizational capabilities, and the born-global firm. *Journal of International Business Studies*, *35*(2), 124–141. doi:10.1057/palgrave.jibs.8400071

Kotzé, L., & Smit, A. (2008). Personal financial literacy and personal debt management: The potential relationship with new venture creation. *The Southern African Journal of Entrepreneurship and Small Business Management*, *1*(1), 35–50. doi:10.4102ajesbm.v1i1.11

Latham, S. F., & Braun, M. (2009). Managerial risk, innovation, and organizational decline. *Journal of Management*, *35*(2), 258–281. doi:10.1177/0149206308321549

Lechner, C., & Gudmundsson, S. V. (2014). Entrepreneurial orientation, firm strategy and small firm performance. *International Small Business Journal*, *32*(1), 36–60. doi:10.1177/0266242612455034

Li, J., & Zhou, S. (2019). Can executives' financial literacy affect the financial exclusion of enterprises? Based on the perspective of financial exclusion of small and medium enterprises. *Journal Central University Finance Economic*, *5*, 19–32.

Ling, Y. A. N., Simsek, Z., Lubatkin, M. H., & Veiga, J. F. (2008). Transformational leadership's role in promoting corporate entrepreneurship: Examining the CEO-TMT interface. *Academy of Management Journal*, *51*(3), 557–576. doi:10.5465/amj.2008.32626023

Liu, B., Wang, J., Chan, K. C., & Fung, A. (2020). The impact of entrepreneurs's financial literacy on innovation within small and medium-sized enterprises. *International Small Business Journal*, *0266242620959073*, 1–19. doi:10.1177/0266242620959073

Lodh, S., Nandy, M., & Chen, J. (2014). Innovation and family ownership: Empirical evidence from India. *Corporate Governance*, *22*(1), 4–23. doi:10.1111/corg.12034

Lusardi, A., Mitchell, O. S., & Curto, V. (2010). Financial literacy among the young. *The Journal of Consumer Affairs*, *44*(2), 358–380. doi:10.1111/j.1745-6606.2010.01173.x

Lusardi, A., & Scheresberg, C. D. B. (2013). *Financial literacy and high-cost borrowing in the United States*. Working Paper (No. w18969). National Bureau of Economic Research.

Macko, A., & Tyszka, T. (2009). Entrepreneurship and risk taking. *Applied Psychology*, *58*(3), 469–487. doi:10.1111/j.1464-0597.2009.00402.x

Malerba, F., & Adams, P. (2014). Sectorial Systems of Innovation. In M. Dodson, D. M. Gann, & N. Phillips (Eds.), The Oxford Handbook of Innovation Management (pp. 183-203). Oxford, UK: University Press.

Mangematin, V., & Nesta, L. (1999). What kind of knowledge can a firm absorb? *International Journal of Technology Management*, *18*(3/4), 149–172. doi:10.1504/IJTM.1999.002771

March, J. G. (1987). Ambiguity and accounting: The elusive link between information and decision making. *Accounting, Organizations and Society*, *12*(2), 153–168. doi:10.1016/0361-3682(87)90004-3

March, J. G., & Shapira, Z. (1987). Managerial perspectives on risk and risk taking. *Management Science*, *33*(11), 1404–1418. doi:10.1287/mnsc.33.11.1404

Marriott, D. N., & Mellett, H. (1996). Health care managers' financial skills: Measurement, analysis and implications. *Accounting Education*, *5*(1), 61–74. doi:10.1080/09639289600000006

Mihalcova, B., Gallo, P., & Lukac, J. (2020). Management of Innovations in Finance Education: Cluster Analysis for OECD Countries. *Marketing and Management of Innovations, 1,* 235–244. doi:10.21272/mmi.2020.1-19

Molina-García, A., Florido-Ruiz, B., Campos-Valenzuela, M., & Diéguez-Soto, J. (2020). The effect of family ownership and generation on financial literacy. *Small Business International Review*, *4*(1), 1–15. doi:10.26784bir.v4i1.236

Moreiras, M. A. N., López, S. F., & Búa, M. V. (2019). El Efecto de la Innovación en el Empleo: Análisis de las Empresas Cotizadas Españolas. *European Journal of Applied Business and Management*, *5*(1).

Morris, M. H., Webb, J. W., Fu, J., & Singhal, S. (2013). A Competency-Based Perspective on Entrepreneurship Education: Conceptual and Empirical Insights. *Journal of Small Business Management*, *51*(3), 352–369. doi:10.1111/jsbm.12023

Mwangi, W. P., & Cheluget, J. (2018). Role of Financial Literacy, Financial Innovation, Financial Inclusion on SME Access to Credit in Kenya: A Case of Kumisa SACCO. *Journal of Finance and Accounting*, *2*(2), 1–18.

Nunnally, J. C. (1978). *Psychometric theory*. McGraw-Hill., doi:10.2307/1161962

OECD. (2005). *Oslo Manual. Guidelines for collecting and interpreting innovation data*. OECD Publishing.

OECD. (2010). *PISA 2012 Financial literacy framework*. OECD Publishing.

OEDE. (2014). *PISA 2012 Results: Students and Money. Financial Literacy Skills for the 21st Century, 6*. OECD Publishing.

Rauch, A., Wiklund, J., Lumpkin, G. T., & Frese, M. (2009). Entrepreneurial orientation and business performance: An assessment of past research and suggestions for the future. *Entrepreneurship Theory and Practice*, *33*(3), 761–787. doi:10.1111/j.1540-6520.2009.00308.x

Ripoll, F. S., & Hervás-Oliver, J. L. (2011). ¿Qué explica la innovación en PyMEs? *Dirección y Organización*, (43), 5–15.

Rosenbusch, N., Brinckmann, J., & Bausch, A. (2011). Is innovation always beneficial? A meta-analysis of the relationship between innovation and performance in SMEs. *Journal of Business Venturing*, *26*(4), 441–457. doi:10.1016/j.jbusvent.2009.12.002

Savlovschi, L. I., & Robu, N. R. (2011). The role of SMEs in modern economy. *Economia. Seria Management*, *14*(1), 277–281.

Shen, C. H., Lin, S. J., Tang, D. P., & Hsiao, Y. J. (2016). Self-control, financial literacy and harmful consumer credit behavior in Taiwan market. *Academia Economic Papers*, *44*(2), 251–294.

Spinelli, S., Timmons, J. A., & Adams, R. J. (2011). *New venture creation: Entrepreneurship for the 21st century* (9th ed.). McGraw-Hill Education.

Stango, V., & Zinman, J. (2009). Exponential growth bias and household finance. *The Journal of Finance*, *64*(6), 2807–2849. doi:10.1111/j.1540-6261.2009.01518.x

Starček, S., & Trunk, A. (2013). The meaning and concept of financial education in the society of economic changes. *International Conference Active Citizenship by Knowledge Management & Innovation*.

Sulaiman, N. (2016). *The Impact of Financial Knowledge and Capabilities on SME Firm Performance in Australia*. RMIT University.

Sung, S. Y., & Choi, J. N. (2018). Effects of training and development on employee outcomes and firm innovative performance: Moderating roles of voluntary participation and evaluation. *Human Resource Management*, *57*(6), 1339–1353. doi:10.1002/hrm.21909

Szirmai, A., Naudé, W., & Goedhuys, M. (2011). *Entrepreneurship, innovation, and economic development*. Oxford University Press. doi:10.1093/acprof:oso/9780199596515.001.0001

Thakur, B. P. S., & Kannadhasan, M. (2019). Corruption and cash holdings: Evidence from emerging market economies. *Emerging Markets Review*, *38*, 1–17. doi:10.1016/j.ememar.2018.11.008

Tian, G., Zhou, S., & Hsu, S. (2020). Executive financial literacy and firm innovation in China. *Pacific-Basin Finance Journal*, *62*, 101348. doi:10.1016/j.pacfin.2020.101348

Tiwari, A. K., Shahbaz, M., & Islam, F. (2013). Does financial development increase rural-urban income inequality? *International Journal of Social Economics*, *40*(2), 151–168. doi:10.1108/03068291311283616

Trencher, G., Yarime, M., McCormick, K. B., Doll, C. N., & Kraines, S. B. (2014). Beyond the third mission: Exploring the emerging university function of co-creation for sustainability. *Science & Public Policy*, *41*(2), 151–179. doi:10.1093cipolct044

Verbano, C., & Venturini, K. (2013). Managing risks in SMEs: A literature review and research agenda. *Journal of Technology Management & Innovation*, *8*(3), 186–197. doi:10.4067/S0718-27242013000400017

Von Gaudecker, H. (2015). How does household portfolio diversification vary with financial literacy and financial advice? *The Journal of Finance*, *70*(2), 489–507. doi:10.1111/jofi.12231

Wang, H., Liang, P., Li, H., & Yang, R. (2016). Financing Sources, R&D Investment and Enterprise Risk. *Procedia Computer Science*, *91*, 122–130. doi:10.1016/j.procs.2016.07.049

Wang, Y., & Poutziouris, P. (2010). Entrepreneurial risk taking: Empirical evidence from UK family firms. *International Journal of Entrepreneurial Behaviour & Research*, *16*(5), 370–388. doi:10.1108/13552551011071841

Wärneryd, K. E. (1988). The psychology of innovative entrepreneurship. doi:10.1007/978-94-015-7791-5_11

Widdowson, D., & Hailwood, K. (2007). Financial literacy and its role in promoting a sound financial system. *Reserve Bank of New Zealand Bulletin, 70*(2).

Wiklund, J., & Shepherd, D. (2005). Entrepreneurial orientation and small business performance: A configurational approach. *Journal of Business Venturing*, *20*(1), 71–91. doi:10.1016/j.jbusvent.2004.01.001

Ye, J., & Kulathunga, K. M. M. C. B. (2019). How does financial literacy promote sustainability in SMEs? A developing country perspective. *Sustainability*, *11*(10), 2990. doi:10.3390u11102990

Zahra, S. A. (2005). Entrepreneurial risk taking in family firms. *Family Business Review*, *18*(1), 23–40. doi:10.1111/j.1741-6248.2005.00028.x

Zhao, Y., & Thompson, P. (2019). Investments in managerial human capital: Explanations form prospect and regulatory focus theories. *International Small Business Journal*, *37*(4), 365–394. doi:10.1177/0266242619828264

ADDITIONAL READING

Bongomin, G. O. C., Ntayi, J. M., Munene, J. C., & Malinga, C. A. (2017). The relationship between access to finance and growth of SMEs in developing economies. *Review of International Business and Strategy*, *27*(4), 520–538. doi:10.1108/RIBS-04-2017-0037

Braunstein, S., & Welch, C. (2002). Financial literacy: An overview of practice, research and policy. *Federal Reserve Bulletin*, *88*(11), 445–457. doi:10.17016/bulletin.2002.88-11

Brinckmann, J., Salomo, S., & Gemuenden, H. G. (2011). Financial management competence of founding teams and growth of new technology–based firms. *Entrepreneurship Theory and Practice*, *35*(2), 217–243. doi:10.1111/j.1540-6520.2009.00362.x

García-Pérez-de-Lema, D., Ruiz-Palomo, D., & Diéguez-Soto, J. (2021). Analysing the roles of CEO's financial literacy and financial constraints on Spanish SMEs technological innovation. *Technology in Society*, *64*, 101519. doi:10.1016/j.techsoc.2020.101519

Ismanto, H., Widiastuti, A., Muharam, H., & Pangestuti, I. R. D. (2020). The Impact of Risk and Financial Knowledge, Business Culture and Financial Practice on SME Performance. *Calitatea*, *21*(179), 3–9.

Klewitz, J., & Hansen, E. G. (2014). Sustainability-oriented innovation of SMEs: A systematic review. *Journal of Cleaner Production*, *65*, 57–75. doi:10.1016/j.jclepro.2013.07.017

Remund, D. L. (2010). Financial Literacy Explicated: The Case for A Clearer Definition in an Increasingly Complex Economy. *The Journal of Consumer Affairs*, *44*(2), 276–295. doi:10.1111/j.1745-6606.2010.01169.x

Stan-Maduka, E. (2013). SME Financial Management: A Risk Management Perspective. In M. Khosrow-Pour, S. Clarke, M. E. Jennex, A. Becker, & A.-V. Anttiroiko (Eds.), *Small and Medium Enterprises: Concepts, Methodologies, Tools, and Applications* (pp. 1107–1119). IGI Global., doi:10.4018/978-1-4666-3886-0.ch054

Wise, S. (2013). The impact of financial literacy on new venture survival. *International Journal of Business and Management*, *8*(23), 30–39. doi:10.5539/ijbm.v8n23p30

KEY TERMS AND DEFINITIONS

Entrepreneurship: Creation of new products, services, processes, or business models that enhance the development and competitiveness of the market and the economic system as a whole.

Financial Literacy: Understanding of financial aspects and the application of this knowledge on a personal and a professional level.

Financial Skills: Skills related to the understanding, evaluation and management of the financial resources needed to set up a firm and develop successful, innovative, and sustainable initiatives within it.

Product and Service Innovation: Improvement in the characteristics or functionalities that allows reaching differentiated performances from other products and services offered by a firm. The introduction of a good or service that is new or significantly improved with respect to its characteristics or intended uses includes significant improvements in technical specifications, components and materials, software, user friendliness or other functional characteristics.

Risk Management: Process of identifying, assessing, and controlling the internal and external risks faced by a company.

Risk-Taking: Propensity to get involved in risky projects and the capacity to manage their inherent uncertainty. Risk-taking is the disposition of an organization to determine and act without a definite knowledge of possible returns and possibly consider personal, financial and business risks.

SMEs: Micro, small, and medium size firms according to the European Union Regulation No. 651/2014. In this regard, to be considered an SME a firm must have fewer than 250 employees and not have a turnover of more than 50 million euros or a total balance sheet of more than 43 million.

Sustainable Innovation Strategies: Decisions and actions developed by a firm to enhance innovative and viable growth, consistent with its objectives and committed to its ecosystem and environment.

Section 2
Business Sustainability

Chapter 5
The Confluence of Sustainability and Governance at the Universidade da Coruña (Spain): A Case Study

Ángeles Longarela-Ares
University of A Coruña, Spain

Estefanía Mourelle
University of A Coruña, Spain

Carmen Gago-Cortés
University of A Coruña, Spain

ABSTRACT

Universities are experiencing a transition to sustainable universities, as addressing environmental concerns has become a cornerstone for the governance of higher education institutions. As responsible for the formation of decision-makers and because of its duty with the society, these institutions must be in line with the current society. This chapter deals with the implementation of sustainable procedures and initiatives in a concrete university: the Universidade da Coruña in Spain. Great efforts have been done regarding raising awareness on environmental issues and the implementation of sustainable procedures, even with limited economic resources. As a result, this university is very well positioned in international rankings and has great potential in the field of sustainable development.

INTRODUCTION

Higher Education institutions (HEIs) are responsible for fostering and building critical thinking of citizens and future decision-makers (Henchen et al., 2019). Therefore, these institutions have the vision, the knowledge required and the power to lead the transition towards sustainable development, promoting the

DOI: 10.4018/978-1-7998-7634-2.ch005

necessary changes (Ramísio, 2019). Hence, it is necessary to include academic activities and projects that promote social and environmental education in their study programmes. Nevertheless, HEIs must also put these initiatives into practice, so their internal management must become a successful benchmark of sustainability for the population (Henchen et al., 2019). Therefore, they must carry out both internal and external activities, which may include awareness campaigns, selection of relevant bibliography, socio-environmental training courses, energy eco-efficiency, responsible consumption, promotion of sustainable means of transport, financial transparency, and treatment of waste, among others.

The in-depth study of the different activities and its implementation process in this type of institution acquires a special relevance given that these activities can become an important reference for other organizations. The objective of this chapter is to carry out this analysis through a case study: The Universidade da Coruña (UDC), a Spanish Higher Education institution.

The UDC's transition towards a sustainable university begins to take shape with the 2013-2020 Strategic Plan, which clearly expresses the university's commitment to sustainable development. Since February 2014, this institution is implementing ecological management procedures under the Green Campus programme. Moreover, the commitment to sustainability is reflected in the UDC Sustainability Campus created in 2018. Other fundamental reference for sustainability is the Office of Environmental Planning, responsible for environmental management, awareness, and participation of the university community in the related issues. Another key objective of the Strategic Plan is the promotion of a quality, innovative and specialized teaching, as well as positioning the UDC as a leading institution in training for sustainability. Apart from the above-mentioned issues, the financial aspect of implementing these measures and the promotion of an efficient use of resources is also taken into account in the analysis. Addressing the sustainability actions from different perspectives and areas ensures that all the main objectives are considered, and this makes the analysis more complete.

Firstly, this study begins with a review on the relevance of sustainable development in today's society. Secondly, the attention turns to education and its role on developing sustainable goals; in particular, the focus is Higher Education (HE) and its transition to sustainability at all levels. At this respect, we depart from a general framework to a particular one, deepening in the specific case of the Universidade da Coruña. This central section is a case study that goes from the institutional framework to the sustainability strategies adopted. From this analysis, the principles behind the implementation of the sustainability strategy of this university are introduced. Due to its importance, a separate section is devoted to the economic and financial implication that the transition to sustainability in HE involves. Finally, a discussion, as well as the most important conclusions, are presented.

BACKGROUND

Sustainability has been gaining importance in recent years. Through sustainability management policies and actions, organizations show their commitment to society and the environment. HEIs should show themselves as an example to follow, given their important role in the society. The Brundtland Report, prepared by different nations in 1987 for the UN, develops this concept based on three essential pillars: social, environmental, and economic. The social part includes aspects such as respect for employees and their families, establishing good relationships with different stakeholders, creating and maintaining jobs, or investing in community activities. The environmental protection part includes the rational use of natural resources, the reduction of consumption, the reduction of waste and its proper management, the control of pollution, or the choice of suppliers through sustainable criteria. Regarding the economic field, actions aimed at economic growth must be matched with social and environmental concerns, giving special relevance to the sustainability of the business. Sustainable management helps to generate value and competitive advantage since consumers increasingly demand efficient use of natural resources by organizations. The rationalization of resources can lead to a decrease in production costs for the organization, so it would be generating economic benefits while improving its image (Henchen et al., 2019).

The inclusion of sustainability in universities has a number of positive consequences from a social and environmental point of view. Universities prepare future decision-makers so that they can face future environmental, social and economic problems from a sustainable point of view (Missiacos Cárdenas, 2016). In this way, the mission of sustainable universities goes beyond concrete actions on campus. Given that students are going to inherit serious problems like climate change, this mission focuses on helping them find solutions. Therefore, the sustainable actions carried out within the universities contribute to making the whole community aware of the problem and learn the different ways of facing it (Atherton, 2011).

The literature also addresses the role of the university as a social actor and its efforts to reach the community more effectively. Nowadays, the activities with which universities can contribute to a broader social transition to sustainability are commonly grouped into four interrelated functions: education, research, operations, and community participation. To these four functions can be added the complementary field of governance (Fischer, 2015). A sustainable university is one that manages its resources to implement these functions to help society make a correct transition towards sustainable lifestyles (Turan, 2016). Through education people are empowered for sustainability. Research provides new solutions to socio-economic and environmental problems. The operations involve the implementation of measures at the university, such as achieving a zero footprint. Through community participation, students and staff are empowered to make sustainable decisions. Governance in this area makes sustainability a priority (Green Office Movement, 2019). Therefore, it is necessary to highlight the importance of universities taking advantage of their potential to implement action strategies at the local level, which allow addressing global problems; by doing this, they become examples for all types of organizations to follow (M'Gonigle, 2006).

"Traditional" universities transitioning to sustainable universities should try to create meaning or "make sense" of the conception of sustainability in order to integrate it within the organization. In this area, academic leaders must face challenges related to the methodology for training students, the manner of doing research, the contribution of the institution to society, or the appropriate way of governance in the context of sustainability. To do this, the generation of a shared vision of change in the organization is an essential requirement. While the defenders of sustainability in HEIs try to make their discourse prevail based on social responsibility and regulations, those who feel threatened by this discourse will try to discredit it based on the traditional academic values of scientific freedom, self-government and objectivity. This resistance to the transition towards sustainability is usually activated when the different reference persons in the institution perceive that autonomy, quality, resources, visibility or influence will be reduced (Bien & Sassen, 2020).

Efficiency in the development of environmental management can only be achieved if all the hierarchical levels of the entity agree on its relevance, integrating and engaging each stakeholder (Henchen et al., 2019).

To face the transition towards environmental sustainability, as in industry and in small businesses, the university can also implement environmental management systems (EMSs). These systems consist of a series of activities aimed at reducing harmful impact on the environment. The key aspects of this management focus on guaranteeing the safety and quality of activities and services. EMSs help meet the interests of those stakeholders who are aware of the importance of environmental responsibility; therefore, they can become a powerful tool to improve the public image of the university. The operations that these systems entail are basically focused on identifying and classifying the environmental impacts of each department, and then trying to prevent, reduce or eliminate them. One of the schemes used to launch EMSs in universities is "Eco Campus". It consists of obtaining recognition stage by stage, obtaining bronze, silver, gold and platinum awards. Manchester Metropolitan University has implemented its EMSs through this scheme, becoming awarded with the platinum ecological campus (only 28% of those registered in Eco Campus have this recognition). The 2014-2020 Environmental Sustainability Strategy of the Manchester Metropolitan University establishes its objectives in order to become a sustainable university. These include establishing a link between environmental sustainability and the employability of graduates, the use of sustainable means of transport, reducing carbon emissions by 50%, reusing and recycling 85% of waste or reducing the consumption of water by 25%. To achieve these objectives, it is essential that staff and students show interest and enthusiasm in participating in the design and implementation of the policies, strategies and management plans of their university (Kralikova & Sobotova, 2019).

The concern for economic efficiency in universities has resulted in the design of different sustainability models aimed at reducing costs while increasing the quantity and quality of service. These institutions are thinking of new educational models designed to modify and better adapt services according to the type of student, increasing student success, improving quality, and providing services at economically sustainable costs. For doing this, alternative models to traditional face-to-face teaching are being introduced in a complementary way (Jones & Johnstone, 2016). In addition, salaries of university members make up the largest item of expenses, so efforts are directed toward making their work as efficient as possible. So as to achieve this, a series of obstacles must be overcome. For example, collective bargaining agreements that associate different types of activities to a single employee, who can be responsible for the design of a course, the selection of learning resources, the evaluation, the establishment of the necessary technology, and probably many more (Jones & Johnstone, 2016). This situation is related to the fact that some regulations specify the staffing of the centres by establishing that a certain number of credits must be taught by full-time teaching staff. But there are other options that use university teaching staff in activities that allow greater efficiency in the service they provide. One example is the model created by the National Centre for Higher Education Management Systems (NCHEMS) of the United States. Its usefulness depends on the freedom institutions have to organize and use their resources in providing learning experiences. The model consists of a matrix in which the activities whose combination results in a teaching-learning experience are represented in columns and the necessary resources to carry out those activities in rows (see Table 1).

Table 1. Structure of the model.

Resource Options	Activities		
	Course/Program Development	**Delivery**	**Program Support**
Faculty			
Other Professionals			
Students			
Non-Staff Costs/Resources			

Source: (Jones and Johnstone, 2016)

Taking into account the different types of resources that can be used to carry out each activity, the model helps to determine the costs of creating and delivering the programme in different ways, so that the most efficient and sustainable can be selected.

Green initiatives at universities are typically bottom-up. Proposals are made by students or staff from different departments, which usually require a significant investment. The acceptance of the proposals and the allocation of the necessary resources would take place at a higher level (Brown, 2010). But mixed bottom-up and top-down approaches are considered more suitable for achieving success in changing organizational culture (Ramísio, 2019). Sustainability policies must be implemented in all areas that make up the mission of the organization. Continuous communication and monitoring of both its implementation and its development are key aspects for success. Among the ways of approaching sustainability in universities, two models predominate: campus operations and institutional initiatives (Leal Filho et al., 2019). The term "Campus Greening" often refers to technical aspects including environmental management, sustainable buildings, renewable energy or carbon footprint. It is sometimes seen as a first step towards a sustainable university, but it is something more complex. To be effective, all activities must be integrated within an institutional framework. The Green Office model and the Sustainability Office model can be distinguished. The Sustainability Office coordinates all activities related to this concept, both campus operations, research and teaching, but it often presents difficulties to involve students, teachers and researchers in the implementation of sustainable actions. Instead, the Green Office is typically student-led in order to integrate sustainability into the curriculum, operations, community, and governance. These initiatives are often limited, as they lack funding and institutional access (Leal Filho et al., 2019).

Once the idea of transition from "traditional" to sustainable universities has been presented, the next section deals with the concrete experience carried out at the Universidade da Coruña (UDC).

THE TRANSITION TOWARDS A SUSTAINABLE UNIVERSITY: MAIN ISSUES

Challenges to Face

Addressing sustainable issues has become a cornerstone for the governance of HEIs. This chapter focuses on how the UDC deals with the sustainability objective by addressing the opportune key actions. After the analysis of the general panorama carried out, a series of questions are raised that must be resolved in order to verify the sustainable transition of this university. Given that the university is taken as a point of reference when implementing sustainable actions, one of the first questions to address is what type of actions this institution has initiated and how it is implementing them (Q1). It is also necessary to contextualize these actions, comparing them with those that are being carried out in other institutions to verify their scope (Q2). Regarding the management for the implementation of sustainable initiatives, both the bottom-up approach and the top-down approach have their drawbacks, as mentioned. The mixed approach is the one that manages to achieve both the necessary resources and structure, as well as the involvement of the different groups of the university community. For this reason, it is necessary to know whether the approach used in this university is top-down or bottom-up (Q3). In order to carry out these initiatives, in addition to motivated human resources, it is also necessary to have the necessary financial resources. Many of these programs and activities require considerable funding. So finally, how the obstacle of the scarcity of financial resources has been overcome to carry out the different sustainable initiatives is an important aspect to consider (Q4).

Sustainability in Higher Education Institutions: General Framework

Sustainability is an internationally agreed goal and, as such, requires strategic lines of work and cooperation in diverse areas. United Nations Sustainable Development Goals advocates for Quality Education to "*ensure that all learners acquire the knowledge and skills needed to promote sustainable development, including, among others, through education for sustainable development and sustainable lifestyles, human rights, gender equality, promotion of a culture of peace and non-violence, global citizenship and appreciation of cultural diversity and of culture's contribution to sustainable development*" (SDSN, 2020, p. 55).

The main mission of universities is to work for society, so they must try to protect it against serious threats such as environmental degradation. The 1972 Stockholm Conference formally recognizes the importance of promoting the protection and care of the environment through education (Henchen et al., 2019). This conference is followed by a series of declarations and agreements that aim to promote sustainable development in academic programmes and to provide advice on how to incorporate sustainable models in institutions (Ramísio, 2019): Declarations of Talloires (1990), Halifax (1991), Swansea (1993), Kyoto (1993), Global Higher Education for Sustainability Partnership (2001) and Abuja (2009).

The United Nations has declared the period 2005-2014 as the Decade of Education for Sustainable Development, establishing an international mandate for the integration of sustainability in all aspects of the educational processes (education, research, operations and evaluation) (UNESCO, 2005). In response, HEIs began to incorporate sustainability in their missions and practices (Ramísio, 2019).

In the Spanish context, education for sustainable development is also included in the Sustainable Economy Law, which has a specific section (3rd) for the university system. According to article 60, universities must facilitate the acquisition of the skills demanded by the jobs market and the capacity to address the longer-term challenges (Boletín Oficial del Estado, 2011).

Spanish universities have gradually taken on board social responsibility contents in the academic process (Ruiz-Corbella & Bautista-Cerro, 2016). The faculties of economics and business were the first to incorporate these contents in their degrees and masters. In the survey conducted by the CRUE[1] (Conferencia de Rectores de las Universidades Españolas) in 2011, the universities point out the presence of subjects about professional ethics, human rights, development cooperation, environmental education, sustainable development and sustainability in their programmes (Ministerio de Educación, 2011). There is also an increase in the chairs of collaboration between companies and universities dedicated to social responsibility and sustainability. In this way, the commitment to social responsibility and sustainable development are a relevant part of the so called *Third Mission* of HE.

Galician University System: Specific Framework

Galicia is a Spanish region located in the country northwest. The university system of this region is made up of three universities: Universidade de Santiago de Compostela (USC), Universidade de Vigo (UVigo), and Universidade da Coruña (UDC). These three institutions have assumed the challenge of sustainability management, although by means of different approaches.

The USC approved a sustainable development plan in 2003. As administrative support of this plan, the Office for Sustainable Development was created in 2011, depending on Vice-Rector's Office for Equality, Culture, and Services. Through this plan, this university intends to include sustainability in university management, research, training, and extension. USC is a pioneer university at the European level in the introduction of environmental subjects in the programmes. Specifically, these subjects were introduced in 1982 in the degree in Pedagogy. It has also been one of the first universities to incorporate an efficient energy management system. It also has a hazardous waste management unit and has carried out a mobility study, among other actions. The plan consists of three main axes (Universidade de Santiago de Compostela, n.d.a):

- Generation of knowledge and environmental education
- Planning, management, and environmental assessment
- Environmental awareness and participation

The USC also participates together with the UVigo and the UDC in the International Chair CSR Santander Galicia-North of Portugal, whose objective is the development of teaching, research, training, and documentation activities in the field of corporate social responsibility (Universidade de Santiago de Compostela, n.d.b).

On the other hand, UVigo expresses its commitment to sustainable development through its Environmental Office (Universidade de Vigo, n.d.d). In 2007, UVigo launches the SuMA plan, its sustainability and environment plan, including seven action programmes:

- Energetic efficiency and sustainability
- Singular R&D facilities
- Recycling and reuse of waste
- Natural and patrimonial contour
- Transportation
- Collaboration and social commitment
- Dissemination and awareness

UVigo specifically monitors energy and environmental sustainability programmes through its Vice-Rector's Office for Planning and Sustainability. The section dedicated to Social Responsibility and the 2030 Agenda shows the role of this university in achieving more sustainable development through its adherence to the Global Compact (Universidade de Vigo, n.d.c). In addition, the Pontevedra Campus of this university has the international "Green Campus" certification, which represents recognition of the environmental education activities carried out (Universidade de Vigo, n.d.b). This university, together with the UDC, are the first in Spain to receive this recognition. UVigo also has chairs for collaboration with companies in the sustainability field, among which are the Unesco Chair for sustainable management of coastal areas, and the Unión Fenosa Chair for studies and activities in the energy economics, environment and sustainable development fields (Universidade de Vigo, n.d.a).

As with the other two universities, the UDC also has an action plan to promote sustainable actions. The Strategic Plan 2013-2020 includes sustainability as a priority area in the field of social responsibility (Universidade da Coruña, 2013). Nevertheless, compared with the other two Galician institutions, UDC has a clearly differentiating feature: its Sustainability Campus. Besides this, the UDC shares some issues with the other two universities, like the existence of an Office of Environmental Planning and several institutional chairs devoted to sustainable actions. These aspects of the sustainable management of the UDC are discussed in more depth in the next section.

Sustainability Management at the UDC

The governance of the UDC consists of the Social Council, the Senate, the Rector, the Governing Council, and the University Ombudsman (Universidade da Coruña, n.d.b). The UDC has two campuses: Campus da Coruña and Campus de Ferrol. It has 14 faculties, and 9 university schools. In 2018, the UDC had 17,064 students, of which 13,887 were full-time equivalent. At that year, there were 1,393 teaching staff; most of them are hired full-time. The administrative staff is composed of 799 workers.

The greater concern about sustainability has encouraged universities to accelerate their efforts to develop their own strategies. In the case of the UDC, the Strategic Plan 2013-2020 is the key document that addresses the main environmental and sustainable concerns the institution has to face. This Plan includes the vision for 2020 of "*open up channels of active solidarity, with a strong commitment to environmental protection and sustainable development through innovation*" (Universidade da Coruña, 2013, p. 16). Among others, the Strategic Plan includes the following values and principles (Universidade da Coruña, 2013, p. 17):

Social responsibility and commitment, as a way of contributing actively to the improvement of the socio-economic situation of our community and the creation of greater economic well-being in society as a whole.

Respect for the environment, as a socially responsible university, maximising and managing the resources at our disposal as efficiently as possible, to minimise environmental impact.

A comprehensive scorecard is established for each of the three major areas of action:

1. Teaching and learning.
2. Research, innovation and transfer
3. Social responsibility.

For each area, the strategic objectives, the lines of action, the person in charge, the objective indicators, its initial value and the goals to be achieved are established.

Regarding the strategic objectives in the social responsibility area, the first one is looking for a university that boosts social change. With this objective in mind, an open university model is promoted in which the activities carried out benefit both university community and society. The second seeks for equal opportunities and the promotion of a culture of non-discrimination; the aim is to make equal opportunities effective, guaranteeing everyone's access to quality HE. And the third consists of a university responsible for its environmental impact. This objective responds to the public service function of the university, providing solutions to the environmental crisis and favoring a more sustainable development (Universidade da Coruña, 2013).

Apart from the strategic objectives stated in the Strategic Plan, each centre may add specific objectives, accompanied by their corresponding indicators. The centre may autonomously establish the quantitative goals and the actions necessary to achieve these objectives, in coherence with the strategies of the UDC. The strategic plan of each centre is integrated in its internal quality assurance system to guarantee internal coordination and supervision.

Following the guidelines of the Strategic Plan, the UDC is placing a big bet on the promotion of sustainability among the university community. One clear proof of this fact is the existence of a Vice-Rectorate exclusively dedicated to Infrastructure and Sustainability matters. In addition, one fact to stand out is the creation of the already mentioned Sustainability Campus. This is a specialisation campus that makes use of the strengths and research capacity of our university in this field. The mission of the Sustainability Campus is that the UDC becomes a knowledge hub that allows for regional, national and international research excellence in those areas more closely related to urbanism, sustainability (economic, social and environmental) and healthy lifestyle. This mission is aligned with the priorities mirrored in the Sustainable Development Goals of the United Nations. By creating this Campus, the UDC pretends to be more attractive from an academic, research and management point of view; moreover, it would also help to develop the so-called "third mission" of the university, by impacting the society and contributing to the economic development.

Sustainability Campus

Figure 1. Sustainability Campus logo.
Source: Sustainability Campus webpage (n.d.).

The Sustainability Campus is organized around four main theme areas: city and territory; circular and sustainable economy; social sustainability and environmental education; and healthy lifestyle. Thus, this campus organises, sponsors and supports the development of many different actions and events. Some examples are seminars on circular economy, promotion of wellness or transition to sustainability in the urban environment. Importantly, some of these events are synchronised with similar initiatives in other countries, in particular when celebrating commemorative Days.

The Sustainability Campus can be seen as an umbrella that fosters and gives support to sustainable initiatives, as well as connects the university with its environment. It also serves as a means of communication between different agents of the university community.

Two theme areas have become particularly relevant in the Universidade da Coruña. First, the creation of the "UDC Saudable", a service that depends on the Vice-Rectorate of Ferrol and Social Responsibility. In 2014, the UDC joined the "Red Española de Universidades Saludables" (REUS, the Spanish network on healthy universities), a membership that is framed within the UDC Strategic Plan 2013-2020. Its commitment is the promotion of healthy lifestyles in the university culture, institutional policies, organization and syllabuses; "UDC Saudable" has its own technical commission, as well as a support network in different faculties and schools. Its role is to participate in the coordination and development of initiatives on healthy lifestyle in the university community. Some of the most outstanding aims of the "Campus UDC≡Universidade Saudable" programme are the promotion of the university as health promoter of the university members and the society as a whole; to foster research and teaching on health promotion; to promote the joint work between public health organisations, community institutions and HEIs; and to encourage the exchange of experiences within the health promotion framework. To be considered as "healthy", the university must have a global commitment on health and develop its potential as promoting agent of health, well-being and quality of life.

Second, the area of social sustainability and environmental education is being particularly fostered as it allows for the transition to a society more concerned on nature conservation. In this sense, the University organises several types of events for training and research in environmental issues. Thus, besides the organisation of seminars, workshops, etc. in the research, innovation and transfer fields, sustainable development has been introduced in the regular offer of training courses (that is, joint with those on teaching-learning methodologies or pedagogical aspects, among others). In this line, an important milestone for the UDC was the first call on MOOCs (Massive Open Online Courses) in 2018. One course from the first edition (launched in its second edition, too) was the one named "Sustainability in the era of Big Data", designed by a group of teachers from the Faculty of Economics and Business. The course deals with environmental, social and economic sustainability matters in today's society, which is characterized by the rapid technological growth. Following the data on enrolment, this MOOC has been a success, so that it has contributed to raising awareness and knowledge on sustainable development from different perspectives.

Green Campus Programme

Related to the UDC initiatives carried out to promote sustainable development, one of the most well-known is the Green Campus programme. This programme involves the introduction of environmental management procedures under a green flag ("Green Campus"). In 2014, the UDC signed an agreement with the "Asociación de Educación Ambiental y del Consumidor" (ADEAC, as member of the international Foundation for Environmental Education, FEE), that is in charge of this international initiative. The Green Campus programme applies the methodology, philosophy and experience of the "Ecoescolas" ("Eco-schools") developed by the FEE to the HE context. Green Campus is widespread among European countries, with dozens of HEIs taking part on it.

Regarding its trajectory in the UDC, the different faculties and schools voluntarily adhere to this programme, although there is a rising participation and interest each year. The different faculties and schools must set up an environmental committee (composed of professors, students and administrative staff, and even ex-students or external members) that analyses the situation of the centre regarding the implementation of sustainable and environmentally friendly initiatives. From this starting point, the faculty or school prepares an Action Plan with the main objectives, resources and deadlines. Moreover, a Declaration of Environmental Commitment is also developed.

The Green Campus programme is thus carried out from each faculty or school, but different areas of the Rectorate (in particular, the Office of Environmental Planning) give support, information and advise to the centres. From the faculty or school, the environmental committee develops the different tasks designed in the Action Plan during the time stipulated until the final completion. In order to certify that the centre has fulfilled all the stated goals and commitments, an external examiner visits the faculty or school and proceeds with the evaluation. In case of positive result, the centre receives the Green Flag recognition of meeting the environmental and sustainable criteria. As of September 2020, seven faculties and schools of the UDC were awarded with this Flag. It is important to highlight that this programme helps to giving visibility and rising concern on environmental and sustainable matters. It can be appreciated how people is now more aware of the importance of a sustainable development within the immediate boundaries of the university and beyond it than before.

Office of Environmental Planning

In the aforementioned works to implant environmental procedures, the Office of Environmental Planning plays a key role. This service is dependent on the Vice-Rectorate of Infrastructures and Sustainability and is in charge of participating in the coordinating and development of actions and initiatives in the environmental field. The main objectives of this Office are to deal with, on the one hand, the environmental governance, and, on the other hand, to raise awareness and participation on environmental issues among the university community. The scope of these goals are: environmental evaluation and dissemination in the different campuses of the UDC; participation and environmental co-responsibility; and sectoral projects related to environmental management and sustainability.

Besides the integration in the different initiatives, the members of the university community can take part in the so-called "environmental volunteering". There are two ways of participation; on the one hand, by taking part in specific volunteer sessions that are published on the Office of Environmental Planning website and, on the other hand, by enrolling in voluntary stable actions throughout the course. The university makes great efforts in the dissemination of these initiatives of participation by means of notices published in the main website, e-mail delivery or social media. Furthermore, notice boards and informative posters were placed to publicize the measures adopted and to raise awareness in the university community in the responsible use of resources. Some examples are: posters on common printers with measures that promote the saving of paper and toner; signage with stickers indicating measures to save water and the flow of the billboards; posters on the elevators and floor encouraging you to climb the stairs, etc. The objective is to encourage centres to develop initiatives and purchases with ecological and responsible criteria and to raise awareness, and encourage students to be an active part of the initiatives.

At this respect, it is important to highlight the existence of the "Cooperation and Volunteerism Office". This office serves for channelling demands for participation and solidarity from the university community and regarding the local and global common good in the area of influence of the UDC. The actions carried out are based on three main pillars: Volunteerism, training and development cooperation.

Institutional Chairs

Other interesting instruments that the UDC employs so as to develop and promote sustainable actions are the institutional chairs. Their main objective is the development of a sort of non-profit activities like training, outreach, research, transfer and knowledge ones in focus areas where companies and universities meet. Two examples are introduced. The first is the "EMALCSA Chair", which focuses on the sustainable management of water resources. EMALCSA is the company that supplies water to the city of A Coruña. Then, a key factor in the collaboration between this company and the UDC is the design of methodologies as well as strategies to apply the integrated water resource management principles in the urban water system to different geographical, social and economic contexts. More in depth, some of the main objectives are to enhance transfer and research activities by supporting joint research lines, achievement of research projects, or the development of doctoral, master and bachelor thesis, among others. In summary, this chair means an opportunity to put into practice and to deliver the scientific and technology advances obtained in the UDC to the citizenship.

The second example is the chair "Hijos de Rivera de Desarrollo Sostenible". "Hijos de Rivera S. A." is a Galician company from the food sector and producer of beer and water. The main aim of this chair has to do with exploring new innovative and disruptive models that guarantee the equilibrium between economic competitiveness, environmental respect and social advances. In order to achieve these objectives, different initiatives will be carried out in the field of sustainable development; for example, research, transfer and training activities, seminars on experiences and socioeconomic transformation models, or meetings between major actors.

Besides the institutional chairs just pointed out, the UDC has several others, some of them related to corporate and social responsibility. Importantly, the completion of the actions proposed by all the existing chairs in the UDC would allow the transfer of knowledge between the university and the society.

FINANCIAL AND EFFICIENCY IMPLICATIONS FOR A SUSTAINABLE UNIVERSITY

In addition to social and environmental aspects, it should be remembered that economic aspects must be taken into account, since improving efficiency in resources management will mean not only greater savings but also less harmful impact on environment. Nonetheless, HEIs need funding in order to improve their level of sustainability, and, unfortunately, the lack of financial resources is more common than expected. In particular, this happens in Spain due to the general decline in funding for HE, which represents a great barrier to sustainable development (Aleixo et al., 2018). Thus, financial sources are a relevant issue to address.

In this sense, the Galician university system has the strengths derived from the collaboration, coordination and complementarity between the three universities. Nevertheless, low funding is a weak point, which prevents the real autonomy that allows Galician HEIs to develop their own policies and a stronger and guaranteed financial sustainability.

As a case of study, we are focusing on the Universidade da Coruña. Public universities receive funding from society to carry out its three functions: teaching, research and transfer. The UDC, as a public university that creates value for society, requires public funding for its structural needs. UDC intends to be a university that manages its resources effectively, efficiently, equitably, transparently, and, furthermore, intends to achieve a sufficient and stable public financing system (Universidade da Coruña, 2013).

The UDC Strategic Plan sets targets and action areas that include financing and efficient use of resources, and focus this strategic area on: the need to diversify income through a proactive capture of resources (income diversification and funding); the efficient, responsible and transparent management of available resources and the implementation of an analytical accounting system, and a system for measuring the use and distribution of resources or for linking their allocation from centres and services to the objectives compliance (efficient management of resources) (Universidade da Coruña, 2013). These aspects are detailed below.

Income Diversification and Funding

Support access to international research funding and international competitive announcements in public-private consortia constitute at the present time the greatest possibility of attracting funding outside the Financing Plan of the University System of Galicia (SUG). Horizon 2020 programme or the elaboration of the RIS3 (especially at the level of Galicia) are also important elements to advance in this line. The Horizon 2020 funds could provide an important step reinforcing priorities, namely: smart growth, sustainable growth and inclusive growth. It is an important financial instrument for the sustainability of HEIs that could serve for two purposes: to support the implementation of sustainability and to address the constraints identified.

The financing for quality improvement in the SUG was endowed with 18,000,000 euros each year of its validity (2011-2015). Although in 2011 the distribution was based on the percentages of participation of each institution in the unconditional fund of the 2005-2010 plan, from 2012 it was linked to compliance with the commitments included in the sustainability plans of each institution in the SUG. Consequently, universities received the amounts resulting from the application of criteria of efficiency and effectiveness in the economic-financial management, of the academic planning and of the measures that had allowed to share resources between the three universities of the SUG, being UDC in the second position (Sistema Universitario de Galicia, 2016).

However, the present context imposes the need for greater attention to fundraising and HEIs needs to generate income and resources that make them less dependent on the State (Aleixo et al., 2018). It is not a question of replacing public funding with private funding, but of complementing structural public funding with income from other sources. The UDC must therefore encourage collaboration with companies and institutions to improve fundraising, value its technology and capital at its disposal, and enhance and exploit its brand. The objective is to maintain the revenues from agreements and contracts with companies until 2015 and subsequent annual increase until 2020. In the case of the UDC, university-company collaborations are relevant, although likely to improve. As an example, moreover the chairs previously mentioned, programmes such as the Edition of the Educating for Sustainability Project have the collaboration of the Alcoa Foundation. Transfer projects are also a source of funding that will allow more research projects to be carried out. These projects are a way of achieving greater development and well-being, as well as it allows moving towards a knowledge-based economy. They become even more relevant in the current adverse economic situation. The spin-offs participated by the UDC, the coordination of the good number of transfer management entities that collaborate with the UDC and the training of the staff in transfer capacities are also strategic lines to account for (Universidade da Coruña, 2013).

Efficient Management of Resources

The UDC, as a manager of public resources, must ensure its use according to efficiency criteria. In a context of resource scarcity and uncertainty about its future availability, efficient management can alleviate, albeit only in part, declining income. The efficiency in operation implies reductions in the cost of production or services in HEIs (World Voices Nexus, n.d.). Working for efficiency and ethic in resources management would allow that universities generate financial savings, while reducing harmful impacts on environment through a proper utilisation and reduction of existing resources waste.

In this sense, the UDC has implemented appropriate mechanisms to control expenditure and measure the costs associated with each centre and service, in particular an analytical accounting system in 2015 and the design of a set of cost indicators for centres and services in 2016. Data availability and cost analysis are the first steps towards the use and efficient distribution of all available resources, both human and material. Therefore, it is necessary to implement the appropriate mechanisms for the available data to be used for decision-making. At the same time, the UDC streamlines the purchase processes through purchasing centres and resources use measurement, using the available information to distribute resources between centre and services.

Regarding financial sustainability, the UDC objective is to differentiate between non-financial income and expenses and achieves a progressive increase in the ratio of current transfers/current expenses in the liquidated budget (up to 0.9 in 2020) (Universidade da Coruña, 2013). The financial support of the strategic plan is included in a multi-year programming, a useful tool to give robustness to the strategic plan and make it credible, by linking it with economic-financial endowments in its period of validity. In the last three months of each year, annual operational plans will be formulated to implement the different lines of action and will have clear annual budgets according to spending programmes that will refer to each of the objectives.

The UDC also adopts rules for the allocation of available resources in order to encourage coordination between centres and services, always ensuring coverage of structural needs, and these allocation rules must be linked to the fulfillment of the strategic objectives of each centre. The decentralized purchase of some specific supplies means an increase in costs and a loss of efficiency. The UDC, through the analysis of the specific situation of each supply, studies the adoption of rationalized measures, like the potential implementation of purchasing centres, as effective mechanisms to improve resource management and to reduce spending and review the procedures for the control and monitoring of external procurement (Universidade da Coruña, 2013).

The UDC is committed to improving the efficiency of the use of resources with the aim of including ecological and responsible criteria in the choice of purchased products and services, as well as to evaluate, adjust and reduce consumption as much as possible. The objectives of the measures adopted in this area are the efficiency, rationalization and containment of expenditure and, through them, the diffusion of a responsibility culture in the use of resources. Within the Green Campus framework, eco-audits were conducted at different centres to assess the need to take actions related to reducing costs and increasing savings.

Furthermore, energy management at the UDC, as in the vast majority of public institutions, is not centralized and is also carried out by Services and Negotiations created for other issues. This warns that these departments have different monitoring protocols, which means that the management of consumption and energy billing is a difficult process to follow jointly and globally. The dispersion and disorganization of energy management made the Campuses, like the Industrial Campus, an ideal environment for a pilot project of energy management; the results drawn from this project can be extrapolated to any other administration or HEI in the community that has been in operation for a few years (Campus de Ferrol, 2017a).

Measures for Waste, Water and Energy Efficiency

The approximate qualitative and quantitative characterization of the waste from the different centres was developed by means of analyses. Among the initiatives taken to manage resources and waste are the following: collecting environmental information on the sustainable products and services offered by companies to adjust purchases progressively, to develop indicators of the percentage of responsible consumer purchases over total and to classify the companies according ecological procurement criteria; selective collection of waste, cork collection boxes and reduction of plastic, paper or cardboard consumption; spaces for the collection of Waste Electrical and Electronic Equipment, and composting and recycling areas for the organic waste generated in the cafeterias, to turn them naturally into a stable and quality fertilizer.

In order to save water, the type of faucets in the centres was studied and replaced for more efficient ones, eco-efficient pearlers were installed, faults were repaired, the water flow was adjusted by means of a tap, the water consumption of the cisterns was reduced and labels with water consumption and cisterns were placed. The water saving achieved were about 70-80% for most of the centres (Campus de Ferrol, 2017a; Campus de Ferrol, 2017b; Facultade de Ciencias da Educación, UDC, 2017; Universidade da Coruña, n.d.a). To save energy, a classroom review programme was conducted to avoid the use of unnecessary lighting; a dissemination programme was created on the importance of leaving lights off in bathrooms and other public spaces and computer equipment, and energy efficiency plans were developed in the centres. These plans consisted of the progressive installation of presence detectors in transit areas of buildings, bathrooms or function rooms, and large classrooms, as well as the replacement of lighting with low-consumption LED lamps (some estimations show that energy savings of 2,750 euros / year can be reached in a building, such as the Faculty of Civil Engineering). Furthermore, automatic thermostats for heating were installed and diesel boilers were replaced by natural gas.

Regarding mobility initiatives, the mode of travel on campuses has been analysed through a survey and the ecological footprint of some faculties has been measured. An attempt has been made to improve the bus service in its timetable and price, offering cards with a discount on prices; private car-sharing promotions have been carried out, bicycle parking has been installed on campus and a bicycle loan programme was created.

Some of the initiatives designed for an efficient use of resources are in the development and implementation phase. This is why it is necessary to carry out a rigorous and analytical study of the savings that the measures adopted in several areas and each centre of the UDC involve. However, there may be difficulties in measuring savings, as some electricity consumption meters are not independent (the same device records the overall consumption of several centres). To date, some reductions in the electricity consumption, water and diesel has been detected with the measures taken; nevertheless, they are not significant or enough. The reasons can be: difficulty in extracting isolated consumption data from the centres, as there is a single meter shared with other centres, some of which are not affiliated with the Green Campus programme; more data would be needed for a more conclusive analysis, such as, for example, activity rates (in relation to the number of students, weekend activities at the centre, etc.), existence of possible breakdowns, etc.; not enough time has elapsed for the measures taken to be reflected in the overall consumption data, as some of the most significant were recently installed (for example, the change from lighting to low-consumption lamps or presence sensors).

SOLUTIONS AND RECOMMENDATIONS

The UDC is placing great efforts in its transition to a sustainable university. The first question that the case analysis has tried to answer is to know what type of actions UDC has undertaken and how it has carried them out (Q1). This analysis has shown as remarkable facts, the creation of Sustainability Campus and the Office of Environmental Planning, that contribute to the sustainability goal with activities focused on information and dissemination on UDC campuses, participation and environmental co-responsibility, and sectoral projects related to management and environmental sustainability. At the faculty level, the creation of the Green Campus initiative should be highlighted, as it has fostered the environmental awareness in the university community. As previously mentioned, this project involves the generation of an Environmental Committee, and the conduct of eco-audits and action plans, procedures that contribute to improve the sustainability dedication. The great advances in the work developed has allowed that seven faculties have already achieved the Green Flag, and more than half of the UDC faculties participate in the Green Campus programme.

Another issue raised is to determine the scope of the measures carried out, in comparison with those of other institutions (Q2). In comparison with the two universities in its closest environment, the analysis has shown common ground such as a strategic plan that promotes sustainable actions, the existence of an Environmental Planning Office or the chairs created in order to exchange experiences in the field of teaching, research, and scientific dissemination related to environment and sustainability. But other aspects differentiate it and show its clear commitment to sustainability, among which its Sustainability Campus stands out. In the area of governance, this commitment is also evident through the creation of a Vice-Rectorate exclusively dedicated to Infrastructure and Sustainability matters. In order to positioning the UDC as a leading institution in training for sustainability, it is important to highlight the great effort made regarding the curriculum greening of HE. For several years now, the sustainable goals are included not only in the syllabuses, but also in the teaching guides of the different subjects. It is also committed to expanding environmental education beyond the university classrooms, with courses such as the MOOC Course "Sustainability in the Era of Big Data".

The efforts have been fruitful, as the UDC is very well positioned in international ranking. Thus, evidence of the UDC's commitment and the success of the procedures and initiatives introduced is its position in international rankings, like Times Higher Education or GreenMetric. Regarding the GreenMetric World University Ranking in 2019, the UDC is the third university at national level and the 85th out of 780 institutions at world level. The GreenMetric World University Ranking was first conducted in 2010; its main goal is to provide a classification according to the environmental policies undertaken within the universities across the world[2]. This success encourages the institution to continue in this vein, although the future needs must be evaluated as we form part of an alive and changing environment.

Other question to be resolved is how the implementation of the transition has been managed (Q3). The analysis shows a mixed model, top-down and bottom-up, already promoted since the 2013-2020 UDC Strategic Plan. In addition to initiatives promoted "from top" to favor more sustainable development, each university centre has the opportunity to establish its own sustainable objectives "from bottom". This opportunity, together with the efforts made by teams directly involved have achieved that the entire university community and others important stakeholders, such as companies and government agencies, walk together towards a sustainable university.

Another challenge to face is obtaining the necessary financing to carry out the transition towards sustainability (Q4). As explained in the previous sections, the UDC has used a financing system based on three main pillars: proactive recruitment of resources, efficient management of the resources obtained, and a system of allocation to the different centres in order to achieve their objectives. The UDC has been very effective in the introduction of environmental procedures with a limited amount of resources. It is especially noticeable the development of an important number of initiatives in a short period of time. These actions are intended to have social projection and they are in line with the objective of sustainable development of the university. They will allow UDC for meeting current and future social challenges.

The main recommendations would be focused on keep working hard on the commitment with sustainable development from the University. The commitment of the university's human capital with sustainable development is undoubtedly essential. The university community is involved in many initiatives and an increasing interest on these topics is clearly observed. Although it is complicated, one way of improvement has to do with the budget devoted to these concerns. The UDC is not a big university, so there are some budgetary constraints, particularly from the economic crisis on. In any case, and as previously stated, the University has done a huge effort with limited budget, so this is a key point to take into account in the next and future challenges.

FUTURE RESEARCH DIRECTIONS

The implementation of the sustainability goal in educational institutions will have a relevant importance in the future, especially considering the role that universities have in the students' sensibilisation and diffusion of knowledge. 2030 is a key date to take conscience about the necessity of making a real change in our way of interacting with our environment if we want to guarantee equality, basic resources access, and sustainable development.

The sustainability analysis at the UDC will let identify strengths, problems and opportunities that help to improve the ongoing initiatives, reflect about them and consider future actions. The comparison with other institutions provides a more global vision of the problem and helps to assess the UDC trajectory on sustainability. An interesting line of future research bases on evaluating and comparing the optimization of resources consumption and responsibility. Other areas of research may revolve around improving sustainable mobility; promoting food sovereignty initiatives; creating new activities around awareness and environmental volunteering and incorporating more activities to promote curricular greening of teaching and research.

CONCLUSION

Sustainable development is a key goal to achieve in today's society. It should be reach at all levels, from individuals to countries. The procedures to be implemented to reach this objective should be well designed, in an effective and efficient way. In any case, this is a long-run project that shows intermediate results in the short and medium rum.

So as to reach the objective of sustainability, education plays a key role. From environmental education to real applications, education must be in the agenda of the different agents, stakeholders and policymakers. In particular, HE, as trainer of future professionals and because of its duties with the society, must be an example in developing sustainable actions. This is already happening. "Traditional" universities are becoming sustainable. In this sense, they are implementing different procedures that can serve as an example for the society. In this chapter, a particular case is posed: the one of the Universidade da Coruña.

This university is putting a lot of effort to achieve the sustainable goals and the process is still going on. Nevertheless, this transition needs the commitment of the individuals and university community as a whole. Human resources are needed, as well as funding for implementing the different procedures and initiatives. The latter is limited, so additional sources must be considered. The university community has shown great interest and involvement in the development of the different actions, and this has been fruitful, as this university has reached a very good position in international rankings in a short period of time.

All the initiatives created and procedures implemented may help achieve the goals of sustainability from all perspectives; from the environment consciousness of our staff and the professional life of our students, to reaching the *Third Mission* of the University, through the curricular greening of teaching and research, among many other activities.

REFERENCES

Aleixo, A. M., Leal, S., & Azeiteiro, U. M. (2018). Conceptualization of sustainable higher education institutions, roles, barriers, and challenges for sustainability: An exploratory study in Portugal. *Journal of Cleaner Production*, *172*, 1664–1673. doi:10.1016/j.jclepro.2016.11.010

Atherton, A., & Giurco, D. (2011). Campus sustainability: Climate change, transport and paper reduction. *International Journal of Sustainability in Higher Education*, *12*(3), 269–279. doi:10.1108/14676371111148054

Bien, C., & Sassen, R. (2020). Sensemaking of a sustainability transition by higher education institution leaders. *Journal of Cleaner Production*, *256*, 120299. doi:10.1016/j.jclepro.2020.120299

Boletín Oficial del Estado. (2011). *Ley 2/2011, de 4 de marzo, de Economía Sostenible.* https://www.boe.es/eli/es/l/2011/03/04/2/con

Brown, G. (2010). Sustainability in higher education. *Perspectives*, *14*(4), 103–104. doi:10.1080/13603108.2010.522888

Campus de Ferrol. (2017a). *Anexo 3. Objetivo 3. Sostenibilidad medioambiental- Unidad de Eficiencia energética.* https://www.udc.es/export/sites/udc/campusindustrial/_galeria_down/PDFs-Creen-Campus-Ferrol/Anexo-3.pdf_2063069239.pdf

Campus de Ferrol. (2017b). *Informe-Memoria I Plan Green Campus Ferrol 2017-2019.* https://www.udc.es/export/sites/udc/sociedade/medio_ambiente/_galeria_down/GreenCampus/FERROL-Informe_Memoria.pdf_2063069239.pdf_2063069294.pdf

Facultade de Ciencias da Educación, UDC. (2017). *Informe-Memoria Plan Green Campus 2017-2019.* https://www.udc.es/export/sites/udc/sociedade/medio_ambiente/_galeria_down/GreenCampus/Ciencias-da-Educacion-Memoria-2017-2019.pdf_2063069294.pdf

Fischer, D., Jenssen, S., & Tappeser, V. (2015). Getting an empirical hold of the sustainable university: A comparative analysis of evaluation frameworks across 12 contemporary sustainability assessment tools. *Assessment & Evaluation in Higher Education*, *40*(6), 785–800. doi:10.1080/02602938.2015.1043234

Green Office Movement. (2019). *What is a sustainable university?* https://www.greenofficemovement.org/sustainable-university/

Henchen, A. V., Moura-Leite, R., & Lopes, J. C. J. (2019). Sustainability and Management of Higher Education Institutions: Scientific Production Analysis. *Revista De Gestão Ambiental e Sustentabilidade*, *8*(1), 38–61. doi:10.5585/geas.v8i1.13763

Higher Education and Research for Sustainable Development. (1991). *Halifax Declaration.* https://www.iau-hesd.net/en/documentation/30-halifax-declaration.html

Higher Education and Research for Sustainable Development. (1993). *Swansea Declaration.* https://www.iau-hesd.net/sites/default/files/documents/the_swansea_declaration.pdf

Higher Education and Research for Sustainable Development. (2009). *Abuja Declaration on Sustainable Development in Africa: The Role of Higher Education.* https://www.iau-hesd.net/sites/default/files/documents/abuja_declaration_rev_20aug.pdf

International Association of Universities. (1993). *Kyoto Declaration on Sustainable Development.* https://iau-aiu.net/IMG/pdf/sustainable_development_policy_statement.pdf

Jones, D. P., & Johnstone, S. M. (2016). Responding to the Challenge of Sustainability. *Change: The Magazine of Higher Learning*, *48*(4), 27–33. doi:10.1080/00091383.2016.1198171

Kralikova, R., & Sobotova, L. (2019). Environmental Management System- A Way to Sustainable Development in Universities. *Acta Technica Corviniensis-Bulletin of Engineering*, *12*(1), 69–72. http://acta.fih.upt.ro/pdf/2019-1/ACTA-2019-1-13.pdf

Leal Filho, W., Will, M., Salvia, A. L., Adomssent, M., Grahl, A., & Spira, F. (2019). The role of green and Sustainability Offices in fostering sustainability efforts at higher education institutions. *Journal of Cleaner Production*, *232*, 1394–1401. doi:10.1016/j.jclepro.2019.05.273

M'Gonigle, M., & Starke, J. C. (2006). Minding place: Towards a (rational) political ecology of the sustainable university. *Environment and Planning. D, Society & Space*, *24*(3), 325–348. doi:10.1068/d3104

Ministerio de Educación. (2011). *La responsabilidad social de la universidad y el desarrollo sostenible.* https://sede.educacion.gob.es/publiventa/detalle.action?cod=14925

Missiacos Cárdenas, S. (2016). ¿Por qué necesitamos construir una universidad sustentable? *UC Maule*, (51), 9.

Ramísio, P., Pinto, L. M. C., Gouveia, N., Costa, H., & Arezes, D. (2019). Sustainability Strategy in Higher Education Institutions: Lessons learned from a nine-year case study. *Journal of Cleaner Production*, *222*, 300–309. doi:10.1016/j.jclepro.2019.02.257

Ruiz-Corbella, M., & Bautista-Cerro, M. J. (2016). La responsabilidad social en la universidad española. *Teoría De La Educación. Revista Interuniversitaria*, *28*(1, 1 (en-jun)), 159–188. doi:10.14201/teoredu2016281159188

SDSN. (2020). *Accelerating Education for the SDGS in Universities. A Guide for Universities, Colleges, and Tertiary and Higher Education Institutions*. New York: Sustainable Development Solutions Network (SDSN). https://irp-cdn.multiscreensite.com/be6d1d56/files/uploaded/accelerating-education-for-the-sdgs-in-unis-web.pdf

Sistema Universitario de Galicia. (2016). *Plan galego de financiamento universitario 2016-2020.* https://www.udc.es/export/sites/udc/goberno/_galeria_down/vepes/documentos/planfinanciamento20162020.pdf_2063069294.pdf

Sustainability Campus Webpage. (n.d.). https://www.udc.es/es/campus_sustentabilidade/

Turan, F., Cetinkaya, S., & Ustun, C. (2016). A methodological framework to analyze stakeholder preferences and propose strategic pathways for a sustainable university. *Higher Education*, *72*(6), 743–760. doi:10.100710734-015-9973-8

ULSF. (1990). *Talloires Declaration.* http://ulsf.org/talloires-declaration/

ULSF. (2001). *Global Higher Education for Sustainability Partnership (GHESP) is Launched in December 2000.* https://ulsf.org/global-higher-education-for-sustainability-partnership-ghesp-is-launched-in-december-2000/

UNESCO. (2005). *United Nations Decade of Education for Sustainable Development (2005-2014): International Implementation Scheme.* https://unesdoc.unesco.org/ark:/48223/pf0000148654

Universidade da Coruña. (2013). *Plan Estratéxico UDC 2020.* https://www.udc.es/export/sites/udc/goberno/_galeria_down/vepes/documentos/PLAN1320.pdf_2063069294.pdf

Universidade da Coruña. (n.d.a). *Informes Green Campus Centros UDC 2019.* https://www.udc.es/es/sociedade/medio_ambiente/GreenCampus/

Universidade da Coruña. (n.d.b). *Organigrama.* https://www.udc.es/es/transparencia/egoberno/organigrama/

Universidade de Santiago de Compostela. (n.d.a). *Desarrollo sostenible.* https://www.usc.gal/es/usc/institucional/desarrollo-sostenible

Universidade de Santiago de Compostela. (n.d.b). *Mecenazgo.* https://www.usc.gal/es/usc/mecenazgo

Universidade de Vigo. (n.d.a). *Cátedras.* https://www.uvigo.gal/es/universidad/contratar-colaborar-universidad/proyectos-abiertos-colaboracion/catedras

Universidade de Vigo. (n.d.b). *Green Campus.* https://www.uvigo.gal/campus/pontevedra-campus-crea/green-campus

Universidade de Vigo. (n.d.c). *Responsabilidad social y Agenda 2030.* https://www.uvigo.gal/es/universidad/conocenos/responsabilidad-social-agenda-2030

Universidade de Vigo. (n.d.d). *Sostibilidade-OMA.* http://oma.webs.uvigo.es/Sostibilidade/Inicio.php

World Voices Nexus. (n.d.). *Own-Income Generation: A Pillar of Financial Sustainability in Institutions of Higher Learning.* https://www.worldcces.org/58/post/2019/11/own-income-generation-a-pillar-of-financial-sustainability-in-institutions-of-higher-learning.html

ADDITIONAL READING

Barlett, P. F., & Chase, G. W. (2013). *Sustainability in higher education: stories and strategies for transformation*. MIT Press. doi:10.7551/mitpress/9418.001.0001

Gomes Teixeira, G. F., & Canciglieri, O. Junior. (2019). How to make strategic planning for corporate sustainability? *Journal of Cleaner Production, 230*, 1421–1431. doi:10.1016/j.jclepro.2019.05.063

Henchen, A. V., Moura-Leite, R., & Lopes, J. C. J. (2019). Sustainability and Management of Higher Education Institutions: Scientific Production Analysis. *Revista De Gestão Ambiental e Sustentabilidade, 8*(1), 38–61. doi:10.5585/geas.v8i1.13763

Leal Filho, W., & Pace, P. (2013). *Teaching Education for Sustainable Development at University Level.* Springer International Publishing.

Ramísio, P., Pinto, L. M. C., Gouveia, N., Costa, H., & Arezes, D. (2019). Sustainability Strategy in Higher Education Institutions: Lessons learned from a nine-year case study. *Journal of Cleaner Production, 222*, 300–309. doi:10.1016/j.jclepro.2019.02.257

SDSN. (2020). *Accelerating Education for the SDGS in Universities. A Guide for Universities, Colleges, and Tertiary and Higher Education Institutions*. New York: Sustainable Development Solutions Network (SDSN). https://irp-cdn.multiscreensite.com/be6d1d56/files/uploaded/accelerating-education-for-the-sdgs-in-unis-web.pdf

KEY TERMS AND DEFINITIONS

Governance: The art or way of governing to achieve lasting economic, social, and institutional development, promoting a healthy balance between the State, civil society and economic market.

Higher Education (HE): Tertiary education leading to award of an academic degree as an optional final stage of formal learning that occurs after completion of secondary education.

Resource Efficiency: The limited resources management in a sustainable manner while minimising environmental impacts.

Strategic Plan: Document that establishes the direction and objectives of an organization and the actions needed to achieve those objectives.

Sustainability: The ability to continue its existence for a long time with activities that do not damage the environment and are in harmony with social and economic concerns.

Sustainable Development: The development achieved considering the needs of all type of stakeholders and that goods and services should be produced in ways that do not use resources that cannot be replaced and that do not damage the environment.

Third Mission (of Universities): HEIs must be able to meet the social demands and to link their activity to the one developed in the socioeconomic context that surrounds them.

ENDNOTES

1 CRUE: association that brings together the majority of Spanish universities (50 public and 26 private), which has been working for decades for the development of this institution and the consolidation of the University's interaction with the productive and social fabric of Spain.

2 Green Metrics website: http://greenmetric.ui.ac.id/.

Chapter 6
Evolution and Future of the Marketing and Sustainability Linkage:
Towards a Civil Marketing Approach

Sandra Lizzeth Hernández-Zelaya
Pontifical University of Salamanca, Spain

Fernando Reyes-Reina
Pontifical University of Salamanca, Spain

María Elena Rodríguez Benito
https://orcid.org/0000-0002-6345-7206
Pontifical University of Salamanca, Spain

ABSTRACT

The pairing of sustainability and marketing has been around for several decades and has opened new standards in management and marketing. The main objective of this chapter is trifold: First, to shed some light on the distinctions between sustainability marketing and analogous terms; second, to review some of the criticisms that have arisen (i.e., greenwashing or green marketing myopia); finally, the authors offer a broader term for the marketing and sustainability link. The chapter will review the evolution of these concepts and present future directions of the sustainability and marketing linkage. Taking as a starting point theories that propose a new relationship between society and companies (civil economy, corporate citizenship) and the new paradigm of marketing, the authors also put forth a wholesome concept: civic marketing. This concept balances the two objectives expected in a marketing approach: positive business results and customer satisfaction in a sustainable economy.

DOI: 10.4018/978-1-7998-7634-2.ch006

INTRODUCTION

As businesses and the market have changed through time to respond to more than mere economic incentives, the marketing field has also undergone through dramatic transformations. Milton Friedman's (1970) claim that "the business of business is business" reflects a vision focused on economic results, financial gains, and in regard to marketing, unsustainable consumption patterns (De Graaf, et al, 2005). This view was oblivious to the effect businesses (and therefore marketing) have on socioeconomic growth, environmental impact and welfare. To address these concerns, the notion of sustainability has gained interest in many disciplines, and among them, marketing.

Before examining this concept, it is important to focus on the integrating concepts of marketing sustainability. First, a commonly used definition of sustainability is provided by the OECD (2002) which defines it as "the consumption of goods and services that meet basic needs and quality of life without jeopardizing the needs of future generations". These definitions associate sustainable development to a series of actions that reflect positive moral and ethical values and are directed towards long term beneficial goals. The other integrating concept, marketing, can therefore be a driver in the business' engagement in sustainability (Tollin et al, 2017). The broad definition of marketing provided by the American Marketing Association (2017) describes marketing as "the activity, set of institutions, and processes for creating, communicating, delivering, and exchanging offerings that have value for customers, clients, partners, and society at large". This reviewed version does not go far enough in how value is created, which hinders the ability of researchers to adequately address the sustainability and marketing nexus (McDonagh & Prothero, 2014).

As an integrative concept, sustainable marketing can be considered a corporate philosophy (Lim, 2016) or an approach that researchers and practitioners recognize its importance but struggle to integrate to their strategies (Greenfield, 2004). A more widely accepted definition of sustainability marketing is provided by Matin & Schouten (2014) who state: "Sustainable marketing is the process of creating, communicating, and delivering value to customers in such a way that both natural and human capital are preserved or enhanced throughout". The ambiguity in the definition of the key concepts allows the question of what the linkage between sustainability and marketing entails to still linger despite the research efforts of the past 50 years (Kilbourne & Beckmann, 1998; Kumar et al., 2013; McDonagh & Prothero, 2014).

While a managerialist approach to marketing has dominated the field, sustainability marketing has become increasingly mainstream (Gordon et al., 2011). Sustainability marketing represents an evolution in the marketing field that combines economic perspectives of traditional marketing with newer concepts of relational marketing and social, ethical, environmental and intergenerational aspects included in a sustainable development agenda (Gali, 2013). It generally implies a change in the consideration of marketing as a tool for management under a more commercial perspective to a tool to recognize and propel social development (Varey, 2010), under a more societal perspective. But in the last decade, as society and the consumer intensify their demand for sustainability, this trend is also embraced by companies that are moved to satisfy the customer's demand under a commercial perspective, without the societal perspective.

Nonetheless, although social and environmental aspects in the development of marketing strategies are emphasized, economic aspects in the development of marketing strategies are also included in the approach of sustainability marketing (Bridges & Wilhelm, 2008). Sustainability marketing comprises many aspects and dimensions, and all of them should be improved, not limited through a strategic plan

(Lim, 2016). This leads to the question: exactly what does sustainability marketing entail? What is and what should the linkage between marketing and sustainability be?

The answer to this question is still elusive. Sustainability research has still to become a widely studied topic in top marketing journals (Chabowski et al., 2011). The main objective of this chapter is to shed some light to the distinctions between sustainability marketing and analogous terms as well as explore some future directions for the linkage of marketing and sustainability. We interpret the concept as a milestone reached in the evolutionary path of a relation between marketing and sustainable development. While there are several nuances presented in the conceptualization of sustainability marketing, we will explore them in this chapter. We see them as part of a process that continues to add depth to the link between marketing and sustainability. In a dynamic market, based on the examination of the evolution of sustainability in marketing, we propose what to expect of the milestones to come in this relationship.

BACKGROUND

Even though there is still no consensus on the definition of sustainability marketing, several studies (Kemper & Ballantine, 2019; Quoquab et al, 2020; Rakic & Rakic, 2015; Thomas, 2018) have tried to pinpoint some of the key aspects that are frequently included in its conceptualization. The different conceptualizations and theoretical approaches (Connelly et al., 2011)) might also be a reason for contradicting results, viewpoints and even opposing opinions as to what exactly does sustainability marketing encompass. To better understand the concept and then provide paths to future research we review the evolution of the concept. While there have been more than two decades of attempts to define the concept of sustainable marketing, research in the topic is still in its infancy (Quoquab et al., 2020). We therefore answer the calls to shed light on what it means to be sustainable in marketing (McDonagh & Prothero, 2014) through an examination on the evolution of the concept and its key features.

There are many concepts that are related to sustainability marketing that are erroneously used as analogous terms. Terms such as green marketing (Oyewole, 2001; Dangelico & Vocalelli, 2017), ecological marketing (Fisk, 1974; Henion & Kinnear, 1976), corporate social responsibility (Brønn & Vrioni, 2001) and social marketing (Kotler & Zaltman, 1971; Lambin, 1986; Andreasen, 1994) have been used previously as interchangeable terms to sustainability marketing. These concepts however have particular distinctions that make them heterogeneous.

A concept that might also seem to be identical and is also used interchangeably to sustainability marketing but is not equivalent, is sustainable marketing. As described by Belz & Peattie (2012), sustainability can be attributed to continuous and long-term relations with customers, whereas sustainable is more clearly referenced to embracing sustainable development, an goal that is very difficult to evaluate and dependent on the sustainability of the society within which it takes place. We agree with this nuance and prefer to use the term sustainability marketing, but we found the terms as interchangeable in many of the previous research.

It is true that sustainability marketing includes several dimensions, and within them environmental and social dimensions are prominent, so sustainability marketing draws on social or green marketing, however, the use of these concepts as equal or interchangeable concepts is not accurate. While there are clear influences of these marketing concepts in sustainability, the latter is a concept that one might say has evolved from these concepts (Peattie, 2001) and has a more holistic approach that includes a change in the intention, from commercial tool to social approach.

Most of the reviews on the conceptualization of sustainability marketing agree on three dimensions: social dimension, environmental dimension and economic dimension, but they fail to state a concept that links them together creating the differential focus, something that we will try to work in this chapter. Herein lies a reason that might explain why terms that focus on only one of these dimensions could be erroneously used as substitutes. The environmental dimension centers on ecological issues and the impact of eco-friendly concerns. There is considerable literature that focuses on this dimension (Gordon et al., 2011) and a multitude of concepts emanate from this approach. Regarding the social dimension, while acknowledging other important objectives in the marketing strategy, social welfare is the pivotal focus. As well as the previous dimension, it is difficult to delineate exactly what this entails. Finally, the economic dimension highlights the deficiencies in the current economic system and unsustainable economic development. This dimension underlines the importance of a balance between short- and long-term economic profit and balanced relations with stakeholders (Sun et al., 2014). A more thorough analysis is made of each dimension throughout this chapter.

Another classification of the dimensions of sustainability marketing proposes three different dimensions: Auxiliary Sustainability Marketing (ASM), Reformative Sustainability Marketing (RSM) and Transformative Sustainability Marketing (TSM) (Kemper & Ballantine, 2019). These dimensions refer to the reach of the strategic goals rather than the area in which the sustainability marketing strategy is focused on. The main difference in these dimensions can be found in who carries the burden of the responsibility to produce the sustainability results. First, ASM dimension credits the consumer sustainable attitude as the cornerstone for the success of the sustainability strategy. This strategy focuses on improving sustainable goals within existing structures. Then, RSM dimension shares this responsibility to both businesses and consumers. This dimension centers on consumption reduction. Passing from a "craving" to a "need" in the promotion of a sustainable lifestyle. Finally, TSM values institutional pressures as the main drivers of the sustainability strategy. This dimension highlights the role of external actors, third sector and a change in the marketing paradigm.

PRESENT STATE OF THE SUSTAINABILITY AND MARKETING LINK

Evolution and Related Terms

In order to be able to understand the linkage between marketing and sustainability and to be able to propose new approaches, we will first try to understand the evolution of the marketing concept in relation with the societal concerns, that start as early as in the 1960s. We will attend the two main dimensions included in sustainability: social and ecological.

We will start by social marketing: the creators of this concept (Kotler & Zaltman, 1971, p. 5) define the term as: "the design, implementation and control of programs calculated to influence the acceptability of social ideas and involving considerations of product, planning, price, communication, distribution and market research". The aim of social marketing is to build a brand or improve the relationship with customers by differentiating its product with the creation of socially responsible attributes. A way to achieve this is through the association with a social cause and, therefore, to an ethical dimension. For Garriga & Melé (2004) this type of marketing with a cause can be interpreted as corporate social responsibility. The concept of social marketing promotes very broad ideas, which can be summarized in four main blocks: 1. to improve health, 2. to prevent harm, 3. to protect the environment and 4. to encourage participation of the community (Lee et al., 2002).

This type of marketing can be seen as a strategy for rethinking the market economy and promoting social change (Lambin, 2016). There are four different levels in which this change can be produced. They are described as cognitive, action, behavior or change of values (Lambin, 1986). The last level seeks to modify the values deeply anchored in a certain culture with respect to any type of conception. By understanding the immense content of change that it entails, social marketing is an invaluable tool that those involved (business, consumer and government) can use to achieve the advances that today's society demands with great effort and almost desperation (Páramo Morales, 2016).

The evolution of social marketing, ethics and corporate social responsibility, to which the term sustainability marketing is closely linked, involves the individual as the main actor within the company (Páramo Morales, 2016). Environmental concern causes changes in the environment, not only due to consumer demands, but also due to national and international regulations, environmental taxes, and other penalties. This would suggest that there are 3 main agents in environmentally focused marketing: businesses, citizens and governments. This is also the case in social marketing, the three main agents are responsible to fully address the marketing goals and changes. Some researchers pose that application of sustainability marketing (in whichever dimension it is focused) is mostly to prevent issues with other stakeholders and penalties (Leonidou et al., 2013).

With a direction towards the care and protection of the environment arise other concepts whose difference is often not clearly identifiable. These are ecological marketing, green marketing and sustainable marketing. Monteiro et al. (2015) state that ecological awareness began in the mid-1960s and early 1970s due to growing concern about the negative impact of consumption patterns and the impact of economic growth and the population on the environment. However, a serious concern with green marketing occurred in the late 1980s, with a rapid rise in consumer awareness of the need to purchase green products. Environmental awareness could be summarized in four stages: 1. an Embryonic Stage (*-1974), 2. Ecological marketing (1975-1989), 3. Green marketing (1990-2000), and 4. Sustainable Marketing Stage (2001-*), the current stage in which ecologically concerned marketing acquires a more holistic and comprehensive vision. We will analyze the four stages and their commonalities, paying special attention to the last stage.

1. **Embryonic Stage:** Green marketing is characterized by classifying companies between those that do good to the environment and those that harm it. The biggest concern that is needed to address for businesses is the increase in legislation, so that for the vast majority of companies' environmental concern was a problem for engineers and lawyers (Peattie, 2001). In this first stage, concepts such as sustainable development, the green consumer, eco-performance, ecological quality or waste-free technologies emerge (Katrandjiev, 2016).
2. **Ecological Marketing Stage:** Días (2008) notes: "ecological marketing is located in the field of social marketing and corporate social marketing and integrates social objectives with those of business commercial marketing with regard to protecting the environment. In this way, ecological marketing can be approached from two perspectives: social marketing or social cause and corporate or commercial social marketing". In this stage, green marketing is developed in parallel with Corporate Social Responsibility. Broader issues are beginning to be considered, leaving the reality of specific problems, such as product manufacture, and a more systemic conception of the company

is promoted. Green marketing is very concerned with the nature of inputs, their reduction, and their impact on the environment and society (Walker & Hanson, 1998).

3. **Green Marketing Stage:** In this stage, the marketing strategy has aspirations to design products that are respectful to the environment, competitive in price and of equal or higher quality than existing ones. This proves to be challenging to businesses due to the consumer's obstacles such as the difficulty in demonstrating the eco-efficiency of a product compared to other characteristics. On the other hand, it faces corporate barriers, due to the impediments that businesses might find when adopting the green philosophy (Katrandjiev, 2016). Many companies begin to adopt and make decisions with an environmental focus because they have realized that a segment of the customer base has an interest in green products (Escobar Moreno, 2012).
4. **Sustainable Marketing Stage:** In this last stage, the concept of sustainable marketing is popularized. This concept applied to marketing requires a philosophical change, to focus on needs and not wants. Furthermore, these needs consider not only those of current consumers but also those of future generations (Peattie, 2001). Belz & Peattie (2010) argue that sustainable marketing arises from the intersection between socio-ecological problems and consumer behavior. Along these lines, Martin Benz et al. (2013), mention that sustainable marketing represents an evolution of traditional marketing with new concepts of relationship marketing and social, ethical, environmental perspectives and the objectives of the sustainable development agenda. Based on the above, sustainable marketing could be perceived as a re-adapted and improved marketing that aims to last over time, ensuring the sustainable development of the current and future planet.

This marketing philosophy is intended to make businesses more aware of their impact on society and the environment and to raise awareness among consumers towards a more responsible consumption. It is aimed at the protection of society and the planet. As Bustillo-Castillejo (2011, p. 170) puts it:

The era of sustainability has not left anyone out of its axis, all people, companies, foundations and institutions are aware of current practices and activities, the planet and society will hold us accountable in the future; that our development and future prosperity will depend on how we take care of and conserve our physical, human and environmental resources.

Sustainable marketing has given a starting point to new ways of managing companies, of operating in markets and offering new products. It has awakened new interests and desires in consumers to demand more responsible products, which allows consumers to take care of the environment, and produce little-to-no environmental footprint and leaves a better planet for future generations. Likewise, many consumers are willing to pay a higher price to purchase this type of product, however, as mentioned by Rodríguez Rad et al. (2018), this continues to be a challenge for companies, since they must justify their price to the eco / green hue that consumers are willing to pay for it.

Issues Regarding the Sustainability and Marketing Link

Several issues arise in the linkage of marketing and sustainability that hamper the consensus of a conceptualization of sustainability marketing. One of the most contentious issues is presented in marketing's dominant model of unsustainable consumption. Several authors question the potential to influence sustainability through marketing precisely because of the economic dimension (that highlights importance of sale and consumption) of sustainability marketing (Kemper & Ballantine, 2019) Most studies on sustainability marketing are oriented towards consumer (Quoquab et al., 2020) highlighting the importance of consumption understanding in academia.

The issue with consumption in sustainability marketing is related to its solidarity value: it does not center on education of citizens or individuals in development goals. Rather, it generates a very comfortable type of solidarity for the consumer who feels that he collaborates by increasing consumption of more socially friendly goods or service. You can access funding to promote a sustainability marketing strategy if you are able to promote consumption, but it so happens that consumerism is precisely one of the main causes of serious planetary problems (Ortiz Nicolás, 2007). In contrast to some practices that companies adopt to integrate a sustainable operation at the business level, other relevant concepts arise that can confuse the correct orientation that sustainability marketing pursues. This is a cynical position that leads us to promote "green" products and services that, by themselves, cannot solve the global environmental problem and that require a reduction in consumption (Wymer & Polonsky, 2015). Nonetheless, research that questions the escalating levels of consumption is gaining traction (Papadas et al., 2017).

Two very relevant terms are identified, such as greenwashing and the green myopia of marketing. Greenwashing was coined by Jay Westervelt (1986) and referred to the hotel industry practice of placing signs to promote reuse of towels as environmental efforts (Rahman et al., 2015). Greenwashing refers to the act of misleading consumers regarding the environmental practices of a company or the environmental benefits of a company product or service. This might negatively affect green consumer behavior as it introduces skepticism of the firm's environmental claims. A company might have a poor environmental performance and communicates this performance in a positive way (Delmas & Burbano 2011). This is closely linked to the issue of corporate social responsibility where companies do not comply with what they communicate to their consumers on issues related to environmental impact.

Green marketing myopia refers to the failure of achieving the goals that marketing that is focused on the environmental dimension should have: improving environmental quality and customer satisfaction (Ottman et al., 2006). If the focus is placed on increasing the *green hue* of their products, leaving aside the expectations of consumers, regulators and activists that may lead to failure. Green marketing must improve the environmental qualities of your products, but also achieve the satisfaction of your customers (Tiwari et al., 2011). A derivative of this term is sustainability marketing myopia, proposed by Villarino & Font (2015), which considers it to be the result of being product focused instead of consumer focused and emphasizing on sustainability legitimacy and credentials over consumer needs.

Sustainability marketing is recognized as being context specific (Minton et al., 2012; Thogersen, 2010; McDonagh & Prothero, 2014; Papadas et al., 2017). Nonetheless, most studies examine sustainability marketing from a single dimension in isolation (Quoquab, 2020) excluding the cultural bases for sustainability. Analysis that examines the variations of marketing sustainability in different cultural, political, social and economic contexts are still scarce, although calls for them have been made previously (Steg & Viek, 2009). Also affecting specific context is industrial settings (Menon & Menon, 1997). This is also a factor that should be considered when reviewing a sustainability marketing strategy.

Finally, another controversial issue in the marketing–sustainability link is the drivers of sustainability marketing. At a consumer level, Groening et al., (2018) identify several potential drivers: values and knowledge, beliefs, attitudes, intentions, motivations, social dimensions or combinations of these drivers. At a business level, reputation, competitive and financial advantage are touted as possible drivers of sustainability marketing (Miles & Covin, 2000; Moravcikova et al., 2017). There are also many ethical and moral drivers that lead to a sustainability marketing approach. This results in an extensive casuistry, more possible correlations and increased heterogeneity that hinders a precise definition of the nexus between marketing and sustainability.

SOLUTIONS AND RECOMMENDATIONS

Until now, the relationship between marketing and sustainability has been mostly passive and reactive, responding to what was identified as a trend or market niche of consumers' sensitive to environmental concerns or following governmental regulations. The discourse of the 'green commodity' (Prothero et al., 2010) by which the consumer changes products without rethinking their habits and consumption levels, not achieving the global sustainability objectives (Varey, 2011; Peattie & Crane, 2005; Kemper & Ballantine, 2019) is part of the dominant social paradigm. Marketing might not offer a clear solution to reigning unsustainability but can help achieve sustainable development through sustainability marketing (Van Dam & Apeldoorn, 1996). That's why, Peattie (2015), proposes to use the term sustainability market instead of the also popular sustainable marketing.

There are numerous audits and certifications related to sustainability that in some cases do not address sustainability through a comprehensive method and with an integral view. The focus of businesses is frequently to achieve the certification as a commercial claim rather than to establish an integral culture of sustainability in the company (Heim, 2018). Although there are also, as we have seen, more holistic approaches, which focus on a triple balance, these are usually based on economic and technological aspects, excluding the sociocultural dimension (McManus, 1996; Sheth & Sisodia, 2005).

Marketing is in a delicate position to lead the environmental revolution of companies, as it is too often considered one of the main factors of the negative impact that goods and services have on the environment (Katrandjiev, 2016). Furthermore, companies that declare themselves sustainable have a difficult challenge, which is to grow in a sustainable way without reducing consumption, something that some authors consider impossible (Kotler, 2011). However, there seems to be evidence that good environmental marketing can benefit to create a reputational advantage that leads to enhanced financial performance (Miles & Covin, 2000; Cantele & Zardini, 2018; De Mendonca & Zhou, 2019).

Although the achievement of sustainability entails an ethical problem to the company, it is relevant from a marketing viewpoint since it can be decisive in the relationship with stakeholders (Baldassare & Campo, 2016), especially future consumers. Marketing can (and from our point of view, should) play a leading role in transforming companies towards sustainable models. To achieve optimal results, the sustainability marketing efforts should also count on a balanced system of regulations and laws (Van Dam & Apeldoorn, 1996). For this reason, despite these paradoxes and difficulties, sustainability is taking hold as a new paradigm, a new philosophy in business and marketing (Kumar et al., 2012; Charter et al., 2002).

This new philosophy was proposed by Achrol & Kotler, (2012) and labeled it as an emerging paradigm. Companies must actively communicate the negative effects of excessive consumption, grow environmentally sustainable consumer segments by developing superior products at competitive prices and do demarketing so that demand is decreased for marginalized products, technologies and consumer segments. The changes analyzed do not exclusively involve marketing, but require a reorientation of business management, social dominant paradigm and even the economic model. To do this, firms must avoid partial and short-term approaches to marketing and establish more holistic strategies.

Table 1 presents the comparison stated by Achrol & Kotler (2012) of the received or dominant paradigm with what the authors labelled as emergent paradigms.

Table 1. Key assumptions of the marketing paradigms

Received/Dominant Paradigm	Emergent Paradigm (2012)
Consumer satisfaction.	Consumer sensations and sense-making.
Cognitive psychology of behavior.	Neurophysiology of consumer behavior and sensory experiences.
Products as "delivered services".	Product and services as sensory experiences.
Massive-scale manufacturing by contract manufacturers (phase one networks) early phase two innovation networks.	Small-scale distributed production-consumption networks. Products built atom-by-atom. Customer co-creation and co-production (phase three networks).
Dominant technologies: digitization and computer-controlled systems.	Dominant technologies: Biotechnology, nanotechnology.
Management as internal coordination of finance, marketing, production, R&D and personnel in the firm.	Management as customer care and network development-interorganizational coordination of finance, innovation and production.
Core competency: idiosyncratic resources, usually technology.	Core competency: focal firm-marketing; Network-relational solidarity, synergy and mutuality.
Management priorities: growth, customer life-time value, targeting middle- and upper-class high value markets.	Management priorities: Sustainable marketing (including demarketing, counter-marketing), growth from lower middle and base-of-the pyramid markets.
Dyad as a unit of analysis: theories of hierarchical control, power, and dependence: early relationship marketing, social norms of behavior.	Multi-level networks as units of analysis: bottom-up networks; "commons", social engagement (proactive).
Corporate social responsibility (reactive, adaptive).	Proactive corporate strategies in ecology and development.
Public policy: laissez-faire capitalism.	Public policy: regulated capitalism (embedded regulation, self-regulation): conscientious capitalism, conscious capitalism, social capitalism.

Source: Achrol and Kotler, (2012, p. 36)

This shift in marketing paradigm to more ethical and sustainable practices seems to have already taken place. In order to consolidate and complement this paradigm we propose a new perspective of approach to sustainability marketing. The proposed paradigm starts from the analysis of both the economy and companies as responsible institutions with social responsibility and that are immersed within the tradition of the civil economy (Bruni & Zamagni, 2007). This paradigm includes the change of the company's "firm" rol to a citizen (Aguadero Fernández, 2010; Wood & Logsdon, 2017) or even activist role (Kotler & Sarkar, 2018; Eilert & Nappier Cherup, 2020).

The civil economy, although invented by Antonio Genovesi in the 18th century, has been updated in the 21st century by Bruni & Zamagni (2007). These authors consider that current socioeconomic problems derive from the neglect by the economic system of the relational dimension of the human being. The individualism imposed by the current system does not allow individuals to overcome the barrier of the suboptimal balance (Zamagni, 2006) in the use of limited resources. Furthermore, it makes it difficult to carry out an economic activity that is profitable and sustainable at the same time (Zamagni, 1999).

In the proposed civil economy model, three basic principles coexist, efficiency, equity and reciprocity that allow the production of private goods, justice goods and relational goods (Bruni & Zamagni, 2007).

Within this civil economy, the business becomes a social institution, a citizen company. The change is "towards a new role that can be beneficial for itself, for interest groups and for society in general" (Aguadero Fernández, 2010). Faced with the concept of corporate citizenship, which represents a continuity perspective and is limited to the company's relations with its community, corporate citizenship proposes a global understanding of the company as a responsible subject, as a social institution. Corporate citizenship implies a long-term strategic vision that takes into account the existing interdependencies and that proposes a new way of valuing the company that includes compliance with ethical, social and environmental responsibilities (Lozano, 2009).

Sarkar & Kotler (2018) go a step further in this conception of the citizen company and urge companies to be activist brands, to activate their purpose: "Brand Activism consists of business efforts to promote, impede, or direct social, political, economic, and/or environmental reform or stasis with the desire to promote or impede improvements in society" (Sarkar & Kotler 2018, p. 574).

In order to nurture their citizenships, companies develop their social activism, which is the company's "willingness to take a stand on social, political, economic and environmental issues to create societal change by influencing the attitudes and behaviors of actors in its institutional environment". (Eilert & Nappier Cherup 2020, p. 463).

This activism differs from CSR because it is driven by a fundamental concern for the biggest and most pressing issues facing society, allowing us to directly connect with sustainability. These two concepts of a company -activist and citizen- involve a more in-depth compromise of businesses to sustainability. As natural evolution seems to be headed in this direction (a more profound compromise of consumers and businesses to sustainability), one might expect that these concepts be at the forefront of the marketing – sustainability linkage.

These perspectives imply that sustainability and corporate social responsibility are not approached from a strategic point of view from which it is expected to achieve certain objectives, but as an inalienable moral duty. It implies an evolution from the first moment in which sustainability was an option, passing through a second stage in which it is considered important in the marketing strategy to achieve a competitive advantage to a third stage, in which sustainability is considered as inherent to the existence of the company. This perspective allows the three dimensions of the triple balance -social, ecological and economic- to be situated and maintained at the same level, as well as considering other aspects such as governance or ethics.

And how does this new concept translate into marketing? Once this conceptual framework, that derives from an ethical conception of the economy has been established, we approach a new perspective for sustainability marketing that is based on seeking an ethical basis for this sustainability that allows guiding its decisions. We propose civil or civic marketing in which sustainability is a moral requirement. Civil marketing has to balance two objectives: positive results for the company and satisfaction of the sensations and the civic sense of the customer. This implies a change throughout the industry, reducing the intensity of competitive rivalry to cooperation and seeking joint solutions (Peattie & Charter, 2003). It consists of considering the physical environment as the base on which societies and economic models are built and, consequently, placing growth within its limits, as is graphically explained in his proposal for the donut economy (Raworth, 2017).

Mimicking the Achrol and Kotler, (2012), we show our proposal for an updated paradigm based on the civil marketing in the Table 2.

Table 2. Proposal for Civil Marketing paradigm

Received Paradigm	Emergent Paradigm (2012)	Proposal for Civil Marketing Paradigm (2020)
Consumer satisfaction.	Consumer sensations and sense-making.	Citizen empowerment and sense-making. Company activism.
Cognitive psychology of behavior.	Neurophysiology of consumer behavior and sensory experiences.	Sociology and ethics applied to neurophysiology.
Products as "delivered services".	Product and services as sensory experiences.	Product and service as social integral experiences. Activism as an expanded product.
Massive-scale manufacturing by contract manufacturers (phase one networks) early phase two innovation networks.	Small-scale distributed production-consumption networks. Products built atom-by-atom. Customer co-creation and co-production (phase three networks).	Small-scale distributed production-consumption networks and direct to consumer paradigm. Social co-creation and co-production (makers).
Dominant technologies: digitization and computer controlled systems.	Dominant technologies: biotechnology, nanotechnology.	Dominant technologies: ethical approach to technology, block chain, biotechnology and artificial intelligence.
Management as internal coordination of finance, marketing, production, R&D and personnel in the firm.	Management as customer care and network development- interorganizational coordination of finance, innovation and production.	Management as stakeholders' care and network development. Coordination of the Triple-Bottom Line (TBL).
Core competency: idiosyncratic resources, usually technology.	Core competency: focal firm-marketing; Network-relational solidarity, synergy and mutuality.	Core competency: reputation management, find how the firm serves the common good, solidarity, synergy and mutuality.
Management priorities: growth, customer life-time value, targeting middle and upper class high value markets.	Management priorities:, sustainable marketing (including demarketing, counter-marketing), growth from lower middle and base-of-the pyramid markets.	Management priorities: sustainable marketing (including demarketing, counter-marketing), purpose and active reputation management, finding the growth scale.
Dyad as a unit of analysis: theories of hierarchical control, power, and dependence: early relationship marketing, social norms of behavior.	Multi-level networks as units of analysis: bottom-up networks; "commons", social engagement (proactive).	Multi-level networks as units of analysis: bottom-up networks; "commons", social engagement (proactive) and projections about future generations.
Corporate social responsibility (reactive, adaptive).	Proactive corporate strategies in ecology and development.	Proactive co created corporate strategies in ecology, social development, governance, and ethics (bottom line).
Public policy: laissez-faire capitalism.	Public policy: regulated capitalism (embedded regulation, self-regulation): conscientious capitalism, conscious capitalism, social capitalism.	Public policy: regulated capitalism (embedded regulation, self-regulation). Corporations and citizens filling the moral void of capitalism.

Source: Adaptation from Achrol and Kotler, (2012, p. 36)

FUTURE RESEARCH DIRECTIONS

The recovery of citizenship is at the base of the proposed marketing model, both that of the citizenship of people, ceasing to consider them merely consumers, seeking an implication that goes beyond their condition of economic institution and that makes it worthy of social credit. Social capital is necessary in order for people to work for the collective good and not only for the individual and this is essential to achieve work towards sustainability (Brandstedt & Emmelin, 2016), we will be all accountable in the future:

The era of sustainability has not left anyone out of its axis, all people, companies, foundations and institutions are aware of current practices and activities, the planet and society will hold us accountable in the future; that our development and future prosperity will depend on how we take care of and conserve our physical, human and environmental resources. (Barry, 2016, p. 10)

This thinking implies a new dimension in the relationship between marketing and sustainability: sustainability marketing must focus on the relationship with stakeholders from a civic point of view, encompassing society as a whole and future societies and establishing a triple line of action. Results in which sustainability is the vision and economic, social and ecological results are at the same level. Sustainability is "'an ideal toward which society and business can continually strive" (Wheeler et al., 2003) and in the case of marketing, "the way firms can strive is by creating value, creating outcomes that are consistent with the ideal of sustainability along social environmental and economic dimensions '' (Wheeler et al., 2003).

CONCLUSION

While the relevance of sustainability marketing appears to be increasing in recent years, the topic is still understudied (Purani, 2014). The definition is unclear, the dimensions it includes (and importance of each) and the interpretation of what the drivers are also dubious. This chapter attempts to contribute to answer calls to more clearly define sustainability marketing (McDonagh & Prothero, 2014) reviewing it as an evolving term in the relationship between sustainability and marketing (Kumar et al., 2012). We also sense that in this evolving nexus, the next logical step is that consumers ask businesses to further pursue the depth in which social, economic and environmental dimensions are addressed in the marketing strategy. Two particular concepts might help shape the future relation between marketing and sustainability which are: civic economy (Bruni & Zamagni, 2007) and brand activism (Sarkar & Kotler, 2018). The inclusion of these concepts into the marketing philosophy will result in the promotion of civic marketing in which the company is more active in the promotion of sustainable development.

Theoretical and practical implications can be made of this chapter's theoretical review. While environmental concerns in sustainability marketing literature is prevalent in studies (Kemper & Ballantine, 2019), it is narrowly focused and does not address the entire scope of sustainability. One important aspect of sustainability marketing research is the contextual factors and institutional influences it might thrive under. While proven to be contextually influenced, sustainability marketing and how it stresses on one or another dimension should respond to the claims of societal requirements.

Sustainability marketing is gaining popularity but is still not the dominant social paradigm (Carrington et al., 2016). Progress can be made by the incorporation of sustainable practices, but the sustainability marketing strategy should focus not only on firms but also consumers (Carrigan & Bosangit, 2016) through the promotion of responsible consumption, stakeholders, and institutions. Due to the various actors, contexts and industries, practitioners should recognize that the sustainability marketing efforts of a business are not standardized strategies. Also, despite being controversial, a civic marketing philosophy should not imply adding costs (Lim, 2016) but opportunities to engage in economic gains and participate in a long-term sustainable development.

Through activism marketing businesses will not only apply a strategy that focuses on social, economic and economic development but will be conceived with this goal. This would then maximize the development goals as the business will use this to partner with other stakeholders which translates to a capitalization of the global or local development goals. As the evolution of the nexus between sustainability and marketing has grown to include all related stakeholders, this next step to a civic marketing paradigm could be the most holistic system approach that some researchers (i.e., Thomas, 2018) have yearned for.

ACKNOWLEDGMENT

This research received no specific grant from any funding agency in the public, commercial, or not-for-profit sectors.

REFERENCES

Aguadero Fernández, F. (2010). La responsabilidad social corporativa como punto de encuentro. *REDMARKA*, *21*(1), 53–70.

AMA. (2013). *Definitions of Marketing*. https://www.ama.org/AboutAMA/Pages/Definition-of-Marketing.aspx

Andreasen, A. R. (1994). Social marketing: Its definition and domain. *Journal of Public Policy & Marketing*, *13*(1), 108–114. doi:10.1177/074391569401300109

Baldassarre, F., & Campo, R. (2016). Sustainability as a marketing tool: To be or to appear to be? *Business Horizons*, *59*(4), 421–429. doi:10.1016/j.bushor.2016.03.005

Barry, J. (2016). Citizenship and (Un)Sustainability: A Green Republican Perspective. In S. M. Gardiner & A. Thompson (Eds.), *The Oxford Handbook of Environmental Ethics*. Oxford University Press.

Belz, F. M., & Peattie, K. (2012). *Sustainability marketing* (2nd ed.). John Wiley & Sons, Ltd.

Brandstedt, E., & Emmelin, M. E. (2016) The concept of sustainable welfare. In Sustainability and the political economy of welfare. Routledge.

Bridges, C. M., & Wilhelm, W. B. (2008). Going beyond green: The "why and how" of integrating sustainability into the marketing curriculum. *Journal of Marketing Education*, *30*(1), 33–46. doi:10.1177/0273475307312196

Brønn, P. S., & Vrioni, A. B. (2001). Corporate social responsibility and cause-related marketing: An overview. *International Journal of Advertising*, *20*(2), 207–222. doi:10.1080/02650487.2001.11104887

Bruni, L., & Zamagni, S. (2007). *Eficiencia, equidad, felicidad pública*. Prometeo.

Bustillo-Castillejo, M. C. (2011). El marketing social es una respuesta del mundo mercantil al desarrollo sostenible 2011. *Saber. Ciencia y Libertad*, *6*(2), 169–176. doi:10.18041/2382-3240aber.2011v6n2.2504

Cantele, S., & Zardini, A. (2018). Is sustainability a competitive advantage for small businesses? An empirical analysis of possible mediators in the sustainability–financial performance relationship. *Journal of Cleaner Production*, *182*(1), 166–176. doi:10.1016/j.jclepro.2018.02.016

Carrigan, M., & Bosangit, C. (2016). The challenges of responsible marketing and consumption. In D. Shaw, M. Carrington, & A. Chatzidakis (Eds.), *Ethics and Morality in Consumption: Interdisciplinary Perspectives* (pp. 75–96). Routledge.

Carrington, M., Zwick, D., & Neville, B. (2016). The ideology of the ethical consumption gap. *Marketing Theory*, *16*(1), 21–38. doi:10.1177/1470593115595674

Chabowski, B. R., Mena, J. A., & Gonzalez-Padron, T. L. (2011). The structure of sustainability research in marketing, 1958–2008: A basis for future research opportunities. *Journal of the Academy of Marketing Science*, *39*(1), 55–70. doi:10.100711747-010-0212-7

Charter, M., Peattie, K., Ottman, J., & Polonsky, M. J. (2002). *Marketing and sustainability. Sustainable Marketing*. Knowledge Network.

Cohen, M. A. (2010). The narrow application of Rawls in business ethics: A political conception of both stakeholder theory and the morality of markets. *Journal of Business Ethics*, *97*(4), 563–579. doi:10.100710551-010-0525-y

Connelly, B. L., Ketchen, D. J. Jr, & Slater, S. F. (2011). Toward a "theoretical toolbox" for sustainability research in marketing. *Journal of the Academy of Marketing Science*, *39*(1), 86–100. doi:10.100711747-010-0199-0

Dangelico, R. M., & Vocalelli, D. (2017). "Green Marketing": An analysis of definitions, strategy steps, and tools through a systematic review of the literature. *Journal of Cleaner Production*, *165*(1), 1263–1279. doi:10.1016/j.jclepro.2017.07.184

De Graaf, J., Wann, D., & Naylor, T. H. (2005). *Affluenza: The All-Consuming Epidemic* (2nd ed.). Berrett-Koehler.

De Mendonca, T., & Zhou, Y. (2019). What does targeting ecological sustainability mean for company financial performance? *Business Strategy and the Environment*, *28*(8), 1583–1593. doi:10.1002/bse.2334

Delmas, M. A., & Burbano, V. C. (2011). The drivers of greenwashing. *California Management Review*, *54*(1), 64–87. doi:10.1525/cmr.2011.54.1.64

Días, R. (2008, June). Marketing ecológico y turismo. *Estudios y Perspectivas en Turismo*, *17*(2), 140–155.

Eilert, M., & Nappier Cherup, A. (2020). The Activist Company: Examining a Company's Pursuit of Societal Change Through Corporate Activism Using an Institutional Theoretical Lens. *Journal of Public Policy & Marketing*, *39*(4), 461–476. doi:10.1177/0743915620947408

Escobar Moreno, N. R. (2012). Las Comunicaciones Integradas de Marketing (CIM) como pilar de la estrategia de marketing verde y sus implicaciones en la gestión ambiental. *Revista Facultad De Ciencias Económicas*, *20*(2), 69–79. doi:10.18359/rfce.2165

Fisk, G. (1974). *Marketing and the ecological crisis*. Harper & Row.

Friedman, M. (1970). A Friedman doctrine: The social responsibility of business is to increase its profits. *The New York Times Magazine*, *13*(1970), 32-33.

Gali, J. M. (2013). *Marketing de sostenibilidad*. Profit Editorial.

Garriga, E., & Melé, D. (2004). Corporate social responsibility theories: Mapping the territory. *Journal of Business Ethics*, *53*(1-2), 51–71. doi:10.1023/B:BUSI.0000039399.90587.34

Gordon, R., Carrigan, M., & Hastings, G. (2011). A framework for sustainable marketing. *Marketing Theory*, *11*(2), 143–163. doi:10.1177/1470593111403218

Greenfield, W. M. (2004). In the name of corporate social responsibility. *Business Horizons*, *47*(1), 19–28. doi:10.1016/j.bushor.2003.11.004

Groening, C., Sarkis, J., & Zhu, Q. (2018). Green marketing consumer-level theory review: A compendium of applied theories and further research directions. *Journal of Cleaner Production*, *172*, 1848–1866. doi:10.1016/j.jclepro.2017.12.002

Heim, L. (2018). Killing Sustainability: Blunt Truths about Corporate Sustainability/Social Responsibility Failures and How to Avoid Them. Academic Press.

Henion, K. E., & Kinnear, T. C. (1976). *A guide to ecological marketing. Ecological Marketing*. American Marketing Association.

Katrandjiev, H. (2016). Ecological marketing, green marketing, sustainable marketing: Synonyms or an evolution of ideas. *Economic Alternatives*, *1*(7), 71–82.

Kemper, J. A., & Ballantine, P. W. (2019). What do we mean by sustainability marketing? *Journal of Marketing Management*, *35*(3-4), 277–309. doi:10.1080/0267257X.2019.1573845

Kilbourne, W. E., & Beckmann, S. C. (1998). Review and critical assessment of research on marketing and the environment. *Journal of Marketing Management*, *14*(6), 513–532. doi:10.1362/026725798784867716

Kotler, P., & Zaltman, G. (1971). Social marketing: An approach to planned social change. *Journal of Marketing*, *35*(3), 3–12. doi:10.1177/002224297103500302 PMID:12276120

Kumar, V., Rahman, Z., & Kazmi, A. A. (2013). Sustainability marketing strategy: An analysis of recent literature. *Global Business Review*, *14*(4), 601–625. doi:10.1177/0972150913501598

Kumar, V., Rahman, Z., Kazmi, A. A., & Goyal, P. (2012). Evolution of sustainability as marketing strategy: Beginning of new era. *Procedia: Social and Behavioral Sciences*, *37*, 482–489. doi:10.1016/j.sbspro.2012.03.313

Lambin, J. J. (1986). *Le marketing stratégique: fondements, méthodes et applications*. McGraw-Hill.

Lambin, J. J. (2016). *Market-driven management: marketing strategico e operativo*. McGraw-Hill Education.

Lee, N., Kotler, P., & Roberto, N. (2002). *Social marketing improving the quality of life*. Sage Publications.

Leonidou, C. N., Katsikeas, C. S., & Morgan, N. A. (2013). Greening the marketing mix: Do firms do it and does it pay off? *Journal of the Academy of Marketing Science*, *41*(2), 151–170. doi:10.100711747-012-0317-2

Lim, W. M. (2016). A blueprint for sustainability marketing: Defining its conceptual boundaries for progress. *Marketing Theory*, *16*(2), 232–249. doi:10.1177/1470593115609796

Lozano, J. M. (2009). *La empresa ciudadana como empresa responsable y sostenible*. Ed Trotta.

Martin Benz, F., Peattie, K., & Gali, J. M. (2013). *Marketing de sostenibilidad*. Profit Editorial.

McDonagh, P., & Prothero, A. (2014). Sustainability marketing research: Past, present and future. *Journal of Marketing Management*, *30*(11-12), 1186–1219. doi:10.1080/0267257X.2014.943263

McManus, P. (1996). Contested terrains: Politics, stories and discourses of sustainability. *Environmental Politics*, *1996*(5), 48–73. doi:10.1080/09644019608414247

Menon, A., & Menon, A. (1997). Enviropreneurial marketing strategy: The emergence of corporate environmentalism as market strategy. *Journal of Marketing*, *61*(1), 51–67. doi:10.1177/002224299706100105

Miles, M. P., & Covin, J. G. (2000). Environmental marketing: A source of reputational, competitive, and financial advantage. *Journal of Business Ethics*, *23*(3), 299–311. doi:10.1023/A:1006214509281

Minton, E., Lee, C., Orth, U., Kim, C. H., & Kahle, L. (2012). Sustainable marketing and social media: A cross-country analysis of motives for sustainable behaviors. *Journal of Advertising*, *41*(4), 69–84. doi:10.1080/00913367.2012.10672458

Monteiro, T. A., Giuliani, A. C., Antonio, C., Cavazos-Arrollo, J., & Kassouf Pizzinato, N. (2015). Mezcla el marketing verde: Una perspectiva Teórica. *Cuadernos del Cimbage*, *17*, 103–126.

Moravcikova, D., Krizanova, A., Kliestikova, J., & Rypakova, M. (2017). Green Marketing as the Source of the Competitive Advantage of the Business. *Sustainability*, *9*(12), 2218. doi:10.3390u9122218

OECD. (2002). *Towards Sustainable Household Consumption? Trends and Policies in OECD Countries*. OECD.

Ortiz Nicolas, P. (2007). *Las cuatro llaves: marketing de cambio social*. Ed Signo.

Ottman, J. A., Stafford, E. R., & Hartman, C. L. (2006). Avoiding green marketing myopia: Ways to improve consumer appeal for environmentally preferable products. *Environment*, *48*(5), 22–36. doi:10.3200/ENVT.48.5.22-36

Oyewole, P. (2001). Social costs of environmental justice associated with the practice of green marketing. *Journal of Business Ethics*, *29*(3), 239–251. doi:10.1023/A:1026592805470

Papadas, K. K., Avlonitis, G. J., & Carrigan, M. (2017). Green marketing orientation: Conceptualization, scale development and validation. *Journal of Business Research*, *80*, 236–246. doi:10.1016/j.jbusres.2017.05.024

Páramo Morales, D. (2016). Una Aproximación al marketing social. *Pensamiento & Gestión.*, *41*, 7–12.

Peattie, K. (2001). Towards sustainability: The third age of green marketing. *The Marketing Review*, *2*(2), 129–146. doi:10.1362/1469347012569869

Peattie, K. (2015). Sustainability marketing. In Handbook of research on sustainable consumption. Edward Elgar Publishing. doi:10.4337/9781783471270.00014

Peattie, K., & Belz, F. M. (2010). Sustainability marketing—An innovative conception of marketing. *Marketing Review St. Gallen*, *27*(5), 8–15. doi:10.100711621-010-0085-7

Peattie, K., & Charter, M. (2003). Green marketing. In The Marketing Book. Academic Press.

Peattie, K., & Crane, A. (2005). Green marketing: Legend, myth, farce or prophesy. *Qualitative Market Research*, *8*(4), 357–370. doi:10.1108/13522750510619733

Prothero, A., McDonagh, P., & Dobscha, S. (2010). Is green the new black? Reflections on a green commodity discourse. *Journal of Macromarketing*, *30*(2), 147–159. doi:10.1177/0276146710361922

Purani, K., Sahadev, S., & Kumar, D. S. (2014). Globalization and academic research: The case of sustainability marketing. *IIM Kozhikode Society & Management Review*, *3*(1), 93–99. doi:10.1177/2277975214520910

Quoquab, F., Mohamed Sadom, N. Z., & Mohammad, J. (2020). *Sustainable Marketing*. The Palgrave Handbook of Corporate Social Responsibility.

Rahman, I., Park, J., & Chi, C. G. Q. (2015). Consequences of "greenwashing": Consumers' reactions to hotels' green initiatives. *International Journal of Contemporary Hospitality Management*, *27*(6), 1054–1081. doi:10.1108/IJCHM-04-2014-0202

Rakic, B., & Rakic, M. (2015). Holistic management of marketing sustainability in the process of sustainable development. *Environmental Engineering and Management Journal*, *14*(4), 887–900. doi:10.30638/eemj.2015.100

Raworth, K. (2017). *Doughnut Economics. Seven Ways to Think Like a 21st-Century Economist*. Random House Business.

Rodríguez Rad, C. J., Sánchez del Rio Vásquez, M. E., Navarro García, A., Rondan Cataluña, F. J., & Pérez Méndez, M. B. (2018). Adaptación de la distribución minorista al consumidor ecológico: el caso de España y Alemania. In J. A. Trespalacios Gutiérrez, R. Vázquez Casielles, E. Estrada Alonso, & C. González Mieres (Eds.), *Nuevos horizontes del marketing y de la distribución comercial* (pp. 355–376). Cátedra Fundación Ramón Areces de Distribución Comercial.

Sarkar, C., & Kotler, P. (2018). *Brand Activism: From Purpose to Action*. Idea Bite Press.

Sheth, J., & Sisodia, R. (2005). A Dangerous Divergence: Marketing and Society. *Journal of Public Policy & Marketing*, *24*(1), 160–162. doi:10.1509/jppm.24.1.160.63896

Sun, Y., Kim, K. H., & Kim, J. (2014). Examining relationships among sustainable orientation, perceived sustainable marketing performance, and customer equity in the fast fashion industry. *Journal of Global Fashion Marketing*, *5*(1), 74–86. doi:10.1080/20932685.2013.866319

Thogersen, J. (2010). Country Differences in Sustainable Consumption: The Case of Organic Food. *Journal of Macromarketing*, *30*(2), 171–185. doi:10.1177/0276146710361926

Thomas, N. J. (2018). Sustainability marketing. The need for a realistic whole systems approach. *Journal of Marketing Management, 34*(17-18), 1530–1556. doi:10.1080/0267257X.2018.1547782

Tiwari, S., Tripathi, D. M., Srivastava, U., & Yadav, P. K. (2011). Green marketing-emerging dimensions. *Journal of Business Excellence, 2*(1), 18.

Tollin, K., Christensen, L. B., & Wilke, R. (2017). Sustainability in business from a marketing perspective. *Journal of Strategic Marketing, 23*(6), 471–496. doi:10.1080/0965254X.2014.991348

Van Dam, Y. K., & Apeldoorn, P. A. (1996). Sustainable marketing. *Journal of Macromarketing, 16*(2), 45–56. doi:10.1177/027614679601600204

Varey, R. J. (2010). Marketing means and ends for a sustainable society: A welfare agenda for transformative change. *Journal of Macromarketing, 30*(2), 112–126. doi:10.1177/0276146710361931

Varey, R. J. (2011). A sustainable society logic for marketing. *Social Business, 1*(1), 69–83. doi:10.1362/204440811X570563

ADDITIONAL READING

Benavides Delgado, J., & Fernández Mateo, J. (2020). *Los límites de la sostenibilidad*. EUNSA.

Cortina, A. (2010). *Por una ética del consumo*. Taurus.

Dyck, B., & Manchanda, R. V. (2021). *Sustainable marketing based on virtue ethics: addressing socio-ecological challenges facing humankind*. AMS Rev.

Gossen, M., Ziesemer, F., & Schrader, U. (2019). Why and how commercial marketing should promote sufficient consumption: A systematic literature review. *Journal of Macromarketing, 39*(3), 252–269. doi:10.1177/0276146719866238

Hall, M. R. (2019). The Sustainability Price: Expanding Environmental Life Cycle Costing to include the costs of poverty and climate change. *The International Journal of Life Cycle Assessment, 24*(2), 223–236. doi:10.100711367-018-1520-2

Hoffman, A. J. (2018). The next phase of business sustainability. *Stanford Social Innovation Review, 16*(2), 34–39.

Kolster, T. (2020). *The Hero Trap: How to Win in a Post-Purpose Market by Putting People in Charge*. Routledge. doi:10.4324/9780429281457

Makower, J. (2020). *2020 state of green business*. GreenBiz Group.

KEY TERMS AND DEFINITIONS

Brand Activism: Term created by Sarkar & Kotler in 2018, referring to an evolution of CSR that allows social change and promotion to be sponsored actively by brands and companies.

Civil Economy: Coined by Antonio Genovesi during the second half of the 18th century, it refers to the economic model capable of responding to the society of the moment seeking a more just and happy society.

Civil Marketing: Marketing model inspired by the civil economy that contributes to the construction of a more fair and overall happy society balancing two objectives: positive results for the company and satisfaction to the civic sense of customers.

Corporate Citizenship: It refers to a company's responsibilities toward society in a broad sense. It is how companies exercises its rights, obligations, privileges, and duties in order to benefit the local environments but also the society as a whole.

Demarketing: The marketing practices that aims to reduce the demand for certain products and services, discouraging customers in general or a segment of customers on a temporary or permanent basis. This concept, coined in the 70s, acquires a new dimension when working in sustainability.

Green Marketing Myopia: The marketing practice that, involves an effort to improve the environmental quality of its product or service, but does not attain customer satisfaction, creating and imbalance between the marketing goals of the company.

Greenwashing: The act of misleading consumers regarding the environmental practices of a company or the environmental benefits of a company product or service. This practice generates skepticism and discourages sustainable consumption.

Social Marketing: Approach to marketing that describes the change in orientation from commercial interest to social good.

Sustainability Marketing Myopia: Similar to green marketing myopia, is the result of being product focused instead of consumer focused and emphasizing on sustainability legitimacy and credentials over consumer needs and satisfaction, losing the balance between marketing goals.

Chapter 7
Breaking Barriers to Promote Sustainable Development in the Wine Industry:
A Theoretical Study on the Role of the Entrepreneurial Ecosystem Approach

Eloi Jorge
https://orcid.org/0000-0002-0523-2762
Universidade de Vigo, Spain

Carlos Herves-Beloso
Universidade de Vigo, Spain

Antonio Monteiro Oliveira
ISCAP, Polytechnic of Porto, Portugal

ABSTRACT

The focus on sustainability is one of the different strategies adopted by companies looking for arguments for their differentiation from other competitors. Implementing this concept in the wine industry implies environmental soundness, social equity, and economic feasibility since when pursuing sustainable development, these companies are protecting the identity of their terroirs. Nevertheless, this is not an easy task because companies have to face several potential barriers to the adoption of sustainable practices. Thus, the objective of this chapter is to introduce the entrepreneurial ecosystem approach (EEA) as an instrument to help to understand and identify the mechanisms to remove the barriers to the adoption of sustainable practices in the wine industry, preparing the ground for a more detailed investigation to assess the effective implementation of the EEA.

DOI: 10.4018/978-1-7998-7634-2.ch007

INTRODUCTION

Environmental degradation, climate change, biodiversity loss, demographic growth, and poverty faced nowadays lead companies to establish awareness of the need to implement and develop sustainable practices. Indeed, the challenges related to this issue affect different firms and industrial sectors. The attention paid to sustainable development does not focus only on less-established industries but also on well-established ones, such as the wine industry, where sustainable development has been awakening more and more attention throughout the years (Willer & Lernoud, 2018). This attention is related to the need to lessen the adverse environmental, social, and economic impact of the increased industrialization of this sector. However, these new responsibilities also translate into business opportunities. The concern to implement these practices can also be seen as a strategy that companies follow to meet the needs of the market more efficiently (Garanti & Berberoglu, 2018) or to differentiate themselves from the other competitors (Gilinsky et al., 2016; Atkin et al., 2011), repositioning their competitive advantages and ensuring their process of economic growth. Furthermore, when implementing sustainability in the wine industry, an evident positive effect occurs: protecting the distinctive capabilities of the *terroir*.

The modern definition of *terroir* refers to the space recognized as capable of conferring distinctive characteristics to products from their originating (Castellucci, 2010), thanks to the combination of natural and human factors (Seguin & Leeuwen, 2006). For its turn, in the wine industry context, sustainability can be referred taking into account the three-dimensional balance of sustainable development as follows: growing and winemaking practices that are sensitive to the environment (planet), respecting the needs and interests of society at large, and promoting equal opportunity (people), and being economically feasible to implement and maintain long-term economic viability (profit; Gilinsky et al., 2016; Sellers-Rubio & Nicolau-Gonzalbez, 2016; Forbes et al., 2009; Zucca et al., 2009). The very definition of the *terroir* encapsulates the three main pillars of sustainable development: natural conditions (environmental), human factors (social), and competitive advantage (profit). This directs our attention to the fact that *terroir* and sustainable development concepts walk side-by-side.

Nevertheless, the need to establish a trade-off between the adoption of sustainable practices in the wine industry and the impact on costs for wine (cost compliance) can lead sustainability-oriented companies to face more barriers than conventional ones[1] (Gast et al., 2017). It is expected for sustainability-oriented companies to find, among others, not only significant financial or market-related barriers (Gast et al., 2017; Trianni et al., 2017) but also regulatory barriers (Champoux & Brun, 2003), which they have to overcome.

From the importance of removing the many obstacles to the adoption of sustainable practices emerges the proposal to structure an approach to ensure sustainability-oriented companies their self-sustaining and self-generating. The development of this theoretical stream grounds on the ecosystem approach. In particular, following an implementation axis that starts in the reasoning of Isenberg's (2010, 2011) entrepreneurial ecosystem approach (EEA). In the literature, "the fundamental ideas behind entrepreneurial ecosystems emerged (…) towards a broader community perspective that incorporates the role of social, cultural, and economic" (Stam & van de Ven, 2019, p. 2) characteristics underlying sustainability. Thus, this study aims to propose a multidimensional sustainability model that allows the characterization of the different development stages, components, and models. Simultaneously, understanding the dynamics of its evolutionary process (Shwetzer et al., 2019), including its antecedents, interdependence, and related concepts (Colombelli et al., 2019; Woolley, 2017). Nevertheless, in hindering a stream of corporate sustainability research that focuses on the design of instrumental strategies aiming to achieve environmental, social, and economic objectives, or to align these objectives pursuing business goals (Voinea et al., 2019), the focus of this study is not capturing the content but the process.

The literature is rich in evidence of the relevant role of the sustainable development concept throughout the business community. Having this in mind, this study went further by focusing specifically on the effects of sustainable development in the wine industry, by offering insights on how more sustainable business models should be leveraged and unfold in *terroir*-based wine business companies, whose long-term survival depends on the resilience of shared common-resources. Besides, it extends this literature highlighting this approach, mainly in the field of geographical indications (protected geographical indications and protected designations of origin), contributing to the literature on the role of territorial identity. Thanks to geographical proximity between players operating there, common learning and knowledge flowing between different actors become frequent phenomena. In this context, the use of the EEA framework establishes it as an appropriate instrument. This is because it has the potential to expand the understanding about sustainability in experiences of specification of territorial assets of wine regions, elaboration of new institutional arrangements evolving throughout time, and the creation of a new network organization. The learning proposed by this study is completely original and integrates a theoretical view; although it addresses a current stream of literature, it has been overlooked by the entrepreneurial ecosystem literature so far in the wine industry.

For the aim of the present study, the methodology adopted is a structured literature review of publications in peer-reviewed academic journals. According to Fink (2013), this methodology can be defined as a systematic design for identifying, assessing, and interpreting the existing literature. Comprehensive bibliographic research was carried out by using keywords (Mayring, 2015). Scopus, an abstract and citation database of peer-reviewed literature—scientific journals, books, and conference proceedings—was used as a search engine. The following keywords were used: *coopetition*, *ecosystem*, *entrepreneurship*, *entrepreneurial ecosystem*, *sustainable development*, *sustainability*, terroir, *wine industry*, *geographical indications*, *protected designations of origin*, and *rural development*. This comprehensive method, through a reasonable evaluation of the literature, allowed us to reach an overview of the present study object, fitting the narrative review defined by Bryman (2008).

The remainder of this article is structured as follows. Section 2 is dedicated to an overview of the literature on the subject. Section 3 explores the main focus of the chapter, while Section 4 discusses solutions and recommendations. Section 5 provides insight into the future of the book's theme from the perspective of the chapter focus. Finally, Section 6 presents the conclusions stemming from the research.

BACKGROUND

In a market where differentiated products are highly valued by consumers (Jorge et al., 2020), the development of strategies based on the specificities granted by certain territories has become an important factor that can be used to qualify a product (Famularo et al., 2010; Espejel & Fandos, 2009). According to Vergamini et al. (2019), regional products have strong links to their production processes, related to specific geographical characteristics and local cultural values. Given the territorial identity and its relationship with territorial development, one of the central issues that has reference with the theme of territorial resources, the main challenge for the development of strategies, is the need to appropriate specific resources and seek what may constitute the identifiable potential of a territory (Barney et al., 2011). For this author, the territorial development model has very precise characteristics and is essentially based on the dynamics of specification of resources by a set of players operating there, which should use their competencies to qualify a region's product. Thus, the process of asset specification is what distinguishes a territory from the other, consisting of this process of the qualification and differentiation of resources (López-Bayón et al., 2018; Singh & Evans, 2010).

Some studies (e.g., Vergamini et al., 2019; López-Bayón et al., 2018; Famularo et al., 2010) start from the understanding that territorial development is directly linked to the relationship between local agents and their ability to foster economic activities based on differentiation. This correlation impacts the territorial development of products that may be associated with a regional brand identity, which differentiates them from others due to their geographical, historical, and sociocultural characteristics. One of the main strategies that articulate the potential of territorial development to the notion of territorial identity is origin certification, where the singularities linked to the territory can be recognized and protected through the geographical indication. This strategy can give the territorial basis agri-food products, greater competitiveness, and the possibility to scope the characteristics of segmentation of consumption resulting from this, a favorable conjuncture to territorial development (Famularo et al., 2010).

To be eligible to use origin certifications, a region must have a historical tradition and geographical, social, and cultural specificity (Vergamini et al., 2019; López-Bayón et al., 2018). This is how the geographical indications, protected designation of origin (PDO), and the protected geographical indication (PGI) emerged: first, to prove the link between natural and human factors of the region of origin unequivocally and second, to ensure that the characteristics and reputation of a product can relate to a region or location. In the face of geographical indications as a strategy of territorial action, Espejel and Fandos (2009) stated that the link between a recognized product with other economic activities in the region corresponding to indicators that may generate advances in the development process for such territory. In this regard, sustainable practices can serve as part of a firm's capabilities that contribute to the performance of the resource-based view (Barney et al., 2011).

Sustainability

Several definitions have been recast throughout the years regarding sustainability and sustainable development concepts without achieving a consensus (Gast et al., 2017; Santillo, 2007). Nevertheless, there seems to be a general understanding that takes into consideration three indivisible pillars, also referred to as the *triple bottom line*: the environment (planet), society (people), and economic performance (profit; Crals & Vereeck, 2005; Elkington, 1998), perfectly integrated and balanced (United Nations, 2015). According to Schaltegger et al. (2016, p. 268), the development of a sustainable business model contributes to managing a company's sustainable value proposition to all other stakeholders, capturing economic value from here while maintaining natural, social, and economic capital advantages. In what concerns the wine industry, the definition of sustainability by the International Organization of Vine and Wine contemplates the processing of grapes and the production systems, aligning these activities in the sustainable development criteria, to preserve consumers' health, environment, and historical and cultural heritage, besides the wine and aesthetic (OIV, 2004). For example, sustainable practices in the wine sector may include environmental factors, such as responsible water management, the non-use of chemical treatments in the vineyard and winery (Gabzdylova et al., 2009), and social responsibility by promoting education and improving the quality of life for all stakeholders (e.g., employees, customers, suppliers, and the community; Zucca et al., 2009; Polèse & Stren, 2000).

The importance of preserving natural resources and promoting the well-being of people is particularly relevant for wine companies, especially for the *terroir*-based ones. When pursuing the goal of sustainable development, they are protecting the identity of the *terroir*, one of their most significant competitive advantages. In a VRIO[3] perspective analysis, it is in the *terroir* that exists the *inimitability factor*—that is to say, that which cannot be replicated by another wine-producing region. It is from the complexity of the interconnection of natural (soil, climate, and biological characteristics) and human (collective know-how) factors that result in the unique characteristics of a wine from a given territory (Capece et al., 2019; Vergamini et al., 2019; Famularo et al., 2010; Gergaud & Ginsburgh, 2010). Furthermore, *terroir* is a landscape-defining element (Castellucci, 2010). In several wine regions, including those in the Euro-region Galicia (Spain) – Northern Portugal, this concept is used as a key ingredient for the commercialization of wines and obtaining competitive advantages over other geographical locations (Vergamini et al., 2019; Gergaud & Ginsburgh, 2010; Espejel & Fondos, 2009).

An emergent stream of research has paid attention to how sustainable practices can play a relevant role in organizational performance (Bollani et al., 2019; Voinea et al., 2019; Trianni et al., 2017). Such practices aim to maximize environmental and social benefits without compromising the generation of financial revenue (Palomares-Aguirre et al., 2018), but firms adopting sustainable business models are also interested in creating competitive advantages. According to Barber et al. (2009), the claim of sustainable wines, together with other factors, is an element that influences the perception of consumers about the value of a wine. As is the case in different industries, companies in the wine sector are involved in complex networks of natural and social relationships (Tait et al., 2019; Vergamini et al., 2019; Sellers-Rubio & Nicolau-Gonzalbez, 2016; Gilinsky et al., 2016; Forbes et al., 2009), expecting that stakeholders, from the private and public sectors, may be positively influenced by the adoption of sustainable practices (Gabzdylova et al., 2009). For it, according to some authors (e.g., Chen et al., 2006), the role of the entrepreneur is considered first and foremost for establishing foundations for sustainable development. However, to generate systemic change, by incorporating the triple bottom line elements in its strategy, there is a need to gradually eliminate the existing barriers, allowing the establishment of company policies that will underpin long-term sustainable economic growth.

Limited knowledge about sustainable development addresses one of the most significant barriers to the widespread adoption of sustainable practices (Su et al., 2019). Furthermore, there are no regulations or official international certifiers for sustainable agricultural products. Nevertheless, there are private companies that carry out this work in promoting and assisting in the certification of sustainable production processes.[2] Besides, many other examples of barriers to the adoption of sustainable development can be found in previous literature, such as the lack of financial and human resources (Ali et al., 2019; Martins et al., 2019); acquisition of capital (Pankov et al., 2019); the complex bureaucracy (Gilinsky et al., 2015; Brammer et al., 2012); market barriers affecting businesses and consumers (Galli et al., 2020; Pankov et al., 2019); entry barriers (Gilinsky et al, 2015; Champoux & Brun, 2003), perceived shortcomings (Pankov et al., 2019); and the state of uncertainty (Pankov et al., 2019). Further, public authorities often assume that sustainability management policies of large firms, commonly more industrialized, can simply be transferred to SME's, usually family-owned companies, tending in this way to ignore contradictory positions of both realities (Fassin, 2008).

All the arguments mentioned above present significant barriers affecting firms to foster sustainable development, requiring the mobilization of resources to address threats and identify business opportunities (Bocken, 2020) and mechanisms that ensure the renewed maintenance of its organizational capabilities (Teece, 2018). Thus, the EEA can act on behalf of organizations' activities as a coordinator to promote their interests by helping to remove barriers, pursuing sustainable development, and offering useful information for planning, evaluation, and decision-making (Shwetzer et al., 2019; Stam & van de Ven, 2019. The main advantage that EEA can represent for sustainable strategy lies in previous studies on the business ecosystem (e.g., Scaringella & Radziwon, 2018; van der Borgh et al., 2012).

Entrepreneurial Ecosystem

The *entrepreneurial ecosystem* is an emergent trend that has awoken the interest of multiple disciplines such as operations management and environment studies (Velt et al., 2020; Scaringella & Radziwon; Maroufkhani et al., 2018). According to Mazzarol (2014), it is a conceptual model designed to foster economic development by encouraging entrepreneurship, balanced business growth, and innovation. Entrepreneurship, which is crucial in the continued growth and development of any organization, lies on two main pillars: on the one hand, as a process in which economic activity is enhanced by having a right and capable management system in an organization promoting creativity and innovation, and on the other hand, mitigating the risk (European Commission, 2003). Concerning the *ecosystem* concept, it is related to an ecological metaphor that explains different system designs linked together in a specific location (Ritala & Almpanopoulou, 2017). The business ecosystem can "vary according to each type of ecosystem" (see Tsujimoto et al. 2018, p. 52; Kuckertz, 2019; Mason & Brown, 2014). This characteristic also appears in the definition of EEA (e.g., Isenberg, 2010, 2011; Stam, 2015, 2018; Stam & van de Ven, 2019).

Following Isenberg's (2010) definition, the entrepreneurship ecosystem consists of a set of individual elements, combined in complex ways, including a set of individual factors such as policy, finance, culture, human capital, leadership, open-minded customers, supports, markets. Following this reasoning, Maroufkhani et al. (2018) stated that the definition of the entrepreneurial ecosystems depends on the research goals, identifying as one of the primary domains the "industrial dynamics." According to the same author, industrial dynamics concentrates on changes of the environmental elements crucial for the survival of organizations, such as consumers' preferences, technology, and competitive situation. Following this, and considering wine industry particularities, EEA could be defined as an evolutionary multilevel process (Spigel, 2017), simultaneously inside-out and outside-in. The inside-out evolutionary process emerges from the creative innovation and the entrepreneurial process, understood according to Fukuda-Parr's (2003) definition of human development and Sen's (1993, 1997, 2004, 2013) definition of the capability approach. The outside-in evolutionary process is framed by the social engagement assured by the fair redistribution of the new value creation, understood according to Hoefnagels's (1962) definition of the social question, more recently developed by Ates et al. (2019), Case (2016), Lettice and Parekh (2010), Stam and van de Ven (2019), among others.

DRAWING LINES IN THE LANDSCAPE

Wine and Territory

As a result of the characteristics of the territory, focusing on this study to the Euro-region Galicia (Spain) – Northern Portugal, specifically in the geographical areas near to Sil, and Douro Rivers, the conditions are all present for the production of distinctive wines, namely those produced in four of the most outstanding PDOs. That is to say, Rías Baíxas (Spain), and the sub-region Monção and Melgaço (Portugal) on the Spanish and Portuguese banks of River Miño, respectively, with the single varietal Albariño, Ribeira Sacra (Spain) on the banks of River Sil, with Godello (white wines) and Mencía (red wines), and the Douro where are cultivated on the terraces of its valley, along the geographic area defined by the Baixo Corgo, Cima Corgo, and Douro Superior, the grapes to produce not only the well-known port wine but also superb whites and reds table wines as well. It is largely because of the existent cultural practices, winemaking methods, nature of the soils, climatic, pedological, and topographic conditions that create a microclimate conducive to the production of such wines in these locations.

Sustainable Development and Terroir: Two Interconnected And Interrelated Concepts

The designation of origin of Ribeira had a total of 93 wineries in 2019, bringing together 2,353 winegrowers. In the case of Rías Baíxas, operating in this designation of origin in that year were 5,177 winegrowers, for a total of 161 wineries—5,177 winegrowers divided among five sub-regions. In the same year, 2,236 economic operators in the wine-producing sector, including independent producers and farmers' cooperatives, were operating in the sub-region of Monção and Melagaço (Portugal), 1,121 in the Douro region (Portugal), not just related to port wine production, but also the production of table wines with PDOs. To these data should be added other productive activities involved along the production chain, from the vineyard to the final product, namely those responsible for producing and supplying glass, labels, corks, vats, barrels, and other oenological articles, not to forget those responsible for marketing and sales, transport, and, last but not least, the maintenance of agricultural activity in these regions. All of this leads this activity to represent an important source of income and responsible for generating a significant number of direct and indirect jobs throughout its production chain (Jones & Alves, 2012).

The presence of the vineyard in the Euro-region Galicia (Spain) – Northern Portugal exerts a positive influence on the achievement of a more balanced territorial development. This agri-food industry means the support of rural development, contributing to offsetting the depopulation process. A significant number of municipalities from this region, on both sides of the border, represent a high dependency on the vineyard. This activity is a relevant source of agricultural income, and even the only technically and economically viable one in some areas, namely due to the rugged terrain and the characteristics of the soil. As shown in Figures 1 and 2, the economic activity focused on vine cultivation of the PDOs Ribeira Sacra and Douro is closely linked to its climatic singularity and the configuration of the land relief. By way of example, the defining feature of Ribeira Sacra is the deep lace of the river network that causes a strong contrast in the valleys of the Sil River with its surroundings. Here, the minimum altitude located at the bottom of the valley barely exceeds 100 m. On the contrary, the maximum height exceeds 1,200 m, south of the Sil River. The middle inclination can exceed 500 m between its bottom and the top in different places of the canyon, generating relief with strong slopes.

Figure 1. Sendeiro (Ribeira Sacra)
Source: Vinetur, 2018

Figure 2. Terraces of Douro Valley
Source: Own elaboration

The relationship between people and the wine practices in these territories is the result of an ancestral coexistence, translated into a cultural legacy in the way it approaches wine culture, habits, procedures, and traditions transmitted from generation to generation. The human factor is a key element that manages the vineyard within the whims of the climate and soil, transforms the grapes into wine, and also monitors its evolution in the cellar. All this makes the human element one of the most responsible for the quality of wines produced in these PDOs. The support of such population settlements means support for the population structure of these regions and the exercise of this agri-food activity, essential for the achievement of regional and social development. Indeed, these regions have a high dependence on the wine industry, due to its economic and social importance (López-Bayón et al., 2018; Rebelo & Caldas, 2013; Jones & Alves, 2012; Espejel & Fandos, 2009).

Table 1. Sustainable development and terroir, two interconnected and interrelated concepts

	Planet	People	Profit	Source References
Sustainable development	Growing and winemaking practices that are sensitive to the environment.	Respecting the needs and interests of society at large, promoting education and equal opportunity.	Maintaining long-term economic viability.	Gilinsky et al. (2016); Sellers-Rubio and Nicolau-Gonzalbez (2016); Forbes et al. (2009); Zucca et al. (2009)
Relation	Protect ↓	Enhance ↓	Contribute ↑	
Terroir	Environmental, biological, climatic, and geologic characteristics.	Collective know-how.	Conferring a competitive advantage.	Castellucci (2010); OIV (2004); Seguin and Leeuwen (2006)

Source: Own elaboration

Thus, the commitment to the sustainable development of this activity, in the above-mentioned region, among others, besides its environmental importance, contributes to support local communities to achieve an improvement in social conditions, and the economic profitability of the players operating in this sector, with other words, pursuing a sustainable development is preserving the essence of the *terroir*. In this regard, through the adoption of sustainable practices, they can achieve competitive advantages (Tait et al., 2019; Sellers-Rubio & Nicolau-Gonzalbez, 2016; Gilinsky et al., 2016; Forbes et al., 2009). Thus, and as mentioned before, *terroir* and sustainable development are concepts that do not just walk side-by-side but also complement each other (see Table 1). In this way, identifying the aspects that confer a competitive advantage should be part of the strategic thinking of a company that seeks to determine the behavior to be adopted to improve its performance and position in the market. Nevertheless, the analysis should consider that the decision to pursue sustainable development is influenced by two contrary forces: the attitude of owners and managers to sustainability and the barriers to its adoption. These two forces have different effects on sustainability. On the one hand, the strong impact of entrepreneur attitudes toward sustainability, that is, concern about the environment and social issues, and on the other hand, the idea that sustainability is a priority in the wine industry and that the industry is moving in this direction. This positive attitude is counterbalanced by the specific perceived barriers, namely, among others, those mentioned previously, the lack of financial and human resources (economic-financial and human capital), and the complex bureaucracy (policy).

Figure 3. Entrepreneurial ecosystems framework
Source: Author's elaboration adapted from Isenberg (2011) and Stam (2015)

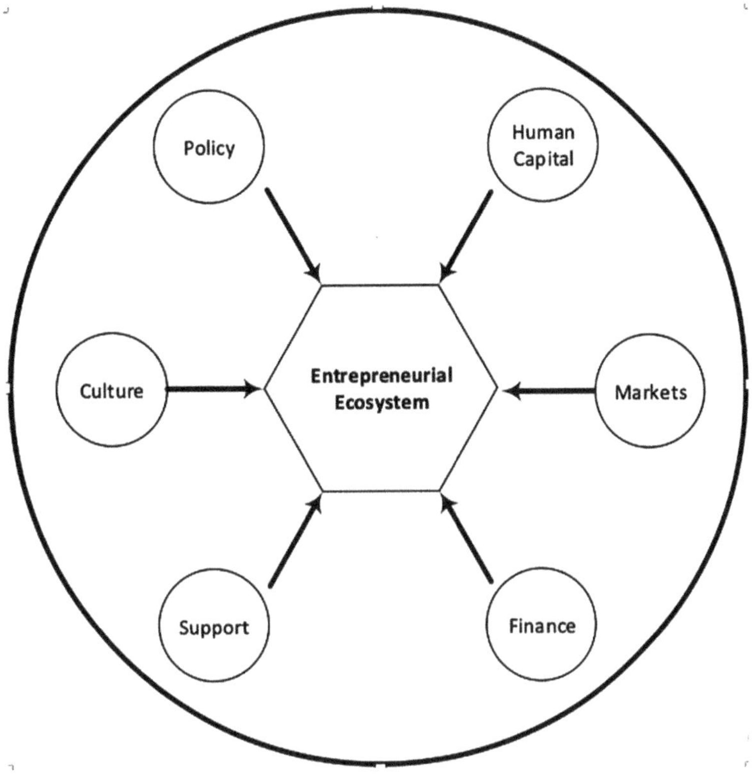

SOLUTIONS AND RECOMMENDATIONS

EEA Framework

In the context of the need to adopt a sustainable development for a territorial balance, the EEA framework emerges as an instrument to help understand and identify the mechanisms to remove the barriers to the adoption of sustainable practices in the wine industry. When talking about the entrepreneurial ecosystem, a distinctive viewpoint is being considered that complements previous studies, not only on the clustering of economic activity but also on the socio-territorial entity (Maroufkhani et al., 2018). According to Isenberg (2011), Stam (2015), and Spigel (2017), the EEA framework is composed of six related attributes, five of them aligned into two major groups organized as follows:

Group 1: Formal institutions or explicit

- Policy (leadership and government)
- Human Capital (labor and educational institutions)
- Finance (financial capitals)

Group 2: Informal institutions or implicit

- Support (infrastructures and support professions)
- Culture (success stories and societal norms)

Besides following Isenberg's (2011), the presented EEA framework includes *markets* as an additional attribute, comprised of early customers and networks, which is frequently omitted on the implementing measures (see Figure 3).

Instrument Conceptualization

Therefore, assuming each of Isenberg's attributes as a conceptual barrier, it will be possible to conceptualize the instrument according to the following: for each of these attributes, a scale from zero to ten is defined, corresponding to the total inadequacy of the organization and its total adequacy, respectively. The adjustment to this scale has two implications: the individualized measurement of each organization and its process of evolution over time. At the same time, it enables global measurement. As an increasing number of organizations reach levels of excellence, so does the average standard. This ensures temporal dynamics.

From the mentioned relationships emerge the distinction between integration and integrality and the commitment to the entrepreneurial ecosystem. Some difficulties can drive toward extinction in the long term. Excessive competition, due to parasitic and predatory behaviors, or excessive adaptability, that implies the mischaracterization of its essence, could compromise the ecosystem. According to Tsujimoto et al. (2018), parasitic and predatory behaviors should be accepted because they underlie the very definition of the ecosystem. But without contradicting the authors, we propose a balanced solution. In this regard, organizations should assume collaborative behaviors or "coopetition." An adaptation to changes in the external environment cannot question the fundamental characteristics of the entrepreneurial ecosystem nor how it is perceived. Therefore, to ensure this balance, we propose to incorporate into the very definition of Tsujimoto et al. (2018) the sociocultural development perspectives of Ates et al. (2019), Stam and van de Ven (2019), and Sen's (2013) human development prospects. Thus, the importance of engagement leads to committed behaviors. In other words, rules and regulations must be accepted and accomplished by everyone. This characteristic defines support that requires robust regulatory frameworks (Isenberg, 2011). This engagement, in turn, is also a function of the set of accepted social values (and beliefs) followed and respected by the community that is defined as *cultural attitude* (Spigel, 2017).

The Evolutionary Process of the EEA

Based on the EEA, wine companies must proceed with the characterization of the strategic competitive position. And so, their specific capabilities and limitations are characterized first, represented by the red line on the illustrative example presented in Figure 4. Next is, aligning objectives and defining specific initiatives to improve the previous situation. This practice should be a continuous, multilevel, integrated, and interdependent evolutionary process, capable of integrating and assimilating the discontinuities caused by the internal and external environmental changes that are inherent to the temporal development of the process itself. This second axis of variability, represented by the blue line in Figure 5, is associated with the evolution of external surroundings. In this way, considering that organizations are framed in a simultaneous inside-out and outside-in interface, wine companies should never neglect the interdependence between changes in the external environment and changes in the internal environment.

In other words, defining strategic positioning as simultaneously inside-out and outside-in will make it easier to overcome the identified barriers.

Figure 4. Entrepreneurial strategic positioning
Source: Own elaboration adapted from Isenberg, 2011 and Stam, 2015

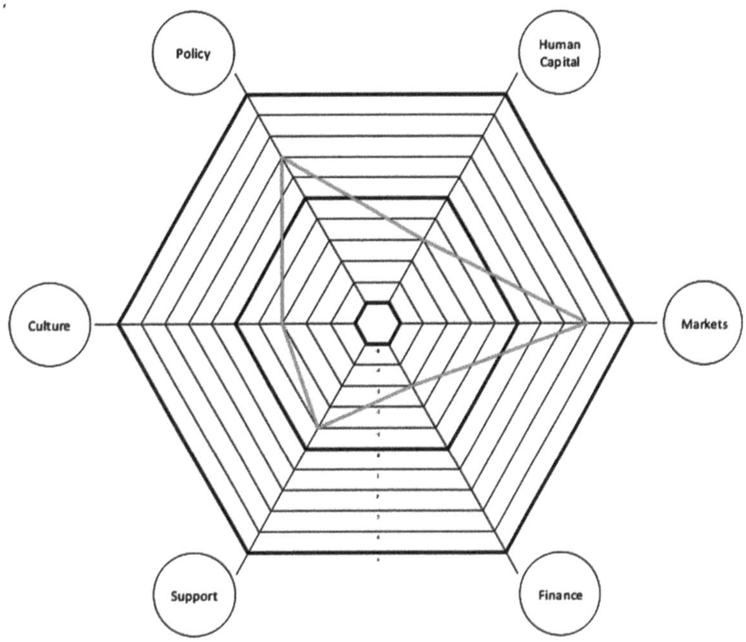

Figure 5. Entrepreneurial strategic positioning evolutionary process
Source: Own elaboration adapted from Isenberg, 2011 and Stam, 2015

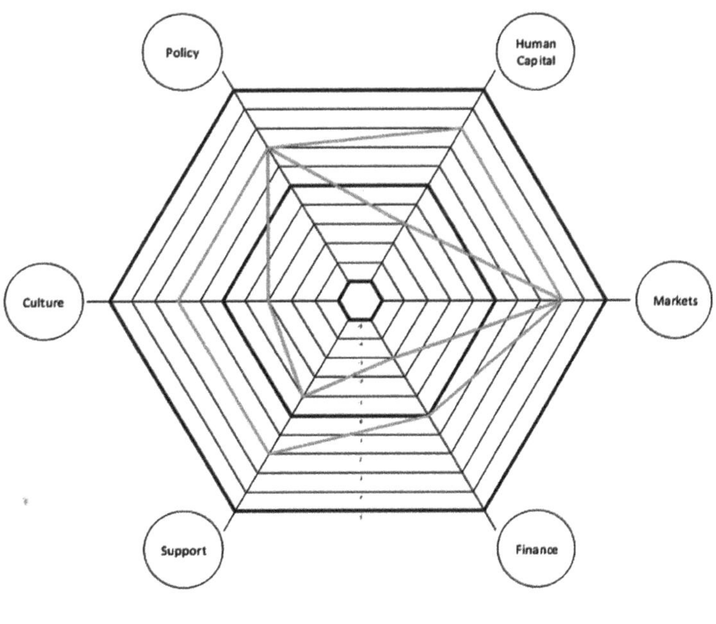

The prevalence of any entrepreneurial ecosystem is dependent on how attractiveness and ability to react, interrelate and counterbalance. Furthermore, the diversity and quantity of players ensure resilience. In this way, the greater the number of old and new companies operating in the PDO, the greater their commitment should be. Consequently, larger and stronger ecosystems are better for ensuring inside-out development. In a large entrepreneurial ecosystem, the ability to adapt to the changes in the external environment will become greater. In this case, the development is outside-in. That has two relevant implications, the first is the development and reinforcement of the framework, and the second is the consequent implementation of risk minimization measures since adaptability ensures regeneration. It is what can be defined as evolution in continuity (see Figure 6).

Figure 6. Entrepreneurial ecosystems evolutionary process
Source: Own elaboration

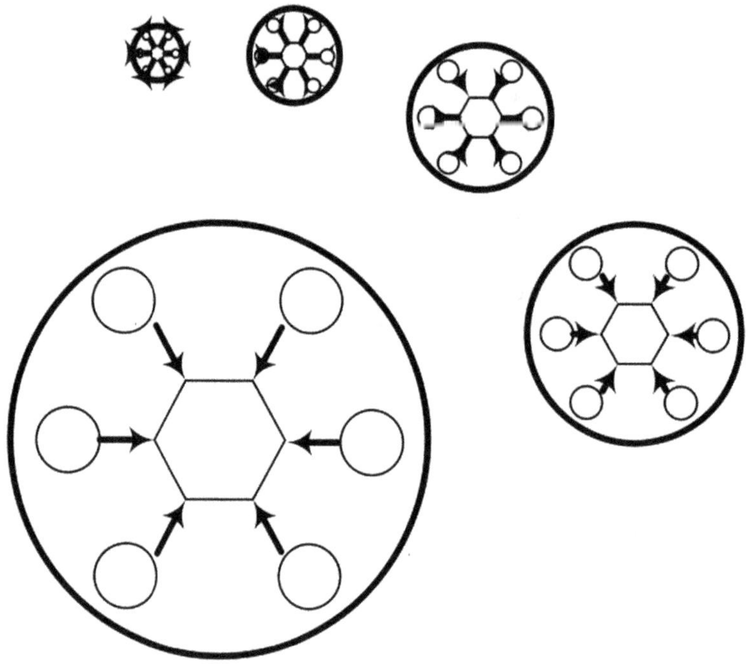

The issue of sustainability in the wine industry lies precisely in the fact that achieving sustainable development cannot be an individual choice of any organization; it is necessarily a sectorial choice. It is this choice that defines the set of beliefs and values accepted, followed, and respected by the community. The operational process, based on the six attributes previously mentioned, takes place in three phases: first, diagnosis and positioning is a general objective to align the individual and the common interest of the community where the company is integrated; the second phase is implementation, in which the guidelines are implemented; and the last phase is the follow-up, in which the implemented measures are monitored closely.

FUTURE RESEARCH DIRECTIONS

The limitation of not identifying causal relationships points out a line of research that can allow progress in the purpose of the present study. The restrictions can be circumvented, at least partially, with a new extension in the treatment of the main issue discussed in this chapter. Following this reasoning, a first approach would be the analysis of business performance, contemplating temporally an entire business cycle of the wine companies operating in each PDO, referred to in the present document, with a streamlined and consistent analysis throughout the entire production chain—from the vine to the shelf. This possibility would contribute to improving the performance of the research in several respects. It would allow us to observe the performance of the EEA framework in a real scenario and, if applicable, incorporate new references of interest to assess business performance based on sustainable development. The inclusion in this analysis of the temporal scope will mitigate the disadvantage of considering EEA framework performance that has been obtained at a specific point in the production chain. This option would allow us to add a more dynamic orientation to the research and undertake objectives related to a substantial contribution of the EEA. Which, it is vital to assess the differences of each regional entrepreneurship ecosystem (the different PDOs) to specify causal paths at specific timelines.

Once results are conditioned by the given situation of context factors, the issue to be resolved does not end with the identification of the determinants of differences in the adoption of sustainable practices between companies but rather with the mechanism that allows each company to learn, change, and adapt to sustainable development—that is to say, how and why companies reach competitive advantages based on sustainable development and can maintain them over time, even though they are caused by internal and external environmental changes, which may also change the relevance of that competitive advantage.

Another line of research is the conduction of confirmatory factor analysis, using partial least squares structural equation modeling (PLS-SEM) for measurement and validation. This methodology, popular in business science (Henseler et al., 2016), allows us to incorporate other business aspects with a more quantitative character. The main contributions of this approach lie in the possibility of contemplating the weight of each attribute that forms the EEA framework and the effects of the independent variables on dependent ones (e.g., EEA → wine company performance), and also to add the indirect consequences derived from the interrelationships between variables (e.g., introduction moderator variables), allowing in this way to reproduce the existing relationships at a more inclusive level.

Furthermore, the foundations for the development of future studies are laid down in deeper detail of some of the concepts addressed in this study. The scarcity of time and the need for other types of approaches have limited the deepening of issues whose understanding may be of high relevance to the projection of future strategies that contribute to the sustainable development of the wine sector. Finally, note that the approach presented here can be replicated in different geographical locations, such as other PDOs and other *terroir*-based products.

CONCLUSION

The globalization of the wine market is changing the profile of the business. The installed capacities make the production of wine on a larger scale possible, giving some producers and production regions competitive advantages in positioning by price in the commercialization of their wine. However, the threat that may represent the highest mainstreamed wine production is not synonymous with the trivialization of the wine product. The *terroir*-based wines are unique, and the territories where they are produced constitute their true factors of differentiation and competitive advantages where inimitability resides.

In a highly competitive global market, with unexpected changes in business characteristics that could undermine producers' communication and marketing strategies, producers are required to focus on quality and differentiation to distinguish themselves from competitors. It is a fact that there may be similarities in the methods and techniques employed by winegrowers and winemakers in different locations. Techniques and technologies can be replicated. However, the inimitable factor always will reside mostly in the *terroir*. If the territories are endowed with a portfolio of natural and cultural resources, some degree of innovative entrepreneurship can, through the mobilization of collective resources, support the competitive advantages of local companies (Singh & Evans, 2010). In this way, promoting local entrepreneurship and innovation will become a promising strategy for the development of rural and less-developed territories. Considering this, producers from the Euro-region Galicia (Spain) – Northern Portugal, in particular, those from the four most outstanding PDOs: Rías Baíxas (Spain), Ribeira Sacra (Spain), the sub-region of Monção and Melgaço (Portugal), and the Douro should be prepared for the new challenges that will arise, starting with the need to delineate strategies for differentiating wines produced in such regions, focusing on the differences that are conferred by each *terroir* of origin compared to that produced in other geographical locations. These geographic, historical, and cultural differences responsible for the edaphoclimatic characteristics of each region and also for the ancestral know-how of the people are being redefined and challenged by increasing commercial interests.

As argued throughout this chapter, the strategies adopted by the producers, pursue sustainable development will have to be one of them. The road toward sustainable development can be interpreted as a means of protecting wine companies' interests or a way to protect the only truly inimitable resource—the *terroir*. However, flexibility and responsiveness represent a market rule that cannot be over-neglected. A sector where modernity must go alongside tradition is the wine industry. The productive efficiency must be achieved by rational resource management and sustainable growth (e.g., the work on the vineyard should be based on non-aggressive practices to nature, and the vinification process must respect the true identity of the grape, avoiding any harmful chemical processes). In this scenario, the possibility of imbalance in natural systems will be reduced, which, in turn, will eventually disrupt the functioning of social and economic structures, and that will affect the balance of the whole *terroir*. Following this reasoning, consolidating a position through sustainable development affects not only the value and versatility of the wines but also the ability, through acquired knowledge, to explore the full potential of the *terroir*.

In this scenario, the success of a region is not enough for the individual success of one of its producers, an allegiance between all players is necessary to build a solid strategy based on the sustainability commitment (Erokhin & Ivolga, 2012). Since the competitive strategy of wine companies that choose price positioning can change the economic structure of the entire industry, local sectorial entities will have to play a crucial role in diversifying market strategies. In the same way, sustainable development objectives should also encourage the provision of private resources, in particular, established companies. To ensure high individual performances and the achievement of objectives requires investing in specific instruments, competencies, and control systems that play a relevant role in the definition of a cooperative strategy.

As an instrument, the EEA is proposed to help understand and remove the barriers to the adoption of sustainable practices in the wine industry, as well as to provide an alternative and effective mechanism to achieve good management results. EEA allows managers to identify and monitor closely six attributes that, by ensuring alignment between the particular interest and the interest of the community, guarantee the commitment that breaks the barrier. The concept of the entrepreneurial ecosystem is active in cooperatives. Through cooperatives, companies can increase business opportunities, get better results, reduce their risks, and provide benefits in the economy at scale.

Nevertheless, managers should always bear in mind that the decision to buy sustainable food products is complex and influenced by several factors (Ghvanidze et al., 2017). One of the main challenges for wine-producing companies is the need to understand whether the consumer recognizes the value of what is offered and is motivated to buy wines from sustainable viticulture. This specificity gives the wine inimitable attributes that distinguish it from the others, so it is important to earn if the final consumer values them and is willing to pay a premium value for such a product. Wine companies and institutions that protect, supervise, and promote the activity are the agents responsible for educating consumers, increasing their level of knowledge about the product.

ACKNOWLEDGMENT

We thank the detailed suggestions of the anonymous reviewers for their careful reading and comments that helped improve previous versions of the chapter.

This research was supported by the RGEAF-ECOBAS (Xunta de Galicia).

REFERENCES

Ates, S. A., Ateş, M., & Yülek, M. A. (2019). Going Beyond GDP: The Role of Social Innovation in Building a Welfare State. In *Handbook of Research on Digital Marketing Innovations in Social Entrepreneurship and Solidarity Economics* (pp. 241–258). IGI Global. doi:10.4018/978-1-5225-8939-6.ch013

Atkin, T., Gilinsky, A., & Newton, S. K. (2011) Sustainability in the Wine Industry: Altering the Competitive Landscape? *Proceedings of the 6th AWBR International Conference.*

Barber, N., Taylor, C., & Strick, S. (2009). Wine consumers' environmental knowledge and attitudes: Influence on willingness to purchase. *International Journal of Wine Research*, *1*, 59–72. doi:10.2147/IJWR.S4649

Barney, J. (1991). Firm Resources and Sustained Competitive Advantage. *Journal of Management*, *17*(1), 99–120. doi:10.1177/014920639101700108

Barney, J. B., Ketchen, D. J. Jr, & Wright, M. (2011). The Future of Resource-Based Theory: Revitalization or Decline? *Journal of Management*, *37*(5), 1299–1315. doi:10.1177/0149206310391805

Bocken, N. M. P., & Geradts, T. H. J. (2020). Barriers and drivers to sustainable business model innovation: Organization design and dynamic capabilities. *Long Range Planning*, *53*(4), 101950. doi:10.1016/j.lrp.2019.101950

Bollani, L., Bonadonna, A., & Peira, G. (2019). The Millennials' Concept of Sustainability in the Food Sector. *Sustainability*, *11*(10), 2984. doi:10.3390u11102984

Brammer, S., Hoejmose, S., & Marchant, K. (2012). Environmental management in SME s in the UK: Practices, pressures, and perceived benefits. *Business Strategy and the Environment, 21*(7), 423–434. doi:10.1002/bse.717

Bryman, A. (2008). *Social research methods*. Oxford University Press.

Capece, A., Pietrafesa, R., Siesto, G., Romaniello, R., Condelli, N., & Romano, P. (2019). Selected Indigenous Saccharomyces Cerevisiae Strains as Profitable Strategy to Preserve Typical Traits of Primitivo Wine. *Fermentation (Basel, Switzerland), 5*(4), 87. doi:10.3390/fermentation5040087

Case, H. (2016). The "social question" 1820-1920. *Modern Intellectual History, 13*(3), 747–775. doi:10.1017/S1479244315000037

Castellucci, F. (2010). *Resolution OIV/VITI 333/2010*. OIV.

Champoux, D., & Brun, J. (2003). Occupational health and safety management in small size enterprises: An overview of the situation and avenues for intervention and research. *Safety Science, 41*(4), 301–318. doi:10.1016/S0925-7535(02)00043-7

Chen, Y. S., Lai, S. B., & Wen, C. T. (2006). The influence of green innovation performance on corporate advantage in Taiwan. *Journal of Business Ethics, 67*(4), 331–339. doi:10.100710551-006-9025-5

Colombelli, A., Paolucci, E., & Ughetto, E. (2019). Hierarchical and relational governance and the life cycle of entrepreneurial ecosystems. *Small Business Economics, 52*(2), 505–521. doi:10.100711187-017-9957-4

Crals, E., & Vereeck, L. (2005). The affordability of sustainable entrepreneurship certification for SMEs. *International Journal of Sustainable Development and World Ecology, 12*(2), 173–183. doi:10.1080/13504500509469628

Elkington, J. (1998). Partnerships from cannibals with forks: The triple bottom line of 21st-century business. *Environmental Quality Management, 8*(1), 37–51. doi:10.1002/tqem.3310080106

Erokhin, V., & Ivolga, A. (2012). How to Ensure Sustainable Development of Agribusiness in the Conditions of Trade Integration: Russian Approach. *International Journal of Sustainable Economies Management, 1*(2), 12–23. doi:10.4018/ijsem.2012040102

Espejel, J., & Fandos, C. (2009). Wine marketing strategies in Spain: A structural equation approach to consumer response to protected designations of origin (PDOs). *International Journal of Wine Business Research, 21*(3), 267–288. doi:10.1108/17511060910985980

European Commission. (2003). *Green paper entrepreneurship in Europe*. Retrieved from https://web.archive.org/web/20040611050753/http://www.europa.eu.int:80/comm/enterprise/entrepreneurship/green_paper/index.htm

Famularo, B., Bruwer, J., & Li, E. (2010). Region of origin as a choice factor: Wine knowledge and wine tourism involvement influence. *International Journal of Wine Business Research, 22*(4), 362–385. doi:10.1108/17511061011092410

Fassin, Y. (2008). SMEs and the fallacy of formalizing. *CSR. Business Ethics (Oxford, England), 17*(4), 364–378. doi:10.1111/j.1467-8608.2008.00540.x

Fink, A. (2013). *Conducting research literature reviews: from the Internet to paper.* Sage Publications.

Forbes, S. L., Cohen, D. A., Cullen, R., Wratten, S. D., & Fountain, J. (2009). Consumer attitudes regarding environmentally sustainable wine: An exploratory study of the New Zealand marketplace. *Journal of Cleaner Production, 17*(13), 1195–1199. doi:10.1016/j.jclepro.2009.04.008

Fukuda-Parr, S. (2003). The human development paradigm: Operationalizing Sen's ideas on capabilities. *Feminist Economics, 9*(2-3), 301–317. doi:10.1080/1354570022000077980

Gabzdylova, B., Raffensperger, J. F., & Castka, P. (2009). Sustainability in the New Zealand wine industry: Drivers, stakeholders and practices. *Journal of Cleaner Production, 17*(11), 992–998. doi:10.1016/j.jclepro.2009.02.015

Galli, F., Prosperi, P., Favilli, E., D'Amico, S., Bartolini, F., & Brunori, G. (2020). How can policy processes remove barriers to sustainable food systems in Europe? Contributing to a policy framework for agri-food transitions. *Food Policy, 96*, 101871. doi:10.1016/j.foodpol.2020.101871

Garanti, Z., & Berberoglu, A. (2018). Cultural perspective of traditional cheese consumption practices and its sustainability among post-millennial consumers. *Sustainability, 10*(9), 3183. doi:10.3390u10093183

Gast, J., Gundolf, K., & Cesinger, B. (2017). Doing business in a Green way: A systematic review of the ecological sustainability entrepreneurship literature and future research directions. *Journal of Cleaner Production, 147*, 44–56. doi:10.1016/j.jclepro.2017.01.065

Gergaud, O., & Ginsburgh, V. (2010). Natural Endowments, Production Technologies and the Quality of Wines in Bordeaux. Does Terroir Matter? *Journal of Wine Economics, 5*(1), 3–21. doi:10.1017/S1931436100001346

Gilinsky, A. Jr, Newton, S. K., & Vega, R. V. (2016). Sustainability in the Global Wine Industry: Concepts and Cases. *Agriculture and Agricultural Science Procedia, 8*, 37–49. doi:10.1016/j.aaspro.2016.02.006

Henseler, J., Hubona, G., & Ray, P. A. (2016). Using PLS path modeling in new technology research: Updated guidelines. *Industrial Management & Data Systems, 116*(1), 2–20. doi:10.1108/IMDS-09-2015-0382

Hoefnagels, H. (1962). *La sociologie face aux "problèmes sociaux". Textes et études philosophiques.* Éditions Desclée de Brouwer, Bruge.

Isenberg, D. (2011). The entrepreneurship ecosystem strategy as a new paradigm for economy policy: principles for cultivating entrepreneurship. Babson Entrepreneurship Ecosystem Project, Babson College.

Isenberg, D. J. (2010). How to start an entrepreneurial revolution. *Harvard Business Review, 88*(6), 40–50.

Jones, G. V., & Alves, F. (2012). Impact of climate change on wine production: A global overview and regional assessment in the Douro Valley of Portugal. *International Journal of Global Warming, 4*(3-4), 383–406. doi:10.1504/IJGW.2012.049448

Jorge, E., Lopez-Valeiras, E., & Gonzalez-Sanchez, M. B. (2020). The importance given to food naturalness attributes by millennial university students. *Sustainability, 12*(2), 728. doi:10.3390u12020728

Kuckertz, A. (2019). Let's take the entrepreneurial ecosystem metaphor seriously! *Journal of Business Venturing Insights, 11*(e00124), 1–7. doi:10.1016/j.jbvi.2019.e00124

Lettice, F., & Parekh, M. (2010). The social innovation process: Themes, challenges and implications for practice. *International Journal of Technology Management, 51*(1), 139–158. doi:10.1504/IJTM.2010.033133

López-Bayón, S., González-Díaz, M., Solís-Rodríguez, V., & Fernández-Barcala, M. (2018). Governance decisions in the supply chain and quality performance: The synergistic effect of geographical indications and ownership structure. *International Journal of Production Economics, 197*, 1–12. doi:10.1016/j.ijpe.2017.12.022

Maroufkhani, P., Wagner, R., & Ismail, W. K. W. (2018). Entrepreneurial ecosystems: A systematic review. *Journal of Enterprising Communities: People and Places in the Global Economy, 12*(4), 545–564. doi:10.1108/JEC-03-2017-0025

Mason, C., & Brown, R. (2014). Entrepreneurial ecosystems and growth oriented entrepreneurship. *Final report to OECD, 30*(1), 77-102.

Mayring, P. (2015). Qualitative Content Analysis: Theoretical Background and Procedures. In A. Bikner-Ahsbahs, C. Knipping, & N. Presmeg (Eds.), *Approaches to Qualitative Research in Mathematics Education. Advances in Mathematics Education*. Springer. doi:10.1007/978-94-017-9181-6_13

Mazzarol, T. (2014). *Growing and sustaining entrepreneurial ecosystems: what they are and the role of government policy*. White Paper WP01-2014. Small Enterprise Association of Australia and New Zealand (SEAANZ). Retrieved from https://www.iicie.com/uploads/White-Paper/1463661660SEAANZ_WP_01_2014_Mazzarol.pdf

OIV. (2004). Resolution OIV/CST 1/2004. Definition of Sustainable Vitiviniculture. Paris: OIV.

Pankov, S., Velamuri, V. K., & Schneckenberg, D. (2019). Towards sustainable entrepreneurial ecosystems: Examining the effect of contextual factors on sustainable entrepreneurial activities in the sharing economy. *Small Business Economics*. Advance online publication. doi:10.100711187-019-00255-5

Polèse, M., & Stren, R. E. (2000). *The Social Sustainability of Cities: Diversity and the Management of Change*. University of Toronto Press. doi:10.3138/9781442682399

Rebelo, J., & Caldas, J. (2013). The Douro wine region: A cluster approach. *Journal of Wine Research, 24*(1), 19–37. doi:10.1080/09571264.2012.717220

Ritala, P., & Almpanopoulou, A. (2017). In defense of 'eco' in innovation ecosystem. *Technovation, 60–61*, 39–42. doi:10.1016/j.technovation.2017.01.004

Santillo, D. (2007). Reclaiming the definition of sustainability. *Environmental Science and Pollution Research International, 14*(1), 60–66. doi:10.1065/espr2007.01.375 PMID:17352129

Scaringella, L., & Radziwon, A. (2018). Innovation, entrepreneurial, knowledge, and business ecosystems: Old wine in new bottles? *Technological Forecasting and Social Change*, *136*, 59–87. doi:10.1016/j.techfore.2017.09.023

Schaltegger, S., Lüdeke-Freund, F., & Hansen, E. (2016). Business models for sustainability: A co-evolutionary analysis of sustainable entrepreneurship, innovation, and transformation. *Organization & Environment*, *29*(3), 264–289. doi:10.1177/1086026616633272

Seguin, G., & Leeuwen, C. V. (2006). The Concept of Terroir in Viticulture. *Journal of Wine Research*, *17*(1), 1–10. doi:10.1080/09571260600633135

Sellers-Rubio, R., & Nicolau-Gonzalbez, J. L. (2016). Estimating the willingness to pay for a sustainable wine using a Heckit Model. *Wine Economics and Policy*, *5*(2), 96–104. doi:10.1016/j.wep.2016.09.002

Sen, A. (1993). Capability and well-being. In M. Nussbaum & A. Sen (Eds.), *The quality of life* (pp. 30–53). Clarendon Press. doi:10.1093/0198287976.003.0003

Sen, A. (1997). Maximization and the Act of Choice. *Econometrica*, *65*(4), 745–779. doi:10.2307/2171939

Sen, A. (2004). Capabilities, lists, and public reason. *Feminist Economics*, *10*(3), 77–80. doi:10.1080/1354570042000315163

Sen, A. (2013). The ends and means of sustainability. *Journal of Human Development*, *14*(1), 6–20.

Shwetzer, C., Maritz, A., & Nguyen, Q. (2019). Entrepreneurial ecosystems: A holistic and dynamic approach. *Journal of Industry-University Collaboration*, *1*(2), 79–95. doi:10.1108/JIUC-03-2019-0007

Singh, I., & Evans, J. (2010). Natural resource-based sustainable development using a cluster approach. In J. Richards (Ed.), *Mining, Society, and a Sustainable World* (pp. 183–201). Springer.

Spigel, B. (2017). The relational organization of entrepreneurial ecosystems. *Entrepreneurship Theory and Practice*, *41*(1), 49–72. doi:10.1111/etap.12167

Stam, E. (2015). Entrepreneurial ecosystems and regional policy: A sympathetic critique. *European Planning Studies*, *23*(9), 1759–1769. doi:10.1080/09654313.2015.1061484

Stam, E. (2018). Measuring Entrepreneurial Ecosystems. In A. O'Connor, E. Stam, F. Sussan, & D. Audretsch (Eds.), *Entrepreneurial Ecosystems. Place-Based Transformations and Transitions* (pp. 173–196). Springer.

Stam, E., & van de Ven, A. (2019). Entrepreneurial ecosystem elements. *Small Business Economics*, 1–24.

Su, J., Watchravesringkan, K., Zhou, J., & Gil, M. (2019). Sustainable clothing: Perspectives from US and Chinese young Millennials. *International Journal of Retail & Distribution Management*, *47*(11), 1141–1162. doi:10.1108/IJRDM-09-2017-0184

Tait, P., Saunders, C., Dalziel, P., Rutherford, P., Driver, T., & Guenther, M. (2019). Estimating wine consumer preferences for sustainability attributes: A discrete choice experiment of Californian Sauvignon blanc purchasers. *Journal of Cleaner Production*, *233*, 412–420. doi:10.1016/j.jclepro.2019.06.076

Teece, D. J. (2018). Business models and dynamic capabilities. *Long Range Planning*, *51*(1), 40–49. doi:10.1016/j.lrp.2017.06.007

Trianni, A., Cagno, E., & Neri, A. (2017). Modeling barriers to the adoption of industrial sustainability measures. *Journal of Cleaner Production*, *168*, 1482–1504. doi:10.1016/j.jclepro.2017.07.244

Tsujimoto, M., Kajikawa, Y., Tomita, J., & Matsumoto, Y. (2018). A review of the ecosystem concept – Towards coherent ecosystem design. *Technological Forecasting and Social Change*, *136*, 49–58. doi:10.1016/j.techfore.2017.06.032

United Nations. (2015, October). *Resolution adopted by the General Assembly on 25 September 2015.* Retrieved 28/02/2018, from General Assembly: http://www.un.org/ga/search/view_doc.asp?symbol=A/RES/70/1&Lang=E

van der Borgh, M., Cloodt, M., & Romme, A. G. L. (2012). *Value creation by knowledge-based Business Ecosystems*. Harper Business.

Velt, H., Torkkeli, L., & Laine, I. (2020). Entrepreneurial Ecosystem Research: Bibliometric Mapping of the Domain. *Journal of Business Ecosystems*, *1*(2), 43–83. doi:10.4018/JBE.20200701.oa1

Vergamini, D., Bartolini, F., Prosperi, P., & Brunori, G. (2019). Explaining regional dynamics of marketing strategies: The experience of the Tuscan wine producers. *Journal of Rural Studies*, *72*, 136–152. doi:10.1016/j.jrurstud.2019.10.006

Vinetur. (2018). *Ribeira Sacra celebrará en octubre el III desafio Vía Romana*. Retrieved from https://www.vinetur.com/2018042246919/ribeira-sacra-celebrara-en-octubre-el-iii-desafio-via-romana.html

Voinea, C. L., Logger, M., Rauf, F., & Roijakkers, N. (2019). Drivers for Sustainable Business Models in Start-Ups: Multiple Case Studies. *Sustainability*, *11*(24), 6884. doi:10.3390u11246884

Willer, H., & Lernoud, J. (2018). *The World of Organic Agriculture: Statistics and Emerging Trends 2018*. Frick: Research Institute of Organic Agriculture (FiBL).

Woolley, J. (2017). *Infrastructure for entrepreneurship*. Oxford Research Encyclopedia of Business and Management. Retrieved and printed from business.oxfordre.com

Zucca, G., Smith, D. E., & Mitry, D. J. (2009). Sustainable viticulture and winery practices in California: What is it, and do customers care? *International Journal of Wine Research*, 189-194.

ADDITIONAL READING

Brandt, U. S., & Svendsen, G. T. (2016). When can a green entrepreneur manage the local environment? *Journal of Environmental Management*, *183*(3), 622–629. doi:10.1016/j.jenvman.2016.09.007 PMID:27637810

Castellini, A., Mauracher, C., & Troiano, S. (2017). An overview of the biodynamic wine sector. *International Journal of Wine Research*, *9*(1), 1–11. doi:10.2147/IJWR.S69126

Chavez, R., Yu, W., Sadiq Jajja, M. S., Lecuna, A., & Fynes, B. (2020). Can entrepreneurial orientation improve sustainable development through leveraging internal lean practices? *Business Strategy and the Environment*, *29*(6), 2211–2225. doi:10.1002/bse.2496

González, P. A., & Dans, E. P. (2018). The 'terroirist' social movement: The reawakening of wine culture in Spain. *Journal of Rural Studies*, *61*, 184–196. doi:10.1016/j.jrurstud.2018.04.014

Jorge, E. (2016). *Da casta ao terroir: Posicionamento estratégico do vinho Alvarinho produzido na Sub-região de Monção e Melgaço para o mercado dos grandes vinhos brancos mundiais*. (Unpublished master's thesis). Instituto Superior de Contabilidade e Administração do Porto, Porto.

Storchmann, K. (2018). Introduction to the Issue: Wine Cooperatives. *Journal of Wine Economics*, *13*(3), 239–242. doi:10.1017/jwe.2018.51

KEY TERMS AND DEFINITIONS

Coopetition: Collaboration between business competitors operating in the same industry with the hope of mutually beneficial results.

Ecosystem: Adapted from biology, referring to a group of living organisms that interact with each other in a specific environment.

Entrepreneurial Ecosystem: A set of different elements, such as culture, policies, and networks, that affects the local or regional creation of new businesses.

Entrepreneurship: An act of creation, where economic activity is enhanced by having a right and capable management system in an organization.

Sustainability: Economic viability with respect for the environment and the needs and interests of society.

Sustainable Development: Ways to meet the present and the future the needs of all.

Terroir: An aspect that defines the landscape, referring to a territory recognized as capable of conferring distinctive characteristics to agricultural production and other food products originating from there.

Wine Industry: An industry comprised of the production of table wines and wines with designation of origin from grapes, also including the mixing, purification, and bottling of wines.

ENDNOTES

1 Conventional companies should be understood as opposed to sustainable ones.

2 These include the Sustainable Agriculture Initiative (SAI), which is the leading global sustainable food and beverage value chain initiative, Sustainability in Practice (SIP), and the Federation Internationale des Vins et Spiritueux (FIVS).

3 An organization's competitive advantage will be sustainable when it can be valuable, rare, not imitated by competitors and manageable by the organization (Barney, 1991).

Chapter 8
Open Innovation as a Strategy to Sustainably Compete in the Textile Industry

Sara Santos
Polytechnic Institute of Cávado and Ave, Portugal

Teresa Dieguez
https://orcid.org/0000-0002-4886-1446
Polytechnic Institute of Cávado and Ave, Portugal

ABSTRACT

Innovation is crucial for business in order to meet consumers' needs and stakeholders' expectations. Innovation emerges as a must for all activity sectors, including the textile industry. Change can be an opportunity for organizations that present competitive advantages and new solutions. However, not all changes are directly visible, and innovation by nature is impossible to quantify and measure. This intangibility requires tools to help managers monitor the results of their investment. The present study applies the Innovation Scoring 1.0, a Portuguese tool for companies to self-evaluate in what concerns innovation, efficiency, and profitability improvement. It is structured in three main sections: literature review, case study, and conclusions. The study showed that a company may improve its results through open innovation, being leadership, and organizational culture determinants in the process.

INTRODUCTION

Innovation becomes, more and more, a significant factor when defining and delimiting business objectives. The literature has been studying its contributions about strategic results and sustainability (Alegre & Chiva, 2008), being today accepted as being "vital to sustain and guarantee the advancement of companies' businesses" (Chesbrough, 2012 p. 1). Innovation systems are important determinants of technological change (Hekkert et al, 2007), requiring companies to improve their capacities and resources

DOI: 10.4018/978-1-7998-7634-2.ch008

to develop new products, services, systems and processes (operational or production), ways of working and technologies, in order to respond to the needs and expectations of its consumers.

In this context, innovation appears as an indispensable requirement for the success and sustainability of all activity sectors, among which is the textile industry (Rech, 2006). Indeed, technological changes have introduced significant changes in the competitiveness of the textile industry, especially with regard to the definition of new areas of competition (more internationalized), sustainability of products and processes (more reduced), as well as product differentiation (increased). In the new competitive standard, regarding technological innovation, product quality, organizational innovation, flexibility, speed of delivery and rationalization of production costs prevail (Rech, 2006).

Companies must obtain competitive advantages through differentiation (Godinho, 2003). Change must be an opportunity and organizations can obtain competitive advantages through new solutions and value added (Poças, 2015). However, results of the change are not always immediately visible, and it is often suggested that innovation, by nature, is impossible to quantify and measure (Cerveira, 2009). This intangibility requires the creation of tools that help managers to monitor the results of their investment, given that developing a business without a consistent image of its performance and objectives increases the degree of uncertainty and risk (Patton, 2007).

This chapter is related with innovation management, more specifically with the need of having a tool to monitor the performance of the company. There is a gap in the literature review between innovation and business performance (González-Fernández & González-Velasco, 2018). One of the many reasons why companies invest strategically in innovation is related to the objective of achieving better performance (Beechler & Woodward, 2009). How can we evaluate and manage innovation is the research question and this study analyses this problematic through Innovation Scoring 1.0, from COTEC, a system that aims to provide organizations with an instrument for self-diagnosis of their capabilities and performance in the field of innovation. Additionally, it assists in the analysis of the organization's performance, identifying and assessing the capabilities and weaknesses in terms of innovation. Above all, it aims to encourage companies to diagnose and develop innovation in a more systematic, efficient, and effective way (COTEC, 2018).

The Innovation Scoring is applied to a Portuguese company in the textile sector for helping the diagnosis and propose suggestions for improvement. It is structured in three main chapters. In the first chapter, a theoretical framework is presented, through a literature review, which addresses three main themes:

1. Innovation.
2. Innovation Scoring.
3. Textile sector.

In the second chapter, the methodology used, the general and specific objectives, the questionnaire used, and the description of data collection are presented. An analysis of the results obtained is obtainable and their discussion is made. In the third and last chapter, the conclusions on the application of Innovation Scoring in the textile company under study are presented, the limitations are pointed out and recommendations for future research are suggested. This study highlights leadership and organizational culture as determinants in the process of innovation.

LITERATURE REVIEW

Innovation

The literature review on the concept of innovation is very vast and has been registering significant evolution in all sectors. The first great academic to address this topic was Schumpeter (1934) who considered innovation as the introduction of a new product or a new product quality, a new production method, opening a new market and / or winning from a source of supply of raw materials or semi-manufactured goods. Later, the same author proposes a new, simpler and more comprehensive definition: Any way of doing things differently in the sphere of economic life (Schumpeter, 1939). In 1982, Freeman argues that innovation stems from invention. Referring to the development of an idea, project, or product, it can be considered an innovation whenever the market in which it is inserted proceeds to its acceptance and validation. Despite considering that innovation stems from invention, the author says that innovation promotes process improvement that is likely to be a real asset to the organization that promoted it. In 1985, Drucker presented innovation as a tool that organizations and entrepreneurs use to promote the transformation of opportunities in business, having as main characteristics the ability to allow their learning and the promotion of their practice.

In this sense, innovation arises as "the implementation of a new or significantly improved product (good or service), or a process, or a new marketing method, or a new organizational method in business practices, in the organization of the workplace or in external relations (OECD, Oslo Manual, p. 55). For Tidd & Bessant (2009), innovation does not correspond only to the ability to improve the position in the market in which the organization operates, as it results from an entire process of seeking opportunities and exploiting them, taking advantage of them. Thus, innovation allows the consolidation of a position in already developed and mature markets, while at the same time allowing integration into new markets. In general, as Pinto (2012) mentions, most researchers on this theme understand that innovation has a meaning arising from demand and discovery, from a process of experimentation and development of products and production processes and, ultimately, from new structures at the level of organizations, based, in general, on customer satisfaction.

Figure 1 illustrates a whole set of elements and assumptions that must be taken into account when addressing innovation, including suitability for the environment in which the company operates, patents and the idealization of projects, tending the creation and development of a certain product, good or service. In addition, the process, marketing and organizational improvement, bases for creating value and customer satisfaction, may also be considered.

Figure 1. Innovation and quality
Source: Adapted from Santos, Braga, Lima, Teixeira, &. Sá, 2018, p. 10.

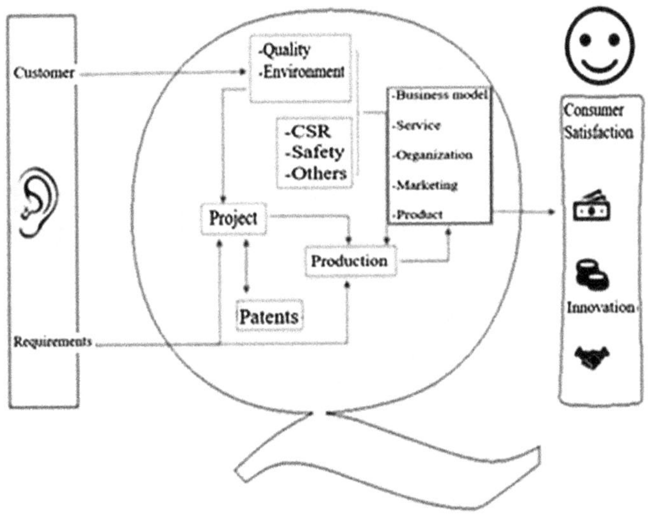

In fact, Santos, Braga, Lima, Teixeira, &. Sá (2018), argue that innovation is primarily responsible for ensuring that organizations are able to maintain their competitive advantages over competitors, ensuring, through it, its maintenance and sustainability. This sustainability is ensured, according to Engel, Dirlea, Dyer and Graff (2015), by the ability of true innovators to think in the long term, projecting broad time horizons and being persistent in the way they face each opportunity. Using this tool, organizations promote not only their own growth, but also general economic growth (Pinto, 2012). Innovation also assumes a very relevant role with regard to the leverage effect, as it promotes the competitiveness of companies, individually and, in an aggregate way, contributing to the good economic performance of a given country or territory (Ramesh, Dieguez, Ferreira, & Silva, 2018). Being a complex process and full of multifactorial challenges, innovation is commonly accepted as vital for the growth of the economy, for the formation of new industries and for the beginning of new social challenges (Sivam, Dieguez, Ferreira, & Silva, 2019). A growing understanding of these factors (at the level of organizations, regions, or countries) is the focus of many research and practice policies (European Commission, 2014).

According to the OECD Oslo Manual (2005), four classifications for innovation are considered: product / service innovation, process innovation, organizational innovation, and marketing innovation (OECD, 2005). Another classification is presented by Henderson & Clark (1990) and is related to the degrees of innovation itself: two degrees of innovation: namely incremental and radical innovation. Faria (2008) argues that innovation comes, to a large extent, from the existence of a system of knowledge networks and from the collaboration verified between them, as organizations do not have the capacity to master all areas of knowledge.

In this sense, as mentioned by Caraça, Ferreira, & Mendonça (2006), an innovative company cannot live outside the context in which it is inserted, since all its actions are conditioned and, in a way, dependent on all the agents that participate in the innovation process. Whether innovation is associated with something new or improved, there are naturally barriers associated with its promotion. In essence, most authors, according to Pinto (2012), consider the existence of internal and external barriers to innovation. Barriers of an internal nature are those that arise within the organization and barriers of an external nature are those that are generated in its external environment but have a contagion effect at the level of its internal environment. Although all are important, Pinto (2012) considers that barriers of human nature tend to be unduly undervalued or underestimated and, therefore, "the biggest barriers to innovation reside within the companies themselves, being deeply rooted in their organizational culture and their work routines, being the result of the company's own activity and the mechanisms and relationships created over time" (Pinto, 2012, p. 14).

With regard to the particular case of the national business fabric, Vieira (2007) argues that the main barriers to innovation are the high risk and economic cost that are associated with innovation, the difficulty in obtaining financing, the rigid way as the generality national organizations are oriented, the lack of information about technology, the rigor of regulation and applicable legal norms and the difficulty of companies, in different situations, to approach customers in order to be able to meet their needs. The recent global economic and financial crises have generated some distrust between the various market agents and Janeiro (2009) argues that the lack of innovation on the part of national companies is due, above all, to the resistance resulting from a rigid organizational structure, both to their culture and strategic development. The conventional rules that are in place and that hinder the introduction and implementation of new methods, the lack of evaluation in terms of the results obtained by the organizations, the need for additional work resulting from the implementation of new ideas, methods and processes and, finally, the lack of appreciation and rewards for taking the risk associated with the change process are also important barriers that must be considered.

Organizations should have a culture of sustained innovation. However, most organizations are averse to this process due associated risks (Rubiano, 2011). The concepts of Management and Innovation symbolize different ideologies, although innovation cannot be separated from the strategic guidelines of the company in general (Rosário, 2011). The process is the set of all these ideologies, interacting in a coordinated way (Myers & Marquis, 1969). Innovation is not only related to the technological innovation and the management of R&D projects, but also with organizational aspects and the processes of retention of tacit knowledge (Simões, 2015). Measuring innovation is complex, as single metrics are not enough. However, it should be an important objective for a company (Manoochehri, 2010). The literature emphasizes the need to identify more results and a measurement structure based only on product indicators (Ylitalo, 2017).

Measuring Innovation

Innovation requires the transformation of knowledge capital or innovation inputs into innovation outputs (Cirera & Muzi, 2020). This means an adequate planning of activities, realistic objectives, constant monitoring of the development of activities and measurement of results (Chesbrough, 2003; European Commission, 2016). For these reasons, when studying innovation, the emphasis should be placed on measuring all innovation inputs and activities, as well as results, with continued attention to minimizing errors, through careful questions and questionnaire design (Snijkers & Willimack, 2011). Due the qualitative character of innovation, its measurement is very difficult (Acs, Anselin & Varga, 2002; COTEC, 2007; Ernest & Young LLP, 2016) and is possible to have inconsistency of the results obtained in previous research (Coombs & Bierly II, 2006).

The literature presents several ways to measure innovation, as well as processes for doing so. Tale 1 presents some of the existing approaches.

Table 1. Process guidelines for measuring innovation

Researcher	Process Guidelines for Measuring Innovation
Buzzell &Wiersema (1981)	• ROI (Return on Investment) • Market share • Investment intensity • Marketing budget • R&D expenses.
Collier, Mong & Conlin (1984)	• R&D expenses affect profitability expressed in ROI. • However, there are two major gaps in the overall result: o It does not eliminate the effect of other factors such as the intensity of investments and o Considers profitability, at a given moment, as the only measure of the company's performance.
Bower (1986)	• The results of investments in innovation are uncertain and may not be reliable, and the ability to predict the financial consequences of introducing new products is very limited.
Gupta (2008)	• Assessing innovation is a challenge, since effective measures are based on understanding the innovation process (unique in each company) and the relationship between inputs and outputs.
Jensen & Webster (2009)	• There are four main points in the problem of measuring innovation: o Namely in terms of delay o Assessment of novelty o Continuous adjustment o Invisibility. • The slowness of the innovation process, from the concept to its commercialization • The difficulty in evaluating the novelty in terms of products and services, as well as the adjustments of the measurements of the process • The continuous adjustment of the measurement of innovation over time • The innovation activity is considered invisible and is not referenced by conventional methods.
Poças (2016)	• Innovation contributes to the company's competitiveness and allows the company to remain as a leader in the market. • It is also verified that innovation is a differentiating factor in the company and this characteristic it essentially involves opening up to change, investing in quality and a service of excellence.
Richtnér (2017)	• Comprehensive measurement of innovation allows managers to follow up on inputs, the innovation process itself, and its outcomes. • However, excessively detailed measurement of everything harms innovation outcomes. As the saying goes, not everything that can be counted counts, and not everything that counts can be counted.
Taques et al, 2020	• The existing scholarly work doubtlessly displays considerable efforts to account for the evolution experienced by innovation measuring systems at companies. • However, some difficulties persist both in the indicators' technical nature and in the detection of certain innovation types in companies with highly intangible activities, due to today's new market dynamics.

Source: Own elaboration

Innovation Scoring System

As previously seen, measuring innovation is a highly complex process. Nowadays, due to the change and dynamics that characterize the markets, companies must have tools that help them in the decision-making process. Innovation is a guarantee for the development of organizations, but it implies, in general, a large investment that, sometimes, only generates financial return in the medium and long term. In this sense, COTEC Portugal (Business Association for Innovation) has developed a model: Innovation Scoring, whose objective is to allow a better and more assertive assessment of the impact of innovation in organizations.

The first version "Innovation Scoring 1.0" was created in 2007, being accessible only in 2008. Since its launch until today, around 700 companies have joined the System to evaluate their performance in innovation. Ten years later, the model was refined and today "Innovation Scoring 2.0" is used to measure innovation. Based on a digital platform (Innovation Scoring platform), the system automatically generates a free feedback report on the company's performance. This feedback is created thanks to the application of an algorithm to the information, making a comparison with the average and the top performers under expert guidance. With the results obtained, it is possible to recognize the company's strengths as well as areas for improvement. Having been developed over different phases, in a first phase, a benchmarking analysis was carried out in order to identify the critical success factors inherent to the implementation of the system, as well as the inherent difficulties. At the same time, relevant information regarding the project implementation process was collected.

The different systems that make up the Innovation Scoring were classified according to their typology, specifically in business-based systems and nationally based systems, according to the approach promoted by each of these systems. In this sense, while business-based systems are oriented towards performance evaluation at the level of innovation, national-based systems have a more complete view. The pilot model was created in 2006 and was driven by COTEC, to aggregate information on all the efforts inherent to business innovation. Thus, a first Innovation Scoring model was created that would essentially serve to measure results in relation to innovation (COTEC, 2007). It was an initiative that aimed at defining a systematic and sustained innovation model that would allow the strengthening of the competitive advantages of the sectors of an economy, increasingly based on knowledge and globalization.

Through the Innovation Scoring system, which COTEC proposed to implement, it would become possible to advance in relation to the certification of R&D and Innovation management. In practice, the system would allow comparison with what was being done in other countries, either through audit procedures or through self-assessment processes. The pilot project started with a limited number of COTEC member companies, although its objective was greater, in order to make it more dynamic and universal. This initiative was financed by the entities included in the pilot project and by COTEC itself and all its implementation was in charge of a commission and different groups of coordinators. More than a dozen pilot companies participated in this initiative, having held several specific meetings with each of the entities and clarifying the existing doubts. At the same time, suggestions were made to reformulate the questions that were being asked.

Available in 2008, Innovation Scoring 1.0 allowed companies to assess their capabilities and vulnerabilities in the relationship they established with innovation. It was a questionnaire that was divided into 43 questions and four major dimensions: conditions, resources, processes, and results. (COTEC, 2007). Its brief representation is made in Figure 2.

The Conditions dimension concerns all issues related to environmental and strategic aspects that are capable of influencing the way companies deal with innovation. In this sense, it incorporates three aspects: Culture, in which the company's culture is evaluated in relation to the innovation processes and the dynamics that the company presents in relation to change projects, Leadership as an evaluation process of how it is likely to promote innovation within the organization and the Strategy in terms of how to implement strategic guidelines in the organization.

The Resources dimension allows an analysis to be made of how the different resources of the organization can promote dynamics and the innovative and entrepreneurial spirit. In terms of Resources, it is necessary to take into account elements such as Human Capital, through which the way human resources develop an action for innovation is evaluated, Organizational Skills that aim to analyze the competences and the organization's capacity to adopt innovation mechanisms that allow the maintenance of its competitiveness, the External Relationships that aim to evaluate the way the company relates and cooperates with entities linked to the phenomenon of innovation and the Organizational Structures as tools to support innovation activities.

The Processes dimension aims to analyze the most important organizational processes in the scope of innovation and its dynamics in this domain. Fundamentally, the Management of RDI Activities are considered as Process Groups, such as the conception of new products or services, the collaboration between different departments within the organization, the constitution of different teams related to projects, among others, Learning and Systematic Improvement as a mechanism for using good practices related to innovation and the Protection and Valorisation of Results, as basic elements in obtaining conclusions and adopting new behaviors.

The Results dimension aims to assess how the previous three dimensions materialize in results for the organization. These results can be observed according to their Financial nature, evaluating the relationship between the adoption of innovation and the company's profitability, with the Market, assessing the effects at the level of changes in the company's share and with the Society at the level the creation of a qualified company and contributions so that it is possible to ensure sustainable development.

Figure 2. Dimensions of Innovation Scoring 1.0
Source: COTEC, 2007

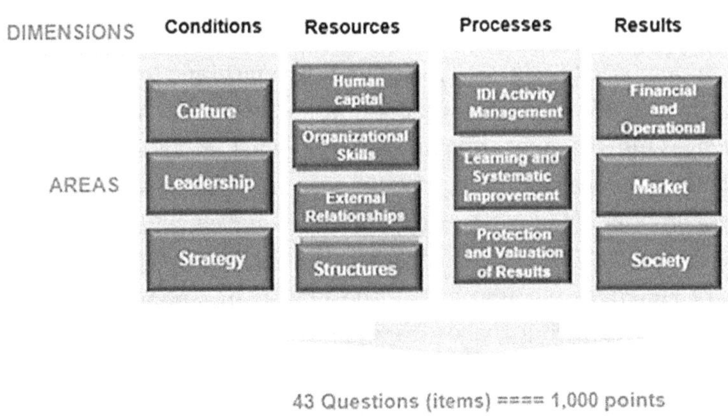

The successful implementation of Innovation Scoring 1.0 induced COTEC to choose to develop the model, promoting an evaluation of the previous model and designed Innovation Scoring 2.0. It has 5 dimensions, divided into several sub-dimensions, making a total of 14 groups. While the dimensions refer to the analysis itself, the sub-dimensions seek to segment the issues that embody the model. The model has 30 main questions (each with maximum associated score) and 16 complementary questions (with closed answer). Are applied 24 accounting indicators and 56 quantitative indicators are. With regard to scoring, Innovation Scoring 2.0 uses a double scale, similar to Innovation Scoring 1.0: approach and application. The approach is focused on the way the company views the different themes and the perspective it has according to the various subjects inherent to it. The application is linked to the way the company effectively operates in the aspects in question and to the involvement of employees. The overall score is the result of all scores from all questions asked. The goal is for the global score to be as high as possible, which can be between 0 (minimum) and 1000 (maximum). Innovation Scoring 2.0 resulted, as previously seen, from the experience and knowledge acquired over the duration of Innovation Scoring 1.0.

According to COTEC (2016, p. 7), entity linked to the genesis and development of this innovation management tool, Innovation Scoring 2.0 presents seven major changes compared to the previous model, more specifically: "(I) new structure with more dimensions and sub-dimensions than the previous model, incorporating new conceptual domains such as financing, diversity and design, however (II) containing 30 questions, less than the 43 of the previous version. The number of justifications required was also reduced (III), with a justification field being available only at the end of each sub-dimension. (IV) The double scale started to be applied also in the dimension of impacts and its descriptive adjusted to each dimension. The possibility of capturing additional relevant information was introduced through the introduction of (V) complementary closed-answer questions and (VI) quantitative indicators. Within the framework of the results shared with each company after completing the respective questionnaire, the new generation of Innovation Scoring will allow (VII) to compare the audited results of the organization with those of other companies, as well as to select the sample and the level of detail of the intended comparisons".

Innovation and Sustainability

More and more companies are interested in firm-based innovation practices and processes for creating value in terms of economic, social, and environmental levels (Gupta, Rudd & Lee, 2014), where economics objectives appears in parallel (Adams et al, 2016; Klewitz & Hansen, 2014). Innovation is one of the most effective strategies for businesses looking for to contribute to sustainable development (Hall & Vredenburg, 2003). Nevertheless, the addition of new social and environmental goals brings in extra complexity and challenges into the innovation process (Hansen, Grosse-Dunker & Reichwald, 2009). To undertake such challenges, companies frequently connect in alliances with other organizations, allowing mutual access and combination of compulsory resources and capabilities (Goodman, Korsunova, & Halme, 2017; Holmes& Smart, 2009; Inigo, Albareda, & Ritala, 2017).

The textile industry generates big impacts on the planet. It generates, for example, big volumes of water (Chen et al., 2017), throwing away toxic metals in the soil, the air and the water (San et al., 2018). In fact, the textile industry is the world's oldest branch of consumer goods manufacturing. It is a diverse and "heterogeneous sector which covers the entire production chain of transforming natural and chemical fibres (such as cotton, wool, and oil) into end-user goods, including garments, household goods, and industrial textiles" (European Comission, 2013). Currently, one main concern is to achieve sustainability in the textile chain (Amindoust & Saghafinia, 2016). Producers and retailers are the mostly driving players responsible for guarantee the need improvements in sustainability of textiles, as well as enhance consumer awareness. The textile industry is clearly ready for innovative solutions, as obvious in the determined sustainability targets set by many large brands and retailers, some of which are not attainable without innovation (Fashion For Good, 2019).

Textile Industry

The importance of the textile sector in global terms is undeniable, as it is widespread in practically all countries in the world, guaranteeing the production of wealth and economic and social development. In this sense, in relation to 2018, the main global textile exporters belonged to different continents, with

China standing out as the world leader in textile exports, followed by the European Union (28), India and the United States, as can be seen on Figure 3. According to data from World Trade Statistic Review 2019, the first three countries together accounted for approximately 66.9% of world textile exports, thus realizing the importance of the textile sector in the global economy.

Figure 3. Top Ten Textile Exporters 2018, Billion USD and Annual Percentage Change
Source: Lu, S. WTO 2019

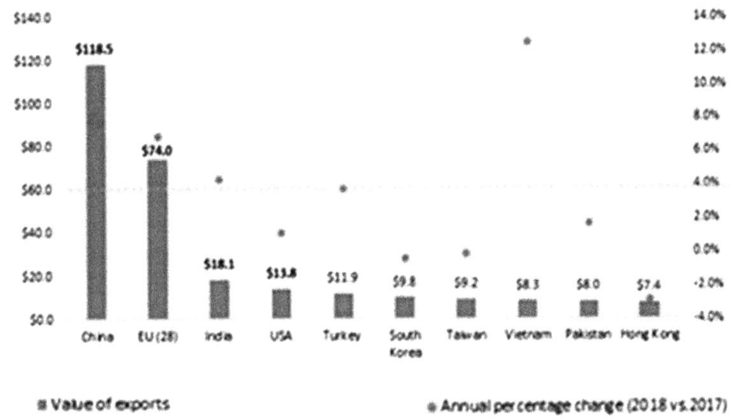

The European Union (28), the United States and China were the three largest textile importers, reaching 37.5% of total imports worldwide in 2018. Although their market shares in 2018 were close to 37.7% a year earlier, however, was much lower in the 2000s, reaching just over 50%.

In national terms, the Portuguese Textile and Clothing Industry, according to AICEP, is characterized by the high "quality, innovation, design and technology" leading to that it can be associated with "development and research that allowed its growing international recognition" (COTEC 2016, p. 7). According to the Textile and Clothing Industry (2012) in the last decades, the Portuguese industry has gone through several obstacles and difficulties, and for this reason it was forced to transform itself, once again, to assert itself. The first signs of difficulty appeared in 2001, with the entry of the People's Republic of China in the World Trade Organization, the enlargement of the European Union to some countries in the East ended up forcing concrete measures, since competition with these countries passes not be bearable.

According to the National Statistics Institute (INE), all the textile companies that survived the 2008 crisis, are distinguished by their flexibility, quality, and timely response. In national terms, the weight of the textile sector in the economy is undeniable. According to AICEP (2018, p. 8) between 2013 and 2018, exports of the Portuguese textile and clothing industry grew by about 5% and, in global terms, these exports represent around 0.75% of total exports. The main export markets for the national textile and clothing industry are Spain (33.8%), France (12.56%), Germany (8.69%) and the United Kingdom (7.96%). The Portuguese textile industry has a strong export component, constituting about 80% of production and destined for 189 countries, according to the referred organization. It employs about 152 thousand direct workers through family-owned SMEs with a strong knowledge of the business and involvement at the management level, according to Silva (2018). Today the Portuguese textile industry is worldwide known for its high quality and innovation. It is a highly demanding sector and the existence of tools to assess its degree of innovation becomes fundamental. Challenges like uncontrolled consumption, rapid climate change, population risks and technological development, among others, led to a change in the profile of companies in the textile sector. This change, namely through Digitization - IoT - (Internet of Things), Dimension, Differentiation, and Capitalization quick change the competitive arena (Textile and Clothing Industry, 2012, p. 17-19).

EMPIRICAL EVIDENCE AND RESULTS

Methodology and Research Question

Methodology and Objectives

In the present research study, it was chose to use a quantitative methodology and the working instrument was the questionnaire of the Innovation Scoring 1.0 system (already tested and validated in about 700 companies), using the Excel support tool to proceed with the calculations made. This version was chosen because it is a version already known by the Director General of the Portuguese textile company and because he was responsible for requesting this particular tool. Although he had references of the added value of its use in competing companies, the Director-General had never had the opportunity to try it in this company and was curious to deepen knowledge that would bring him quick answers to real problems.

The research question that gave rise to this study was "How can Textile ABC improve its performance, aiming at efficiency and increasing profitability?". In addition to the research question, as general objectives, it was proposed: 1) to carry out two diagnoses to a company in the textile sector in two different time periods (July 2018 and July 2019); 2) to propose suggestions for improvement for the company, in order to maximize its effectiveness / profitability. With the specific objectives, it is additionally intended: 1) to explore the complexity of the theme related to innovation management; 2) to theoretically compare the Innovation Scoring 1.0 system with the Innovation Scoring 2.0 system and 3) to apply the Innovation Scoring 1.0 system to the company's reality.

Questionnaire Description

The questionnaire used was the questionnaire developed by COTEC for the Innovation Scoring 1.0 system. With the questionnaire, a User Manual was sent, sufficiently descriptive, in order to avoid misunderstanding about the content of the topics to be addressed. The questionnaire is divided into 4 dimensions (Conditions, Resources, IDI Processes and Results) and presents 43 questions. All main questions are scored according to a double scale, which aims to characterize each theme from two different perspectives:

1. **Approach**: how the organization views each theme and its perspective on the various issues related to it.
2. **Application**: how the organization acts in relation to the aspects in question and the degree of involvement of employees in this implementation.

In the present study, it was only approached the "Application" perspective. In order to facilitate the understanding of each question, the scoring scale is also specific to each dimension, with a weighted value associated with each question, a value to which each selected option is given a weight. Throughout the questionnaire, the cumulative scores for each dimension are calculated, which result from the sum of the weightings assigned to the questions, by dimension.

The overall score (that is, the final innovation score) is the sum of the scores for all the asked questions.

Data Collection

The data were collected in a textile company, located in the north of Portugal and operating in the national and international market. It is a Small and Medium Company in the Dyeing and Finishing sector, with about 100 workers, most of whom have the High School. It began by conducting a face-to-face interview with the Director General, where the objectives of the study were explained, and authorization was requested to send the questionnaire. The questionnaire was sent electronically, accompanied by a supporting document, with a brief explanation about the Innovation Scoring system.

The questionnaire was completed by the company's General Director, responsible at the highest level and who knew the system, although he never applied it in the organization. This analysis was carried out in two different periods, the first in July 2018 and the second in July 2019.

After data collection and before the diagnosis was made, there was a new face-to-face meeting to try to understand what, in the opinion of the person in charge, could have happened and which could justify any deviations that might be verified.

Analysis of Results

As previously saw, each question in the questionnaire has an associated weighted value; according to this value, a weight is assigned to each selected option, in this specific case, within the "Application" sector. Dividing the weighting value by 5, since there are 5 possible answer options (weak, poorly developed, reasonable, very developed, and excellent). The obtained value corresponds to the selection of the first option, '' Weak '' (values represented by the pink column). It was essential that the questionnaire was carefully completed and as detailed as possible, so that the result of the audit can be carried out based on all relevant data.

COMPANY GLOBAL SCORE

With regard to the company's Global Score in 2018, the score was obtained through the weighted average of the score of the 43 questions analyzed in the four dimensions of the Innovation Scoring System and respective aspects; the value rises to 834 points, corresponding to 83.4% (Figure 4).

Next figure (Figure 5), represents, in an intuitive way, the comparison of the different classifications attributed to the analyzed dimensions in the Innovation Scoring. The dimension Results achieved the best classification, with 268 (89.3%) of the score, followed by the dimensions Processes and Conditions, with 227 (87.3%) and 176 (80.0%), respectively. Finally, there is the Resources dimension, which obtained 163 (74.1%).

About the company's Global Score in 2019, the score was obtained in a similar way as Global Score in 2018. The total value rises to 752 points, corresponding to 75,2% (Figure 6). It reveals a decrease of 8.2% when compared to 2018.

Figure 4. Global Company Score in 2018 (bar chart)
Source: own elaboration

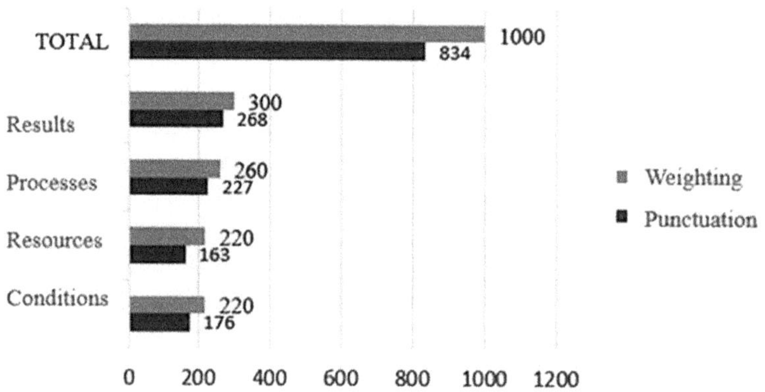

Figure 5. Global Company Score in 2018 (radar chart)
Source: Own elaboration

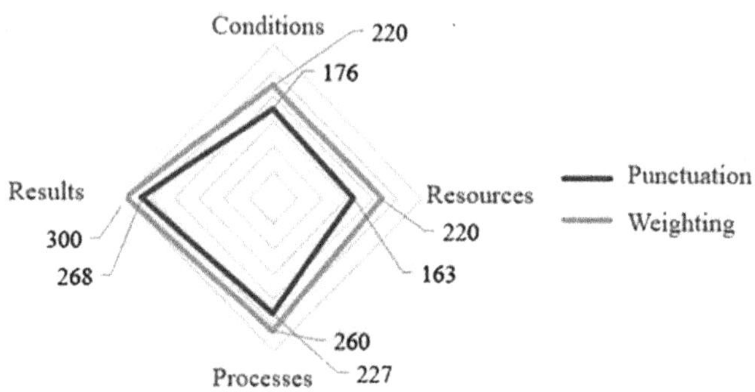

Figure 6. Global Company Score in 2019 (bar chart)
Source: Own elaboration

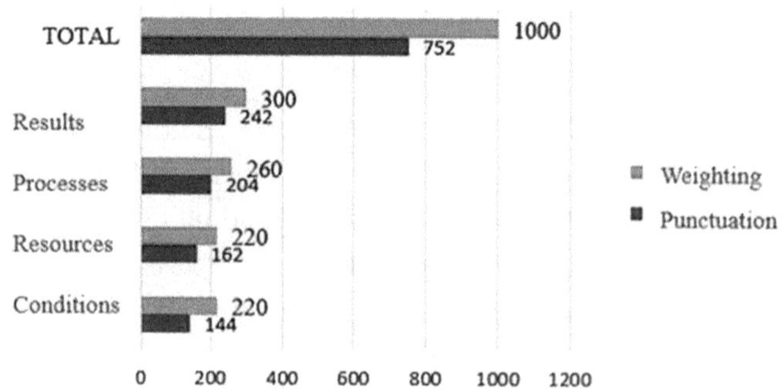

Next figure (Figure 7), represents, in an intuitive way, the comparison of the different classifications attributed to the analysed dimensions in the Innovation Scoring. The dimension Results achieved the best classification, with 242 (80,7%) of the score, followed by the dimensions Processes and Resources, with 204 (78.5%) and 162 (73.6%), respectively. Finally, there is the Conditions dimension, which obtained 144 (65.5%). In relation to the previous year, the most significant drop is seen in the Conditions dimension, with a difference of 14.5%.

Figure 7. Global Company Score in 2019 (radar chart)
Source: Own elaboration

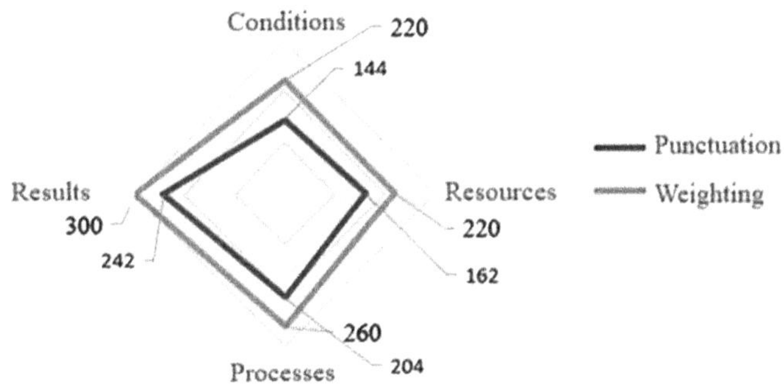

The Processes and Results dimensions registered an equally sharp drop, reaching 78.5% and 80.7%, respectively. The Resources dimension is where there is a smaller fall, obtaining the classification of 73.6%, with the registered fall being only 0.5%. In summary, the change observed (Table 2) leads us to conclude that the Conditions and Resources dimensions are those with the lowest values in both 2018 and 2019, which is why we have chosen to only scrutinize the results of these dimensions.

Table 2. Comparison of Quotients obtained in 2018 and 2019

Dimension	2018	2019
	Quotient	**Quotient**
Conditions	0,8	0,655
Resources	0,741	0,736
Processes	0,873	0,785
Results	0,893	0,807
TOTAL	0,834	0,752

Source: Own elaboration

SCORE OF RESOURCES DIMENSION

The Resources dimension encompasses Human Capital, Skills, External Relationships and Structures. Table 3 represents the values obtained in July 2018.

When analyzing the Resources dimension, it appears that the company does not properly promote the external links it has. Human Capital (with three questions) and External Relationships (with two questions) were the sub-dimensions that had the lowest score, obtaining a rating of 54.5% and 60% respectively (Figure 8).

Table 3. Company Resources Dimension Results on 2018

Dimension	Subgroup	Punctuation	Weighting	Quotient
Resources 74,1%	Human Capital	30	55	54,5%
	Skills	75	90	83,3%
	External Relationships	18	30	60,0%
	Structures	40	45	88,9%

Source: Own elaboration

Figure 8. Positioning of the Enterprise Resources Dimension on Results on 2018
Source: Own elaboration

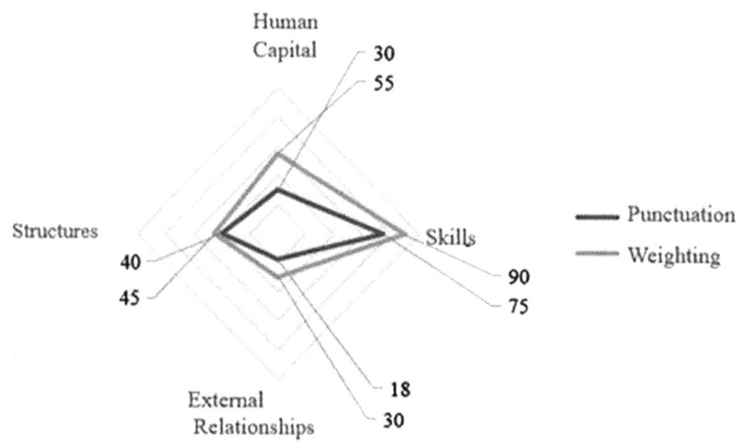

In 2019, the values recorded were substantially different, with the following Table (Table 4) and Figure (Figure 9) representing the values obtained in July 2019.

Table 4. Results of the Enterprise Resources Dimension in 2019

Dimension	Subgroup	Punctuation	Weighting	Quotient
Resources 73,6%	Human Capital	30	55	54,5%
	Skills	69	90	76,7%
	External Relationships	30	30	100,0%
	Structures	33	45	73,3%

Source: Own elaboration

Results pointed a small decrease in the Resources dimension in the order of 0.5%, compared to the previous year (2018). Although there has been no major change, it is useful to try to understand what may have resulted in this result. In this sense, the following paragraphs will analyze, in detail, each of the sub-dimensions considered, namely Human Capital, Skills, External Relationships and Structures.

Figure 9. Positioning of the Enterprise Resources Dimension in 2019
Source: Own elaboration

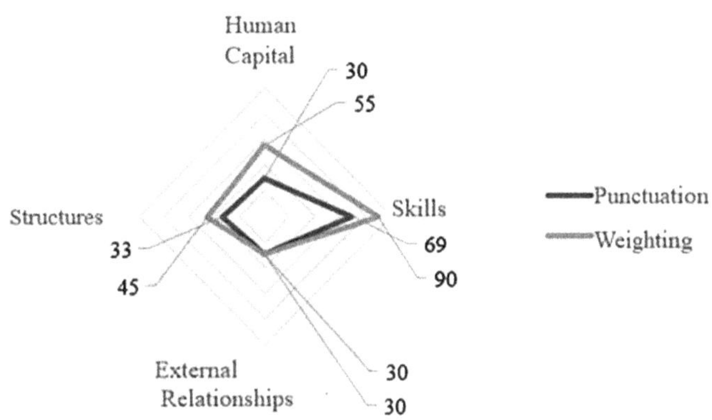

Human Capital

The analysis of this vector has as main objective to evaluate the way in which the organization's human resources management is directed towards innovation, mainly with regard to the human capital policy, the training policy and the way the company stimulates and invests in the creativity and initiative of its employees (COTEC, 2007). This vector is analyzed according to three questions having obtained the classification of 30 points in the two analyzed periods (2018 and 2019), which, in turn, correspond to 54.5%, as shown in Table 5, being the vector with the lowest classification of the Resources dimension.

Table 5. Human Capital Subgroup

Subgroup	2018	2019
Human Capital	54,5%	54,5%

Source: Own elaboration

Table 6. Skills Subgroup

Subgroup	2018	2019
Skills	83,3%	76,7%

Source: Own elaboration

Skills

The observation of the Skills vector includes the analysis of the competences and capacities inherent to the company, which are more relevant to promote its innovative performance and consequently its competitive affirmation (COTEC, 2007). This assessment aims to assess the identification of the company's specific and technical skills for the management and performance of RDI, production and service and marketing activities. This subgroup was analyzed through five questions and was classified with 75 points, corresponding to 83.3% in 2018, being marked by a decrease this year, obtaining a classification of 69 points, corresponding to 76.7%, as can be seen verify by observing Table 6.

External Relationships

When analyzing this aspect, we seek to ascertain how the company promotes and takes advantage of external links with different entities to boost innovation (COTEC, 2007). This aspect is analyzed through two questions having obtained the classification of 18 points, in the year 2018, which correspond to 60% (Table 7). Note that there is a great evolution of this vector from the previous year to this year, having obtained the classification of 3 points, corresponding to 100% (Table 6), it should be noted that this vector has the best result within the dimension Resources, thus being able to affirm that the company has been systematically developing cooperation actions in innovation with external entities.

Table 7. External Relationships Subgroup

Subgroup	2018	2019
External Relationships	60%	100%

Source: Own elaboration

Structures

The Structures vector, the last of the Resources dimension, has the main objective of identifying the organizational structures of the company that support the activities of innovation and knowledge management, including the information and communication system (COTEC, 2007). This vector is analyzed based on three questions and was classified with 40 points in 2018, which corresponds to 88.9%. There is a decrease of 15.6%, since it obtains only 73.3% of classification in the year 2019 (Table 8).

Table 8. Structures Subgroup

Subgroup	2018	2019
Structures	88,9%	73,3%

Source: Own elaboration

SCORE OF DIMENSION CONDITIONS

In the Conditions dimension of the Innovation Scoring system, the main objective is to verify the extent to which the company's attitudes and behaviors in the domain of innovation dynamics are influenced by its environmental and strategic aspects (COTEC, 2007). This dimension is subdivided into three subgroups, namely Culture, Leadership and Strategy. The following table (Table 9) and Figure 10 represent the values obtained in July 2018.

Table 9. Results of the Company Conditions Dimension in 2018

Dimension	Subgroup	Punctuation	Weighting	Quotient
Conditions 80,0%	Culture	64	75	85,3%
	Leadership	66	70	94,3%
	Strategy	46	75	61,3%

Source: Own elaboration

Figure 10. Positioning of the Company Conditions Dimension in 2018
Source: Own elaboration

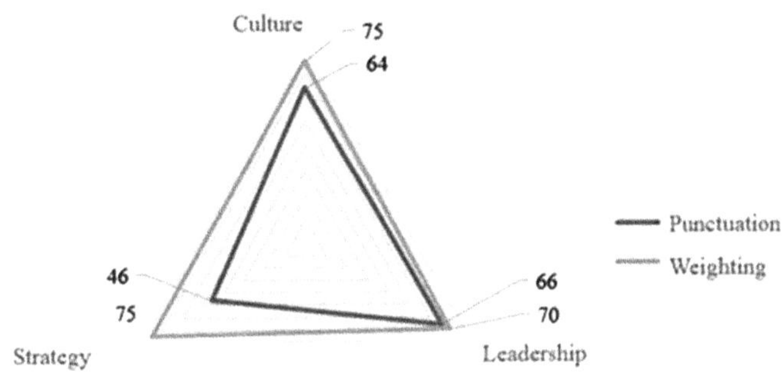

Table 10. Results of the Company Conditions Dimension in 2019

Dimension	Subgroup	Punctuation	Weighting	Quotient
Conditions 65,5%	Culture	64	75	85,3%
	Leadership	42	70	60,0%
	Strategy	38	75	50,7%

Source: Own elaboration

Figure 11. Positioning of the Company Conditions Dimension in 2019
Source: own elaboration

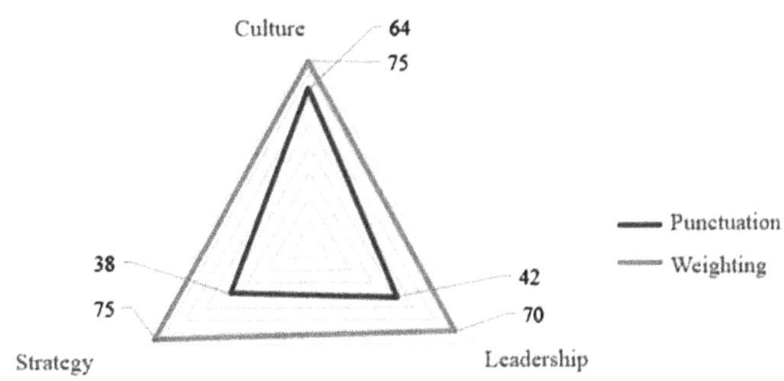

From reading Table 8 and Figure 10, this dimension obtained a classification of 80% in 2018, being considered the second dimension with the worst classification in relation to the four dimensions analyzed in the Innovation Scoring system.

In 2019, the recorded values were substantially different, representing the following table (Table 10) and Figure 11 the values obtained in July 2019.

By observing Table 9 and Figure 11, it is possible to affirm that there is a drop of 14.5%, in relation to the previous year, and the classification obtained in 2019 is 65.5%. The following paragraphs will analyze, in detail, each of the sub-dimensions considered, namely Culture, Leadership and Strategy.

Culture

The company's culture can be defined as the set of values and beliefs shared by all its employees (COTEC, 2007). This vector is analyzed based on 4 questions having in the present study obtained, in the 2 analyzed periods, the classification of 64 points, corresponding to 85.3%.

The analysis of this vector allows us to conclude that the company has, in a linear and constant manner, a well-defined and disseminated culture, with its positioning in the third quantile (Table 11).

Table 11. Subgroup Culture

Subgroup	2018	2019
Culture	85,3%	85,3%

Source: Own elaboration

Leadership

With the analysis of Leadership, we intend to assess how the characteristics and leadership style of the company are likely to stimulate its innovation process, particularly with regard to the attitudes and obligations assumed by top management and the way in which the structures of leadership promote, or not, the emergence of leaders (COTEC, 2007). This subgroup is evaluated based on 4 questions. In 2018, we obtained 66 points, corresponding to 94.3% (Table 17). It was the vector that represented the highest relative classification of the Conditions dimension, in the year 2018. This may mean that the company has a strong capacity to adapt to changes in the market. In 2019, the same is not true, since this vector suffers a drop in its classification, having then 42 points, corresponding to 60% (Table 12).

Table 12. Subgroup Leadership

Subgroup	2018	2019
Leadership	94,3%	60%

Source: Own elaboration

Strategy

This vector acts to evaluate the way the company creates its strategy and executes the respective strategic guidelines. This theme comprises the innovation and marketing strategy and the monitoring of the external environment by the Company (COTEC, 2007). The strategy is analyzed based on 4 questions. Through the observation of the following Table (Table 13) it is possible to see that the Strategy vector fell by 10.6% in relation to the previous year (2018), having obtained a classification in 2019 of 38 points, corresponding to 50.7%.

Table 13. Subgroup Strategy

Subgroup	2018	2019
Strategy	61,3%	50,7%

Source: own elaboration

DISCUSSION

According to the dimensions analyzed, it appears that the worst results are in terms of Resources and Conditions, as can be confirmed by observing the following Table (Table 14). In view of the scenario, we try to understand with the responsible person, what are the possible events that could possibly have happened and that justified the obtained results.

Table 14. Main differences between 2018 and 2019

Dimensions	Subgroup	2018	2019
Resources	Human Capital	54,50%	54,50%
	Skills	83,30%	76,70%
	External Relationships	60%	100%
	Structures	88,90%	73,33%
Conditions	Culture	85,30%	85,30%
	Leadership	94,30%	60%
	Strategy	61,30%	50,70%

Source: Own elaboration

A possible justification for recording relatively low values in the Resources dimension, in the Human Capital subgroup, may be the lack of motivation of employees, not only due to the death of two colleagues, but also due to changes that the company has been undergoing since 2018 at the level of the initial part of the process, since the machinery in this sector is being replaced and the employees are still in an adaptation phase.

The Skills subgroup has decreased, and one of the reasons that may have led to these values may be the fact that in the company employees receive mandatory training (30 hours per year), but this does not take into account the profile and the role of the employee.

As for the External Relationships subgroup, there was a marked growth, with the company systematically developing cooperation actions in innovation with external entities and participating in Sector and Trade Fairs, which leads to an increase in new external contacts. Its participation in business missions was an asset, in the sense that it helped to realize that the challenges of the textile industry are a reality today, forcing it to work more closely with its suppliers and customers.

As for the Structures subgroup, it should be noted that the company's organizational structure underwent unexpected changes in 2019, due to the death of two employees who held leadership positions in the departments where they were inserted. As long-term employees in the company and with no prompt replacement, it appears as a solution to unite these departments, which may have justified, according to the company's General Director, the decrease that occurred in this subgroup.

About the Conditions dimension, the Culture subgroup maintained a considerably high value, leading to the conclusion that the company follows a defined and well-publicized culture. As for the Leadership subgroup, the change in the results can be justified by the fact that unexpected changes were made in management positions in two sectors of the company, as above mentioned.

About the Strategy subgroup, everything seems to conclude, based on the recorded values, that the company does not currently have a well-defined and structured innovation strategy. After carrying out the analysis of the different dimensions, having discussed the results and talked to the Director General of the company under study, the suggestions we proposed were as follows. Thus, the company must:

- Develop cooperation actions with other companies / partners; in order to create synergies for eventual cost reductions and increase in solutions for market needs.
- Develop and establish partnerships or alliances with other National or International Companies to share knowledge relevant to Innovation and cooperate in terms of Research and Development. The approach to companies upstream or downstream of the value chain may facilitate access to trends and technological surveillance. In the case of the company in question, it may be interesting to study the hypothesis of product innovation, in order to evolve in the value chain and add highly differentiating results.
- Support programs to promote Research in the Business Environment with hosting Universities or other areas of Education and Technological Centres.
- Promote innovation activities and encourage employees to integrate these activities.
- Develop skills and create conditions for the implementation of a more dynamic and structured strategy.
- Make a diagnosis of the type of training required and promote training actions (internal and external) accordingly.
- Promote and encourage collaboration between different departments, while simultaneously implementing other practices, such as Brainstorming and internal workshops for generating ideas and involving managers at different levels.
- Promote the systematic evaluation of the company's innovation activities, considering its continuous monitoring as a priority.
- Sensitize employees to the process of adopting good practices and the competitive advantages they can bring, both at an individual and organizational level.

To complement in a more structured way all the proposed above suggestions, and in order to combat the different flaws that exist in the company, it is also proposed to develop Benchmarking system, so that it is implemented as a tool management of the company's analysis and comparative performance. In this sense, a team of managers with the necessary skills and knowledge must be created in order to interweave the company's strategy with the desired results.

SOLUTIONS AND RECOMMENDATIONS

As the main limitations it is pointed out the fact that the questionnaire must be filled by other departments, being not enough the opinion of a singular (the Director General in the present case). Alternatively, the study could have been carried out by an external team. Another limitation is related to the fulfilment of perspective ''Application'' instead of filling in the two aspects (Application and Approach). Being a Textile Dyeing and Finishing company, the study should have focused more the product component and development.

FUTURE RESEARCH DIRECTIONS

For future studies, we recommend the application of Innovation Scoring 2.0. Whenever possible, it would be interesting for the questionnaires to be filled out by the different departments of the company. Additionally, it is suggested that the Innovation Scoring system presents a part exclusively oriented towards the product component, depending on the importance it presents in terms of innovation.

CONCLUSION

The use of the Innovation Scoring tool can be a valuable tool for the diagnosis of a company, in what concerns innovation. In the present study, the application of the Innovation Scoring 1.0 allowed company to evaluate its performance regarding innovation. The worst identified results were linked with Resources and Conditions. A possible justification maybe linked with the lack of motivation of employees and the lack of adaptability to technological change. The mandatory training does not consider the employee's profile and function, a weakness that can generate very negative results in the medium and long term. The company has been systematically developing cooperation actions in innovation with external entities and participates in Sector and Trade Fairs. Therefore, it increases the network of external contacts and sensitizes the manager to the challenges of the textile industry – a good tactic for competing in the medium and long term.

The study also showed that teamwork is necessary and the dissemination of knowledge by all is essential so that the unexpected absence of a manager does not cause irreversible damage to the entire production unit. The company studied has a defined and well-publicized culture. Being, in general, associated with the values that govern actions and behaviours within a company, its Human Resources do their work better and contribute to the growth of the organization. People seem to be satisfied with this sub-dimension. There is a strong leadership, which may mean that top management is truly involved, knows the business, and understands that innovation is also one of the competitive advantages that can guarantee the company's sustainability. However, company does not currently have a well-defined and structured innovation strategy.

In general, it is possible to conclude that Innovation Scoring allows comparative analysis of the results to be made, identifying the evolution registered in the companies in terms of innovation and the profile of existing innovation in companies according to the obtained classifications. As an added value, this system has the advantage of allowing companies to know, in a very deep way, their skills and limitations in terms of innovation, allowing the leverage of the former and the correction of the latter, thus obtaining advantages competitive.

REFERENCES

Acs, Z., Anselin, L., & Varga, A. (2002). Patents and innovation counts as measures of regional production of new knowledge. *Research Policy*, *31*(7), 1069–1085. doi:10.1016/S0048-7333(01)00184-6

Adams, R., Jeanrenaud, S., Bessant, J., Denyer, D., & Overy, P. (2016). Sustainability-oriented innovation: A systematic review. *International Journal of Management Reviews*, *18*(2), 180–205. doi:10.1111/ijmr.12068

AICEP. (2018). Indústria Têxtil e de Vestuário - Uma referência a nível mundial. *Revista Portugal Global*, *113*, 8–9.

Alegre, J. & Chiva, R. (2008). Assessing the impact of organizational learning capability on product innovation performance: an empirical test. *Technovation*, *28*(1:2), 315-326.

Amindoust, A., & Saghafinia, A. (2016). Textile supplier selection in sustainable supply chain using a modular fuzzy inference system model. *Journal of Industrial Textiles*, *108*(7), 1250–1258.

Beechler, S., & Woodward, I. (2009). The global "war for talent". *Journal of International Management*, *15*(3), 273–285. doi:10.1016/j.intman.2009.01.002

Bower, J. (1986). *When Markets Quake Cambridge*. M.A. Harvard.

Buzzell, D., & Wiersema, F. (1981). Modelling changes in market share: A cross-sectional analysis. *Strategic Management Journal*, *2*(1), 27–42. doi:10.1002mj.4250020104

Caraça, J., Ferreira, J., & Mendonça, S. (2006). *Desenvolvimento Sustentado da Inovação Empresarial - Modelos de Inovação*. COTEC Portugal.

Cerveira, A. (2009). *Empreendedorismo e inovação. O caso da Crioestaminal*. Relatório de Estágio. Faculdade de Economia da Universidade de Coimbra.

Chen, L., Wang, L., Wu, X., & Ding, X. (2017). A process-level water conservation and pollution control performance evaluation tool of cleaner production technology in textile industry. *Journal of Cleaner Production*, *143*, 1137–1143. doi:10.1016/j.jclepro.2016.12.006

Chesbrough, H. (2003). *Open Innovation: The New Imperative for Creating and Profiting from Technology*. Harvard Business Press.

Chesbrough, H. (2012). *Inovação aberta: como criar e lucrar com a tecnologia*. Porto Alegre: Bookman.

Cirera, X., & Muzi, S. (2020). Measuring innovation using firm-level surveys: Evidence from developing countries. *Research Policy*, *49*(3), 1039122. doi:10.1016/j.respol.2019.103912

Clayton, T., Borgo, M. D., Haskel, J., & Franklin, M. (2010). *Measuring Creativity and Innovation Based on Knowledge Capital Investment*. Publications Office of the EU.

Collier, D., Mong, J., & Conlin, J. (1984), How effective is technological innovation? *Research Management*, *27*(5), 11-16.

Coombs, J., & Bierly, I. I. P. (2006). Measuring technological capability and performance. *R & D Management*, *36*(4), 421–438. doi:10.1111/j.1467-9310.2006.00444.x

COTEC. (2007). *Manual de Apoio ao Preenchimento do Sistema de Innovation Scoring da COTEC*. COTEC Portugal.

COTEC. (2016). *Innovation Scoring – Relatório de Avaliação do modelo*. COTEC Portugal.

Drucker, P. (1985). Opportunities to innovate: the seven sources. Innovation and Entrepreneurship. Butterworth Heinemann.

Engel, K., Dirlea, V., Dyer, S., & Graff, J. (2015). *Strategy & Leadership*. Newcastle University. Emerald Insight.

Ernest & Young LLP. (2016). R*&D investment execution*. Author.

European Comission. (2013). *Sustainability of textiles*. Retail Forum for Sustainability. Paper nº 11, August 2013.

European Commission. (2016). *Open Innovation Open Science Open to the World - a vision for Europe*. European Commission, Directorate-General for Research and Innovation.

Faria, A. (2008). *Redes de conhecimento e inovação*. Rede 2020.

Fashion For Good. (2019). *Investing in Textile Innovation. The opportunities for investors in the textile and apparel innovation ecosystem*. Author.

Freeman, C. (1982). *The economics of industrial revolution*. MIT Press.

Godinho, M. (2003). Inovação: conceitos e perspectivas fundamentais. In M. J. Rodrigues, A. Neves, & M. M. Godinho (Eds.), Para uma política de inovação em Portugal. Lisboa: Publicações Dom Quixote, Lda.

González-Fernández, M., & González-Velasco, C. (2018). Innovation and Corporate Performance in the Spanish Regions. *Journal of Policy Modelin*.

Goodman, J., Korsunova, A., & Halme, M. (2017). Our collaborative future: Activities and roles of stakeholders in sustainability-oriented innovation. *Business Strategy and the Environment*, *26*(6), 731–753. doi:10.1002/bse.1941

Gupta, P. (2008). *Inovação empresarial no século xxi*. G. E. Económica.

Gupta, S., Rudd, J., & Lee, N. (2014). Special Issue on Integrating marketing and operations for business sustainability. *Industrial Marketing Management*, *43*(1), 1–176. doi:10.1016/j.indmarman.2013.10.004

Hall, J., & Wagner, M. (2012). Integrating Sustainability into Firms' Processes: Performance Effects and the Moderating Role of Business Models and Innovation. *Business Strategy and the Environment*, *21*(3), 183–196. doi:10.1002/bse.728

Hansen, E. G., Grosse-Dunker, F., & Reichwald, R. (2009). Sustainability Innovation Cube – A Framework to Evaluate Sustainability-Oriented Innovations. *International Journal of Innovation Management*, *13*(4), 683–713. doi:10.1142/S1363919609002479

Hekkert, M. P., Suurs, R. R. A., Negro, S. A., Kuhlmann, S., & Smitsa, R. E. (2007). Functions of innovation systems: A new approach for analysing technological change. *Technological Forecasting and Social Change*, *74*(4), 413–432. doi:10.1016/j.techfore.2006.03.002

Henderson, R. & Clark, K. (1990). Architectural Innovation: The reconfiguring of existing product, technologies and the failure of established firms. *Administrative Science Quaterly*, 9-30.

Homes, S., & Smart, P. (2009). Exploring open innovation practice in firm-nonprofit engagement: A corporate social responsability perspective. *Research for Development*, *39*(4), 394–409.

Indústria Têxtil e do Vestuário. (2012). *Roadmap para a Inovação 2012>>2020*. Academic Press.

Inigo, E. A., & Albareda, I. (2019). Sustainability oriented innovation dynamics: Levels of dynamic capabilities and their path-dependent and self-reinforcing logics. *Technological Forecasting and Social Change*, *139*, 334–351. doi:10.1016/j.techfore.2018.11.023

Janeiro, P. (2009). *Barreiras à Inovação*. Editora de Negócios.

Jensen, P., & Webster, E. (2009). Another Look at the Relationship between Innovation Proxies. *Australian Economic Papers*, *48*(3), 252–269. doi:10.1111/j.1467-8454.2009.00374.x

Klewitz, J., & Hansen, E. G. (2014, February). Sustainability-oriented innovation of SMEs: A systematic review. *Journal of Cleaner Production*, *65*(15), 57–75. doi:10.1016/j.jclepro.2013.07.017

Lu, S. (2019). *FASH455 Global Apparel & Textile Trade and Sourcing*. WTO Reports World Textile and Apparel Trade in 2018.

Manoochehri, G. (2010). Measuring Innovation: Challenges and Best Practices. California. *Journal of Operations Management*, *8*(1).

Myers, S. & Marquis, D.G. (1969). *Successful industrial innovations. A study of factors Underlying Innovation in Selected Firms*. Academic Press.

OCDE. (2005). *Manual de Oslo: Diretrizes para a recolha e interpretação de dados sobre a inovação* (3rd ed.). Paris: Author.

Patton, J. (2007). Metrics for Knowledge-based project organizations. *Advanced Management Journal*, *71*(1).

Pinto, H. (2012). *Inovação estratégica na indústria têxtil e do vestuário nacional: estudo de caso.* Dissertação de Mestrado. Universidade do Minho.

Poças, A. (2015). *O contributo da inovação para a competitividade das organizações Estudo de caso.* Instituto Politécnico de Viana do Castelo.

Ramesh, B., Dieguez, T., Ferreira, L. P., & Silva, F. J. G. (2018). A Strategy to Reinforce the Textile and Clothing Sector Cluster in Portugal. *Transdisciplinary Engineering Methods for Social Innovation of Industry 4.0: Proceedings of the 25th ISPE.*

Rech, S. R. (2006). *Cadeia produtiva da moda: um modelo conceitual de análise da competitividade no elo confecção.* Tese (Doutorado em Engenharia de Produção). Universidade Federal de Santa Catarina – Programa de Pós-Graduação em Engenharia de Produção.

Richtnér, A. (2017). *Creating Better Innovation Measurement Practices.* Academic Press.

Rosário, I. (2011). *Gestão de Inovação numa empresa de serviços de engenharia civil.* Dissertação de Mestrado da Faculdade de Engenharia da Universidade do Porto, Mestrado em Engenharia Civil – Especialização em Construções.

Rubiano, D. (2011). *Risco, Incerteza e aversão à inovação: o Setor de Automação Industrial e a Demanda Tecnológica da Indústria de Petróleo e Gás Natural no Brasil.* Dissertação de Mestrado do Instituto de Economia da Universidade Federal do Rio de Janeiro, Mestrado em Ciências Económicas.

San, V., Spoann, V., & Schmidt, J. (2018). Industrial pollution load assessment in Phonm Penh, Cambodia using an industrial pollution projection system. *The Science of the Total Environment, 615*, 990–999. doi:10.1016/j.scitotenv.2017.10.006 PMID:29751449

Santos, G., Braga, A., Lima, V., Teixeira, P., & Sá, J. (2018). Value creation through quality and innovation - a case study on Portugal. *The TQM Journal.*

Schumpeter, A. J. (1934). *The Theory of Economic Development: An Inquiry into Profits, Capital, Credit, Interest, and the Business Cycle.* Harvard Economic Studies.

Schumpeter, A. J. (1939). *Business Cycle: A Theoretical, Historical, and Statistical Analysis of the Capitalist Process.* McGraw-Hill.

Silva, C. (2018). *Os desperdícios da Indústria Têxtil.* Dissertação de Mestrado. Instituto Politécnico do Cávado e do Ave.

Simões, V. C. (2015). *Gestão da Inovação.* Apontamentos do Mestrado em Gestão e Estratégia Industrial. Instituo Superior de Economia e Gestão.

Sivam, A., Dieguez, T., Ferreira, L., & Silva, F. (2019). Key settings for successful Open Innovation Arena. *Journal of Computational Design and Engineering, 6*(4), 507–515. doi:10.1016/j.jcde.2019.03.005

Snijkers, G., & Willimack, D. (2011). The missing link: from concepts to questions ineconomic surveys. *Proceedings of the 2nd European Establishment StatisticsWorkshop (EESW11).*

Taques, F.H., López, M.G., Basso, L.F. & Areal, N. (2020). Indicators used to measure service innovation and manufacturing innovation. *Journal of Innovation & Knowledge.* . doi:10.1016/j.jik.2019.12.001

Tidd, J., & Bessant, J. (2009). *Managing Innovation - Integrating Technological, Market and Organizational Change*. John Wiley & Sons.

Vieira, F. (2007). *Distritos industriais e inovação: o setor dos moldes em Portugal*. Tese de Doutoramento. Universidade do Minho.

Ylitalo, P. (2017). *Value creation metrics in systematic idea generation*. Tese Doutoral de Tecnologia e Ciências Naturais da Universidade de Oulu, Linnanmaa.

ADDITIONAL READING

Brau, E., Reinhardt, R., & Gurtner, S. (2013). Measuring the success of open innovation. In *Evolution of Innovation Management* (pp. 52–74). Palgrave Macmillan. doi:10.1057/9781137299994_3

Chesbrough, H., Vanhaverbeke, W., & West, J. (Eds.). (2006). *Open innovation: Researching a new paradigm*. Oxford University Press on Demand.

Saebi, T., & Foss, N. J. (2015). Business models for open innovation: Matching heterogeneous open innovation strategies with business model dimensions. *European Management Journal*, *33*(3), 201–213. doi:10.1016/j.emj.2014.11.002

KEY TERMS AND DEFINITIONS

Conditions Dimension: Relates to environmental and strategic aspects that might influence business attitudes and behaviour.

Innovation Scoring 1.0: A system from COTEC that aims to provide organizations with an instrument for self-diagnosis of their capabilities and performance in the field of innovation.

Innovation Scoring 2.0: The evolution of Innovation Scoring 1.0 model.

Processes Dimension: Relates to the most relevant organizational processes innovation dynamics and its performance.

Resources Dimension: Relates to the different resources of organization in order to ensure the execution and consequent performance of the innovation practices.

Results Dimension: Relates what extent conditions, innovation-oriented resources and processes translate into value as much as measurable as possible.

Chapter 9
The Country-Level Determinants of Sustainability Reporting in Emerging Markets

Sinem Ates
Yalova University, Turkey

ABSTRACT

This chapter examines the role of the institutional environment in the adoption of GRI-based sustainability reporting in emerging markets. Panel data analysis of the relevant data of firms from 20 emerging markets provides evidence that environmental, social, and governance performance, financial structure, and cultural dimensions are the institutional drivers of corporate social responsibility disclosure which was measured by publishing a GRI-based sustainability report. Overall findings of the study show that strategic decisions regarding CSR disclosure of companies are shaped by the institutional context in which they operate.

INTRODUCTION

Sustainability report, also called by various terms such as corporate responsibility (CR), corporate social responsibility (CSR), triple bottom line (TBL), environmental, social, and governance (ESG), social or sustainable development report, was defined as: "*public reports by companies to provide internal and external stakeholders with a picture of corporate position and activities on economic, environmental and social dimensions*" by the World Business Council for Sustainable Development (WBCSD, 2002).

Sustainability reporting satisfies the stakeholders' requirements of the disclosure about environmental, social, and governance outputs of the business activities. Sustainability reports also provide companies with the opportunities for the legitimacy of their activities, products, and services, improvement of brand value and reputation, competitive advantage, corporate transparency and accountability, and increasing employee motivation (Herzig and Schaltegger, 2006). Despite the increasing adoption and recognized importance of sustainability reporting, there has not been a commonly held way of collecting, evaluating, and reporting non-financial data of companies (Kolk and Perego, 2010). As an attempt to provide

DOI: 10.4018/978-1-7998-7634-2.ch009

guidance to companies on reporting their sustainability performance and thereby enhancing the quality, transparency, and comparability of the worldwide sustainability reports, Global Reporting Initiative (GRI) has released some set of guidelines. Between 2000 – 2013, GRI published 5 sets of guidelines as GRI – G1/G2/G3/G3.1/G4, and finally in 2016 Global Sustainability Standards Board (GSSB) has developed GRI Standards as "*the first global standards for sustainability reporting*" (GRI, 2020a).

According to the KPMG's Survey of Corporate Responsibility (CR) Reporting in 2017, CR reporting rate of the N100 companies (the top 100 companies by revenue in the sample covering 49 countries) and the G250 companies (the top 250 companies by revenue in the list of Fortune 500 in 2016) was 75% and 90%, respectively. As a result of this survey, the Global Reporting Initiative (GRI) was specified as the most commonly used framework by companies for their sustainability reporting. More precisely, 63% of the sustainability reports of the N100 companies and 75% of the G250 reports were prepared based on GRI standards (KPMG, 2017).

GRI developed the GRI Sustainability Disclosure Database (SDD) to enable companies to add their sustainability reports on the database and make them accessible for the users. Based on the data-driven from GRI SDD, some academic papers investigated the determinants of GRI-based sustainability reporting. While some of these papers searched for company-level drivers of GRI-based sustainability reporting (Karaman et al., 2018), some addressed country-level characteristics which may affect the likelihood of publishing a GRI-based report for specific industries (Karaman et al., 2020; Kılıç et al., 2019; Uyar et al., 2019).

Unlike the above-mentioned studies, this study focused on not only a specific industry but all the companies from 20 emerging countries that have a sustainability report in the GRI SDD. Focusing on a group of emerging countries instead of a diverse group of countries could provide a better understanding of the country-level determinants of corporate social responsibility disclosures (De Villiers and Marques, 2016). From this point of view, this study seeks to investigate the country-level drivers of the adoption of GRI-based sustainability reporting in emerging markets listed in the Morgan Stanley Capital International (MSCI) Emerging Markets Index. The country-level factors addressed in this study are mainly environmental, social, and governance performances of the countries, the structure of the financial system, and cultural factors. Furthermore, the country's trade openness and the number of listed companies were used as country-level control variables throughout the statistical analyses.

The main results of the study reveal that the companies in the countries with higher environmental, social, and governance performances and a market-oriented financial system are more likely to publish GRI-based sustainability reports. Additionally, cultural factors were also found to be significant determinants of GRI-based sustainability reporting.

Contribution of this study is twofold: First, identifying the level of both GRI and non-GRI based sustainability reporting in emerging markets would provide insight into the adoption level of sustainability reporting requirements in the markets with high economic growth potential. Second, highlighting the country-level drivers of the adoption of GRI-based sustainability reporting would be a guide for the efforts to encourage sustainability reporting adoption by companies.

The remainder of the chapter is organized as follows: The relevant literature is reviewed in the next section. The third section outlines the theoretical framework and research hypotheses. The research methodology is explained in the fourth section. After presenting and discussing the empirical findings in the fifth section, an overall conclusion is provided in the last section.

BACKGROUND

Even though GRI is the most commonly used framework by firms for their sustainability reporting, it is not unexpected that the level of adoption and usage of GRI-based sustainability reporting will vary depending on both company and country-level characteristics. It is known that CSR reporting is a newer concept for emerging markets compared to developed markets. This situation is mainly due to the less pressure from stakeholders, weak governance mechanism to enforce CSR and prevalence of economic concerns (Jamali et al., 2007). However, emerging markets have also been exposed to CSR matters by means of financial market regulations and supply chain relations (Garcia-Johnson, 2000). Moreover, emerging market firms can benefit from CSR reporting to achieve international visibility and thus attract foreign investors. The emerging market firms which adopted GRI can attain this objective by informing international investors regarding their policies on environmental or social concerns (Marimon et al., 2012).

Since sustainability reporting is not mandatory for firms in most countries around the world (Haffar and Searcy, 2018), companies need some driving factors to issue sustainability reports at the expense of their time and money. The underlying motivation of companies for issuing sustainability reports may be due to company or country-specific factors.

One of the studies investigating the company-level drivers of GRI-based sustainability reporting in an emerging market belongs to Kuzey and Uyar (2017). Handling a sample of listed Turkish firms, the authors found that manufacturing firms, larger firms, and firms with lower leverage and current ratio are more likely to issue GRI-based sustainability reports. Orazalin and Mahmood (2018) examined the determinants of GRI-based sustainability reporting in the Russian oil and gas industry. Based on their empirical analyses, the authors indicated that issuing a standalone sustainability report, firm age, the type of auditing company, and the language used for sustainability report determine the quality of a sustainability report which was measured by the extent of the disclosure using GRI guidelines. In another study, while firm size and leverage ratio were found to be positively correlated with GRI-based sustainability reporting, a negative association was found between diffused ownership and GRI-based reporting in the aviation industry (Karaman et al., 2018). Mafudi and Suyono (2018) found that firm profitability has a positive effect on GRI-based disclosure of listed Indonesian companies from the manufacturing and mining sectors. On the other hand, leverage and liquidity were determined as the company-specific factors which do not affect the GRI-based disclosure.

In the extant literature, various country-level factors have also been examined to determine their effect on the existence or level of GRI-based sustainability reporting of firms. Addressing an international sample of firms from the aviation industry Kılıç et al. (2019) showed that the firms from the countries having higher governance quality, social and environmental performance are more likely to issue GRI-based sustainability reports. The economic development of the country and the size of the aviation industry were also found to have a positive effect on the likelihood of publishing GRI-based sustainability reports. Using the same methodology with Kılıç et al. (2019), Uyar et al. (2020) got somewhat similar results for the tourism sector. The authors found that not social but governance and environmental performance of the countries have a positive relationship with GRI-based sustainability reporting. Karaman et al. (2020) examined mainly the link between green logistics performance of the countries and GRI-based sustainability reporting in the logistics sector. Based on the empirical results, the authors concluded that the relationship between GRI-based reporting and green logistics performance is significant and positive and gets stronger in countries having weak corporate governance. Bollas-Araya et al. (2019) analyzed the data of cooperative and mutual organizations from 28 countries and showed that the firms in the countries having a more stakeholder-oriented governance model are more likely to issue GRI-based sustainability reports. Utilizing Hofstede's cultural dimension scores, Sannino et al. (2020) investigated the effect of cultural dimensions on the GRI commitment level of the Organisation for Economic Co-operation and Development (OECD) banks. While masculinity was found to have a negative association with GRI commitment level, uncertainty avoidance, long-term orientation and indulgence are the cultural dimensions that were found to have a positive effect on GRI commitment level.

While some of the above-mentioned studies utilized panel data regression methods (Kılıç et al., 2019; Sannino et al., 2020; Uyar et al., 2020) some carried out just pooled regression models (Bollas-Araya et al., 2019; Karaman et al., 2020). These studies showed that much of the available literature on the link between GRI-based reporting and country-specific factors deals with either a specific industry or just a few country-specific factors. This study contributes to the literature by focusing on emerging markets which may differ from the developed markets in terms of sustainability practices and covering a wide range of country-specific factors to analyze their effects on GRI-based sustainability reporting.

THEORETICAL FRAMEWORK AND HYPOTHESES

The research hypotheses of this study, developed to explore the effect of institutional factors on the adoption of GRI-based sustainability reporting, are mainly grounded on the institutional theory which has frequently been used in accounting research to understand the accounting practices of organizations (Dillard et al., 2004).

The institutional theory deals with the interaction between an organization and its institutional environment and the ways through which the social expectations are integrated into organizational practices (Martinez, 1999). The institutional theory explains this process by three types of mechanisms, namely coercive, mimetic, and normative isomorphism. Coercive isomorphism means the organizational change due to the pressure exerted on an organization by other organizations upon which they are dependent. Coercive pressure may arise from policies and regulations of governments or some other regulatory institutions or just expectations of society or employees. Mimetic isomorphism occurs when the organizations imitate other organizations due to environmental uncertainties. Finally, normative isomorphism is the adoption of particular practices and procedures established by professionalists (DiMaggio and Powell, 1983)

Corporate social responsibility (CSR) practices of companies can also be explained utilizing coercive, mimetic, and normative isomorphism under institutional theory. Coercive pressure on CSR issues may come from either regulators or stakeholders. Governmental regulations on CSR issues, stakeholders' expectations regarding transparency of business activities are just a few examples of this type of pressure. On the other hand, companies may imitate counterparties with best practices on CSR or follow the norms of the society within which they operate (Vaz et al., 2016). Based on the institutional theory, the following institutional factors were hypothesized as the determinants of GRI-based sustainability reporting.

Environmental, Social, and Governance (ESG) Performance

ESG performance of countries shows *the degree to which a country pays attention to ESG matters* (Stellner et al., 2015). In an institutional environment that pays higher attention to ESG issues, pressure on companies regarding their CSR activities would also be higher. In a country with high social and environmental performance, stakeholders regard CSR activities as a duty but not a superiority of companies (Xiao et al., 2018). In order to meet stakeholder expectations in such an institutional environment, companies would engage in more CSR activities and report them (Uyar et al., 2019). Furthermore, the failure to follow the regulations on CSR matters would be served with a fine in the countries highly committed to CSR (De Villiers and Marques, 2016).

Governance infrastructure of a country covers governmental policies and institutions which establish a framework for economic, legal, and social relations (Globerman and Shapiro, 2003). This institutional framework, which company managers confront, impose some formal and informal constraints on strategic choices of companies (Peng et al., 2008). Governments with high governance quality, which is mainly measured through the level of regulatory quality, enforcement of rule of law, freedom of press and speech, control of corruption, and government effectiveness, are more likely put pressure on businesses to conform to CSR matters (Kühn et al., 2018).

Above mentioned theoretical arguments have been empirically confirmed through some academic studies. Firms from the countries with a high governance quality measured by the level of investor protection, democracy, the effectiveness of governmental services, quality of regulations, and press freedom were found to have higher levels of GRI-based disclosure (De Villiers and Marques, 2016). ESG disclosure was found to be negatively correlated with the level of corruption in a country, while the unemployment rate was enhancing CSR disclosure (Baldini et al., 2018). Grauel and Gotthardt (2016) showed that voluntary carbon disclosure is higher in countries with a higher level of environmental regulations. Alrazi et al. (2016) found that firms from countries highly concerned with environmental protection and carbon emissions are more likely to have more comprehensive environmental disclosure.

In line with these theoretical arguments and empirical findings, the following hypotheses were developed:

- **H_1**: GRI-based sustainability reporting is higher in countries with a higher level of environmental performance.
- **H_2**: GRI-based sustainability reporting is higher in countries with a higher level of social performance.
- **H_3**: GRI-based sustainability reporting is higher in countries with a higher level of governance performance.

Financial System

International Monetary Fund measures the level of financial development via the indicators related to the depth, access, and efficiency of the countries' financial institutions and financial markets (IMF, 2019). This method of measurement complies with the traditional classification of financial systems of the countries as bank-oriented and market-oriented. While the capital market is the main provider of the funds for companies in market-oriented financial systems, bank-oriented financial systems are characterized by higher dependence on banks to meet financing needs (Berglof, 1990). In market-oriented financial systems, companies need to satisfy the expectations of investors holding the fund which the company needs. However, banks which are the leading actors of the bank-oriented financial systems care mostly about the repayment ability of the company. In line with this argument, it is expected CSR reporting will be more common in market-oriented financial systems in comparison to bank-oriented financial systems.

The study of Pucheta-Martínez and Gallego-Álvarez (2018) provides empirical support for the theoretical arguments above. Through their study, the authors showed that environmental disclosure is higher in countries where the capital markets are the leading capital providers.

In order to test the correlation between the financial structure of the country and the level of GRI-based reporting, the following hypothesis was developed:

- **H_4**: GRI-based sustainability reporting is higher in countries with a market-oriented financial system.

Cultural Factors

Since a country's culture shapes the values and norms of the society, cultural factors constitute a part of the informal side of the institutional framework (Redding, 2005). Organizations are expected to comply with cultural norms and values to gain legitimacy for their business activities (Perez-Batres et al., 2011). Hofstede's cultural dimensions have frequently been used in the studies examining the link between cultural factors and CSR disclosure (e.g. Gallén and Peraita, 2018; Garcia-Sanchez et al., 2016; Sannino et al., 2020) and/or corporate social performance (Ho et al., 2012; Ioannou and Serafeim, 2012; Ringov and Zollo, 2007). Hofstede's cultural dimensions are power distance, individualism versus collectivism, masculinity versus femininity, uncertainty avoidance (Hofstede, 1980), long-term orientation versus short-term normative orientation, (Hofstede, 2001), and indulgence versus restraint (Hofstede et al., 2010).

Hofstede et al. (2010) define the power distance index as: "*the extent to which the less powerful members of institutions and organizations within a country expect and accept that power is distributed unequally*." Based on this definition, it is possible to comment that in societies with a high power distance, stakeholders' requirements for CSR disclosure will be low since they perceive inequality as normal and feel that they have no right to demand an explanation from the ones with power.

- **H_5:** GRI-based sustainability reporting is lower in countries with a higher level of power distance.

Individualism/collectivism stands for a society's preference for "I" or "we." Members of an individualistic society prefer "I" over "we" which means they only care about themselves and their immediate families. On the other hand, in a collectivist society people see themselves as group members, have a tight link to those groups, thereby they favor the interests of groups rather than their individual interests. In collectivist societies, it is expected that firms concern with the effect of their business activities on society, therefore, the relevant hypothesis is developed as follows:

- **H*6*:** GRI-based sustainability reporting is lower in countries with a higher level of individualism.

The distinction between masculinity and femininity is based on the preference in society for masculine or feminine values. Societies with a high level of masculinity prefer the values of achievement, heroism, assertiveness, and material rewards for success whereas femininity refers to the preference for cooperation, modesty, caring for the weak, and quality of life. Since masculine societies focus on material success, they are expected to ignore the needs of society. However, societies with high levels of femininity have also high levels of social orientation thereby they are expected to be more socially responsible.

- **H_7:** GRI-based sustainability reporting is lower in countries with a higher level of masculinity.

Uncertainty avoidance measures the level of a society's tolerance for uncertainty and ambiguity. Societies exhibiting a high level of uncertainty avoidance are deeply committed to codes of belief and behavior, rules, and regulations, thereby less tolerant of anomalous behaviors. In this regard, firms in societies with a high level of uncertainty avoidance may benefit from CSR disclosures to reduce the uncertainty regarding the effect of business activities on society, sustainable development of the business, or future expectations of business performance.

- **H_8:** GRI-based sustainability reporting is higher in countries with a higher level of uncertainty avoidance.

Long- versus short-term orientation deals with how societies prioritize the present and future. Short-term oriented societies attach more importance to past and present, are not inclined to save for the future, and are bound up with traditions. In contrast, long-term oriented societies focus on success in the future, thereby save and prepare for the future, may sacrifice today for the future. Since long-term oriented societies care about future goals and success, CSR reporting which provides insights into the future of the business would be more common and valuable in those societies.

- **H_9:** GRI-based sustainability reporting is higher in countries with a higher level of long-term orientation.

Indulgence versus restraint refers to society's approach to the gratification of basic and natural human drives regarding the enjoyment of life and having fun. While indulgent societies allow free gratification of human desires, restrained societies regulate and control human desires via strict social norms. Corporate social responsibility can be seen as a control mechanism for the selfish desires of firms thereby may not be adopted in indulgent societies.

- **H_{10}:** GRI-based sustainability reporting is lower in countries with a higher level of indulgence.

RESEARCH METHODOLOGY

Sample and Data

The initial sample of this study includes the firms from emerging markets listed in the MSCI Emerging Markets Index and had a sustainability report in the GRI SDD between 2000-2016. GRI SDD includes sustainability reports uploaded by companies and classifies these reports as GRI-G1, G2, G3, G3.1, G4, Standards, Citing-GRI, and Non-GRI in terms of the GRI guidelines applied in the report. "Citing-GRI" represents the reports which "*make explicit reference to being based on the GRI Guidelines but for which there is no GRI Content Index*" and Non-GRI stands for the *reports that do not satisfy the database requirements of the GRI-Standards report type* (GRI, 2020b). In line with this classification of GRI SDD, in this study the report types "GRI-G1, G2, G3, G3.1, G4, Standards" were classified as GRI-based reports while the report types "Citing-GRI, Non-GRI" were coded as Non-GRI reports.

The firm-level dataset derived from GRI SDD was matched with the country-level data gathered from several sources such as Ecological Footprint (EF) of Global Footprint Network, Human Development Index (HDI) of United Nations Development Programme, World Governance Indicators (WGI) of World Bank, cultural dimensions of Hofstede, Financial Structure Dataset and World Development Indicators of World Bank. Since the country-level variables were not available for Egypt, Qatar, Saudi Arabia, South Africa, Taiwan, and the United Arab Emirates these countries were excluded from the initial sample.

The final sample covers 3,457 firms and 10,622 firm-years from 20 countries. The classification of the final sample is presented in Table 1. As seen in Table 1, China (22.11%) and Brazil (14.91%) have the highest number of firm-years in the sample and constitute approximately 37% of the total sample. Non-GRI firm-years in Table 1 represent the firm-years where the companies did not have a GRI-based report in GRI SDD during the sample period. On the contrary, GRI firm-years stand for the years when the companies published a GRI-based report. GRI firm-years represent 67.49% of total firm-years in the sample.

Research Model and Variables

The model developed to test the research hypotheses of the study is as follows:

$$GRI_{it} = \beta_0 + \beta_1 EF_{it} + \beta_2 HDI_{it} + \beta_3 GQ_{it} + \beta_4 MARKET_{it} + \beta_5 CULTURE_i + \beta_6 CONTROL_{it} + a_i + u_{it} \quad (1)$$

In the equation above, GRI is a binary variable that takes the value of "1" if the firm has a GRI-based report, and "0" otherwise. EF is the ecological footprint of the country used as a proxy for environmental performance. HDI represents the Human Development Index of the country and was introduced into the model as a proxy for social performance. GQ stands for the governance quality of the country which was used as a proxy for governance performance. MARKET is the ratio of "stock market capitalization" to "private credit by deposit money banks" which was calculated to determine whether the financial system of the country is market or bank-oriented. CULTURE represents the Hofstede's cultural dimensions of the country. CONTROL covers both country- and firm-level control variables. Country-level control variables include trade openness of the country (TRADE), which was calculated as the ratio of the sum of exports and imports of goods and services to GDP, and the number of listed domestic companies (LCOMP). Firm-level control variables are the SIZE and INDUSTRY of the company. YEAR was also added to the model in order to control the time effect. While β_0 represents the constant term, $(a_i + u_{it})$ is the composite error term and i and t stand for the firm and year, respectively.

The data related to GRI and Non-GRI-based sustainability reporting of the firms were gathered from GRI SDD. If the firm's report in GRI SDD had one of the report types of "GRI-G1, G2, G3, G3.1, G4, Standards" then this report was coded as GRI-based report and the dependent variable of the Equation (1) took the value of "1". On the other hand, for the cases in which the firm had a "Citing GRI" or "Non-GRI" type-report, then the dependent variable took the value of "0".

Table 1. Sample by Country

Country	NON-GRI Firm-years		GRI Firm-years		ALL firm-years	
	N	%	N	%	N	%
ARGENTINA	98	2.84	410	5.72	508	4.78
BRAZIL	203	5.88	1,381	19.26	1,584	14.91
CHILE	24	0.70	351	4.90	375	3.53
CHINA	1,675	48.51	674	9.40	2,349	22.11
COLOMBIA	299	8.66	594	8.29	893	8.41
CZECH R.	50	1.45	17	0.24	67	0.63
GREECE	83	2.40	248	3.46	331	3.12
HUNGARY	89	2.58	139	1.94	228	2.15
INDIA	140	4.05	401	5.59	541	5.09
INDONESIA	74	2.14	290	4.05	364	3.43
KOREA	40	1.16	668	9.32	708	6.67
MALAYSIA	75	2.17	131	1.83	206	1.94
MEXICO	126	3.65	431	6.01	557	5.24
PAKISTAN	12	0.35	32	0.45	44	0.41
PERU	26	0.75	305	4.25	331	3.12
PHILIPPINES	28	0.81	125	1.74	153	1.44
POLAND	45	1.30	189	2.64	234	2.20
RUSSIA	132	3.82	339	4.73	471	4.43
THAILAND	151	4.37	194	2.71	345	3.25
TURKEY	83	2.40	250	3.49	333	3.14
TOTAL	3,453	100	7,169	100	10,622	100

The independent variables of the research model are mainly country-level variables that may affect the GRI-based reporting practices of the companies in those countries. EF, HDI, and GQ are the proxies for the environmental, social, and governance performances of the country, respectively. The ecological footprint (EF) shows "*the total area of productive land and water required by an individual, population, or activity to produce the resources it consumes and to absorb the waste it generates, using prevailing technology and resource management practices.*"(Global Footprint Network, 2020). Global Footprint Network database was utilized to collect the ecological footprints of the countries measured in global hectares per person. Human Development Index (HDI) of the United Nations Development Programme is an aggregated measure of three indices: life expectancy, education, and Gross National Income (GNI) (UNDP, 2020). Worldwide Governance Indicators of the World Bank report on six dimensions of governance: voice and accountability, political stability and absence of violence, government effectiveness, regulatory quality, rule of law, and control of corruption (World Bank, 2020). Governance Quality (GQ) of the countries was measured by the average of the country score on these six dimensions in this study. MARKET is a proxy for the financial structure of the country. It was calculated by the ratio of "stock market capitalization" to "private credit by deposit money banks" which were derived from the World

Bank Financial Structure Dataset. CULTURE covers Hofstede's six cultural dimension scores on power distance, individualism, masculinity, uncertainty avoidance, long-term orientation, and indulgence. Country-level control variables i.e. trade openness and the number of listed domestic companies were gathered from World Development Indicators of the World Bank. Finally, SIZE and INDUSTRY data of the firms were found in GRI SDD.

RESULTS AND DISCUSSION

Descriptive Statistics

Table 2 provides the number of observations, mean, and standard deviation figures for both Non-GRI and GRI firm-years. Additionally, Table 2 presents the results of t-test and Mann-Whitney tests applied to test the equality of means and mean ranks of variables for Non-GRI and GRI firm-years. According to the Mann-Whitney test, there are significant differences in all variables between Non-GRI and GRI firm-years. Similarly, t-test results indicate significant differences in all variables except trade openness between two groups.

Figure 1 shows the trend of GRI-based reporting during the sample period. From the data in Figure 1, it is apparent that there were sharp increases in the number of GRI-based reports during 2010-2013. The number of GRI-based reports remained constant in 2014 and experienced a small increase in 2015. However, in 2016, the number of GRI-based reports fell back nearly to the level of 2014.

Figure 1. The Trend of GRI-Based Reporting During 2010-2016

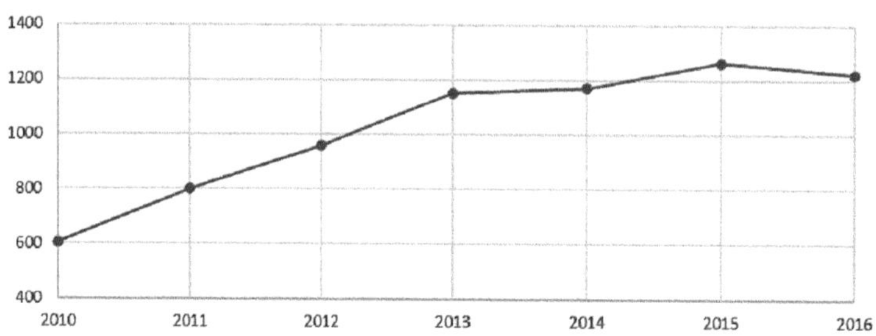

The correlation between the variables to be included in the regression model was checked for the multicollinearity problem and the results were reported in Table 3. As seen from Table 3, the correlations between Human Development Index (HDI) and uncertainty avoidance (UAI), indulgence (IVR) and long-term orientation (LTOWVS), LTOWVS and number of listed companies (LCOMP), IVR and LCOMP, which are all above 0.7, indicate a strong correlation. Therefore, these variables which were found to be highly correlated were used one at a time in the regression models not to disturb the predictive value of the model.

Table 2. Descriptive Statistics

	NON-GRI Firm-Years			GRI Firm-Years			T-test	Mann -Whitney Test
	Obs.	Mean	Std. Dev.	Obs.	Mean	Std. Dev.	t-stat	z-stat
EF	3,453	3.28	0.98	7,169	2.87	1.20	18.87***	20.09***
HDI	3,453	75.12	5.10	7,169	76.91	6.93	-14.93***	-17.48***
GOV	3,453	43.57	11.00	7,169	50.68	14.34	-28.16***	-30.81***
MARKET	3,453	0.68	0.44	7,169	0.96	0.53	-28.53***	-30.69***
PDI	3,453	74.91	10.95	7,169	70.01	11.63	21.19***	24.08***
IDV	3,453	26.85	13.96	7,169	30.70	14.04	-13.29***	-12.07***
MAS	3,453	59.79	11.37	7,169	52.03	12.49	31.88***	33.22***
UAI	3,453	53.21	26.19	7,169	72.97	21.10	-38.68***	-36.85***
LTOWVS	3,453	63.50	27.82	7,169	49.23	26.41	25.17***	22.91***
IVR	3,453	38.78	22.28	7,169	49.73	22.00	-23.81***	-29.86***
TRADE	3,453	54.94	33.43	7,169	56.04	32.33	-1.61	-4.12**
LISTEDCOMP	3,453	1715.04	1461.63	7,169	950.56	1361.32	25.81***	25.12***
SIZE	3,453	2.00	0.49	7,169	2.07	0.50	-6.90***	-6.86***

Notes: EF: Ecological Footprint, HDI: Human Development Index, GOV: Governance Quality, MARKET: The ratio of "stock market capitalization" to "private credit by deposit money banks", PDI: Power Distance, IDV: Individualism, MAS: Masculinity, UAI: Uncertainty Avoidance, LTOWVS: Long-term orientation, IVR: Indulgence, TRADE: The ratio of exports and imports of goods and services to GDP, LISTEDCOMP: Number of listed domestic companies, SIZE: A variable with three categories ("0" for SME, "1" for Large, and "3" for MNE). *, **, *** stand for 0.10, 0.05, 0.01 significance levels, respectively

Regression Results and Discussion

The dependent variable of the regression model in Equation (1) is a binary variable that takes the value of "1" or "0", hence logistic regression model was used to estimate the Equation (1). Additionally, random effects estimator was preferred over the fixed effects estimator since the cultural dimensions included in the model are time-constant variables that do not change by time and it is impossible to get the coefficient of time-constant variables via fixed effects estimator. Finally, Equation (1) was estimated with standard errors that are robust to autocorrelation and heteroskedasticity. Due to high collinearity between long-term orientation (LTOWS) and indulgence (IVR) (-0.84, $p<0.01$), it was decided to include the cultural dimensions one at a time in the regression model, thereby Equation (1) was estimated 6 times in total, including only 1 cultural dimension at a time. Additionally, since the correlation between uncertainty avoidance (UAI) and Human Development Index (HDI) is greater than 0.7, the third model including UAI does not include HDI. The results of the estimation of Equation (1) with random effects logistic regression model and robust standard errors are reported in Table 4 in 6 columns including power distance, individualism, masculinity, uncertainty avoidance, long-term orientation, and indulgence, respectively.

As Table 4 shows, Ecological Footprint (EF) has a significant and negative coefficient in all models. This means that the higher the country's ecological footprint the lower the level of GRI-based reporting. Since the ecological footprint was used as a proxy for the country's environmental performance, in more general terms, it is possible to say that the lower the environmental performance of the country the lower the level of GRI-based reporting in that country. This finding confirms the first research hypothesis (H_1) and also the findings of other studies (Alrazi et al., 2016; Kılıç et al., 2019; Uyar et al., 2020).

Table 3. Pairwise Correlations

Variable	*GRI*	*EF*	*HDI*	*GOV*	*MARKET*	*PDI*	*IDV*	*MAS*	*UAI*	*LTOWVS*	*IVR*	*TRADE*	*LCOMP*	*TRADE*
GRI	**1.00**													
EF	**-0.19**	**1.00**												
HDI	**0.17**	**0.24**	**1.00**											
GOV	**0.30**	**-0.21**	**0.53**	**1.00**										
MARKET	**0.30**	**-0.52**	**-0.17**	**0.22**	**1.00**									
PDI	**-0.23**	**0.24**	**-0.50**	**-0.58**	0.00	**1.00**								
IDV	**0.12**	**0.34**	**0.18**	**0.15**	**-0.10**	0.00	**1.00**							
MAS	**-0.32**	**0.19**	**-0.30**	**-0.36**	**-0.32**	**0.40**	**-0.04**	**1.00**						
UAI	**0.36**	**0.06**	**0.73**	**0.47**	**0.24**	**-0.54**	**0.23**	**-0.48**	**1.00**					
LTOWVS	**-0.22**	**0.13**	**-0.10**	**-0.25**	**-0.52**	**0.25**	**-0.09**	**0.07**	**-0.42**	**1.00**				
IVR	**0.29**	**-0.27**	**0.26**	**0.51**	**0.48**	**-0.38**	-0.00	**-0.10**	**0.43**	**-0.84**	**1.00**			
TRADE	**0.04**	0.00	**0.28**	**0.22**	**0.09**	**-0.08**	**-0.08**	**-0.08**	**0.22**	**0.16**	**-0.16**	**1.00**		
LCOMP	**-0.24**	**0.03**	**-0.43**	**-0.31**	**-0.26**	**0.42**	**-0.05**	**0.11**	**-0.67**	**0.76**	**-0.75**	**0.03**	**1.00**	
SIZE	**0.07**	**0.03**	**0.07**	**0.04**	0.01	**-0.05**	**0.10**	-0.02	**0.05**	-0.02	**0.03**	**0.05**	**-0.03**	**1.00**

Notes: GRI: a binary variable which takes the value of "1" if the firm has a GRI-based report, "0" otherwise, EF: Ecological Footprint, HDI: Human Development Index, GOV: Governance Quality, MARKET: Ratio of "stock market capitalization" to "private credit by deposit money banks", PDI: Power Distance, IDV: Individualism, MAS: Masculinity, UAI: Uncertainty Avoidance, LTOWVS: Long-term orientation, IVR: Indulgence, TRADE: the ratio of exports and imports of goods and services to GDP, LCOMP: number of listed domestic companies, SIZE: a variable with three categories ("0" for SME, "1" for Large, and "3" for MNE). The correlations in bold indicate a significant correlation at 0.01 level.

The human development index (HDI), which was used as a proxy for the social development of countries, has a positive and significant coefficient in all models. Supporting H_2, this finding indicates that socially developed countries have higher levels of GRI-based reporting. Similar findings exist in the relevant literature (Alrazi et al., 2016; Kılıç et al., 2019).

Consistent with H_3, all models produced a significant and positive coefficient for governance quality (GOV) which means that the firms in the countries with a higher level of governance quality are more likely to publish GRI-based sustainability reports. Governance quality was found to be positively correlated with CSR disclosure in some other studies also (Bollas-Araya et al., 2019; Kılıç et al., 2019; Kühn et al., 2018; Uyar et al., 2020).

"MARKET" which is an indicator of the country's financial structure has a significant and positive coefficient in all models. Since the higher MARKET ratios represent a more market-oriented financial system, in line with H_4, it is expected that the higher the "MARKET" ratio the higher the level of GRI-based reporting. Thus, the results of the models provide support for H4. This finding is also consistent with those of Pucheta-Martínez and Gallego-Álvarez (2018).

The first model includes power distance (PDI) as a cultural dimension and provides a negative coefficient for PDI. Consistent with H_5, the results of Model 1 confirm that the countries with higher levels of power distance are more likely to have lower levels of GRI-based reporting. There are studies in the

Table 4. Panel Logistic Regression Results

	Model 1	Model 2	Model 3	Model 4	Model 5	Model 6
EF	-0.79***	-1.10***	-0.76***	-0.72***	-0.82***	-0.83***
	(0.09)	(0.09)	(0.09)	(0.08)	(0.08)	(0.09)
HDI	0.07***	0.11***	0.05**		0.22***	0.19***
	(0.02)	(0.02)	(0.02)		(0.02)	(0.02)
GOV	0.08***	0.05***	0.08***	0.05***	0.05***	0.06***
	(0.01)	(0.01)	(0.01)	(0.01)	(0.01)	(0.01)
MARKET	1.52***	1.49***	1.17***	1.03***	1.15***	1.42***
	(0.21)	(0.20)	(0.19)	(0.18)	(0.21)	(0.21)
PDI	-0.02*					
	(0.01)					
IDV		0.07***				
		(0.01)				
MAS			-0.07***			
			(0.01)			
UAI				0.08***		
				(0.00)		
LTOWVS					-0.04***	
					(0.00)	
IVR						0.03***
						(0.00)
TRADE	-0.02***	-0.03***	-0.02***	-0.01***	-0.02***	-0.02***
	(0.00)	(0.00)	(0.00)	(0.00)	(0.00)	(0.00)
LCOMP	-0.00***	-0.00***	-0.00***			
	(0.00)	(0.00)	(0.00)			
SIZE						
Large	0.77***	0.83***	0.56**	1.07***	0.80***	0.59**
	(0.27)	(0.26)	(0.27)	(0.26)	(0.27)	(0.27)
MNE	0.82**	0.62**	0.79**	0.88***	0.71**	0.68**
	(0.33)	(0.32)	(0.33)	(0.32)	(0.33)	(0.33)
Constant	-4.80***	-8.76***	-0.19	-6.39***	-13.90***	-16.00***
	(1.72)	(1.49)	(1.68)	(0.75)	(1.38)	(1.47)
INDUSTRY	YES	YES	YES	YES	YES	YES
YEAR	YES	YES	YES	YES	YES	YES
N	10,622	10,622	10,622	10,622	10,622	10,622
Wald chi2	595.56***	640.28***	629.06***	636.49***	595.63***	553.71***

Notes: EF: Ecological Footprint, HDI: Human Development Index, GOV: Governance Quality, MARKET: The ratio of "stock market capitalization" to "private credit by deposit money banks", PDI: Power Distance, IDV: Individualism, MAS: Masculinity, UAI: Uncertainty Avoidance, LTOWVS: Long-term orientation, IVR: Indulgence, TRADE: The ratio of exports and imports of goods and services to GDP, LCOMP: number of listed domestic companies, SIZE: A variable with three categories ("0" for SME, "1" for Large, and "3" for MNE). INDUSTRY and YEAR are dummy variables created for each type of industry and year in the sample. Robust standard errors are in parenthesis. *, **, *** stand for 0.10, 0.05, 0.01 significance levels, respectively.

literature that both support (Gallén and Peraita, 2018; Garcia-Sanchez et al., 2016) and contradict (Sannino et al., 2020) this finding indicating a negative correlation between power distance and CSR disclosure.

Contrary to H_6, individualism (IDV) was found to be positively correlated with GRI-based reporting according to the estimation results of Model 2. This means that the higher the level of individualism of the country the higher the level of GRI-based reporting. Indeed, it is not a fully surprising finding since the motivation behind CSR activities may differ between different institutional contexts. Matten and Moon (2008) describe CSR practices within the implicit-explicit CSR framework. The main driver to engage in implicit CSR activities is to act in line with the values, norms, and rules of the society and fulfill the stakeholders' requirements. On the other hand, companies engaging explicit CSR activities aim to inform the society regarding their CSR activities which are often based on deliberate and strategic decisions (Porter and Kramer, 2006). From this point of view, it may be expected that societies with a higher level of individualism are expected to engage in explicit CSR activities for their individualistic goals. Ioannou and Serafeim (2012) provided empirical evidence for this argument by showing that the companies from the countries with higher levels of individualism have higher corporate social performance scores.

The negative coefficient of the variable masculinity (MAS) in Model 3 provides support for H_7 which suggests that GRI-based sustainability reporting is lower in countries with a higher level of masculinity. The same conclusion was obtained in several studies (Gallén and Peraita, 2018; Garcia-Sanchez et al., 2016, Sannino et al., 2020).

As the results of the estimation of Model 4, uncertainty avoidance (UAI) was found to be positively correlated with GRI-based reporting which is consistent with H_8 and also the findings of Gallén and Peraita (2018) and Sannino et al. (2020).

The results of Model 5 reveal the exact opposite of H_9. More precisely, GRI-based sustainability reporting was found to be lower in countries with a higher level of long-term orientation. Although there have been some studies indicating a positive relationship between long-term orientation and CSR disclosure (Garcia-Sanchez et al., 2016; Sannino et al., 2020), Gallén and Peraita (2018) obtained a negative relationship for the countries with middle GDP per capita. The mixed results for the link between long-term orientation and CSR disclosure may be due to the changing expectations regarding the short- and long-term benefits from CSR reporting. When a long-term oriented society believes that the costs related to CSR reporting would be higher than its benefits in the long-term, it may not prefer to engage in CSR activities and/or reporting.

Finally, H_{10} could not be confirmed according to the results of Model 6 in which the variable Indulgence (IVR) was introduced. Contrary to H_{10}, GRI-based reporting was found to be higher in countries with a higher level of indulgence. Similar to long-term orientation, there have been mixed results also for indulgence in terms of its correlation with CSR disclosure. Gallén and Peraita (2018) found a negative relationship between indulgence and CSR disclosure for only countries with middle GDP per capita. However, the authors indicate that this relationship turns to positive when the sample covers all countries or countries with higher GDP per capita. Sannino et al. (2020) provide evidence for a positive link between the level of indulgence and CSR reporting.

Concerning the control variables, the results of the relevant models produced significant coefficients for both country- and firm-level control variables. As the country-level control variables, trade openness (TRADE) and the number of listed domestic companies (LCOMP) have a negative coefficient which means that the countries with a higher percentage of exports and imports of goods and services to GDP and a higher number of listed companies are less likely to publish GRI-based reports. Hu and Sholtens (2014) suggest that in a country with an open economy, CSR policies are already advanced thereby there is a limited chance to provide additional benefits from CSR activities. The authors also confirmed their argument by their empirical research indicating a negative relationship between openness and CSR performance. The results regarding the number of listed companies can be interpreted in the same way as trade openness. More clearly, since the number of listed companies can be considered as an indicator of the potential number of adherents to CSR activities (Lim and Tsutsui, 2012), the higher the number of companies engaging in CSR activities the lower the marginal benefit from CSR disclosure. Finally, SIZE and INDUSTRY dummy variables, which were introduced into the models to control the firm-level factors, were also found to have significant correlations with GRI-based reporting.

To sum up the results, confirmation of the first 3 hypotheses which claim that the GRI-based sustainability reporting is higher in the countries with higher ESG performance can be attributed to the both coercive and mimetic isomorphism mentioned in the institutional theory. Countries with higher ESG performance indicate higher regulations on CSR issues and these regulations put coercive pressure on the companies to perform CSR activities and report them. Moreover, in an institutional environment where there are many examples of superior CSP, companies may tend to imitate these examples in order to gain a competitive advantage. The hypothesis suggesting that GRI-based sustainability reporting is higher in countries with a market-oriented financial system was also confirmed through the empirical analyses. Since the main capital provider in market-oriented financial systems is the capital market, companies should satisfy the expectations of the players in the capital market to raise the fund they need. Finally, although not all the hypotheses related with cultural factors were confirmed but confirmation of some of them reveals that cultural factors play a significant role in determining in GRI-reporting behavior of companies. Cultural factors constitute the norms in a society and companies as one of the members of those societies need to follow these norms to gain legitimacy.

CONCLUSION

This study was designed to identify the country-level determinants of GRI-based sustainability reporting in emerging markets. The sample of the study covers 3,457 firms and 10,622 firm-years from twenty emerging markets listed in the MSCI Emerging Markets Index having a sustainability report in the GRI SDD between 2000 and 2016. Country-level data of the emerging countries in the sample was derived from several sources such as Ecological Footprint of Global Footprint Network Human Development Index of United Nations Development Programme, World Governance Indicators of World Bank, cultural dimensions of Hofstede, Financial Structure Dataset and World Development Indicators of World Bank. The relationship between the country-level variables gathered from these databases and GRI-based reporting of the firms were analyzed through the logistic regression model estimated with a random effects estimator and robust standard errors.

The results of this investigation show that GRI-based reporting is higher in the countries with higher environmental, social, and governance performances and a market-oriented financial system. Furthermore, the cultural dimensions of the country were also found to be correlated with GRI-based reporting. Taken together, these results provide evidence for the role of the institutional context in explaining the differences of GRI-based reporting between countries.

The present study has both theoretical and practical contributions. By highlighting the institutional factors which have a role in the adoption of a global framework for sustainability reporting, this study contributes to the institutional theory. Companies in the countries with higher ESG performance or market-oriented financial system may be exposed to higher coercive pressure in terms of CSR matters. Similarly, mimetic isomorphism may come into play for the companies who want to achieve competitive advantage in an institutional environment having high sensitivity to CSR activities. Finally, cultural dimensions of a country constitute the norms of the society which the companies should take into consideration to be able to gain legitimacy in the eyes of stakeholders.

From a practical point of view, the findings of this study help businesses and investors understand the underlying factors of CSR disclosure practices of firms in different institutional environments and take into account these institutional factors when making their decisions. Finally, policymakers can benefit from the findings of this study while developing CSR disclosure policies and accommodating a favorable institutional context for the adoption of these policies.

The most important limitation of this study lies in the proxies used to measure country-level ESG performance. Although this study utilized the proxies for ESG performance of the countries which have commonly been used in the literature, it would be more reliable to diversify the type of proxies and investigate whether the results change depending on the proxies used in empirical analyses. It is also recommended that further study be undertaken to assess the differences in the GRI application level (such as A+, A, B, and so on) between countries in different institutional environments.

ACKNOWLEDGMENT

This research received no specific grant from any funding agency in the public, commercial, or not-for-profit sectors.

REFERENCES

Alrazi, B., De Villiers, C., & Van Staden, C. J. (2016). The environmental disclosures of the electricity generation industry: A global perspective. *Accounting and Business Research*, *46*(6), 665–701. doi:10.1080/00014788.2015.1135781

Baldini, M., Dal Maso, L., Liberatore, G., Mazzi, F., & Terzani, S. (2018). Role of country-and firm-level determinants in environmental, social, and governance disclosure. *Journal of Business Ethics*, *150*(1), 79–98. doi:10.100710551-016-3139-1

Berglof, E. (1990). Capital Structure as a Mechanism of Control: a Comparison of Financial Systems. In A. Masahiko, B. Gustafsson, & O. E. Williamson (Eds.), *The Firm as a Nexus of Treaties* (pp. 237–262). Sage Publications.

Bollas-Araya, H. M., Polo-Garrido, F., & Seguí-Mas, E. (2019). Determinants of CSR reporting and assurance: An analysis of top cooperative and mutual organisations. *Australian Accounting Review*, *29*(4), 692–707. doi:10.1111/auar.12244

De Villiers, C., & Marques, A. (2016). Corporate social responsibility, country-level predispositions, and the consequences of choosing a level of disclosure. *Accounting and Business Research*, *46*(2), 167–195. doi:10.1080/00014788.2015.1039476

Dillard, J. F., Rigsby, J. T., & Goodman, C. (2004). The making and remaking of organization context. *Accounting, Auditing & Accountability Journal, 17*(4), 506–542. doi:10.1108/09513570410554542

DiMaggio, P. J., & Powell, W. W. (1983). The iron cage revisited: Institutional isomorphism and collective rationality in organizational fields. *American Sociological Review, 48*(2), 147–160. doi:10.2307/2095101

Gallén, M. L., & Peraita, C. (2018). The effects of national culture on corporate social responsibility disclosure: A cross-country comparison. *Applied Economics, 50*(27), 2967–2979. doi:10.1080/00036846.2017.1412082

Garcia-Johnson, R. (2000). *Exporting Environmentalism: US Multinational Chemical Corporations in Brazil and Mexico*. MIT Press. doi:10.7551/mitpress/2941.001.0001

Garcia-Sanchez, I. M., Cuadrado-Ballesteros, B., & Frias-Aceituno, J. V. (2016). Impact of the institutional macro context on the voluntary disclosure of CSR information. *Long Range Planning, 49*(1), 15–35. doi:10.1016/j.lrp.2015.02.004

Global Footprint Network. (2020). Retrieved from http://data.footprintnetwork.org/?_ga=2.85860889.1426762603.1589453027-229816858.1589453027#/abouttheData

Global Reporting Initiative (GRI). (2020a). *GRI's History*. Retrieved from https://www.globalreporting.org/information/about-gri/gri-history/Pages/GRI's%20history.aspx

Global Reporting Initiative (GRI). (2020b). *Sustainability Disclosure Database Data Legend*. Retrieved from https://www.globalreporting.org/SiteCollectionDocuments/GRI-Data-Legend-Sustainability-Disclosure-Database-Profiling.pdf

Globerman, S., & Shapiro, D. (2003). Governance infrastructure and US foreign direct investment. *Journal of International Business Studies, 34*(1), 19–39. doi:10.1057/palgrave.jibs.8400001

Grauel, J., & Gotthardt, D. (2016). The relevance of national contexts for carbon disclosure decisions of stock-listed companies: A multilevel analysis. *Journal of Cleaner Production, 133*, 1204–1217. doi:10.1016/j.jclepro.2016.05.182

Haffar, M., & Searcy, C. (2018). The use of context-based environmental indicators in corporate reporting. *Journal of Cleaner Production, 192*, 496–513. doi:10.1016/j.jclepro.2018.04.202

Herzig, C., & Schaltegger, S. (2006). Corporate Sustainability Reporting. An Overview. In S. Schaltegger, M. Bennett, & R. Burritt (Eds.), *Sustainability Accounting and Reporting* (pp. 301–304). Springer. doi:10.1007/978-1-4020-4974-3_13

Ho, F. N., Wang, H. M. D., & Vitell, S. J. (2012). A global analysis of corporate social performance: The effects of cultural and geographic environments. *Journal of Business Ethics, 107*(4), 423–433. doi:10.100710551-011-1047-y

Hofstede, G. (1980). *Cultures Consequences: International Differences in Work-Related Values*. Sage Publications.

Hofstede, G. (2001). *Culture's Consequences: Comparing Values, Behaviors, Institutions, and Organizations across Nations*. Sage Publications.

Hofstede, G. H., Hofstede, G. J., & Minkov, M. (2010). *Cultures and organizations: Software of the Mind*. McGraw-Hill.

Hu, V. I., & Scholtens, B. (2014). Corporate social responsibility policies of commercial banks in developing countries. *Sustainable Development*, *22*(4), 276–288. doi:10.1002d.1551

International Monetary Fund (IMF). (2019). *Financial Development Index Database*. Retrieved from https://data.imf.org/?sk=F8032E80-B36C-43B1-AC26-493C5B1CD33B

Ioannou, I., & Serafeim, G. (2012). What drives corporate social performance? The role of nation-level institutions. *Journal of International Business Studies*, *43*(9), 834–864. doi:10.1057/jibs.2012.26

Jamali, D., & Mirshak, R. (2007). Corporate social responsibility (CSR): Theory and practice in a developing country context. *Journal of Business Ethics*, *72*(3), 243–262. doi:10.100710551-006-9168-4

Karaman, A. S., Kilic, M., & Uyar, A. (2018). Sustainability reporting in the aviation industry: Worldwide evidence. *Sustainability Accounting. Management and Policy Journal*, *9*(4), 362–391.

Karaman, A. S., Kilic, M., & Uyar, A. (2020). Green logistics performance and sustainability reporting practices of the logistics sector: The moderating effect of corporate governance. *Journal of Cleaner Production*, *258*, 120718. doi:10.1016/j.jclepro.2020.120718

Kılıç, M., Uyar, A., & Karaman, A. S. (2019). What impacts sustainability reporting in the global aviation industry? An institutional perspective. *Transport Policy*, *79*, 54–65. doi:10.1016/j.tranpol.2019.04.017

Kolk, A., & Perego, P. (2010). Determinants of the adoption of sustainability assurance statements: An international investigation. *Business Strategy and the Environment*, *19*(3), 182–198.

KPMG. I. (2017). *The KPMG Survey of Corporate Responsibility Reporting 2017*. Retrieved from https://assets.kpmg/content/dam/kpmg/xx/pdf/2017/10/kpmg-survey-of-corporate-responsibility-reporting-2017.pdf

Kühn, A. L., Stiglbauer, M., & Fifka, M. S. (2018). Contents and determinants of corporate social responsibility website reporting in Sub-Saharan Africa: A seven-country study. *Business & Society*, *57*(3), 437–480. doi:10.1177/0007650315614234

Kuzey, C., & Uyar, A. (2017). Determinants of sustainability reporting and its impact on firm value: Evidence from the emerging market of Turkey. *Journal of Cleaner Production*, *143*, 27–39. doi:10.1016/j.jclepro.2016.12.153

Lim, A., & Tsutsui, K. (2012). Globalization and commitment in corporate social responsibility: Cross-national analyses of institutional and political-economy effects. *American Sociological Review*, *77*(1), 69–98. doi:10.1177/0003122411432701

Mafudi, M., & Suyono, E. (2018). Firm specific attributes and corporate social responsibility disclosure in manufacturing and mining companies: Evidence from Indonesia. *Journal of Economics & Management Perspective*, *12*(4), 14–27.

Marimon, F., del Mar Alonso-Almeida, M., del Pilar Rodríguez, M., & Alejandro, K. A. C. (2012). The worldwide diffusion of the global reporting initiative: What is the point? *Journal of Cleaner Production*, *33*, 132–144. doi:10.1016/j.jclepro.2012.04.017

Martinez, R. J., & Dacin, M. T. (1999). Efficiency Motives and Normative Forces: Combining Transactions Costs and Institutional Logic. *Journal of Management*, *25*(1), 75–96. doi:10.1177/014920639902500104

Matten, D., & Moon, J. (2008). "Implicit" and "explicit" CSR: A conceptual framework for a comparative understanding of corporate social responsibility. *Academy of Management Review*, *33*(2), 404–424. doi:10.5465/amr.2008.31193458

Orazalin, N., & Mahmood, M. (2018). Economic, environmental, and social performance indicators of sustainability reporting: Evidence from the Russian oil and gas industry. *Energy Policy*, *121*, 70–79. doi:10.1016/j.enpol.2018.06.015

Peng, M. W., Wang, D. Y., & Jiang, Y. (2008). An institution-based view of international business strategy: A focus on emerging economies. *Journal of International Business Studies*, *39*(5), 920–936. doi:10.1057/palgrave.jibs.8400377

Perez-Batres, L. A., Miller, V. V., & Pisani, M. J. (2011). Institutionalizing sustainability: An empirical study of corporate registration and commitment to the United Nations global compact guidelines. *Journal of Cleaner Production*, *19*(8), 843–851. doi:10.1016/j.jclepro.2010.06.003

Porter, M. E., & Kramer, M. R. (2006). Strategy and society: The link between competitive advantage and corporate social responsibility. *Harvard Business Review*, *84*(12), 78–88. PMID:17183795

Pucheta-Martínez, M. C., & Gallego-Álvarez, I. (2018). Environmental reporting policy and corporate structures: An international analysis. *Corporate Social Responsibility and Environmental Management*, *25*(5), 788–798. doi:10.1002/csr.1494

Redding, G. (2005). The thick description and comparison of societal systems of capitalism. *Journal of International Business Studies*, *36*(2), 123–155. doi:10.1057/palgrave.jibs.8400129

Ringov, D., & Zollo, M. (2007). Corporate responsibility from a socio-institutional perspective. The impact of national culture on corporate social performance. *Corporate Governance*, *7*(4), 476–485. doi:10.1108/14720700710820551

Sannino, G., Lucchese, M., Zampone, G., & Lombardi, R. (2020). Cultural dimensions, Global Reporting Initiatives commitment, and corporate social responsibility issues: New evidence from Organisation for Economic Co-operation and Development banks. *Corporate Social Responsibility and Environmental Management*, *27*(4), 1–11. doi:10.1002/csr.1914

Stellner, C., Klein, C., & Zwergel, B. (2015). Corporate social responsibility and Eurozone corporate bonds: The moderating role of country sustainability. *Journal of Banking & Finance*, *59*, 538–549. doi:10.1016/j.jbankfin.2015.04.032

United Nations Development Programme (UNDP). (2020). Retrieved from http://hdr.undp.org/en/content/human-development-index-hdi

Uyar, A., Karaman, A. S., & Kilic, M. (2019). Institutional drivers of sustainability reporting in the global tourism industry. *Tourism Economics*, 1–24. doi:10.1177/1354816619886250

Vaz, N., Fernandez-Feijoo, B., & Ruiz, S. (2016). Integrated reporting: An international overview. *Business Ethics (Oxford, England)*, *25*(4), 577–591. doi:10.1111/beer.12125

World Bank. (2020). *Worldwide Governance Indicators*. Retrieved from https://info.worldbank.org/governance/wgi/

World Business Council for Sustainable Development (WBCSD). (2002). *Sustainable development reporting: Striking the balance*. Retrieved from http://docs.wbcsd.org/2002/12/SustainableDevReporting-StrikingTheBalance.pdf

Xiao, C., Wang, Q., van der Vaart, T., & van Donk, D. P. (2018). When does corporate sustainability performance pay off? The impact of country-level sustainability performance. *Ecological Economics*, *146*, 325–333. doi:10.1016/j.ecolecon.2017.11.025

ADDITIONAL READING

Adnan, S. M., Hay, D., & van Staden, C. J. (2018). The influence of culture and corporate governance on corporate social responsibility disclosure: A cross country analysis. *Journal of Cleaner Production*, *198*, 820–832. doi:10.1016/j.jclepro.2018.07.057

Ali, W., Frynas, J. G., & Mahmood, Z. (2017). Determinants of corporate social responsibility (CSR) disclosure in developed and developing countries: A literature review. *Corporate Social Responsibility and Environmental Management*, *24*(4), 273–294. doi:10.1002/csr.1410

De Bakker, F. G., Groenewegen, P., & Den Hond, F. (2005). A bibliometric analysis of 30 years of research and theory on corporate social responsibility and corporate social performance. *Business & Society*, *44*(3), 283–317. doi:10.1177/0007650305278086

De Villiers, C., & Marques, A. (2016). Corporate social responsibility, country-level predispositions, and the consequences of choosing a level of disclosure. *Accounting and Business Research*, *46*(2), 167–195. doi:10.1080/00014788.2015.1039476

Dorfleitner, G., Halbritter, G., & Nguyen, M. (2015). Measuring the level and risk of corporate responsibility–An empirical comparison of different ESG rating approaches. *Journal of Asset Management*, *16*(7), 450–466. doi:10.1057/jam.2015.31

Isaksson, R., & Steimle, U. (2009). What does GRI-reporting tell us about corporate sustainability? *The TQM Journal*, *21*(2), 168–181. doi:10.1108/17542730910938155

Jamali, D., & Karam, C. (2018). Corporate social responsibility in developing countries as an emerging field of study. *International Journal of Management Reviews*, *20*(1), 32–61. doi:10.1111/ijmr.12112

Lélé, S. M. (1991). Sustainable development: A critical review. *World Development*, *19*(6), 607–621. doi:10.1016/0305-750X(91)90197-P

Wood, D. J. (2010). Measuring corporate social performance: A review. *International Journal of Management Reviews*, *12*(1), 50–84. doi:10.1111/j.1468-2370.2009.00274.x

KEY TERMS AND DEFINITIONS

Corporate Social Performance: An organization's performance in fulfilling its responsibilities to its stakeholders.

Corporate Social Responsibility: An organization's responsibilities to its stakeholders other than its business activities.

ESG Performance: An organization's performance in fulfilling its responsibilities regarding environmental, social, and governance issues.

Governance Quality: The measurement of how well an organization performs at governance dimensions, namely control of corruption, government effectiveness, political stability and absence of violence/terrorism, regulatory quality, rule of law, and voice and accountability.

Institutional Context: The set of institutional characteristics such as rules, regulations, policies, cultural factors and so on.

Sustainability: The ability to continue its existence for a long time with activities that are in harmony with environmental, social and governance concerns.

Sustainable Development: The development that achieved without ignoring the needs of all type of stakeholders.

Chapter 10
Advancement of Circular Economy:
The European Perspective

Barbara Bradač Hojnik
https://orcid.org/0000-0002-1314-9088
Faculty of Economics and Business, University of Maribor, Slovenia

ABSTRACT

This chapter provides an overview of the topic circular economy from a European perspective. It focuses on the actual implementation of circular models and processes. Although the European Commission has been trying to address the issue for years and provides many measures, the results of different indicators show a lack of implementation. Therefore, the main challenge of the next stage of development of Circular Economy 4.0 is to develop an inclusive system that involves all relevant stakeholders. This is because only through the efforts of limited groups of stakeholders (e.g., companies), the concept cannot be fully implemented in practice. Instead, the circular economy must become part of the broader culture, the way of thinking and acting of all stakeholders involved. This issue represents the main challenges for the next 10-year period in Europe.

INTRODUCTION

The circular economy has become a global trend that is unstoppable. Over the last decade, the concept of the circular economy has become one of the leading policy issues European Commission. As a result, EU Member States are following it. During this period, the circular economy has become well known to the general public, and in policy terms the concept has been broadened from an initial focus on aspects of waste management to a more comprehensive concept. It should be emphasized that major efforts are still needed to increase the scale of the measures introduced, both at EU and global level, in order to fully close the linear loops and exploit the competitive advantages that the circular economy offers to EU companies (EC, 2020a).

DOI: 10.4018/978-1-7998-7634-2.ch010

The concept of circular economy is an economic concept that can lead to solving current environmental and socio-economic problems and creating a more sustainable society (Witjes & Lozano, 2016). In recent years, it is recognized as a tool to achieve sustainable development. The circular economy promotes the responsible and cyclical use of resources that can contribute to sustainable development. The circular economy can be seen as an umbrella concept (Blomsma & Brennan, 2017; Homrich et al., 2018) that encompasses various content concepts, from reducing material inputs to minimizing waste generation (EASAC, 2016; EEA, 2016), with the aim of achieving economic growth independent of natural resource use (Cullen, 2017; EASAC, 2016; Pauliuk, 2018; Moraga et al., 2019). The concept of circular economy can be divided into several stages of development:

- Circular Economy 1.0 (1970-1990): focus on waste management.
- Circular Economy 2.0 (1990-2010): development of strategies linking inputs and outputs to achieve ecological efficiency.
- Circular Economy 3.0 (2010-2020): increasing the retention of product values in an era of resource scarcity.
- Circular Economy 4.0 (2020 onwards): Integrating sub-concepts into an overall system.

In the first stage of development of the circular economy, the focus was primarily on waste management. In the second stage, the concept was expanded to include the development of strategies that incorporate and link inputs and outputs. The third stage focuses on preserving product values for as long as possible due to resource depletion. In our study, we add a fourth stage, Circular Economy 4.0, which needs to integrate all partial implementation concepts, approaches and models and involve all stakeholders in a single comprehensive approach to maximize the effects of circular economy. Currently, two main directions of implementation can be distinguished in the circular economy field: (1) a systemic implementation across the whole economy, e.g., at local, regional, national and transnational levels, and (2) an implementation focusing on a selected group of sectors, products, materials and substances.

The state of the circular economy at the global level report notes that the world is 8.6% circular (Circle Economy, 2019). Considering the efforts policymakers have been making for decades to build a circular economy not only locally but also globally, the results are quite worrying and require all stakeholders to commit to adopting circular approaches as much as possible.

The chapter focuses mainly on the last five-year period. During this period, the European Commission has focused its policies on putting the circular economy into practice and measuring the impact of the implementation of various policies in this context. The aim of the chapter is therefore to provide an overview of the most current aspects of dealing with the circular economy at EU level. The key questions we try to answer in this chapter are: (1) what is the implementation of the circular economy at EU level; (2) how is the adoption of circular practices perceived by companies; and (3) how can the implementation of the circular economy in companies be promoted in society.

The content is based on the analysis of primary and secondary data from various international studies, research, project results and articles. Primary data from empirical studies at national and international levels are used. The chapter is organized as follows. First, the theoretical background and literature review of circular economy is presented. This is followed by an insight into the EU policy on the circular economy with an overview of the initiatives and measures that have been adopted in recent years. Thirdly, the circular economy is discussed from the point of view of implementation in order to reach its full potential. Fourth, empirical evidence on the implementation of the circular economy at EU level is provided. The chapter ends with further research directions and a conclusion.

THE CIRCULAR ECONOMY CONCEPT

Definition of Circular Economy

The definition of the circular economy concept is very complex, but the bottom line is to transform the prevailing linear economic systems based on predominantly direct material flows and the assumption that resources are infinite (Preston, 2012; EMF, 2013a; Allwood, 2014) into an economic system that uses circular approaches. The concept dates back to the 1960s when it became clear that we had to deal with limited resources in a closed system. Pearce and Turner (1990) were the first to use the concept of circular economy and their work goes back to the findings of Boulding (1966) who was the first proponent of moving from a linear model to a circular economy. The linear model is based on ignoring the environment, following the system of "take, make, use and throw away". Such a model is not sustainable. Therefore, to ensure sustainable development, a change in mentality and attitude towards the use of resources is required. The latter proposes the concept of a circular economy based on systemic thinking towards solutions for a sustainable life for humanity in the coming decades and beyond (Yang et al., 2014).

Most recent studies summarize the definition of the circular economy according to the interpretations of the Ellen MacArthur Foundation (EMF), which, in collaboration with McKinsey & Company, has published several extensive papers in recent years under the umbrella title "Towards the Circular Economy" (EMF, 2013, 2014, 2015a). The basic idea shows how technological and biological products and materials circulate in the economic system. The concept of circular economy is represented by completed material flows at different levels, representing the circulation of the material during the life of the product. The shorter the path of the material embedded in the products from the user who no longer uses the product to the new user, the greater the savings in embedded material, labor, energy, capital and associated external costs (EMF, 2013, p. 30). The proposed approach is based on three fundamental principles (EMF, 2015a), provided in Figure 1:

Principle 1: Preserve and strengthen natural capital by controlling the limited stocks of non-renewable resources and balancing the flows of renewable resources.

Principle 2: Optimize the profitability of resources by circulating materials, components, and products in the technical and biological cycles and ensuring their maximum usability.

Principle 3: Promote system efficiency through openness and design in a way that avoids negative externalities.

Figure 1. Key principles of circular economy
Source: EMF, 2015

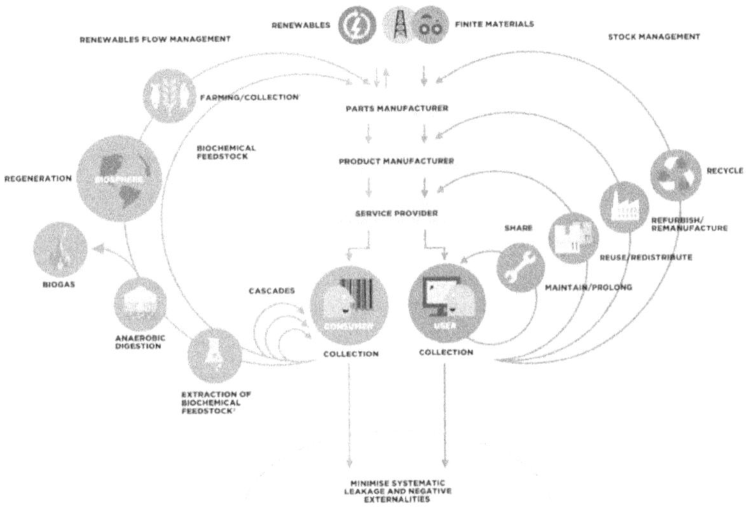

The above-mentioned principles and basic features of the circular economy have four sources of value creation (EMF, 2015a, p. 8; Bešter, 2017, pp. 16-17):

- **Inner circularity**: Means a reduction in material consumption compared to linear models. The tighter the circle, the more valuable the strategy. By repairing and maintaining a certain product (e.g., a car), we maintain most of its value. When this is no longer possible, the individual components can be reused or recycled. In this way, more value is maintained than when materials are recycled. Internal circles maintain more product integrity, its complexity and built-in work and energy.
- **Longer cycle**: Refers to increasing the number of consecutive cycles and extending the duration of individual cycles (reuse). Each extended life cycle means avoiding the use of material, energy and labor to create a new product.
- **Cascade reuse power:** Refers to the diversification of reuse in the value chain (e.g., cotton clothing is first reused as second-hand clothing, then in the furniture industry as padding for upholstered furniture and in the next cascade as insulation for building materials).
- **Power of the clean cycle**: Refers to the fact that uncontaminated materials are better suited for collection and redistribution and reuse, resulting in an extension of the life of products and an increase in the productivity of materials.

The circular economy can thus be defined as a model whose core is that all materials, products and processes are planned and designed from the outset in such a way that no waste is generated. In the ideal version, materials circulate all the time within the same or different uses.

The concept of circular economy has been attempted to define and interpret by many authors. Table 1 provides an overview of some of the definitions given by different authors and organizations over the last decade. The definitions of circular economy have in common that the concept allows to minimize the need for new resources and thus helps to reduce pressures on the environment by reducing resource extraction, waste disposal and emissions. In other words, the concept goes beyond just recycling and waste disposal. Of course, all these efforts are aimed at cost efficiency, economic growth and new business models for companies, as well as a different lifestyle for individuals.

Table 1. Overview of definitions of circular economy

Definition	Authors
The circular economy is an approach that would change the resource function in the economy. Factory waste would become a valuable input to other processes - and products could be repaired, reused or upgraded rather than thrown away.	(Preston, 2012)
The focus of the circular economy is gradually expanding beyond materials management issues to include other aspects such as energy efficiency and conservation, as well as land management, soil and water protection.	(Su et al., 2013)
The transition to a circular economy is essential condition for a resilient industrial system that enables new types of economic activity, strengthens competitiveness and creates jobs.	(Bastein et al.,2013)
The circular economy refers to a self-renewing economic system based on the principles of the cradle-to-cradle concept and the sustainable use of materials. Resources are used for high-quality design without contaminating the biosphere.	(WEF,2013)
The circular economy is an industrial system that is restorative or regenerative in purpose and design. It replaces the concept of waste with renewal, requires a transition to renewable energy sources, eliminates the use of toxic chemicals that harm reuse, and strives to eliminate waste through superior design of materials, products, systems, and, within that, business models. The overall goal is to enable the efficient flow of materials, energy, labor, and information so that natural and social capital can be restored.	(Ellen MacArthur Foundation 2013; 2015a)
The circular economy refers mainly to the physical and material resources of the economy - it focuses on recycling, limiting and reusing physical inputs to the economy, and using waste as a resource leading to a reduction in the consumption of primary resources.	(EEA, 2014)
A circular economy is one "in which the value of products, materials, and resources is maintained in the economy for as long as possible and waste is minimized." The transition to a more circular economy would "make a significant contribution to the EU's efforts to develop a sustainable, low-carbon and competitive resource-efficient economy. Such a transition represents an opportunity to transform our economy and create new and sustainable competitive advantages for Europe".	(European Commission, 2015)
The circular economy is an alternative to the traditional linear economy (take, manufacture, use and discard), in which we keep resources in use for as long as possible and try to make the most of their value during use, then reprocess and use products and materials.	(Mitchell, 2015)
The circular economy refers to the production and consumption of goods through closed-loop material flows that internalize the environmental externalities associated with the extraction of unprocessed resources and the generation of waste (including pollution).	(Sauvé et al.,2016)
The circular economy offers opportunities to create wealth, growth and jobs while reducing pressures on the environment. The concept can in principle be applied to all types of natural resources, including biotic and abiotic materials, water and soil.	(EEA, 2016)
Radical transformation of all product life cycle processes carried out by innovative actors has the potential not only to achieve material or energy recovery, but also to improve the overall life and economic model.	(Ghisellini et al., 2016)

Models and Processes of Circular Economy

Based on the review of definitions and interpretations of the circular economy concept, selected processes and models of the circular economy concept are presented below. They can serve companies and countries to generate economic, environmental and social benefits. At the company level, these processes represent various circular practices that help companies transition from a linear to a circular business model. The description of circular economy processes and models should be used to understand how companies and industries can implement the circular economy concept in practice. Two different approaches are presented below.

The first model was proposed by the Ellen MacArthur Foundation based on analysis and collaboration with companies. They undertook an assessment of the opportunities offered by the circular economy through six types of different activities. The concept is called "ReSOLVE" and combines the principles of regeneration, sharing, optimization, looping, virtualization and exchange. It is a tool that helps companies develop strategies for circular operation and non-linear growth. All activities of the model increase the utilization and efficiency of resource use, extend the life span and ensure that products are reused after the end of their useful life and are further processed in the next production processes or appear as a source (EMF, 2015a, p. 9). The ReSOLVE model is shown in Table 2.

Table 2. Model Resolve

Principe	Outcome
Regenerate	• Transition to renewable energy sources and materials, • Preservation and restoration of ecosystem health, • Return of renewable biological resources to the biosphere
Sharing	• Asset sharing services (e.g., cars, rooms, appliances); • Reuse / use of used items; • Extending the life-time of products through maintenance, creating greater durability, upgradeability
Optimize	• Increasing product efficiency; • Disposal and collection of waste in production and supply chains; • Impact of database use, automation, remote control and management
Loop	• Restoration and processing of products or components; • Recycling of materials / products; • Degradation of anaerobic materials; • Extract of biochemicals from organic waste
Virtualize	• Direct dematerialization (e.g., books, CDs, travel); • Indirect dematerialization (e.g., online shopping)
Exchange	• Replacement of the old with advanced and renewable materials; • Use of new technologies (e.g., 3D printing); • Choosing a new product or service (e.g., multimodal transport)

Source: EMF, 2015

The second model is summarized according to Rizos and co-authors (2017), who identify eight processes that can be further classified into three different categories, namely:

1. **Less** use of primary resources
2. Maintaining the **maximum value** of materials and products
3. **Changing** usage patterns.

The three umbrella categories and their processes are presented in Table 3. It should be emphasized that the categories of circular processes are not mutually exclusive. Many processes are often linked, and in some cases, companies may adopt a strategy that involves multiple circular processes.

Table 3. Processes of circular economy

Less use of primary resources	Recycling
	Efficient use of resources
	Utilization of renewable energy sources
Maintaining the highest value of materials and products	Processing, recovery and reuse of products and components
	Extending the lifetime of the product
Changing patterns of use	Product as a service
	Sharing models
	Shifting consumption patterns

Source: Rizos et al., 2017

The first category of less use of primary resources includes three processes:

1. **Recycling**: Recycling has been defined by the (United Nations et al., 2003, p. 79) as "the reintroduction of residual materials into production processes so that they can be transformed into new products". Recycling has been the most traditional way of implementing the principles of the circular economy for decades, by preserving the value of existing products and helping to reduce the need to extract raw materials from nature and to preserve the environment (Preston, 2012, p. 3). The European Environment Agency (EEA, 2016a) also points out that reducing the use of primary resources through recycling can provide further environmental benefits and help reduce greenhouse gas emissions associated with the use of material resources. Recycling should be understood not only as the reuse of materials, but also as the repurposing of recycled materials into their next life cycle.
2. **Efficient use of resources**: Another process that can lead to a reduction in the use of primary resources is the efficiency of their use. This process is related to the concept of cleaner production, which focuses on the efficiency of material and energy resources in processes (UNEP & Sida, 2006) and can include both the sparing use of resources and the replacement of hazardous or short-lived resources (Nilsson et al., 2007). Cleaner production refers to improvements in industrial production processes and products. Improving resource efficiency is also linked to the concept of eco-design, which can include not only elements related to recycling, processing and extending product life, but also other aspects such as dematerialization and material selection (Almeida et al., 2010). In the construction sector, for example, improved concrete design, careful material selection and improved technological and construction processes can enable the use of less or less CO2-intensive materials (Bribián et al., 2011).
3. **Utilization of renewable energy sources**: As we have already pointed out in the definition of the concept of the circular economy itself, the increasing use of renewable energy sources is a fundamental prerequisite for the transition to a circular economy. The burning of fossil fuels for energy

production is by definition non-renewable. Yet oil, natural gas and coal still account for almost three quarters of total energy consumption in the EU-28 (EC, 2016). The negative side effects are numerous, including pollution, greenhouse gas emissions and dependence on imports. Various renewable energy technologies exist to replace fossil fuels in the power, construction and transport sectors. Currently, biomass, renewable waste fractions, hydro, wind and solar energy dominate among renewable energy sources in the EU (EC, 2016).

The second category of maintaining the highest value of materials and products involves two processes:

1. **Processing, recovery, and reuse of products and components**. There are three ways we give our products a "next life" after their use. Restoration and remanufacturing involve restoring the basic components of products to retain the added value of the material. While the terms "restoration" and "remanufacturing" are both used, the latter term implies the idea of a deeper process that aims to restore the product to a "new" state. On the other hand, refurbishment is understood to refer to a less in-depth product processing (Van Weelden et al., 2016). Product remanufacturing is the direct reuse and/or resale of all or part of a product. All of these processes can change a company's revenue by allowing it to earn a second or third (or more) income from the sale of the product. Further processing is often used for certain, often high-priced parts of products, such as computers or cars (EMF, 2013). Such practices are closely related to the eco-design (eco-design) of products: for example, when recycling options are considered at the product design stage, it facilitates its disassembly and the reuse of parts (Prendeville & Bocken, 2015).
2. **Extending the lifetime of the product**. The concept of rotation can be implemented through the practice of extending the life of the product. Similar to the case of processing, extending the life of a product requires more emphasis on the planning phase of the product life cycle (Bocken et al., 2016). This means, for example, standardizing components by size or material. In the construction sector, product life extension is used, for example, in the design of modular components. These standardized components can be reused in new buildings or repaired and used in infrastructure or other industries (ARUP, 2016). It should be noted that life extension goes beyond the design of products for processing or reuse. It can also apply to products and components designed for long-term durability and long life.

The third category of changing usage patterns includes three processes:

1. **Product as a service**: A product as a service refers to the concept of offering a product as a service and represents a different business approach from the traditional sale of tangible products. It can be implemented through leasing, renting, payment for use, or performance-based business models. Tukker (2004) identified eight categories of business product models as service such as:

    a. Payment per unit of service (payment for copies.
    b. Renting or sharing a product where a consumer purchases access to a product for an agreed period of time.
    c. Leasing a product where the consumer has continuous access to the product.
    d. Grouped products where the majority of customers use the product at the same time (car sharing).

Figure 2. Strategies for achieving circular economy
Source: Potting et al., 2017

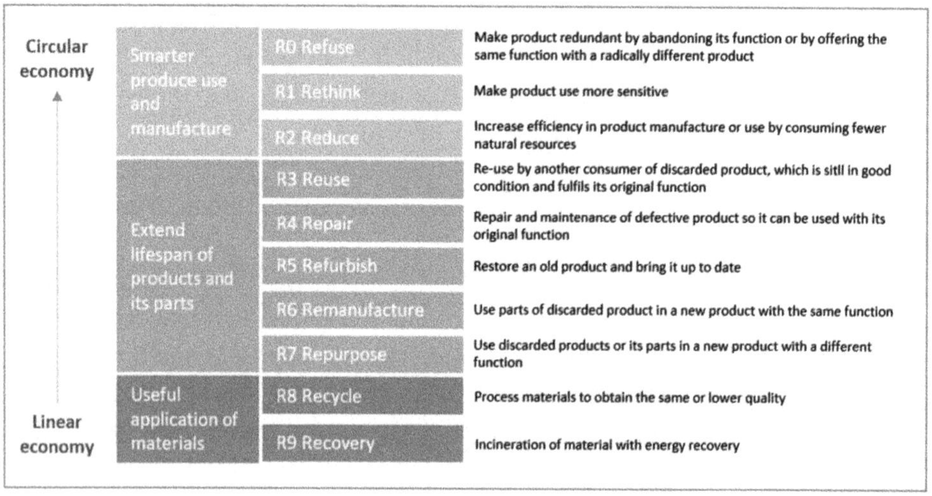

In most cases, the company retains ownership of the product in question and gives customers access to the product. In this way, the company conserves tangible assets. Such practices can have environmental benefits as the model encourages the company to repair and maintain a product that has been in use over time (Accenture, 2014).

2. **Sharing models**: Sharing models are inextricably linked to the concept of circular economy as they aim to reduce the underutilization of products and thus support more efficient use of resources. Sharing models can also contribute to the creation of genuine social capital (JRC, 2016). In addition to the exchange of products and services between individuals, this circular process can also take the form of the exchange of technologies and infrastructure between industry partners (Balanay & Halog, 2016). Sharing models have become established in the exchange of cars (e.g. Uber) and accommodation (e.g. Airbnb) due to advances in digital technologies. They are sometimes referred to as 'collaborative consumption' as they are often implemented through social platforms. Although it is generally accepted that these models can fundamentally change our consumption patterns in favor of the environment, these assessments remain quite vague and more research will be needed in the future to better assess the expected environmental benefits of such models.
3. **Shifting consumption patterns**: Technological advances and better consumer information are leading to shifts in demand patterns. For example, many consumers are opting for products or services that provide practical benefits rather than materials. Examples include digital books, smartphones, music, and online stores. At the same time, companies can make their products practical through virtual channels (e.g., selling digital products through online stores) and increasingly communicate with customers through online advertising, email, and social media (EMF, 2015b; Lewandowski, 2016). These shifts can lead to resource savings and productivity gains, but there are also concerns about the extent of the sustainability of such effects, as these products and services also consume large amounts of electricity in data centers (Whitehead et al., 2014).

In business practice, the circular economy often focuses on basic and traditional strategies such as exchange, recycling, recovery. However, real long-term impact can be achieved mainly through strategies at a higher level of sustainability, such as sharing economy, new business models. Figure 2 shows the strategies to achieve different levels of the circularity, based on an approach called "9R".

At the lowest level (R9), no circularity is achieved at all, while the highest level of circularity is achieved with strategies at the highest levels (R0). The strategies in Figure 15 show the levels of circularity that can be achieved with individual strategies. The strategies are arranged from high circularity (low R number) to low circularity (high R number). An analysis of circular economy practices has shown that companies mainly successfully implement the strategies that are at lower levels of achieving circularity (e.g. recycling strategy, R8) (Potting et al., 2017), while higher rates remain untapped and represent potential and goal, which can also be achieved by introducing different incentives for companies.

EU POLICY ON CIRCULAR ECONOMY

The European Commission has been promoting the development and implementation of a circular economy for many years, which has led to the concept being included in several EU strategies. A review of the last five years shows that in 2014, European Commission significantly transformed its strategy, which was previously based mainly on the waste aspect, into a more comprehensive concept and approach.

The previous circular economy proposal included the following initiatives:

- Towards a Circular Economy: a Zero Waste Program for Europe (EC, 2014a).
- Legislative proposal to review recycling and other waste-related targets in the EU (EC, 2014b).
- Ex-post evaluation of the Five Waste Streams Directives (EC, 2014c).

In 2015, the European Commission adopted an ambitious Circular Economy Action Plan, which includes measures to promote Europe's transition to a circular economy, increase global competitiveness, promote sustainable economic growth and create new jobs (EC, 2020a). The EU Action Plan for the Circular Economy (EC, 2015) sets out a concrete and ambitious program of 54 actions covering the whole cycle: from production and consumption to waste management and the market for secondary raw materials and the revised legislative proposal on waste. The annex to the Action Plan sets out the timeframe for the implementation of each measure. Its aim is to contribute to "closing the loop" of product life cycles through more recycling and reuse, thus making a positive contribution to the environment and the economy (EC, 2020a). By January 2019, more than 90% of the program's planned measures had been implemented.

The EU Circular Economy Action Plan is based on a joint partnership, starting from the idea that an efficient circular economy can only be achieved if public authorities, businesses and civil society work together. The aim of Action Plan is to implement the principles of the circular economy in all policy areas. Another feature is the combination of legislative, financial and supportive incentives, which places a strong emphasis on achieving progress in society and companies and involving all stakeholders. The Action Plan is a response to the 2030 Agenda as it empowers public authorities and stakeholders to accelerate the transition to a circular economy. The circular model can create jobs in Europe, foster innovation, create competitive advantages for EU companies and protect the environment in Europe and beyond.

The circular economy strategy of European Commission benefits and supports the achievement of several Sustainable Development Goals (SDGs), including SGD 6 on energy, SDG 8 on economic growth, SDG 11 on sustainable cities, SDG 12 on sustainable consumption and production, SDG 13 on climate change, SDG 14 on oceans and SDG 15 on life on land.

In 2018, a revised regulatory framework on waste came into force, setting clear waste reduction targets and an ambitious long-term pathway for waste management and recycling.

Three years after its adoption, the Circular Economy Action Plan is fully completed. At EU level, 54 measures have been adopted and will continue beyond 2019. In 2019, the European Commission adopted a comprehensive report on the implementation of the Circular Economy Action Plan. The report presents the main achievements of the Action Plan and identifies future challenges in shaping our economy to pave the way for a climate-neutral circular economy while minimizing pressure on natural and freshwater resources and ecosystems. As part of the final package for the circular economy, the key documents (EC, 2020a) are:

- Report on the Implementation of the Circular Economy Action Plan.
- Working document detailing the 54 actions of the Action Plan.
- Working document on sustainable products in the circular economy.
- Working document on the evaluation of voluntary commitments under Annex III to Plastics Strategy.
- Management and promotion of best practices in mining waste management plans.
- Summary of public consultation on the link between chemicals, products and waste legislation.
- Report on improving access to finance for circular economy projects.
- Report on Horizon 2020 R&D projects to support the transition to a circular economy.
- Circular Economy for Plastics.

In March 2020, the European Commission published a New Action Plan for a Circular Economy: Towards a Cleaner and More Competitive Europe (EC, 2020b; EU, 2020a). It announces initiatives for the coming years covering the whole life cycle of products, aiming for example at their design, the promotion of circular processes in the economy, the promotion of sustainable consumption and the objective of preserving the resources used in the EU economy. The Action Plan provides for legislative and non-legislative measures targeting areas where action at EU level brings real added value, and has the following objectives when adopting measures in the coming years (EC, 2020b). Based on the new Action Plan, the European Commission plans a series of measures over the next two years to develop a cleaner and more competitive Europe.

The New Action Plan introduces legislative and non-legislative measures targeting areas where action at EU level brings real added value and pursues the following objectives when adopting measures in the coming years (EC, 2020b):

- Making the design and production of sustainable products and services the norm in the EU.
- Empower consumers and customers.
- Focus on the most resource-intensive and high-potential sectors (e.g., electronics and information and communication technology, batteries and vehicles, packaging, plastics, textiles, construction and buildings, food, water...).
- Ensuring less waste.

- Establishing a circular economy that benefits people, regions and cities.
- Leading global efforts to establish a circular economy.

Based on the New Action Plan, European Commission plans a series of measures over the next two years to develop a cleaner and more competitive Europe. In this context, changes in legislation and other measures will address the following areas (EU, 2020a), which are presented in Table 1 and relate to five groups of measures. All measures are to be implemented over the next three years in order to achieve the desired effects as quickly as possible.

FRAMEWORK FOR IMPLEMENTATION OF CIRCULAR ECONOMY

Since the circular economy is an inclusive concept that needs to be introduced at all levels and in all parts of society, it also includes different stakeholder groups. They consist of stakeholders who have different roles in the economy and society and therefore have different objectives (see Figure 3). In efforts to introduce a circular economy, it is important to set different objectives and associated action plans, depending on the stakeholders and the level of analysis involved (WBCSD, 2018, 10):

- **Macro level**: this is the highest level, which includes cities, countries and international organizations;
- **Meso level**: represents all inter-industry networks;
- **Micro level**: represented by businesses and consumers;
- **Nano level**: is the lowest possible level of analysis, consisting of products and components.

Figure 3. The framework of stakeholders and levels of analysis for circular economy implementation
Source: WBCSD, 2018

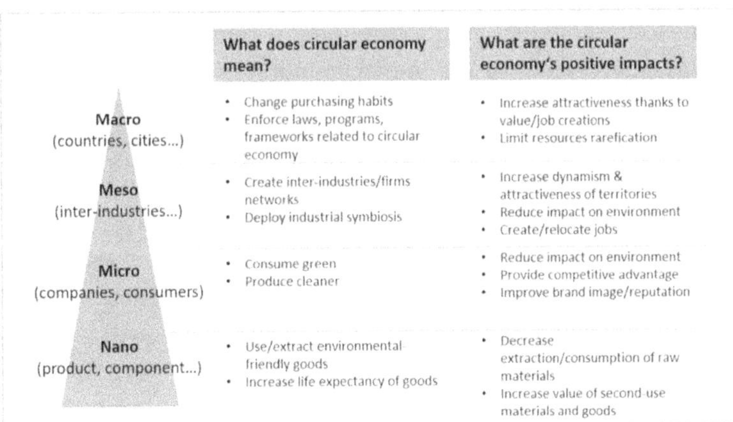

Building a circular economy requires complex efforts at local, national, regional and global levels. To move from the current linear to circular orientation, European economies and companies need to implement the concept of different circular principles. To ensure that the circular economy actually develops in a national context, it is crucial to determine the management of the development and implementation of circular economy strategies. Three steps are crucial to initiate a comprehensive process in the business community and to achieve broader support and involvement of different stakeholders:

- Who are the key partners and stakeholders that can **participate** and why?
- How can stakeholders be **involved** in the circular economy?
- How best to **organize** joint actions and ensure their effective implementation?

Figure 4. Framework for measurement and implementation of the circular economy concept
Source: Elia et al., 2017

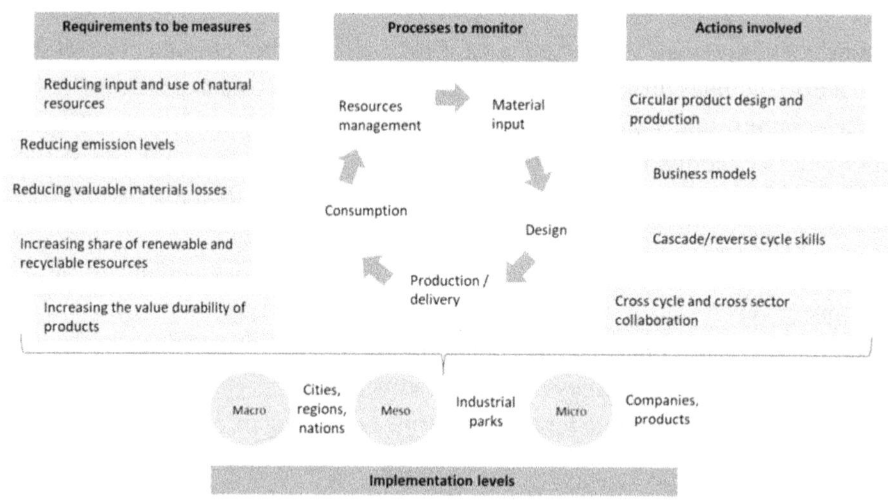

Implementing actions to develop the circular economy requires the involvement of many different stakeholders. This is particularly true for the implementation of a coherent, comprehensive strategy, which needs to involve a wide range of stakeholders, including local businesses, NGOs, social enterprises, academic and research centers, and consumers. Once the governance structure for developing and implementing circular economy strategies is in place, it is important to add a fourth important step and establish a system for monitoring and evaluating the circular economy, i.e., a framework for reviewing the implementation of the strategy and mechanisms for monitoring and evaluating its results.

The circular economy is based on the combination of environmental and sustainability concepts and on the development of an economic ecosystem in which economic growth is separated from resource and waste consumption and end-of-life emissions, the latter becoming sources rather than waste (Sauvé et al., 2016). This means closing material loops, reducing the need for raw materials and reducing waste.

In order to identify effective ways to measure the acceptance and implementation of the circular economy concept, it is necessary to evaluate and analyze the main related issues. To this end, a framework consisting of four elements was developed to assist in measuring the acceptance and implementation of the circular economy concept (see Figure 4). The four elements are:

1. The processes we monitor.
2. The measures included.
3. The requirements we measure and monitor.
4. The degree of circular economy implementation.

Starting from the first category, the processes we monitor, the circular economy usually includes five main phases:

1. Material input.
2. Design or construction.
3. Production or execution.
4. Consumption.
5. Resource management, which provides inputs to the first phase in closed-loop logic.

Within the proposed framework, these phases represent the processes whose performance needs to be measured in order to assess how circular the whole system is.

The second category of measures included consists of the basic building blocks identified by the Ellen McArthur Foundation (EMF, 2015a) and defines the basic building blocks to support the adoption of the circular economy. Four categories of measures are included:

1. **Circular design and manufacturing of products**: several measures can be placed in this category, starting with eco-design methods that aim to facilitate reuse, recovery and recycling, as well as product design and processes with less hazardous substances.
2. **Business models**: this category mainly includes the incorporation of new models, such as renting products instead of owning them, shared consumables.
3. **Cascade/reverse circular capabilities and skills:** developing closed-loop systems, e.g., with innovative technologies for high-quality recycling or cascading use of materials where high-quality recycling is not possible, and supporting the secondary raw materials market.
4. **Cross-sectoral cooperation**: actions in this category focus on strengthening cooperation in value chains, including by engaging new stakeholders in effective industrial symbiosis, preventing by-products from becoming waste but being used by different stakeholders in the processes.

In the third category, the requirements we measure and monitor include the creation of favorable systemic conditions for the transition to a circular economy through incentives and regulatory frameworks, as well as awareness raising and knowledge transfer (EEA, 2016, EMF, 2015a). Five groups of actions fall into this category (EEA, 2016):

1. **Reducing inputs and use of natural resources**: the main objective is to reduce the quality of natural ecosystems currently caused by linear models in the economy. The basic goal is to create more value by using less material. The direct consequence is also the conservation of natural resources through the efficient use of raw materials, water and energy.
2. **Reduction of emissions**: the aim is to reduce direct and indirect emissions.

3. **The reduction of the loss of valuable materials**: by introducing closed-loop models for the recovery and recycling of products and materials with return flows, the generation of waste can be avoided, incineration and landfill reduced, and energy and material losses reduced.
4. **Increasing the share of renewable and recyclable resources**: the aim is to reduce emissions throughout the materials cycle by using fewer raw materials and more sustainable sources, and to achieve a lower environmental impact by using cleaner materials.
5. **Increasing product sustainability**: This goal can be achieved by extending product life cycles, introducing new business models based on service-oriented services (e.g., leasing or renting products), or reusing products.

The fourth category is represented by three basic levels of circular economy actions (Ghisellini et al., 2016):

- **Micro level**, which refers to individual companies or customers and products.
- **Meso level**, which refers to industrial parks.
- **Macro level**, which covers the level from cities to regions and countries.

EMPIRICAL EVIDENCE ON CIRCULAR ECONOMY IN EU

In recent years, policy efforts have focused on implementing a circular economy throughout society. Measuring the circular economy has become one of the highlights. In the context of measurement, a number of approaches and methodologies have been developed to measure the circular economy at different levels, from the macro level (including the transnational level), the level of companies, users and other stakeholders, to the level of products and their components, materials and raw materials. As noted by European Commission (EC, 2018), monitoring progress towards a circular economy is a challenging task, as the transition is not limited to a few types of materials, products or sectors, but requires a systemic change that encompasses the whole economy; products and services, and involves all stakeholders of the company.

At the European Union level, the transition to a circular economy is monitored using a range of indicators, as there is no universally accepted 'circular economy indicator' and the scale of the concept makes it impossible to adequately monitor the circular economy using just one indicator (EC, 2018). To this end, a framework for monitoring the circular economy has been developed, as shown in Figure 5. The framework consists of ten indicators classified into four groups or domains of the circular economy:

1. Production and consumption
2. Waste management
3. Secondary raw materials
4. Competitiveness and innovation.

Figure 5. Framework for monitoring the circular economy in the EU
Source: EC, 2018

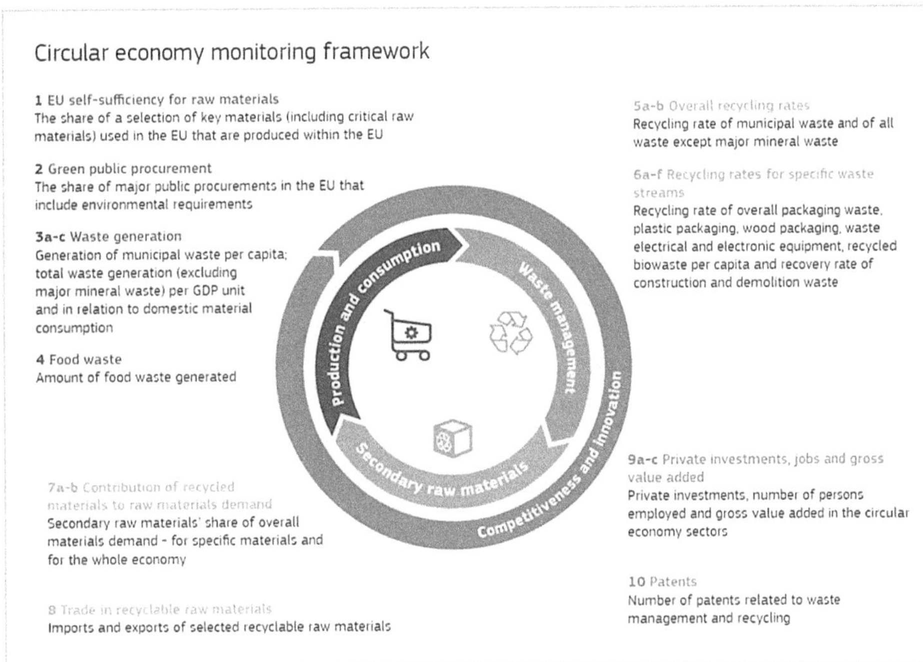

Table 4 presents empirical data on circular economy indicators for the EU-27 average. They are divided into four groups as shown in Figure 5.

The EU Monitoring Framework for the Circular Economy, presented in Table 4, includes 10 key indicators covering each stage of the life cycle of products as well as aspects of competitiveness. Regarding the first group of indicators, the transition to a circular economy requires active engagement of citizens in changing consumption patterns. Regarding the second group of indicators, EC supports Member States in the implementation of waste legislation in order to increase the implementation of circular economy opportunities in all Member States, especially those lagging behind in meeting the above targets. As regards the third group of indicators, one of the objectives of the Circular Economy Action Plan is to promote the use of secondary raw materials. In order to accelerate the transition to a circular economy and to maintain the global competitive position, it is necessary to invest in innovation and to support the adaptation of the industrial base.

SOLUTIONS AND RECOMMENDATIONS

As we have shown in the chapter, in order to fully implement the circular economy, it is essential to use the holistic approach and develop an appropriate policy and strategy with clearly stated objectives that involve all stakeholders. To start a comprehensive process in the economy and to support the different stakeholders involved, some key questions should be answered:

Table 4. Circular economy indicators for the EU average

Indicators		EU-27 Average
(A) Production and consumption		
1	EU self-sufficiency for raw materials (percentage), 2016	36.4
2	Green public procurement	N/A
3a–c	Waste generation	
3a	*Generation of municipal waste per capita (Kg per capita), 2018*	492
3b	*Generation of waste excluding major mineral wastes per GDP unit (Kg per thousand-euro, chain linked volumes 2010), 2018*	66
3c	*Generation of waste excluding major mineral wastes per domestic material consumption (percentage), 2018*	13
4	Food waste (million tons), 2016	70
(B) Waste Management		
5a–b	Recycling rates	
5a	*Recycling rate of municipal waste (percentage), 2018*	47
5b	*Recycling rate of all waste excluding major mineral waste (percentage), 2016*	56
6a–f	Recycling / recovery for specific waste streams	
6a–f	*Recycling rate of overall packaging (percentage), 2017*	67.5
6b	*Recycling rate of plastic packaging (percentage), 2017*	41.7
6c	*Recycling rate of wooden packaging (percentage), 2017*	41.2
6d	*Recycling rate of e-waste (percentage), 2018*	34.8
6e	*Recycling of biowaste (kg per capita), 2018*	83
6f	*Recovery rate of construction and demolition waste (percentage), 2018*	88
(C) Secondary raw materials		
7a–b	Contribution of recycled materials to raw materials demand	
7a	*End-of-life recycling input rates (EOL-RIR) (percentage)*	N/A
7b	*Circular material use rate (percentage), 2017*	11
8	Trade in recyclable raw materials	
8a	*Imports from non-EU countries (tons), 2019*	8,877,945
8b	*Exports to non-EU countries (tons), 2019*	25,467,976
8c	*Intra EU trade (tons), 2019*	47,905,897
(D) Competitiveness and innovation		
9a–c	Private investment, jobs and gross value added related to circular economy sectors	
9a	*Gross investment in tangible goods (percentage of GDP at current prices), 2017*	0.12
9b	*Persons employed (percentage of total employment), 2017*	1.72
9c	*Value added at factor cost (percentage of GDP at current prices), 2017*	0.96
10	Number of patents related to recycling and secondary raw materials, 2015	337.74

Source: EU, 2020b

- Who are the **key** stakeholder partners you can involve in the why?
- How can you **engage** stakeholders in the circular economy?

- How can **shared** services best be organized to implement them effectively?

As Dragoi et al. (2018) found, it is important to transform the paradigm of the national economy and implement the circular economy because it adds economic value through its environmental and social dimensions. In addition, Hysa et al. (2020) found that the circular economy should be supported by the main stakeholders of the sustainable economy, namely academia, government, business and civil society. Similarly, Khan and Khan (2020) found that the government needs to play a leading role and actively guide the circular economy in order to implement it efficiently in the economy.

Therefore, according to the analysis in this chapter and the findings of other authors, we can conclude that the implementation of a development-oriented circular economy policy requires the participation of various stakeholders. To be particularly relevant for the implementation of coherent, comprehensive policies, a wide range of stakeholders must be involved, including local businesses, non-governmental organizations, social enterprises, academic and research centers, and consumers. citizens. Once the policy for the implementation of the circular economy strategy is established, a fourth important step should be added to set up a monitoring and evaluation system for the circular economy, i.e., a framework to check the coherence of the strategy implementation in mechanisms to monitor and evaluate its results.

In planning for the comprehensive development of the circular economy at the national level, it is important to identify the different stakeholders or interest groups that will be involved in the implementation of the circular economy. It is important to involve as many different stakeholders as possible, as the implementation of the circular economy requires the participation of all stakeholders. The circular economy concept encompasses all types of sectors and affects lifestyles, production and consumption in many ways. Therefore, taking a systemic approach and seizing every opportunity to collaborate with different stakeholders that can promote circular economy initiatives is crucial. The private sector plays a key role in the circular economy. As providers of products and services, and in many cases as polluters, SMEs and larger companies need to be among the first to reap the benefits of more efficient resource use or to open up new markets with their eco-innovative products and services. At the same time, the circular economy can also be an unlimited source of innovation. Developing an entrepreneurial ecosystem around the circular economy by encouraging companies to collaborate and work with innovators or R&D institutions to develop green products and services can be a path to success. Establishing or fostering collaborations between established companies and start-ups or involving universities in the development of programs in this area are some of the ways to encourage the participation of different stakeholders for the benefit of the circular economy. In addition, raising awareness and informing the public about the benefits of the circular economy is becoming increasingly important. In this regard, urban communities, for example, as well as educators, academics and knowledge providers, play a key role in spreading positive messages and demonstrating the benefits of the circular economy and sustainable practices, as well as engaging more and more citizens in daily circular activities. Government and public institutions can become promoters of the circular economy and provide a platform for regional actors to participate in depth in circular economy projects. Government can facilitate the learning and development processes of shifting production and consumption to a circular economy by providing funding sources and improving regulations.

The development of an appropriate combination of policies at the national level for the development of the circular economy depends on the framework conditions defined by policies, regulations, taxes and other measures; the socio-cultural openness of people and businesses; the availability of infrastructure for circular economy activities (recycling, reuse, repair, processing); and the characteristics of entrepreneurship, research and development and innovation in the economy. The right combination of government policies is crucial to provide a clear long-term framework for the transition to circular economy models. This includes policy instruments to promote resource efficiency (waste reduction, recycling, reuse, recovery, etc.), to create demand for sustainably designed resource-efficient products and services, and to support resource conservation and eco-innovation in SMEs. The Ellen McArthur Foundation (2015b) proposes the following model as an implementation tool to enable a faster transition to a circular economy. The methodology is designed to allow countries to develop policy-level strategies to accelerate this process consists of three pillars:

1. Matching **starting points**, **ambition** and **focus**:
    a. Baseline level of circular economy and policy support.
    b. Defining desired level of ambition.
    c. Selecting sectors to focus on.
2. Assessing **opportunities** for individual activities:
    a. Outlining circular economy opportunities in each focus sector.
    b. Identification of circular economy opportunities.
    c. Quantify sector impacts.
    d. Identify barriers.
    e. Sector definition of actions.
3. Whole economy **impact** analysis:
    a. Quantitative assessment of economic impacts.
    b. Whole economy policy options maps.
    c. Identification of priorities, packages of measures and different policy options.

Several sets of measures should be introduced for the successful development of the circular economy, including regulatory and economic instruments, support for research and innovation, support for information, education and networking, and voluntary instruments.

CONCLUSION AND FUTURE RESEARCH DIRECTION

The chapter provides the current overview of the circular economy from the perspective of European Union. We have noted that the concept of the circular economy has evolved through several developmental phases, the most recent of which we have identified as the Circular Economy 4.0, which begins with a new program perspective in 2020. While the first phases of circular economy development focused on waste management, Circular Economy 4.0 requires the integration of sub-concepts into a more comprehensive concept, both in terms of the content and actors involved, as well as the level of implementation of the concept, in order to maximize the impact of the circular economy. Currently, it is estimated that the world is only 8.6% circular (Circle Economy, 2019). All circular economy development and implementation models are based on comprehensive approaches and the development of circular economy strategies that are measurable, regardless of the level of analysis.

Regarding the efforts of European Commission to implement a circular economy, we found that they have changed their strategy from a waste-based strategy to a more comprehensive approach in the strategy called EU Circular Economy Action Plan. It is based on a joint partnership of different stakeholders across society to introduce the circular economy. In addition to building a comprehensive circular economy system, EU efforts also focus on developing appropriate indicators to measure the circular economy. As a result, a set of indicators has been developed in the EU, comprising ten sets of indicators in four areas. They are available for each Member State to show the actual results of the implementation of the circular economy for the respective indicator.

Nevertheless, there are still gaps and challenges to overcome in the implementation of the circular economy. There are still no clearly defined indicators for measuring the implementation of the circular economy. Even the circular economy strategies we use to promote it do not include clear measurement criteria. For example, reduction can refer to different stages in the life cycle process, waste generation, raw material use, eco-design or consumption. For example, the reuse framework includes a varying number of strategies that increase the degree of circularity: discard, reconsider, reduce, reuse, repair, refurbish, restore, reinstall, recycle, and recover (Potting et al., 2017). Furthermore, the circular economy can refer to different levels of circular provision, from products or their parts to materials and energy. Circular economy strategies can also promote innovative business models that go beyond keeping products in use for the long term. Strategies to reduce redundancy, multi-functionality or intensify product use promote the circular economy by preventing the consumption of new products or creating new consumption patterns (Potting et al., 2017). Examples of such strategies are rental, sharing (e.g. car sharing), after-sales services to extend product life, virtualization (e.g. virtual meetings instead of travel), which are important tools to promote the circular economy as products are used more intensively (Tukker, 2015).

The EU still faces a challenge in implementing the circular economy. To achieve its wider application, society as a whole needs to be involved. However, for the successful implementation of the circular economy, collaboration between different stakeholders, such as government, civil society and private companies, is essential (CIRAIG, 2015). Thus, companies cannot implement it alone, but must be operationalized on a larger scale, regionally or nationally. Building on this, various stakeholders (CIRAIG, 2015) developed a proposal to overcome barriers to the implementation of the circular economy and a set of measures divided into niche measures (bottom-up approach) and basic measures (top-down approach), whose implementation is complementary. These measures would need to be initiated within the national economy if a circular economy was to be achieved. Only by involving different stakeholders could it be fully implemented in society. Therefore, future research on the circular economy should be based on the implementation level of the circular economy, strategies to involve and engage all stakeholders in society, and the broader levels of circular economy implementation.

REFERENCES

Accenture. (2014). *Circular Advantage: Innovative Business Models and Technologies to Create Value in a World without Limits to Growth*. Retrieved from https://tinyurl.com/hdu6tff

Allwood, J. M. (2014). Squaring the Circular Economy: The Role of Recycling Within a Hierarchy of Material Management Strategies. In E. Worrel & M. A. Reuter (Eds.), *Handbook of Recycling State-of-the-art for practitioners, analysts, and scientists*. Elsevier.

Almeida, C. M. V. B., Rodrigues, A. J. M., Bonilla, S. H., & Giannetti, B. F. (2010). Emergy as a tool for Ecodesign: Evaluating materials selection for beverage packages in Brazil. *Journal of Cleaner Production*, *18*(1), 32–43. doi:10.1016/j.jclepro.2009.03.019

ARUP. (2016). *The Circular Economy in the Built Environment.* Retrieved from https://tinyurl.com/gq79eno

Balanay, R., & Halog, A. (2016). Charting Policy Directions for Mining's Sustainability with Circular Economy. *Recycling*, *1*(2), 219–230. doi:10.3390/recycling1020219

Bastein, T., Roelofs, E., Rietveld, E., & Hoogendoorn, A. (2013). *Opportunities for a Circular Economy in the Netherlands*. Ministry of Infrastructure and Environment.

Bešter, J. (2017). *Ekonomsko učinkovito krožno gospodarstvo.* Ljubljana: Inštitut za ekonomsko raziskovanje.

Blomsma, F., & Brennan, G. (2017). The emergence of circular economy: A new framing around prolonging resource productivity. *Journal of Industrial Ecology*, *21*(3), 603–614. doi:10.1111/jiec.12603

Bocken, N. M. P., de Pauw, I. C., Bakker, C., & van der Grinten, B. (2016). Product design and business model strategies for a circular economy. *Journal of Industrial and Production Engineering*, *33*(5), 308–320. doi:10.1080/21681015.2016.1172124

Boulding, K. (1966). The Economics of the Coming Spaceship Earth. In H. Jarrett (Ed.), *Environmental Quality in a Growing Economy.* Johns Hopkins University.

Bribián, I. Z., Capilla, A. V., & Usón, A. A. (2011). Life cycle assessment of building materials: Comparative analysis of energy and environmental impacts and evaluation of the eco-efficiency improvement potential. *Building and Environment*, *46*(5), 1133–1140. doi:10.1016/j.buildenv.2010.12.002

CIRAIG. (2015). *Circular economy: a critical literature review of concepts*. Retrieved from https://www.ciraig.org/pdf/CIRAIG_Circular_Economy_Literature_Review_Oct2015.pdf

Circle Economy. (2019). *The circularity gap report 2020.* Retrieved from https://www.circularity-gap.world/2020

Cullen, J. M. (2017). Circular economy: Theoretical benchmark or perpetual motion machine? *Journal of Industrial Ecology*, *21*(3), 483–486. doi:10.1111/jiec.12599

Dragoi, M. C., Popescu, M. F., Andrei, J. V., & Mieila, M. (2018). Developments of the Circular Economy in Romania under the New Sustainability Paradigm. *Economic Computation and Economic Cybernetics Studies and Research*, *52*(2), 125–138.

EASAC. (2016). Indicators for a circular economy. Halle: European Academies' Science Advisory Council.

EC. European Commission. (2014a). T*owards a circular economy: A zero waste programme for Europe, COM/2014/0398 final/2*. Retrieved from https://eur-lex.europa.eu/legal-content/EN/TXT/?uri=CELEX:52014DC0398R%2801%29

EC. European Commission. (2014b). *Legislative proposal to review recycling and other waste-related targets in the EU*. Retrieved from https://ec.europa.eu/environment/waste/pdf/Legal%20proposal%20review%20targets.pdf

EC. European Commission. (2014c). *Ex-post evaluation of Five Waste Streams Directives, SWD/2014/0209 final*. Retrieved from https://eur-lex.europa.eu/legal-content/EN/TXT/?uri=CELEX:52014SC0209

EC. European Commission. (2015). *Closing the loop – An EU action plan for the Circular Economy, COM/2015/0614 final*. Retrieved from https://eur-lex.europa.eu/legal-content/EN/TXT/?uri=CELEX:52015DC0614

EC. European Commission. (2016). *EU Energy in Figures - Statistical Pocketbook 2016*. Retrieved from https://publications.europa.eu/en/publication-detail/-/publication/c3d179b2-9a82-11e6-9bca-01aa75ed71a1

EC. European Commission. (2018). *Communication on a monitoring framework for the circular economy, COM/2018/029 final*. Retrieved from https://eur-lex.europa.eu/legal-content/EN/TXT/?qid=1516265440535&uri=COM:2018:29:FIN

EC. European Commission. (2020a). *Circular Economy*. Retrieved from https://ec.europa.eu/environment/circular-economy/index_en.htm

EC. European Commission. (2020b). *A new Circular Economy Action Plan For a cleaner and more competitive Europe, COM/2020/98 final*. Retrieved from https://eur-lex.europa.eu/legal-content/EN/TXT/?qid=1583933814386&uri=COM:2020:98:FIN

EEA. European Environment Agency. (2014). Resource-efficient Green Economy and EU policies. Luxembourg: Publications Office of the European Union.

EEA. European Environment Agency. (2016). *Circular Economy in Europe - Developing the knowledge base. EEA Report No. 2/2016*. Luxembourg: European Environment Agency.

Elia, V., Gnoni, M. G., & Tornese, F. (2017). Measuring circular economy strategies through index methods: A critical analysis. *Journal of Cleaner Production*, *142*(4), 2741–2751. doi:10.1016/j.jclepro.2016.10.196

EMF. Ellen MacArthur Foundation. (2013). T*owards the Circular Economy. Economic and business rationale for an accelerated transition*. Cowes: Ellen MacArthur Foundation.

EMF. Ellen MacArthur Foundation. (2015a). *Towards the Circular Economy. Business rationale for an accelerated transition*. Cowes: Ellen MacArthur Foundation.

EMF. Ellen MacArthur Foundation. (2015b). *Delivering the Circular Economy – A Toolkit for Policymakers*. Retrieved from https://www.ellenmacarthurfoundation.org/assets/downloads/government/Delivering_the_circular_economy_A_toolkit_for_policymakers.pdf

EU. (2020a). *Circular Economy Action Plan*. Retrieved from https://ec.europa.eu/environment/circulareconomy/pdf/new_circular_economy_action_plan.pdf

EU. (2020b). *Circular economy indicators*. Retrieved from https://ec.europa.eu/eurostat/cache/scoreboards/CE/index.html

Euroflash Barometer. (2018). *SMEs, resource efficiency and green markets*. Retrieved from https://ec.europa.eu/commfrontoffice/publicopinion/index.cfm/survey/getsurveydetail/instruments/flash/surveyky/2151

Ghisellini, P., Cialani, C., & Ulgiati, S. (2016). A review on circular economy: The expected transition to a balanced interplay of environmental and economic systems. *Journal of Cleaner Production, 114*, 11–32. doi:10.1016/j.jclepro.2015.09.007

Homrich, A. S., Galvão, G., Abadia, L. G., & Carvalho, M. M. (2018). The circular economy umbrella: Trends and gaps on integrating pathways. *Journal of Cleaner Production, 175*, 525–543. doi:10.1016/j.jclepro.2017.11.064

Hysa, E., Kruja, A., Rehman, N. U., & Laurenti, R. (2020). Circular Economy Innovation and Environmental Sustainability Impact on Economic Growth: An Integrated Model for Sustainable Development. *Sustainability, 12*(12), 4831. doi:10.3390u12124831

JRC. (2016). *Scoping the Sharing Economy: Origins, Definitions, Impact and Regulatory Issues*. Retrieved from https://ec.europa.eu/jrc/sites/jrcsh/files/JRC100369.pdf

Khan, S. S., & Khan, S. A. (2020). Construction of New Circulation Model for Green Supply Chain of Agricultural Products in China. In S. A. Khan (Ed.), *Global Perspectives on Green Business Administration and Sustainable Supply Chain Management* (pp. 220–230). IGI Global. doi:10.4018/978-1-7998-2173-1.ch014

Lewandovski, M. (2016). Designing the Business Models for Circular Economy–Towards the Conceptual Framework. *Sustainability, 8*(43), 1–28. doi:10.3390u8010043

Mitchell, P. (2015). *Employment and the circular economy - Job Creation through resource efficiency in London*. London Sustainable Development Commission, the London Waste and Recycling Board and the Greater London Authority.

Moraga, G., Huysveld, S., Mathieux, F., Blengini, G. A., Alaerts, L., Van Acker, K., de Meester, S., & Dewulf, J. (2019). Circular economy indicators: What do they measure? *Resources, Conservation and Recycling, 146*, 452–461. doi:10.1016/j.resconrec.2019.03.045 PMID:31274959

Nilsson, L., Persson, P. O., Rydén, L., Darozhka, S., & Zaliauskiene, A. (2007). *Cleaner Production: Technologies and Tools for Resource Efficient Production*. Baltic University Press.

Pauliuk, S. (2018). Critical appraisal of the circular economy standard BS8001:2017 and a dashboard of quantitative system indicators for its implementation in organizations. *Resources, Conservation and Recycling, 129*, 81–92. doi:10.1016/j.resconrec.2017.10.019

Potting, J., Hekkert, M., Worrell, E., & Hanemaaijer, A. (2017). *Circular economy: measuring innovation in the product chain. Policy report*. PBL Netherlands Environmental Assessment Agency.

Prendeville, S., & Bocken, N. (2017). Design for Remanufacturing and Circular Business Models. In M. Matsumoto, K. Masui, S. Fukushige, & S. Kondoh (Eds.), *Sustainability Through Innovation in Product Life Cycle Design. EcoProduction (Environmental Issues in Logistics and Manufacturing)*. Springer. doi:10.1007/978-981-10-0471-1_18

Preston, F. (2012). *A Global Redesign? Shaping the Circular Economy. Briefing Paper*. Chatham House.

Rizos, V., Tuokko, K., & Behrens, A. (2017). *The Circular Economy: A review of definitions, processes and impacts*. CEPS Research Report No 2017/8, April 2017.

Sauvé, S., Bernard, S., & Sloan, P. (2016). Environmental sciences, sustainable development and circular economy: Alternative concepts for trans-disciplinary research. *Environmental Development*, *17*, 48–56. doi:10.1016/j.envdev.2015.09.002

Su, B., Heshmati, A., Geng, Y., & Yu, X. (2013). A review of the circular economy in China: Moving from rhetoric to implementation. *Journal of Cleaner Production*, *42*, 215–227. doi:10.1016/j.jclepro.2012.11.020

Tukker, A. (2004). Eight types of product–service system: Eight ways to sustainability? Experiences from SusProNet. *Business Strategy and the Environment*, *13*(4), 246–260. doi:10.1002/bse.414

Tukker, A. (2015). Product services for a resource-efficient and circular economy - A review. *Journal of Cleaner Production*, *97*, 76–91. doi:10.1016/j.jclepro.2013.11.049

UNEP & Sida. (2006). Applying Cleaner Production to MEAs – Global Status Report. United Nations Environment Programme, Division of Technology, Industry and Economics.

United Nations, European Commission, International Monetary Fund, Organisation for Economic Cooperation and Development, & World Bank. (2003). Handbook of National Accounting: Integrated Environmental and Economic Accounting 2003. United Nations.

Van Weelden, E., Mugge, R., & Bakker, C. (2016). Paving the way towards circular consumption: WBCSD. *Circular Metrics: Landscape Analysis*. Retrieved from https://www.wbcsd.org/Programs/Circular-Economy/Factor-10/Metrics-Measurement/Resources/Landscape-analysis

Whitehead, B., Andrews, D., Shah, A., & Maidment, G. (2014). Assessing the environmental impact of data centres part 1: Background, energy use and metrics. *Building and Environment*, *82*, 151–159. doi:10.1016/j.buildenv.2014.08.021

Witjes, S., & Lozano, R. (2016). Towards a more Circular Economy: Proposing a framework linking sustainable public procurement and sustainable business models. *Resources, Conservation and Recycling*, *112*, 37–44. doi:10.1016/j.resconrec.2016.04.015

World Economic Forum. (2013). *Young Global Leaders: Circular Economy Innovation & New Business Models Dialogue*. Retrieved from http://www3.weforum.org/docs/WEF_YGL_CircularEconomyInnovation_PositionPaper_2013.pdf

Yang, Q. Z., Zhou, J., & Xu, K. (2014). A 3R Implementation Framework to Enable Circular Consumption in Community. *International Journal of Environmental Sciences and Development*, *5*(2), 217–222. doi:10.7763/IJESD.2014.V5.481

ADDITIONAL READING

Bocken, N. M. P., de Pauw, I., Bakker, C., & van der Grinten, B. (2016). Product design and business model strategies for a circular economy. *Journal of Industrial and Production Engineering*, *33*(5), 308–320. doi:10.1080/21681015.2016.1172124

Geissdoerfer, M., Savaget, P., Bocken, N. M. P., & Hultink, E. J. (2017). The Circular Economy – A new sustainability paradigm? *Journal of Cleaner Production, 143*, 757–768. doi:10.1016/j.jclepro.2016.12.048

Ghisellini, P., Cialani, C., & Ulgiati, S. (2016). A review on circular economy: The expected transition to a balanced interplay of environmental and economic systems. *Journal of Cleaner Production, 114*, 11–32. doi:10.1016/j.jclepro.2015.09.007

Kirchherr, J., Reike, D., & Hekkert, M. (2017, December). Conceptualizing the circular economy: An analysis of 114 definitions. *Resources, Conservation and Recycling, 127*, 221–232. doi:10.1016/j.resconrec.2017.09.005

Lewandowski, M. (2016). Designing the Business Models for Circular Economy—Towards the Conceptual Framework. *Sustainability, 8*(43), 43. doi:10.3390u8010043

Moreno, M., De los Rios, C., Rowe, Z., & Charnley, F. (2016). A Conceptual Framework for Circular Design. *Sustainability, 8*(937).

Morseletto, P. (2020). Targets for a circular economy. *Resources, Conservation and Recycling, 153*, 104553. doi:10.1016/j.resconrec.2019.104553

Rajput, S., & Singh, S. P. (2019). Connecting circular economy and industry 4.0. *International Journal of Information Management, 49*, 98–113. doi:10.1016/j.ijinfomgt.2019.03.002

KEY TERMS AND DEFINITIONS

Circular Economy: An economic model that takes into account the use of resources and seeks to minimize the need for new resources and consequently helps to reduce pressure on the environment by reducing resource extraction, waste disposal and emissions.

Circular Economy Policy: A set of rules, measures and laws that define the implementation of the circular economy at different strategic levels (international, national, regional, local).

Indicators of Circular Economy: Specific indicators that aim to measure the implementation of different aspects of the circular economy. As the concept is broad, a range of indicators are used in practice to measure it.

Models of Circular Economy: Models that provide companies and other stakeholders with different ways to implement circular economy practices.

Processes of Circular Economy: Processes implemented by different actors of the circular economy concept, especially companies. These processes represent different circular practices that help companies to achieve a shift from linear to circular business processes.

Stakeholders: All groups of different interest groups of entities (e.g., individuals, organizations, local community, policy) associated with and responsible for the implementation of the circular economy. Different stakeholders have different objectives; therefore, the circular economy policy must address all of them.

Chapter 11
The Corporate Social Responsibility on Capital Market:
Myth or Reality?

Mirela Panait
https://orcid.org/0000-0002-5158-753X
Petroleum-Gas University of Ploiesti, Romania & Institute of National Economy, Romanian Academy, Romania

Razvan Ionescu
Independent Researcher, Romania

Irina Gabriela Radulescu
https://orcid.org/0000-0002-2551-1363
Petroleum-Gas University of Ploiesti, Romania

Husam Rjoub
https://orcid.org/0000-0001-6536-8971
Cyprus International University, Cyprus

ABSTRACT

The challenges generated by climate change have led to a greater involvement of companies in promoting the principles of sustainable development, one of the tools used being social responsibility programs. International organizations have launched various initiatives or principles to support companies in this complex process of transition to the green economy. The authors focused their analysis on the involvement of stock exchanges in the process of promotion of corporate social responsibility. The objective of this chapter is to identify the main tools used by stock exchanges in order to model the behavior of listed companies. In particular, the activity of the Bucharest Stock Exchange was analyzed. Even if it is an emerging market, the efforts made by this stock exchange and the results obtained can be used as a benchmark by stock exchanges in the region.

DOI: 10.4018/978-1-7998-7634-2.ch011

INTRODUCTION

The concept of Corporate Social Responsibility (CSR) appeared in the United States in the 1950s (Bowen, 1953), but charitable or philanthropic actions of business people can be detected in the early 15th century (Metaxas & Tsavdaridou, 2010). The social involvement of the companies generated a negative reaction from the local communities who were discontent with the negative consequences of the economic agents' activity. The literature retains the pros and cons of specialists on the honesty of companies, being voices that emphasize the artificial nature of social involvement of companies (Friedman, 1970) and consider companies to be innocent puppets of intellectual forces that undermine the basis of contemporary free society and preach in undisguised socialism (Ionescu, 2006). In addition, the programs of social responsibility which are promoted are considerd a mask to justify certain expenses and actions. Despite such opinions, gradually, the concept begins to be taken into account by companies and stakeholders. Moreover, the concept has evolved, and CSR acquires various forms of manifestation depending on the object of activity of the company, the level of development of country, origin of capital, etc.

The involvement of companies in the economy aims not only to maximize profit for shareholders, but also to support local communities, creating better working conditions for employees, protecting the environment (Piciocchi et al., 2009;Grigorescu & Saseanu, 2010;Matei, 2013;Deigh, et al., 2016). Moreover, stakeholders such as portfolio investors or corporate clients are increasingly paying attention to the involvement of companies in CSR programs and they sanction the inappropriate behavior of some companies through decisions to buy products or sell securities.

There are more and more voices who believe that the seemingly non-profit actions of companies (Friedman, 1970; Manne, 2006) are generated by the need to maximize profits given the economic, social and political pressures to which they are subject to. The motivation behind the initiation of CSR programs is difficult to establish, often being a combination of the need to maximize profits, to fit the market trend, to respond to pressures from consumers or portfolio investors (Zaman et al., 2020). In this way, in fact, companies have become aware of the need for their involvement in promoting sustainable development and we are currently witnessing a rebalancing of the relationship between economic, social and environmental performance (Dobrea, 2006).

CORPORATE SOCIAL RESPONSIBILITY - A NEW CONCEPT THAT SHAPES THE BEHAVIOR OF COMPANIES AND OTHER ENTITIES

Growing in importance over the years, the concept of Corporate Social Responsibility (CSR) is today synonymous with successful business and must be the basis of the strategy of all companies that want to conduct successful activities nationally or globally. CSR ensures a harmonization of the economic, social and environmental objectives of the companies, which are no longer in conflict, being integrated in the business strategy. (Porter& Kramer 2002; Ciutacu et al., 2005;Hoi et al., 2013;Matei, 2013;Pici et al., 2014;Brezoi, 2018;Barić et a., 2020;Gurtu, 2020;Hysa et al., 2020;Kim and Lee, 2020).

The financial scandals in which various large corporations were involved, the ecological disasters caused by the oil companies, the continuous pollution generated by the transport and industry companies have highlighted the negative externalities that the economic activity has and the negative impact on many categories of stakeholders such as employees, shareholders, local communities (Matei, 2013;Zaman et al., 2020). Today, almost 70 years after its conception, the term remains difficult to define, because currently there is no universal consensus when it comes to a definition for Corporate Social Responsibility. The authors will take advantage of this consensual vacuum to define Corporate Social Responsibility as the voluntary self-regulation of a company's business practices to minimize the negative impact, in the present and in the future, on society and human beings and also to maximize the positive potential on the environment, local communities, employees and other categories of stakeholders.

In addition, Social Responsibility is a concept in the process of crystallization considering that it can be applicable to several categories of entities such as public institutions, universities, portfolio investors, etc. The involvement of international organizations in promoting the concept and developing principles to guide the activity of companies and other entities have generated the popularization of the concept of Social Responsibility internationally (Matei et al., 2012; Ortas et al. 2015; Brown et al. 2018; Duca& Gherghina, 2018;Kim, 2018;ElAlfy et al., 2020;Monteiro et al., 2020). The launch of the Millennium Development Goals and subsequent, of the Sustainable Development Goals by the United Nations has led to a rethinking of the role of companies in the world economy and the possibilities generated by CSR programs in achieving these goals.

However, Corporate Social Responsibility should not be seen as a static and immovable strategy, universally applicable to all companies, but as a set of principles, values and measures that each company adapts to its own business model, field of activity, micro and macro economic and social environment.

Social responsibility strategies must anticipate and prevent negative events that may affect society, the environment and the economy and not just appear as a reactionary measure to them. Therefore, CSR involves not only reactive but also proactive actions, which should focus on maximizing the positive impact that a business has.A good CSR strategy can be the most effective marketing technique as long as it has a belief based on solid values and is motivated by a real desire to do good. But the reverse of the medal is also valid.

In the age of information that circulates almost instantaneously, critical thinking, and distrust of unethical practices often used by companies, misleading CSR strategies can give rise to hostile responses from society. Greenwashing strategies specific to companies in polluted industries are known and sanctioned as such by stakeholders (Vollero et al., 2016). The adoption of Corporate Social Responsibility policies must be accompanied by the assumption of a set of ethical principles that provide clear directions for action in the present, but also in the future. The development of programs to be implemented, funded or supported by a company must take into account real social needs and not just a marketing strategy hidden in good intentions. In this way, CSR is an essential component of business strategy that should not be confused with peripheral philanthropic actions (Bhattacharya et al., 2004;Sahay, 2011;Matei, 2013;Vukić et al., 2020).

Table 1. The five dimensions of CSR

Environment size	companies must consider protecting and conserving the environment as well as building a sustainable business, focused on a rational use of natural resources, avoiding waste, recycling and avoiding overproduction (Kolk, 2016)
Social size	Through the practiced social CSR policies, the company must be a catalyst for positive changes from a social point of view in the area in which it operates and beyond. According to the Global Compact Principles launched by the United Nations, corporate social responsibility must also address issues related to human rights and labor standards. (Wettstein, 2012;Matei, 2013;Ramasastry, 2015)
Economic size	The economic dimension refers to the impact that CSR policies have on the smooth running of the business by directly contributing to the process of sustainable economic development (Raimi et al., 2015). More and more studies published in reference journals the direct relationship between CSR programs and economic performance of companies (Timbate, & Park, 2018;Khan et al., 2019;Siminica et al., 2019;Sichigea et al., 2020)
Stakeholders size	Interaction with stakeholders refers on the one hand to ethical and moral behaviors in the interaction with employees, customers, suppliers, and on the other hand to a high level of transparency regarding the business. Keep in mind that any member of society can become, at one time or another, interested in a particular business, even if only from the perspective of the citizen affected by certain practices of the company. For this reason, at international level the emphasis is on the transparency of the activities carried out by the companies, these being encouraged or obliged to insert in the annual activity report aspects related to social involvement or environmental impact. (Khan et al., 2019;Matuszak&Różańska, 2017;Atlı et al., 2018;Aybars et al., 2019;Uysal et al., 2019;Nour et al., 2020;Zaman et al., 2020)
Voluntary size	The voluntary dimension refers to the actions that a company carries out, voluntarily, without being obliged by law or without being influenced by social pressure, in the field of CSR.

Source: Own elaboration based on Dahlsrud, 2008 and specific papers mention in the table.

However, the five dimensions represent only the conceptual framework around which an action plan must be built, materialized through initiatives implemented by companies (Dahlsrud, 2008). Corporate social responsibility involves several types of initiatives (Dahlsrud, 2008;de Jong& van der Meer, 2017):

1. Corporate **philanthropy** that includes the involvement of a company in charitable causes by donating money, goods or services. Large companies often set up foundations that run charitable events on their behalf.
2. Corporate **volunteering** involves the participation of a company's employees in volunteering actions. Companies established in Romania have begun to give special importance in recent years to corporate volunteering programs, employees being motivated to participate in such actions by providing benefits such as bonuses or days off. Vodafone Romania carries out the corporate volunteering program "Build for tomorrow" with 600 employees, hundreds of MOL Romania employees carry out voluntary work activities in seven dormitories belonging to the Saint Francis Foundation in Deva, OMV Petrom employees actively and constantly participate in training reforestation programs organized by the social responsibility platform "Andrei's Country".
3. **Socially responsible** business practices through which companies try to minimize the impact of their operations on the environment and society. In 2017, the retailers of DIY products Horrnbach, Brico Depot and Leroy Merlin gave up the collaboration with Holzindustrie Schweighofer, following the scandal regarding illegal deforestation.

4. **Corporate activism** through which companies promote through their own efforts various social causes to bring them to the attention of the public and attract social, corporate or institutional involvement.
5. **Cause-related marketing - an increasingly** common type of initiative that involves donating funds to a cause or charity event, funds that depend on the sale of a particular product or service (Matei, 2013).
6. **Corporate social marketing - campaigns** financed by companies that try to change certain behaviors and attitudes in society (Hessekiel et al., 2012;Matei, 2013).

These types of initiatives are a good starting point for formulating a coherent corporate social responsibility strategy. However, managers need to take many variables into account when developing an action plan. The size of the company and the sector of activity in which it operates will also dictate the expectations of the company in the field of social responsibility. For example, a company with a high turnover and a high profit margin, whose operations have a major impact on the environment will have to be much more involved in social responsibility projects than a small company operating in the renewable energy sector (Ioana-Maria & Adriana, 2012;Matei, 2013;Kumar et al., 2020). A coherent plan for social responsibility actions must go through the following steps:

Table 2. The steps of CSR plan

Defining goals
Employee involvement at all levels
Harmonization of the social responsibility strategy with the general business strategy
Creating partnerships with non-governmental organizations
Constant monitoring of activities
Assessing the impact of taken actions
Reporting in a transparent manner the activities in the field of CSR in the annual activity report

Source: Own elaboration based on Ioana-Maria & Adriana, 2012, Matei, 2013, Kumar et al., 2020

The EU stands out through its initiatives to promote sustainable development and CSR in corporate activity. In addition to general concerns about sustainable development, CSR has become an area of interest for European authorities who, being aware of the potential of CSR to promote sustainable development, seek to create a legal framework and establish guidelines for European companies (Matei, 2013;Volosevici, 2013). Starting with the document entitled "Manifesto of Enterprises against Social Exclusion", CSR issues have been included in the EU's concerns. CSR Europe was created - a network that supports dialogue between companies and the exchange of good practices in the field of social responsibility. In 2001, the Green Paper of the Social Responsibility "*Promoting a European framework for corporate social responsibility*" was published. The sustainable development strategy adopted in 2001 considers that environmental protection, social cohesion and economic growth are interdependent. Through the measures taken, the EU has become an international leader in promoting CSR starting from the ambitious goal set in 2006 by the Communication of the European Commission of 23.03.2006 "*To make Europe a pole of excellence in the field of Corporate Social Responsibility*".

In addition, the European Union is a signatory to the United Nations 2030 Agenda for Sustainable Development, a position from which it undertakes to draw up a concrete plan on sustainable financing in the context of the Capital Markets Union, for the benefit of the planet and society. In presenting the strategy for implementing the 2030 Agenda, Frank Timmermans, First Vice-President of the European Commission, said: "*The transition to a greener and more sustainable economy is good for job creation, for people and for the planet. Today we make sure that the financial system also participates in achieving this goal. Our proposals will enable investors and citizens to make the right choice so that their money is used more responsibly and supports sustainability.*" (Sustainable funding: The Commission's Action Plan for a Greener and Cleaner Europe).

The key elements of the European Union's action plan for implementing the 2030 Agenda for a greener and cleaner economy are:

1. Establish a **common language** at European Union level that clearly defines what is meant by sustainability and identifies areas where these practices can have the greatest impact. A consensus on the taxonomy of sustainability would increase investor confidence and give entrepreneurs a better ability to understand and identify sustainable investments.
2. **Clarification of the debt of institutional investors** and **asset managers** to invest taking into account sustainability. They are in a unique position to direct capital flows towards sustainable investment.
3. **Introducing sustainability advice** as a mandatory requirement for investment firms in relation to their clients.
4. **Integrate sustainability** into prudential requirements for banks, pension funds and insurance companies. They will be able to be allowed, for example, to make larger investments in sustainable activities.
5. **Reviewing transparency** requirements for corporate reporting as well as developing universally accepted standards for measuring the impact on the environment and society at large.

Thus, the European Union is trying to place sustainability at the heart of the financial system, making systemic changes that will not only help implement the principles of Social Responsibility and Corporate Governance but also stimulate inter-state cooperation and protect the European economy from possible shock waves (Méndez-Suárez et al., 2020).

CSR ON THE FINANCIAL MARKET. INSIGHTS FROM STOCK EXCHANGES

The changing attitude of society and investors towards capital market investments and companies' practices as well as the growing concern for the impact that economic activities have on the environment have set in motion a number of international initiatives that seek to promote and support more sustainable business models based on caring for human life, society as a whole, the rational use of natural resources and minimizing the impact on the environment. Corporate governance and good business practices are today a mandatory criterion for companies that want to attract attention, as well as for portfolio investors (Matei, 2013;Andrei et al., 2018;Ionescu, 2019;Pejić Bach et al., 2020;Raimi et al., 2020).

Financial markets are in a metamorphosis process, fueled by financial innovations generated by technical progress but also by the need to promote the principles of sustainable development. In various forms, financial market participants - banks, brokerage firms, stock exchanges, portfolio investors can generate concrete actions that protect the environment and use resources more rationally (Matei, 2013;Ionescu & Radulescu, 2019). The most relevant initiatives belonging to international institutions to promote sustainable development are Green Investment Principles, Equatorial Principles, Compact Global Principles for Portfolio Investors, and are addressed to private companies that carry out various CSR programs, portfolio investors and stock exchanges.

Financial institutions play an important role because they can shape the behavior of listed companies, clients or investors who act on different components of the financial market (Lee & Kim, 2020;Panait et al., 2020). Banks run multiple CSR programs aimed at local communities, supporting cultural or sports activities for young people or people with disabilities and are also involved in financial education programs. Financial education has gained particular importance in recent decades given the importance and repercussions of financial decisions made by individuals (eg, taking out a 30-year mortgage) or initiating an investment plan for the post-retirement period (Ene &Panait, 2017;Voica, 2017). The international financial crisis triggered in 2008 but also the multiple scandals in which the banks were involved have determined the decrease of the financial consumers' confidence in the banking and capital system, reason for which the CSR programs are welcome to improve their image among the stakeholders (Hinson et al., 2010; Armeanu et al. 2016). The unethical behavior of banks is sanctioned by financial consumers who have become aware of their strength and who use the levers offered by state institutions (consumer protection authorities, courts). The regional crisis of the Swiss franc in Central and Eastern European countries has affected a large number of consumers who have tried to restore the balance of power by suing banks that have used various unfair commercial practices or imposed abusive contractual clauses to customers. Financial consumer confidence in banks has deteriorated considerably in recent decades, which is why credit institutions are now in a complex process of improving their image by running financial education and financial inclusion programs that aim to strengthen customers' financial knowledge and skills and attracting vulnerable groups into the banking circuit .

International financial institutions such as the International Bank for Reconstruction and Development or the International Finance Corporation are also involved in the process of greening financial markets, coming up with technical solutions or specific financial support.

The process of financial innovation so blamed in the last ten years (after the onset of the 2008 crisis) for the emergence and expansion of toxic assets now looks different, as new financial products are being launched to support environmental protection, local community development or inclusion and to decrease the financial risk of vulnerable consumers.

In the battle between banks to attract new customers, the concept of financial inclusion has emerged and gained ground. Financial innovation allows the attraction in the financial circuit of new categories of clients, considered until recently, vulnerable due to low incomes or limited access to traditional financial services.

Another level on which banks can act to promote sustainable development is the use of ESG criteria that are imposed on customers (companies) who want to obtain loans (eg Equator Principles). Environmental, Social and Governance (ESG) criteria are a set of standards for a company's operations that socially conscious investors use to screen potential investments. Environmental criteria consider how a company performs as a steward of nature. Social criteria examine how it manages relationships with employees, suppliers, customers, and the communities where it operates. Governance deals with a company's leadership, executive pay, audits, internal controls, and shareholder rights. Due to the effectiveness and importance of ESG in credit worthiness evaluation, recently Fitch Rating issued Environmental, Social and Governance- Relevance scores (ESG.RS). ESG been used by banking sector for credit application since it help to determine the collateral values.

Portfolio investors have become increasingly aware of their importance in promoting sustainable development, because through concrete actions of divestment or acquisition of securities sanction companies with a negative externalities on the environment or encourage companies that have a positive attitude towards the environment, local communities, etc. The presentation of some examples of good practices from European and Asian countries will provide additional information on the involvement of different categories of stakeholders to achieve the SDGs launched by United Nations. In addition, the new European regulations on the non-financial reporting of large companies help portfolio investors who have more sources of information on the involvement of companies in promoting the principles of sustainable development (Sierra-Garcia et al., 2018;Szadziewska et al.;2018, Banța, 2019)

Stock markets also play an important role in promoting sustainable development because through their position on the capital market, they can impose codes of conduct, guidelines, the principle of corporate governance or CSR, they can establish listing rules or they can create trading markets for companies that meet certain ESG criteria or trading segments for certain products such as carbon and stock indices with a specificity, such as sustainability indices. Together with consulting firms, issuers and rating agencies, stock exchanges are significantly involved in the process of financial innovation that generates financial products that have different components that try to combat the negative effects of climate change or that generate environmental benefits (tools like green, blue and sustainability bonds). Several international bodies UN PRI, UNCTAD and UN Global Compact have launched the "Sustainable Stock Exchanges" initiative to improve the relationship between stock exchanges, listed companies, investors, capital market authorities to promote socially responsible investment (Panait et al., 2014;SSE, 2020).

Intended to encourage sustainability and sustainable development, green bonds finance environmentally friendly and low impact projects such as clean energy and transportation, sustainable agriculture and pollution prevention (Deschryver & De Mariz, 2020;Lebelle et al, 2020;Liaw, 2020). A financial novelty, ***green bonds*** issuance has soared in recent years. Only 2.6 billion dollars of green bonds had been issued in 2012. However, as of 2019, global green bonds issuance has exceeded 200 billion dollars with the United States and China on top of the leaderboard.

And with growing concern over environmental issues, the green bonds market is only set to rise. With the European Union leading the way in the global race to cut carbon emissions, the European Commission is considering issuing green bonds for the first time as part of its 750 billion dollars borrowing plan for the mitigation of the economic impact of the SARS CoV-2 pandemic (FT, 2020a).

Sustainable finance seems to be more than just a trend. It appears to be the future of investing. **ESG funds** gain traction quickly as more and more investors place sustainability, accountability and transparency ever higher on their list of priorities in the investment decision making process. Bank of America Merrill Lynch predicts that up to another 20 trillion dollars will be invested in ESG funds over the next three decades as more and more capital moves away from non sustainable industries with a high level of negative environmental and social impact (Bank of America, 2020). The process of fossil fuel divestment is the perfect example of this new trend (Dordi & Weber, 2019). As of April 2020, over 14 trillion dollars worldwide are in the process of being divested from the fossil fuel industry.(GFF, 2020) During the global health crisis generated by the SARS CoV-2 pandemic, ESG funds have managed to attract a record number of investors, with net inflows of 71,1 billion dollars between April and June 2020 (FT, 2020b). And the trend is gaining momentum. An analysis by Deloitte estimates that by the year 2025, half of all managed assets in the United States will be ESG-mandated. (Deloitte, 2020) And

ESG funds don't offer investors just peace of mind from an ethical perspective. They are performers as well and manage to offer consistent returns. In 2019, nine of the biggest ESG mutual funds in the US outperformed the S&P 500 index. Here are the five top performing US-based ESG funds ranked by percentage of total return in 2019:

Figure 1. Value of green bonds market worldwide in 2019 by major country (in billion US dollars).
Source: Statista, 2019

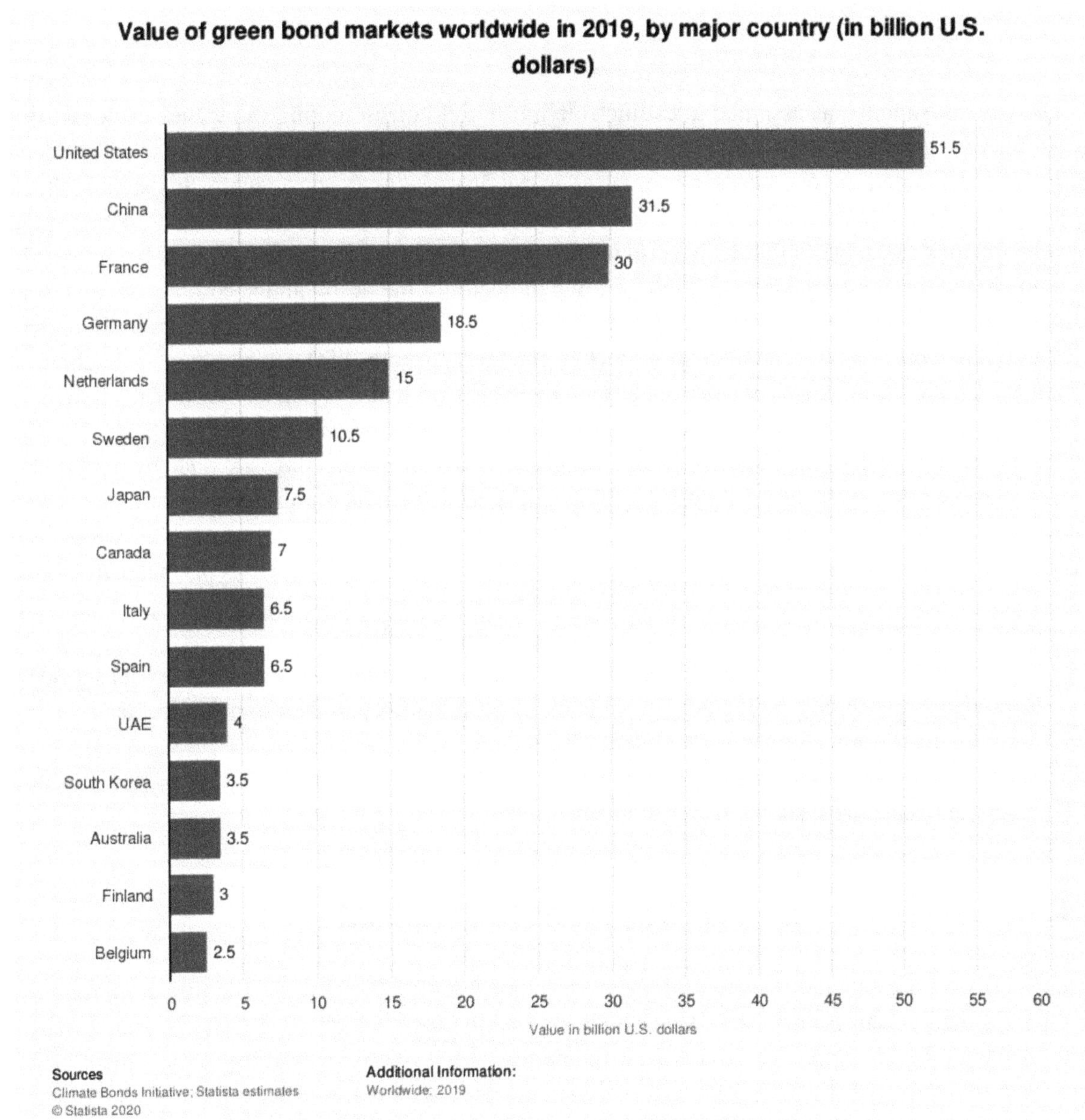

Table 3. US based ESG funds with the highest returns in 2019

Name	Assets $M	1-Year Total Return (%)
Ave Maria Growth Fund	878	+37.09
Calvert Equity Fund	3,766	+36.50
Putnam Sustainable Leaders Fund	4,941	+35.84
Morgan Stanley Institutional Fund - Global Opportunity Portfolio	3,846	+35.03
Brown Advisory Sustainable Growth Fund	2,086	+34.88

Source: Bloomberg, 2020

The United Nations has assumed a leading role in the field of promoting the values of Social Responsibility in the field of capital markets. Thus, in addition to the Global Compact Principles launched by the United Nations, the organization is involved in the financial sector through the Sustainable Stock Exchanges Initiative (Matei, 2013;SSE, 20200). Launched in 2009, this initiative aims to increase the capacity of stock exchanges around the world to support sustainable development. The global interest in participating in this program has been high, a strong indicator of the desire and need for change present throughout the planet. Thus, among the partners of the initiative are the stock exchanges in Shanghai, Santiago, New York as well as the Bucharest Stock Exchange. Currently, the Sustainable Stock Exchanges Initiative includes 96 stock exchanges from around the world, on which financial instruments issued by 52,132 companies are traded, whose total capitalization exceeds 87 million US dollars.

The modus operandi of the initiative consists of global and regional meetings attended by representatives of partner stock exchanges, investors, company leaders as well as representatives of national and international regulatory bodies in the field of capital markets. According to its statement of principles, the Sustainable Stock Exchanges initiative has identified five sustainable development goals that it promotes:

1. **Equal opportunities** for the rise of women in leadership positions.
2. Development of **small** and **medium-sized enterprises** by facilitating access to financial services.
3. **Encourages companies** to include information on sustainability in their annual reports.
4. Adapting to **climate change** and counteracting its effects.
5. Encouraging **global partnerships** between stakeholders to share information, technology and expertise to support sustainable development.

BUCHAREST STOCK EXCHANGE - REGIONAL PLAYER

Stock exchanges are a vital component of a well-developed market economy. In the former communist countries, stock exchanges appeared after 1990, being mainly stock markets. The first companies traded were the state owned companies. In this way, the public authorities supported the development of local capital markets, but the stock exchange-specific mechanisms for the privatization of state-owned companies was used with moderation. The interest of private companies is quite low for the capital market, they continue to use bank credit as the main financing mechanism. The launch of municipal and state bonds was another moment that contributed to the development of capital markets in Central and

Eastern Europe. The derivatives markets are small, and the product offer is modest compared to the big American or European stock exchanges. In some countries, such as Romania, futures and options are no longer traded.The small size of these stock exchanges can be seen both from the volume of transactions with shares and bonds (Annex 1) and from the data on stock market capitalization relative to GDP. The Stock Market Capitalization-to-GDP ratio is a metric made popular by American investor Warren Buffet and subsequently came to be known as the "Buffet Indicator". The indicator helps determining whether a certain market is undervalued or overvalued by comparing the value of an economy's stocks to the value of its total output. The Stock Market Capitalization-to-GDP ratio is calculated using the following formula:

Table 4. Stock Market Capitalization-to-GDP for specific Central and Eastern European countries

Country	Stock Market Capitalization (EUR m)	GDP (EUR m)	Stock Market to Capitalization Ration
Bulgaria	14267	61239	23%
Croatia	20039	54237	37%
Czech Republic	23426	223945	10%
Hungary	29366	146061	20%
Poland	135035	532329	25%
Romania	23331	223337	10%

Source: Own elaboration based on Fese.eu and Eurostat.eu

Market Captalization to GDP = (SMC/GDP)*100

Where:

SMC – Stock market capitalization
GDP – Gross domestic product

Figure 2. Market capitalization visualised in comparison to the GDP of Bulgaria, Croatia, Czech Republic, Hungary, Poland and Romania.
Source: Own elaboration based on Fese.eu and Eurostat.eu

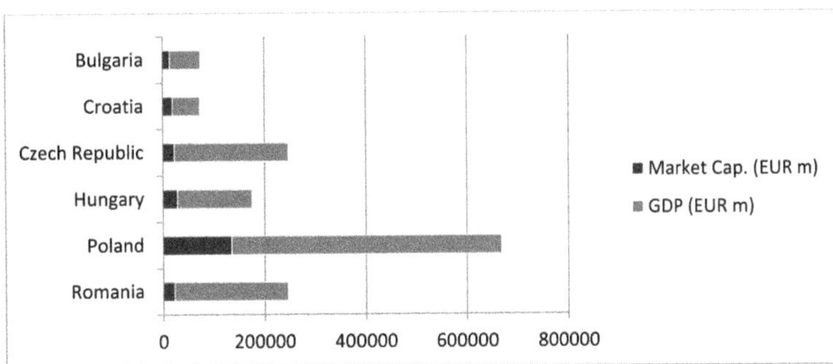

Generally, a ratio greater than 1 or 100% indicates an overvalued market while a ration below 0.5 or 50% suggests that the market of that certain economy is undervalued.[1]

The Stock Market Capitalization-to-GDP ratio in 2019 is calculated for the following six countries: Bulgaria, Croatia, Czech Republic, Hungary, Poland and Romania (table 4).

The chart above suggests that the stock markets of all six countries are currently undervalued, displaying potential for future growth (figure 2).

Judging from the perspective of Social Responsibility, stock market institutions can be considered a mirror of the national business environment, a mirror that externally reflects the degree of sustainability of an economy (Matei, 2013;Panait et al., 2014, Garcia-Sanchez et al., 2019; Pérez& López-Gutiérrez, 2019). As the sole administrator of the securities markets in Romania, the Bucharest Stock Exchange (BSE) can be compared only with similar institutions from other states to highlight the degree of involvement in the activities of Corporate Governance, Social Responsibility and sustainability.In the most recent market classification report, published in September 2019, the British group FTSE Russel (a stock index provider operated by the London Stock Exchange), announced that Romania's capital market will be reclassified from the status of Frontier Market to that of Secondary Emerging Market. The decision will become effective as of September 2020.

Box 1. BSE. Structural landmarks.

The company operates the only capital market in Romania, the Bucharest Stock Exchange, currently composed of two distinct markets: the Regulated Market (Main Market) and the AeRO market (Alternative Exchange Romania - Alternative Trading System). The two markets differ in terms of the requirements that must be met by companies that want to be listed. The AeRO market is mainly dedicated to start-ups and small companies that want to attract financing from the capital market but do not meet the requirements, much stricter, necessary for listing on the main market. The listing on the AeRo market is made on the basis of a presentation document, the costs being also much lower compared to the listing on the Main Market.

Currently, on the Main Market of the BSE are listed 85 companies (Annex 1), while on the AeRO Market there are shares issued by 289 companies. However, the shares are not the only movable asset that can be traded on the BSE. Below is a complete list of financial instruments that can be sold or bought using the Bucharest Stock Exchange platform.

As can be seen, the Bucharest Stock Exchange offers investors a wide range of financial instruments that meet all investment needs and address different degrees of appetite or risk aversion. Stock indices can form a good starting point for creating an investment portfolio and the possibility to trade bonds and government securities is available to investors, whether private or institutional looking for safe investments, with a previously known result.

Source: bvb.ro

Upgrading to the status of Secondary Emerging Market will increase the confidence of international investors as well as the inflow of foreign capital into the Romanian economy.

Starting with 2018, with the merger between the Sibiu Monetary-Financial and Commodity Exchange (SIBEX) and the Bucharest Stock Exchange, the latter remained the only stock exchange in Romania where securities are traded. The Romanian capital market, although a young one, had to adapt quickly to the new European and global standards in terms of Social Responsibility and Corporate Governance (Matei, 2013;Panait et al., 2014). Thus, the Bucharest Stock Exchange, under the supervision of the Financial Supervisory Authority, adopted and implemented rules and regulations meant to create a sustainable and attractive capital market for investors, be they Romanian or foreign.

The Financial Supervisory Authority has made public its strategic objectives for the period 2019-2023. From the perspective of the capital markets, they focus, as expected, taking into account Romania's status as a member of the European Union, on sustainability and the promotion of socially responsible investment as well as on the imposition of the principles of Corporate Governance. The strategic role that the institution plays in the supervision of the securities market requires the correlation of the national provisions with the legislation adopted at European level. (ASF Strategic Objectives 2019-2023).

In this part of the paper, the authors have decided to compare, from the points of view listed above, the Bucharest Stock Exchange with other stock exchanges from region. However, the comparison with similar institutions in highly developed countries, with mature market economies, and with capital market institutions with a long uninterrupted existence would have generated disproportionate results. The authors therefore chose four other stock exchanges, from Eastern and South-Eastern Europe, comparable stock exchanges in terms of development stage, capitalization and number of listed companies. It must be specified that all four stock exchanges are members of the Sustainable Stock Exchanges initiative. The stock exchange institutions that are analyzed and compared are: the Athens Stock Exchange, the Belgrade Stock Exchange, the Bucharest Stock Exchange, the Budapest Stock Exchange and the Warsaw Stock Exchange. Before moving on to the analysis of institutions from the point of view of Social Responsibility and Corporate Governance, a brief review of them is made from their position of capital markets to provide a clearer picture of the region in terms of stock market development.

Table 5. Stock markets and main stock market indicators

Institution	Country	Year of Establishment	Number of Listed Companies	Number of Indices	Market Capitalization
Athens Stock Exchange	Greece	1876	203	30	55.588 million USD
Belgrade Stock Exchange	Serbia	1894, reopened in 2003	597	2	5.058 million USD
Bucharest Stock Exchange	Romania	1882, reopened in 1995	374	9	23.621 million USD
Budapest Stock Exchange	Hungary	1864, reopened in 1990	42	3	29 million USD
Warsaw Stock Exchange	Poland	1874, reopened in 1991	883	15	161.428 million USD

Source: Own elaboration based on statistical data published on the websites of the mentioned stock exchanges.

As can be observed, the five stock exchanges are relatively balanced in terms of market statistics and four of them (with the exception of the Athens Stock Exchange) have been reopened relatively recently (table 5).

In the following section, the five institutions are compared in terms of compliance with the principles of Social Responsibility and Corporate Governance, as well as how they manage to impose them on listed companies. The comparison is made on the basis of six universal items accepted as relevant for measuring the degree of sustainability of a capital market.

These are:

1. Annual sustainability report
2. Compliance with the principles of CSR and Corporate Governance as a mandatory requirement for listing

3. Written rules on CSR reporting
4. Providing CSR training
5. Sustainable stock market index
6. Market segment dedicated to the trading of sustainable bonds.

Table 6. Comparison in terms of compliance with the principles of Social Responsibility and Corporate Governance

Institution	Annual Sustainability Report	Compliance With the Principles of CSR and Corporate Governance as a Mandatory Requirement for Listing	Written Rules on CSR Reporting	Providing CSR Training	Sustainable Stock Market Index	Market Segment Dedicated to the Trading of Sustainable Bonds
Athens Stock Exchange	Yes	No	No	Yes	No	No
Belgrade Stock Exchange	No	No	No	Yes	No	No
Bucharest Stock Exchange	No	No	No	No	No	No
Budapest Stock Exchange	No	No	No	No	No	No
Warsaw Stock Exchange	No	No	No	Yes	Yes	No

Source: Own elaboration based on statistical data published on the websites of the mentioned stock exchanges.

As can be seen from the table 6, the Bucharest Stock Exchange fails to tick any of the items but is in line with the general trend of the region, which does not excel in terms of Social Responsibility and Corporate Governance, at least not when it is compared to large stock exchanges in Western Europe, the United States or some Asian stock exchanges (Dobre et al, 2015;Simionescu& Dumitrescu, 2018;Carp et al. 2019). The London Stock Exchange, for example, the 7th largest in the world and one of the oldest (founded in 1571), with a capitalization of 4.59 trillion USD, has an annual sustainability report, does not require compliance with the principles of CSR and Corporate Governance as a mandatory listing requirement, has written rules on CSR reporting, provides CSR training, operates four sustainable indices, and has a dedicated market segment for sustainable bond trading.

In Romania, Corporate Social Responsibility still remains, unfortunately, a little known concept, very little understood and rarely applied. Often the prerogative of large companies and multinational corporations, which have imported into our country, along with Western business practices and mentalities, more ethical and responsible, Corporate Social Responsibility shyly cuts its way into a still very young market economy such as Romania.

The Bucharest Stock Exchange, in its capacity as a pillar of the free market, makes constant efforts to promote Social Responsibility and Corporate Governance basic principles of Romanian business, and not just substantive footnotes, inserted in activity reports only out of obligation .

Table 7. The ten principles listed in the Code of Ethics of the Bucharest Stock Exchange

Obey the laws and regulations in force
Act with integrity, honesty and respect
Demonstrates professional behavior
Builds trust in business relationships
Focus on social responsibility
Fit into the work environment
Avoid conflicts of interests
Ensures the confidentiality of information
Excludes illegal behavior
Report violations of the Code of Ethics

Source: Code of ethics – Bucharest Stock Exchange 2016

The double role that the BSE plays, on the one hand as an independent company and on the other as that of administrator of the Romanian capital market, places the company in a unique but also difficult position, forcing it to set an example, but to impose good business practices on others. For a small stock exchange, such as the one in Bucharest, attracting investors is crucial, and foreign capital is the Holy Grail. However, foreign capital cannot be attracted by onerous business practices, suspicions of corruption, blatant indifference to the environment and to society. Foreign investors want to come to Bucharest, but to make a profit, knowing their capital is safe. Not to lure the names of their multi-billion dollar corporations into corruption scandals, not to invest in companies that lack transparency, and not to suffer stinging losses from unsustainable business practices.

The status of "Frontier Market", which Romania currently has according to FTSE Russel is not flattering, the term finding its etymology in the borders of the Wild West, where only the brave dared to venture, due to high risks.

The implementation of good practices of Social Responsibility and Corporate Governance by Romanian companies in general and those who want to attract funds on the stock market in particular can get rid of this stigma.

The Bucharest Stock Exchange can be the catalyst for change. The road of the BSE is taking is a good one, but the pace needs to become faster. The capital market remains a nebula for most of the Romanian society and the exit of the Stock Exchange from anonymity so that it can fulfill its mission of promoting change is imperative (Ene, 2017;Panait et al., 2020). Unfortunately, according to the annual report published in 2018, spending on marketing, advertising and promotion has dropped dramatically, from 468,562 lei in 2017 to 136,842 in 2018. The lack of visibility of the Stock Exchange also translates into a lack of visibility of its efforts in terms of promoting good business practices.

Social responsibility is a basic pillar of the policies of the Bucharest Stock Exchange, this aspect being specified in the Code of Ethics of the Bucharest Stock Exchange approved by the Decision of the board of directors of the BSE no. 53 / 07.09.2016. The BSE is committed to being involved in solving community problems and acting responsibly towards society. The Bucharest Stock Exchange acts in terms of Social Responsibility on two fronts, both as an independent economic entity and as a capital market operator. In its actions, the Bucharest Stock Exchange is guided by its own Code of Ethics, a document that reflects the high standards that the BSE undertakes to comply with, both in internal relations, between employees of the company and in relations with partners outside the company.

As can be seen in table 7, the fifth principle mentioned in the Code of Ethics refers directly to Social Responsibility, thus emphasizing the importance it plays in the policies that the BSE is guided by. Evidence of the proactive attitude that the BSE has towards everything related to Social Responsibility are the numerous programs developed, the imposition of the requirements in terms of Corporate Governance for companies wishing to be listed on the Stock Exchange as well as the activities of international cooperation in Social Responsibility and Corporate Governance.

Taking into account the low level of financial literacy specific to former communist countries (Ene, 2017;Iacovoiu, 2018), The Bucharest Stock Exchange has implemented many financial education programs dedicated to individual investors or corporate investors (business environment):

- The **seminar program** and the **Fluent** in **Finance** educational platform.
- **7/24 capital** - the online video production of the Bucharest Stock Exchange, which aims to promote the capital market in a way that is easy to understand and attractive to the general public. The videos can be watched on BSE's Youtube channel.
- **Monthly seminars** that the BSE organizes together with other business partners.
- The **Individual Investors Forum** is a workshop dedicated to private investors who work or want to work on the Romanian capital market and offer them the opportunity to meet face to face with representatives of the Bucharest Stock Exchange and financial intermediation companies.
- The **Entrepreneurs Forum** is a workshop for entrepreneurs. During this event, the entrepreneurial community meets to share their experiences and to find solutions to the problems faced by the Romanian business environment.
- **Made in Romania:** BSE League, a program whose goal is to contribute to the growth of the Romanian economy by identifying and promoting top companies.

Referring to the importance of financial education, Adrian Tănase, CEO of the BSE said:

We cannot have more investors if we do not have financial education. We want the capital market to become accessible to as many people as possible, regardless of their specialization in the financial field. We will continue financial education programs so that the capital market is not an exotic place for retail investors, but a regular place for their capital. "(Bursa.ro) Lucian Anghel, the chairman of the board of directors of the BSE stated:"Financial education cannot be achieved overnight. It is a continuous process that we constantly support through multiple educational initiatives: the Individual Investors Forum, the National Investment Day, the Fluent in Finance seminars, the book My First Investment and the online show 7/24 capital.

The Individual Investors Forum is without a doubt the most ambitious and complex financial education project dedicated to individuals who are or want to become investors on the Romanian capital market. The forum brings together investors and representatives of companies involved in capital market activity, giving them the opportunity to discuss savings and investment strategies on the capital market, in investment funds or in private voluntary pension funds. Among the business partners of the latest edition of the Forum (held on May 18, 2019 in Cluj Napoca) were: Banca Transilvania, BCR, BRD Asset Management, BT Capital Partners, NN, Tradeville and OTP Asset Mangement. The media partners of the event were Agerpres, Digi24 and Radio Romania Actualitati.The commendable and currently unique initiative in Romania can be a catalyst for the rebirth of the Romanian society's trust for financial investments, confidence lost in the 1990s and early 2000s due to a long series of financial frauds disguised under the guise of legitimate investment programs.

The Bucharest Stock Exchange recognizes the major role that the business environment plays in the development of Romanian society and therefore aims to support Romanian entrepreneurs through two special programs dedicated to them: Entrepreneurs Forum and Made in Romania: BSE League. The two programs want to identify and support Romanian companies with high potential that can become engines of the national economy. Made in Romania program: The BSE League takes place in four stages:

- Submission by Romanian entrepreneurs of nomination applications.
- Selection by the BSE and the Nomination Committee of 50 companies from all applications received.
- Selection of 15 winning companies by a jury of 12 experts and their award at the Made in Romania Gala.
- The last stage, in which the Stock Exchange and its partners offer the winning companies a mentoring program consisting of training programs and workshops specially adapted to the needs of each business (training programs include areas such as: branding, marketing and marketing techniques, sales, product development, management consulting, financing alternatives, financial reporting, etc.).

The most recent edition of the Made in Romania Program announced its winners, the 15 finalist companies, during the Awards Gala on May 14, 2019.

The Made in Romania program started in 2017 with 166 nominated companies. At the 2018 edition, the number of nominations reached 201, so that in 2019 the number of registered companies will reach 295, almost double compared to the first edition. Entrepreneurs' interest in participating in the program is justified by the many benefits offered by BSE and its partners such as:

- **Promoting the image of the company and the brand** by presenting its story in the Made in Romania book, launched at the end of each edition.
- **Possibility to participate in networking activities** with other entrepreneurs, consultants and potential investors.
- **Creating new partnerships** and identifying new business opportunities in the informal quarterly meetings between BSE, Made in Romania partners and the management of finalist companies from all previous editions.
- **Free seminars** and **assistance** from BSE and its partners in areas such as: business strategies, marketing and advertising, accounting and auditing

It should also be noted that the program is a major networking opportunity that the BSE provides to the Romanian business environment, taking into account the fact that on the agenda of many business leaders are new technologies and start-ups with potential, but many companies they do not have a coherent strategy for identifying them.

Although difficult to quantify numerically, the effects of the program, related to Social Responsibility are easy to intuit and are reflected in the real economy: increasing turnover, creating new jobs and providing a platform to support new Romanian start-up programs and streamlining and developing old business by opening up new business opportunities.

Figure 3. Evolution of Tesla price stock
Source: Tesla, Inc. Common Stock

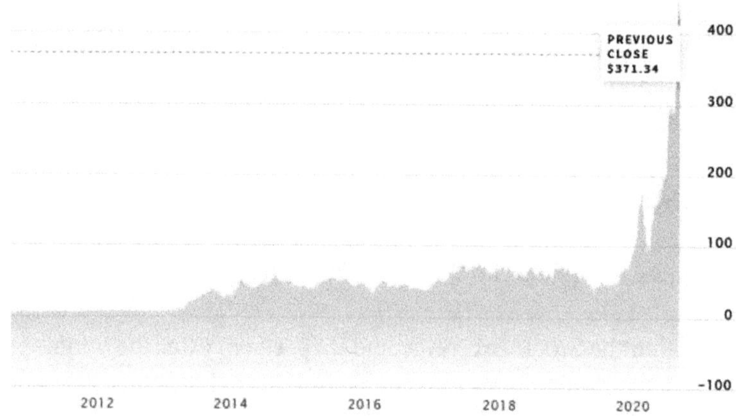

As a member of the "Sustainable Stock Exchanges" initiative, the Bucharest has committed itself to participating in its actions on Social Responsibility, a commitment that it fulfills brilliantly. During the "Ring the Bell" events, the Bucharest Stock Exchange conducts awareness campaigns on current social issues. Ring the Bell with Global Money Week and Ring the Bell for Gender Equality are two of the events organized simultaneously by the partner exchanges of "Sustainable Stock Exchanges" in which the BSE also takes part.

- **Ring the Bell with Global Money Week** is an event organized by the BSE together with the Financial Supervisory Authority on the occasion of World Money Week which aims to raise awareness among children and young people about the importance of financial education.
- **Ring the Bell for Gender Equality** is a global event, organized every year on March 8 on the occasion of International Women's Day. The BSE participates in the event, along with 65 other stock exchanges from around the world in order to draw attention to the important role that women play in economic life as well as in global efforts to create a sustainable future.

Participation in these activities promotes some noble causes and at the same time increases the visibility of the Bucharest Stock Exchange internationally. The fact that the Stock Exchange co-opts and involves in the development of events other partners, from the sphere of the capital market as well as from outside it, extends the sphere of the social impact of the events.

SUSTAINABLE STOCK EXCHANGE INDICES

Investors 'growing concern about companies' environmental policies and their desire to invest in sustainable business for the future has led to the creation of sustainable indices (Matei, 2013;Batista & Francisco, 2018;Simionescu& Dumitrescu,2018). Socially responsible investment is becoming more and more attractive as nations worldwide are trying to promote, aid and reward companies with high environmental standards while at the same time making business more and more difficult for those who fail to adhere to government standards in regards to pollution and Carbon emissions. The process of fossil fuel divestment coupled with the shift in capital towards companies in the alternative energy sector highlights a new trend in stock market investing. And perhaps the most relevant example of this new trend is the American electric vehicle and clean energy company Tesla. The company's shares have skyrocketed in value as the demand for cleaner, more environmental friendly vehicles has increased.

With the shares of companies like Tesla boosting big returns and ESG considerations ranking high in the eyes of investors, it should come as no surprise that sustainable indices, Green Funds and ETFs are quickly gaining traction, with stock markets across the world racing to become regional hubs for sustainable finance. The FTSE4Good Index Series The Dow Jones Sustainability Indices are perfect examples of the emerging trends in responsible investing.The two indices families focus heavily on ESG data and constituents become part of the indices following a complex screening process. Dow Jones Sustainability World Index and FTSE4Good All-World Index are two of the biggest global sustainable indices. The main constituents by index weight are presented in the table 8.

Table 8. Constituents of DJSWI and FTSE4Good All-World Index

Dow Jones Sustainability World Index		FTSE4Good All-World Index	
Constituent	**Sector**	**Constituent**	**Sector**
Microsoft Corp	Information Technology	Apple Inc.	Technology Hardware & Equipment
Alphabet Inc C	Communication Services	Microsoft Corp	Software & Computer Services
Nestle SA Reg	Consumer Staples	Alphabet Class A	Software & Computer Services
Unitedhealth Group Inc	Health Care	Alphabet Class C	Software & Computer Services
Taiwan Semiconductor Manufacturing Co Ltd	Information Technology	Johnson & Johnson	Pharmaceuticals & Biotechnology
Adobe Inc.	Information Technology	Taiwan Semiconductor Manufacturing	Technology Hardware & Equipment
Roche Hldgs AG Ptg Genus	Health Care	Nestle	Food Producers
Salesforce.com	Information Technology	Visa	Financial Services
Novartis AG Reg	Health Care	Procter & Gamble	Household Goods & Home Construction
Bank of America Corp	Financials	Unitedhealth Group	Health Care Equipment & Services

Source: Spglobal, 2020

As a partner of the "Sustainable Stock Exchanges" initiative, the Bucharest Stock Exchange is committed to creating a stock market index that includes companies that meet the highest standards in terms of corporate governance and Social Responsibility. Sustainable indices have become a standard in recent years for the world's major capital markets, investors, especially young people, showing an increased interest in investing in companies that show a proactive attitude in trying to protect the environment and society from the impact negative impact of their own operations.

Also, institutional investors and investment fund managers who are often looking for long-term investment opportunities to the detriment of short-term speculation, thus demonstrating a lower risk appetite, are also more prone to investments in companies that demonstrate sustainable business. So far, this index has not been created. One of the reasons why the BSE sustainable index has not yet been created is undoubtedly the lack of a common understanding and a clear methodology for listing a particular company in such a stock index.

A sustainable stock market index must be made up of companies that adhere to the highest principles of corporate Social Responsibility, defined in the European Commission's sense as: *"A concept by which companies integrate social and environmental concerns in their business operations and in their interaction with stakeholders, in a voluntary manner"* (Communication from the Commission concerning Corporate Social Responsibility: A business contribution to Sustainable Development 2002).

In order to evaluate a company from the point of view of Social Responsibility, the authors analyze its behavior in the economic and social spheres, referring to universally accepted principles as representing the foundation of a sustainable business (Arribas et al., 2019;Lupu et al., 2020). In the following section, the authors analyze five companies listed on the Bucharest Stock Exchange to evaluate their potential to be part of a future sustainable index of BSE. For the evaluation of companies, the authors use a system that takes into account the following factors:

1. The **rating** system of the European Bank for Reconstruction and Development on the inclusion of economic activities in social and environmental risk categories.
2. Involvement in **environmental** projects.
3. Involvement in **social** and charitable projects.
4. Involvement in **educational** projects.
5. **Adherence** to the principles of corporate governance.

Companies ineligible to be part of a sustainable index are those that carry out activities that have or may have a significant negative impact from a social, economic or environmental point of view. These activities, often grouped in investment jargon as "sin stocks" (Matei, 2013;Arribas et al., 2019;Lupu et al., 2020) are:

1. Production, marketing or distribution of tobacco products.
2. Production of spirits.
3. Gambling and betting activities.
4. Production, sale or distribution of firearms, ammunition and offensive military equipment.
5. Nuclear energy production.
6. Production, marketing, distribution or use of genetically modified organisms.

The five companies analyzed are: OMV Petrom S.A., Banca Transilvania S.A., MedLife S.A., Conpet S.A. and Biofarm S.A. The reasons why these companies were chosen was their representativeness for the Romanian market:

- **OMV Petrom**: Biggest player in the Romanian oil sector. The company's stock makes up almost 30% of the BSE's BET-NG Index (BUCHAREST EXCHANGE TRADING ENERGY & RELATED UTILITIES INDEX).
- **Banca Transilvania**: Biggest Romanian bank. Makes up almost 20% of the BSE's main index, the BET.
- **MedLife**: Biggest private healthcare provider in Romania. The only healthcare company included in the BSE's main index, the BET.
- **Conpet**: The sole operator of Romania's National Oil Transport System which comprises 3800 km of pipelines.
- **Biofarm**: One of Romania's biggest pharmaceuticals manufacturers with a presence in 12 other countries - Azerbaijan, Czech Republic, Cyprus, Georgia, Iraq, Lithuania, Malta, Moldova, Russia, Hungary, Ukraine and Kyrgyzstan. The company is a constituent of the BSE's BET PLUS index. Initially, the authors identified the risk category in which each company falls, according to the main object of activity, according to the rating system of the European Bank forReconstruction and Development (EBRD Environmental and Social Risk Categorization List - revised 2014). The data were centralized in the table 9.

Table 9. Grade of risk for selected companies

Company Name	Sector	Environmental Risk	Social Risk	Aggregate Risk
OMV Petrom S.A.	Crude oil extraction	High risk	High risk	High risk
Banca Transilvania S.A.	Banking	Low risk	Low risk	Low risk
MedLife S.A.	Healthcare	Medium risk	Medium risk	Medium risk
Conpet S.A.	Pipeline transport	High risk	Riscmediu	High risk
Biofarm S.A.	Pharmaceutical products	High risk	High risk	High risk

Source: Own elaboration based on pubic information available.

OMV Petrom S.A.

- Social and environmental risk category according to the EBRD rating system for the company's object of activity - High Risk
- Involvement in environmental projects: OMV Petrom finances numerous environmental projects through its Social Responsibility platform, "Andrei's Country", the 57,000 volunteers of the association managing for example to plant 700,000 trees in the last 12 years - the equivalent of 150 hectares reforested.
- Involvement in social and charitable projects: OMV Petrom finances the program "Made in Andrei's country" through which it provides expertise, financing and consulting for business development that solves social problems and creates new jobs.

- Involvement in educational projects: Through the "Ro-Smart in Andrei's Country" program, OMV provides funding for numerous educational projects throughout the country.
- Adherence to corporate governance principles: OMV Petrom adhered to the Corporate Governance Code of the Bucharest Stock Exchange, whose principles it adheres to almost entirely.

Banca Transilvania S.A.

- Social and environmental risk category according to the EBRD rating system for the company's object of activity - Low risk
- Involvement in environmental projects: Through the "More Green" association, founded in 2008, Banca Transilvania is involved in numerous environmental projects.
- Involvement in social and charitable projects: Over time, Banca Transilvania has been involved in numerous social and charitable projects such as the financing of the Free Polyclinic in Cluj-Napoca and the charity event "Golden football, from the soul for children!".
- Involvement in educational projects: The company has been involved over time and continues to be involved in numerous educational projects focused on financial education and beyond. It is also a partner of the Bucharest Stock Exchange in the programs of the Individual Investors Forum and the Entrepreneurs Forum.
- Adherence to corporate governance principles: Banca Transilvania adheres to the highest principles of corporate governance.

MedLife S.A.

- Social and environmental risk category according to the EBRD rating system for the company's object of activity - Medium risk
- Involvement in environmental projects: Together with the Carpathia Conservation Foundation, MedLie launched the program "Let's make Romania green!" through which it participates in reforestation actions of the deforested areas in the Făgaraş Mountains.
- Involvement in social and charitable projects: MedLife runs the Parents' School program through which it advises future parents on the pregnancy, birth and care of the future child.
- Involvement in educational projects: MedLife funds the SF Social Center. Dimitrie which deals daily with the education of forty children from disadvantaged families who have a high degree of risk of social exclusion.
- Adherence to corporate governance principles: MedLife adheres to the highest principles of corporate governance, the company guiding its activity according to its own code of ethics and conduct.

Conpet S.A.

- Social and environmental risk category according to the EBRD rating system for the company's object of activity - High Risk
- Involvement in environmental projects: Complies with legal requirements for environmental protection, does not carry out other environmental projects.

- Involvement in social and charitable projects: Conpet S.A. supported and financed the development of cultural and artistic projects such as the National Competition for Interpretation and Musical Creation "Paul Constantinescu" and the National Theater Festival "Toma Caragiu".
- Involvement in educational projects: The company has sponsored and continues to sponsor the conduct of numerous competitions and school Olympics.
- Adherence to corporate governance principles: Conpet S.A. adheres to the highest principles of corporate governance, including adopting its own integrity plan.

Biofarm S.A.

- Social and environmental risk category according to the EBRD rating system for the company's object of activity - High risk
- Involvement in environmental projects: Biofarm S.A. complies with the legal provisions on environmental protection, does not carry out other environmental projects.
- Involvement in social and charitable projects: Does not carry out or finance social and charitable projects.
- Involvement in educational projects: Does not carry out or finance educational projects.
- Adherence to corporate governance principles: Biofarm S.A. adheres to the highest principles of corporate governance.

According to the above analysis, we propose a formula for calculating the degree of sustainability of a company that takes into account the four principles analyzed as well as the category of social and environmental risk according to the EBRD rating system as follows (table 10).

Table 10. Scoring methodology

Analyzed Principle	Involvement	No Involvement
Involvement in environmental projects	2.5	0
Involvement in social and charitable projects	2.5	0
Involvement in educational projects	2.5	0
Compliance with the principles of corporate governance	Complies	Does not comply
	2.5	0

Table 11. Risk category

Social and environmental risk category according to the EBRD's rating system for the company's object of activity		
Low Risk	**Medium Risk**	**High Risk**
1	0.9	0.8

Thus, involvement in environmental, social and charitable or educational projects will bring each company 2.5 points, as well as compliance with the principles of corporate governance. The amount of the score obtained will be multiplied by a coefficient depending on the category of social and environmental risk in which each company falls, according to the EBRD.

The calculation formula is the following:

(P1+P2+P3+P4) x Q

Where P1, P2, P3,P4 represent the fouranalyzed principles and Q is the risk factor coefficient.

Thus, the scores obtained by the analyzed companies are:

- OMV Petrom S.A. = (2.5+2.5+2.5+2.5)x0.8= 8
- Banca Transilvania S.A. =(2.5+2.5+2.5+2.5)x1= 10
- Medlife S.A. =(2.5+2.5+2.5+2.5)x0.9= 9
- Conpet S.A. =(0+2.5+2.5+2.5)x0.8= 6
- Biofarm S.A. =(0+0+0+2.5)x0.8= 2

As can be seen, the risk coefficient a company falls into can have a negative impact on the final sustainability score. Thus, we can have a company involved in many projects in the field of Social Responsibility that is disadvantaged in the rating system only by the degree of risk of its main object of activity. However, we can take this variable out of the equation and set up a "best in class" system that evaluates companies in the same sector of activity and chooses to include in a sustainable index only those that prove to be very active in the field of CSR. . The responsibility for the constant empirical analysis of CSR practices and projects and the way in which the principles of Corporate Governance are followed can be attributed, in the perspective of creating a sustainable index, to the Indices Commission within the Bucharest Stock Exchange.

The above analysis, based on five basic criteria of Social Responsibility, reveals that, on the Bucharest Stock Exchange, there are indeed companies that meet the highest standards of Social Responsibility and could be included without doubt in a future sustainable index. Of the five companies analyzed, only Biofarm S.A. stands out due to the lack of projects specific to good Social Responsibility practices, and Conpet S.A. lags behind in the absence of concrete projects for the protection of the environment, despite the high-risk activity it carries out. However, it should be noted that Social Responsibility cannot be calculated with a universally applicable mathematical formula and can only be difficult to quantify numerically. Therefore, the inclusion of a company in a future sustainable index should be done only after analyzing its behavior and following a screening process that eliminates from the start the companies that, behind a facade responsible for the environment and society hide reprehensible practices such as of greenwashing. The screening process must be constant and companies that are committed to complying with the principles of Social Responsibility in order to be included in a sustainable stock market index must be warned that the risk of being excluded from that index is high if there are deviations from the desired behaviors. An example of this came recently from the United States where Facebook's shares were excluded from the S&P ESG 500 sustainable index due to deviations from corporate governance principles that led to the use of personal data of Facebook social networking platform users for purposes other than provided in the terms and conditions of use.

SOLUTIONS AND RECOMMENDATIONS

Taking in account the analysis made, a series of recommendations can be presented to increase and speed up the implementation of the principles of Social Responsibility and Corporate Governance by the Bucharest Stock Exchange, as the main player of the Romanian capital market.

- Increasing the **visibility** of the BSE through marketing campaigns addressed to both institutional and private investors, be they Romanian or foreign. The stock market must be promoted as a safe place for financial investments, a regulated and supervised market, with strict rules that reduce, as much as possible, the risks assumed by investors.
- **Urging the implementation of a sustainable stock** market index, which would translate into a positive signal to international investors, signaling to them that in Bucharest, the sustainability of the capital market can offer them the opportunity for secure investments.
- **Offering sustainable financial products**, such as green bonds, by creating a specialized market or market segment and by supporting companies wishing to list such products on the Bucharest Stock Exchange.
- **Continuing and intensifying financial education** programs, both among entrepreneurs and investors, but especially among children and young people, to help them understand the importance of saving, investing and making rational use of money.

FUTURE RESEARCH DIRECTIONS

Starting from the analysis performed, a future research direction would be the analysis of the impact of the European directive (Directive 2014/95 / EU of the European Parliament and of the Council amending Directive 2013/34 / EU) on the publication of non-financial information in the annual activity report for large companies (with over 500 employees) listed on the stock exchange. The KPMG experts noticed that in about half of EU countries, national authorities have been late in transposing the provisions of this directive into national law by the end of 2016 (KPMG, 2017).

This analysis will focus in a first phase on all companies listed on the Bucharest Stock Exchange for which the European directive is applicable. The aim is to determine the influence of factors like the size of the company, the home country, the field of activity (Matei, 2013; Matuszak, & Różańska, 2017;Szadziewska et al., 2018; Sierra-Garcia et al., 2018, Badea et al., 2020) on the reporting of non-financial data by companies. The second analysiswill focus on the origin of the capital - local or foreign. These studies will complete the image of Romanian capital market in terms of sustainability (Siminica, & Sichigea;2018, Popescu & Popescu, 2019;Petrescu et al., 2020). In our next projects, we intend to measure the level of commitment of the firms and their involvement in sustainable programs (like the number of program beneficiaries or the reduction in greenhouse gas emissions).

CONCLUSION

CSR is a concept with long roots in the philanthropic actions of Western European entrepreneurs that has gained ground in recent decades as a result of efforts by international organizations to promote the principles of sustainable development. The challenges generated by climate change and the repeated regional or international financial crises have demonstrated the need to involve more and more entities to promote environmental protection, respect for human rights, the fight against corruption, etc. The efforts are huge and any help is welcome, even from consumers or portfolio investors. Slowly, portfolio investors have become the force that amends the behavior of companies through decisions made on the capital market. More and more investors are selling their shares in companies that pollute the environment or have unethical behavior. Thus, the divestment process has grown, being is also supported by stock exchanges that meet investors with alternative products such as green bonds or sustainability indices. The Romanian capital market, under the aegis of the Bucharest Stock Exchange is on the right path to a more sustainable economic future as efforts are constantly being made to ensure compliance with international CSR standards and principles. ESG focused stock market initiatives provide investors with more insight than ever before and incentivize companies to opt for more sustainable business practices. We believe that the Bucharest Stock Exchange should expedite the process of creating comprehensive sustainable investment products which would attract even more domestic and foreign capital.

REFERENCES

Andrei, J. V., Panait, M., & Voica, C. (2018). Challenges and Approaches for the Corporate Social Responsibility and Human Resource Management in the Financial Sector. *Economics, Management and Financial Markets*, *13*(3), 415–431.

Armeanu, D. S., Enciu, A., Obreja, C., & Cioacă, S. I. (2016). The Financial Crisis' Impact on the Central and Eastern Europe Capital Markets. *Revista de Management Comparat International*, *17*(5), 420.

Arribas, I., Espinós-Vañó, M. D., García, F., & Morales-Bañuelos, P. B. (2019). The inclusion of socially irresponsible companies in sustainable stock indices. *Sustainability*, *11*(7), 2047. doi:10.3390u11072047

Atlı, D., Vidović, M., & Omazić, M. A. (2018). Communicating Corporate Social Responsibility on the Web: A Content Analysis of Sustainability Reports in World's Best Multinational Workplaces. *International Journal of Sustainable Entrepreneurship and Corporate Social Responsibility*, *3*(2), 1–17. doi:10.4018/IJSECSR.2018070101

Aybars, A., Ataünal, L., & Gürbüz, A. O. (2019). ESG and Financial Performance: Impact of Environmental, Social, and Governance Issues on Corporate Performance. In Handbook of Research on Managerial Thinking in Global Business Economics (pp. 520-536). IGI Global.

Badea, L., Armeanu, D. Ş., Nițescu, D. C., Murgu, V., Panait, I., & Kuzman, B. (2020). A Study of the Relative Stock Market Performance of Companies Recognized for Supporting Gender Equality Policies and Practices. *Sustainability*, *12*(9), 3558. doi:10.3390u12093558

Bank of America. (2020), https://newsroom.bankofamerica.com/system/files/2019_Environmental_Social_Governance.pdf

Banța, V. C. (2019). Performance evaluation of the implementation of the 2013/34/EU directive in Romania on the basis of corporate social responsibility reports. *Sustainability*, *11*(9), 2531. doi:10.3390u11092531

Barić, A., Omazić, M. A., Aleksić, A., & Pejic-Bach, M. (2020). Influence of CSR Activities on Stakeholders in Foreign Markets. In *Recent Advancements in Sustainable Entrepreneurship and Corporate Social Responsibility* (pp. 16–36). IGI Global. doi:10.4018/978-1-7998-2347-6.ch002

Batista, A. A. D. S., & Francisco, A. C. D. (2018). Organizational sustainability practices: A study of the firms listed by the corporate sustainability index. *Sustainability*, *10*(1), 226. doi:10.3390u10010226

Bhattacharya, C. B., Smith, N. C., & Vogel, D. (2004). Integrating social responsibility and marketing strategy: An introduction. *California Management Review*, *47*(1), 6–8. doi:10.2307/41166283

Bowen, H. R. (1953). *BOWEN: Social responsibilities of the businessman.* Harper & Row.

Brezoi, A. G. (2018). Ethics and Corporate Social Responsibility in the Current Geopolitical Context. *Economic Insights - Trends and Challenges*, *7*, 45–52.

Brown, J. A., Clark, C., & Buono, A. F. (2018). The United Nations global compact: Engaging implicit and explicit CSR for global governance. *Journal of Business Ethics*, *147*(4), 721–734. doi:10.100710551-016-3382-5

Carp, M., Păvăloaia, L., Afrăsinei, M. B., & Georgescu, I. E. (2019). Is sustainability reporting a business strategy for firm's growth? Empirical study on the Romanian capital market. *Sustainability*, *11*(3), 658. doi:10.3390u11030658

Ciutacu, C., Chivu, L., & Preda, D. (2005). The social responsibility of the company–a challenge for the contemporary world. *The Romanian Economics Magazine*, *2*, 79.

Dahlsrud, A. (2008). How corporate social responsibility is defined: An analysis of 37 definitions. *Corporate Social Responsibility and Environmental Management*, *15*(1), 1–13. doi:10.1002/csr.132

de Jong, M. D., & van der Meer, M. (2017). How does it fit? Exploring the congruence between organizations and their corporate social responsibility (CSR) activities. *Journal of Business Ethics*, *143*(1), 71–83. doi:10.100710551-015-2782-2

Deigh, L., Farquhar, J., Palazzo, M., & Siano, A. (2016). Corporate social responsibility: Engaging the community. *Qualitative Market Research*, *19*(2), 225–240. doi:10.1108/QMR-02-2016-0010

Deloitte. (2020). https://www2.deloitte.com/us/en/insights/industry/financial-services/esg-investing-performance.html

Deschryver, P., & De Mariz, F. (2020). What Future for the Green Bond Market? How Can Policymakers, Companies, and Investors Unlock the Potential of the Green Bond Market? *Journal of Risk and Financial Management*, *13*(3), 61. doi:10.3390/jrfm13030061

Deschryver, P., & De Mariz, F. (2020). What Future for the Green Bond Market? How Can Policymakers, Companies, and Investors Unlock the Potential of the Green Bond Market? *Journal of Risk and Financial Management*, *13*(3), 61.

Dobre, E., Stanila, G. O., & Brad, L. (2015). The influence of environmental and social performance on financial performance: Evidence from Romania's listed entities. *Sustainability*, *7*(3), 2513–2553. doi:10.3390u7032513

Dordi, T., & Weber, O. (2019). The impact of divestment announcements on the share price of fossil fuel stocks. *Sustainability, 11*(11), 3122. doi:10.3390u11113122

Duca, I., & Gherghina, R. (2018). Corporate Social Responsibility and Sustainable Business. *International Journal of Innovation in the Digital Economy, 9*(2), 26–39. doi:10.4018/IJIDE.2018040103

Dupont, G., Ojo, M., & Rossi, J. (2016). Corporate Social Responsibility and Financial Development: Promoting Global Economic Development. In Analyzing the Relationship between Corporate Social Responsibility and Foreign Direct Investment (pp. 115-126). IGI Global.

ElAlfy, A., Palaschuk, N., El-Bassiouny, D., Wilson, J., & Weber, O. (2020). Scoping the Evolution of Corporate Social Responsibility (CSR) Research in the Sustainable Development Goals (SDGs) Era. *Sustainability, 12*(14), 5544. doi:10.3390u12145544

Ene, C. (2017). Current Issues Regarding The Protection Of Retail Investors On The Capital Market Within The European Union. *The USV Annals of Economics and Public Administration, 17*(1 (25)), 35–44.

Ene, C., & Panait, M. (2017). The financial education-Part of corporate social responsibility for employees and customers. *Revista Romana de Economie, 44*(1), 145–154.

Ene, C., & Panait, M. (2017). The financial education-Part of corporate social responsibility for employees and customers. *Revista Romana de Economie, 44*(1), 145–154.

Financial Times. (2020a). https://www.ft.com/content/7a893f6d-08c9-426c-8f19-aa19d434b018

Financial Times. (2020b). https://www.ft.com/content/27025f35-283f-4956-b6a0-0adbfd4c7a0e

Friedman, M. (1970). The social responsibility of business is to maximise its profits. *New York Times Magazine, 13*, 33.

Garcia-Sanchez, I., Ferrero, J., & Azevedo, T. (2019). Does Capital Market Distrust CSR Reporting?: Economic Benefits in Presence of Complementary Monitoring Mechanism. *Economic Benefits in Presence of Complementary Monitoring Mechanism.*

Go Fossil free. (n.d.). https://gofossilfree.org/divestment/commitments/

Grigorescu, A., & Saseanu, A. (2010). The social responsibility influence of corporations on sustainable development, published in: Analele Universităţii Ovidius Constanţa. *Seria: Ştiinţe Economice,* (1), 1049–1054.

Gurtu, A. (Ed.). (2020). *Recent Advancements in Sustainable Entrepreneurship and Corporate Social Responsibility*. IGI Global. doi:10.4018/978-1-7998-2347-6

Hinson, R., Boateng, R., & Madichie, N. (2010). Corporate social responsibility activity reportage on bank websites in Ghana. *International Journal of Bank Marketing, 28*(7), 498–518. doi:10.1108/02652321011085176

Hoi, C. K., Wu, Q., & Zhang, H. (2013). Is corporate social responsibility (CSR) associated with tax avoidance? Evidence from irresponsible CSR activities. *The Accounting Review, 88*(6), 2025–2059. doi:10.2308/accr-50544

Hysa, E., Kruja, A., Rehman, N. U., & Laurenti, R. (2020). Circular Economy Innovation and Environmental Sustainability Impact on Economic Growth: An Integrated Model for Sustainable Development. *Sustainability, 12*(12), 4831. doi:10.3390u12124831

Iacovoiu, V. B. (2018). An Empirical Analysis of Some Factors Influencing Financial Literacy. *Economic Insights - Trends and Challenges, 70*(2).

Ioana-Maria, D., & Adriana, T. T. (2012). The impact of the business and organizational size of a company along with GRI and CSR adoption on integrating sustainability reporting practices. *The Annals of the University of Oradea*, 910.

Ionescu, G. G. (2006). Misiunea si responsabilitatea sociala a organizatiei de afaceri. *Management & Marketing-Bucharest*, (2), 53–72.

Ionescu, R. (2019). Corporate Social Responsibility Programs of the Bucharest Stock Exchange. *Economic Insights - Trends and Challenges.*

Ionescu, R., & Rădulescu, I. D. (2019). Behavioral Finance and the Fast Evolving World of Fintech. *Economic Insights - Trends and Challenges.*

Khan, S. A. R., Yu, Z., Golpîra, H., & Sharif, A. (2019). The nexus between corporate social responsibility and corporate performance: An empirical evidence. *LogForum, 15.*

Kim, R. C. (2018). Can creating shared value (CSV) and the United Nations Sustainable Development Goals (UN SDGs) collaborate for a better world? Insights from East Asia. *Sustainability, 10*(11), 4128. doi:10.3390u10114128

Kim, S., & Lee, J. (2020). Accounting Treatment of R&D for Environmentally Responsible Firms: Evidence from South Korea. *Sustainability, 12*(8), 3418. doi:10.3390u12083418

Kolk, A. (2016). The social responsibility of international business: From ethics and the environment to CSR and sustainable development. *Journal of World Business, 51*(1), 23–34. doi:10.1016/j.jwb.2015.08.010

Kumar, A., Moktadir, A., Liman, Z. R., Gunasekaran, A., Hegemann, K., & Khan, S. A. R. (2020). Evaluating sustainable drivers for social responsibility in the context of ready-made garments supply chain. *Journal of Cleaner Production, 248*, 119231. doi:10.1016/j.jclepro.2019.119231

Lebelle, M., Lajili Jarjir, S., & Sassi, S. (2020). Corporate Green Bond Issuances: An International Evidence. *Journal of Risk and Financial Management, 13*(2), 25. doi:10.3390/jrfm13020025

Lee, J., & Kim, E. (2020). The Influence of Corporate Environmental Responsibility on Overinvestment Behavior: Evidence from South Korea. *Sustainability, 12*(5), 1901. doi:10.3390u12051901

Liaw, K. T. (2020). Survey of Green Bond Pricing and Investment Performance. *Journal of Risk and Financial Management, 13*(9), 193. doi:10.3390/jrfm13090193

Lupu, I., Bobirca, A. B., Miclăuş, P. G., & Ciumara, T. (2020). Risk management of companies included in the Euro stoxx sustainability index. An investors' perception. *Amfiteatru Economic, 22*(55), 707–725. doi:10.24818/EA/2020/55/707

Manne, H. G. (2006). Milton Friedman Was Right. "Corporate social responsibility" is bunk. *Wall Street Journal, 24*.

Matei, M. (2013). *Responsabilitatea socială a corporaţiilor şi instituţiilor şi dezvoltarea durabilă a României*. Expert Publishing House.

Matei, M., & Voica, M. C. (2013). Social Responsibility in the Financial and Banking Sector. *Economic Insights - Trends and Challenges*, *65*(1).

Matuszak, Ł., & Różańska, E. (2017). CSR disclosure in Polish-listed companies in the light of Directive 2014/95/EU requirements: Empirical evidence. *Sustainability*, *9*(12), 2304. doi:10.3390u9122304

Méndez-Suárez, M., Monfort, A., & Gallardo, F. (2020). Sustainable Banking: New Forms of Investing under the Umbrella of the 2030 Agenda. *Sustainability*, *12*(5), 2096. doi:10.3390u12052096

Metaxas, T., & Tsavdaridou, M. (2010). Corporate social responsibility in europe: Denmark, Hungary and Greece. *Journal of Contemporary European Studies*, *18*(1), 25–46. doi:10.1080/14782801003638679

Mieila, M. (Ed.). (2017). *Measuring Sustainable Development and Green Investments in Contemporary Economies*. IGI Global. doi:10.4018/978-1-5225-2081-8

Monteiro, S., Ribeiro, V., & Lemos, K. (2020). Linking Corporate Social Responsibility Reporting With the UN Sustainable Development Goals: Evidence From the Portuguese Stock Market. In Conceptual and Theoretical Approaches to Corporate Social Responsibility, Entrepreneurial Orientation, and Financial Performance (pp. 134-151). IGI Global.

Nour, A. I., Sharabati, A. A. A., & Hammad, K. M. (2020). Corporate Governance and Corporate Social Responsibility Disclosure. *International Journal of Sustainable Entrepreneurship and Corporate Social Responsibility*, *5*(1), 20–41. doi:10.4018/IJSECSR.2020010102

Ortas, E., Álvarez, I., & Garayar, A. (2015). The environmental, social, governance, and financial performance effects on companies that adopt the United Nations Global Compact. *Sustainability*, *7*(2), 1932–1956. doi:10.3390u7021932

Palazzo, M., Vollero, A. & Siano, A. (2020). From strategic corporate social responsibility to value creation: an analysis of corporate website communication in the banking sector. *International Journal of Bank Marketing*. doi:10.1108/IJBM-04-2020-0168

Panait, M., Radulescu, I., & Brezoi, A. (2020). Financial Markets–Under the Sign of CSR. Some Evidences Regarding Financial Education. *LUMEN Proceedings, 11*, 96-106.

Panait, M., Voica, M. C., & Radulescu, I. (2014). The activity of capital market actors: Under the sign of social responsibility. *Procedia Economics and Finance*, *8*, 522–528. doi:10.1016/S2212-5671(14)00123-3

Pejić Bach, M., Starešinić, B., Omazić, M. A., Aleksić, A., & Seljan, S. (2020). m-Banking Quality and Bank Reputation. *Sustainability*, *12*(10), 4315. doi:10.3390u12104315

Pérez, A., López-Gutiérrez, C., & García de los Salmones, M. M. (2019). Do all CSR news affect market value equally? *Social Responsibility Journal*, *16*(8), 1107–1123. doi:10.1108/SRJ-03-2019-0116

Petrescu, A. G., Bîlcan, F. R., Petrescu, M., Holban Oncioiu, I., Türkeş, M. C., & Căpuşneanu, S. (2020). Assessing the Benefits of the Sustainability Reporting Practices in the Top Romanian Companies. *Sustainability*, *12*(8), 3470. doi:10.3390u12083470

Pici, E., Pasmaciu, J., Hysa, E., Hoxhaj, J., & Hodo, M. (2014). Evaluation of millennium development goals process: Case of Albania. *Mediterranean Journal of Social Sciences*, *5*(14), 33. doi:10.5901/mjss.2014.v5n14p33

Piciocchi, P., Vollero, A., & Palazzo, M. (2009). Towards the integration between corporate community relations and CSR communication strategies. The ENEL case study. *Esperienze d'Impresa*, *17*(2).

Popescu, C. R. G., & Popescu, G. N. (2019). An exploratory study based on a questionnaire concerning green and sustainable finance, corporate social responsibility, and performance: Evidence from the Romanian business environment. *Journal of Risk and Financial Management*, *12*(4), 162. doi:10.3390/jrfm12040162

Porter, M. E., & Kramer, M. R. (2002). The competitive advantage of corporate philanthropy. *Harvard Business Review*, *80*(12), 56–68. PMID:12510538

Raimi, L., Akhuemonkhan, I., & Ogunjirin, O. D. (2015). Corporate Social Responsibility and Entrepreneurship (CSRE): Antidotes to poverty, insecurity and underdevelopment in Nigeria. *Social Responsibility Journal*, *11*(1), 56–81. doi:10.1108/SRJ-11-2012-0138

Raimi, L., Fadipe, A. O., & Shokunbi, M. O. (2020). Responsible Investment (RI): An Alternative Funding Option for Roads-Bridges Management in Nigeria Under the Public-Private Partnership Framework. *International Journal of Economic Behavior*, *5*(1), 43–57.

Ramasastry, A. (2015). Corporate social responsibility versus business and human rights: Bridging the gap between responsibility and accountability. *Journal of Human Rights*, *14*(2), 237–259. doi:10.1080/14754835.2015.1037953

Sahay, A. (2011). Philanthropy, CSR and sustainability. In Green Technologies: Concepts, Methodologies, Tools and Applications (pp. 1281-1304). IGI Global.

Sichigea, M., Siminica, M. I., Circiumaru, D., Carstina, S., & Caraba-Meita, N. L. (2020). A Comparative Approach of the Environmental Performance between Periods with Positive and Negative Accounting Returns of EEA Companies. *Sustainability*, *12*(18), 7382. doi:10.3390u12187382

Sierra-Garcia, L., Garcia-Benau, M. A., & Bollas-Araya, H. M. (2018). Empirical analysis of non-financial reporting by Spanish companies. *Administrative Sciences*, *8*(3), 29. doi:10.3390/admsci8030029

Siminica, M., Ionascu, C., & Sichigea, M. (2019). Corporate Social Performance versus Financial Performance of the Romanian Firms. *Prague Economic Papers*, *28*(1), 49–69. doi:10.18267/j.pep.687

Siminica, M., & Sichigea, M. (2018). Corporate Social Responsibility as a Voluntary Initiative but a Mandatory Non-financial Reporting Link Between the Social and Financial Performance of Romanian Companies. In *Current Issues in Corporate Social Responsibility* (pp. 77–96). Springer. doi:10.1007/978-3-319-70449-4_6

Simionescu, L. N., & Dumitrescu, D. (2018). Empirical study towards corporate social responsibility practices and company financial performance. Evidence for companies listed on the Bucharest Stock Exchange. *Sustainability, 10*(9), 3141. doi:10.3390u10093141

SSE. (2020). *Sustainable Stock Exchanges*. https://sseinitiative.org/

Szadziewska, A., Spigarska, E., & Majerowska, E. (2018). The disclosure of non-financial information by stock-exchange-listed companies in Poland, in the light of the changes introduced by the Directive 2014/95/EU. *Zeszyty Teoretyczne Rachunkowości, 2018*(99), 65–95. doi:10.5604/01.3001.0012.2933

Timbate, L., & Park, C. K. (2018). CSR performance, financial reporting, and investors' perception on financial reporting. *Sustainability, 10*(2), 522. doi:10.3390u10020522

Uysal, T. U., Kurt, G., & Karabulut, A. N. (2019). Are Social Marketing Investments Used as a Tool for Voluntary Reporting or Disclosure? In *Advanced Methodologies and Technologies in Digital Marketing and Entrepreneurship* (pp. 597–609). IGI Global.

Voica, C., & Panait, M. (2017). Foreign Banks' Activity in Romania - Under the Sign of Ethics and CSR or Under the Profit's Sign? *Journal of Financial and Monetary Economics, 4*, 439–447.

Voica, M. C. (2017). Financial inclusion as a tool for sustainable development. *Romanian Journal of Economics, 44*(1), 121–129.

Vollero, A., Palazzo, M., Siano, A., & Elving, W. J. (2016). Avoiding the greenwashing trap: Between CSR communication and stakeholder engagement. *International Journal of Innovation and Sustainable Development, 10*(2), 120–140. doi:10.1504/IJISD.2016.075542

Volosevici, D. (2013). Corporations—between Governance and Social Responsibility: The European Commission Approach. *Economic Insights - Trends and Challenges, 65*(2).

Vukić, N. M., Omazić, M. A., Pejic-Bach, M., Aleksić, A., & Zoroja, J. (2020). Leadership for Sustainability: Connecting Corporate Responsibility Reporting and Strategy. In Leadership Styles, Innovation, and Social Entrepreneurship in the Era of Digitalization (pp. 44-72). IGI Global.

Wettstein, F. (2012). CSR and the debate on business and human rights: Bridging the great divide. *Business Ethics Quarterly*, ▪▪▪, 739–770.

Zaman, G., Panait, M. C., Voica, M. C., & Ene, C. (2020). Corporate Social Responsibility in the Agri-Food Sector. Recent Advancements in Sustainable. doi:10.4018/978-1-7998-2347-6.ch003

Zamfir, A. M., Mocanu, C., & Grigorescu, A. (2017). Circular economy and decision models among European SMEs. *Sustainability, 9*(9), 1507. doi:10.3390u9091507

ADDITIONAL READING

Cavaco, S., & Crifo, P. (2014). CSR and financial performance: Complementarity between environmental, social and business behaviours. *Applied Economics, 46*(27), 3323–3338. doi:10.1080/00036846.2014.927572

Fatemi, A. M., & Fooladi, I. J. (2013). Sustainable finance: A new paradigm. *Global Finance Journal, 24*(2), 101–113. doi:10.1016/j.gfj.2013.07.006

Friedman, A. L., & Miles, S. (2001). Socially responsible investment and corporate social and environmental reporting in the UK: An exploratory study. *The British Accounting Review, 33*(4), 523–548. doi:10.1006/bare.2001.0172

Lehner, O. M. (Ed.). (2016). *Routledge handbook of social and sustainable finance*. Routledge. doi:10.4324/9781315772578

Lozano, J. M., Albareda, L., & Balaguer, M. R. (2006). Socially responsible investment in the Spanish financial market. *Journal of Business Ethics, 69*(3), 305–316. doi:10.100710551-006-9092-7

Ortas, E., Moneva, J. M., & Salvador, M. (2010). Conditional volatility in sustainable and traditional stock exchange indexes: Analysis of the Spanish market. *Journal of Globalization, Competitiveness & Governability/Revista de Globalización, Competitividad y Gobernabilidad/Revista de Globalização. Competitividade e Governabilidade, 4*(2), 104–129.

Schoenmaker, D., & Schramade, W. (2018). *Principles of Sustainable Finance*. Oxford University Press.

Sparkes, R., & Cowton, C. J. (2004). The maturing of socially responsible investment: A review of the developing link with corporate social responsibility. *Journal of Business Ethics, 52*(1), 45–57. doi:10.1023/B:BUSI.0000033106.43260.99

KEY TERMS AND DEFINITIONS

CSR: The voluntary self-regulation of a company's business practices to minimize the negative impact, in the present and in the future, on society and human beings and also to maximize the positive potential on the environment, local communities, employees and other categories of stakeholders.

Green Bonds: Are debt instruments used to finance environmental investments.

Green Finance: Are finance focused on the promotion of business that could not be damaging to the environment for present or future generations.

Social Responsible Investment: Is investment that in addition to the traditional criterion for evaluating investments, namely risk return, take in account ESG issues.

Sustainable Index: Is index constructed using only listed companies with a sustainable corporate behavior.

Sustainable Stock Exchange: Is stock exchange that promote sustainable development principles among listed companies and other stakeholders.

APPENDIX

Figure 4. Statistics regarding shares and bonds trade.
Source: Bucharest Stock Exchange

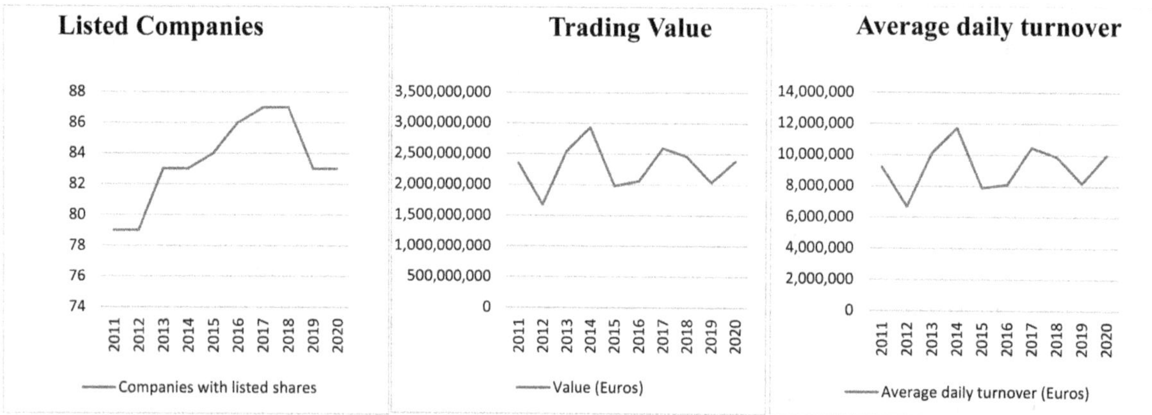

Figure 5. Bonds statistics.
Source: Bucharest Stock Exchange

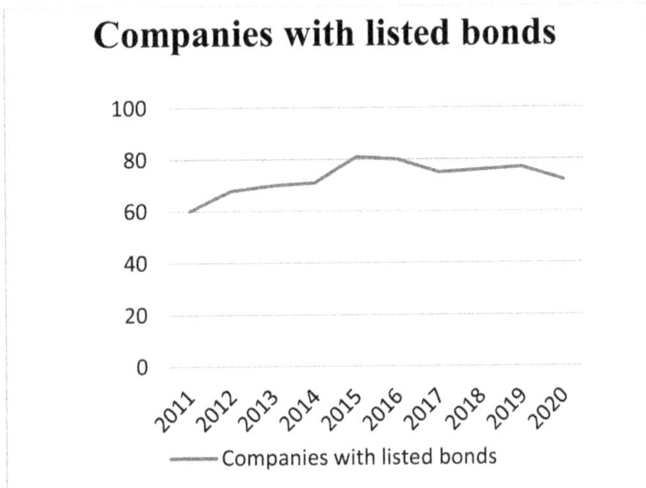

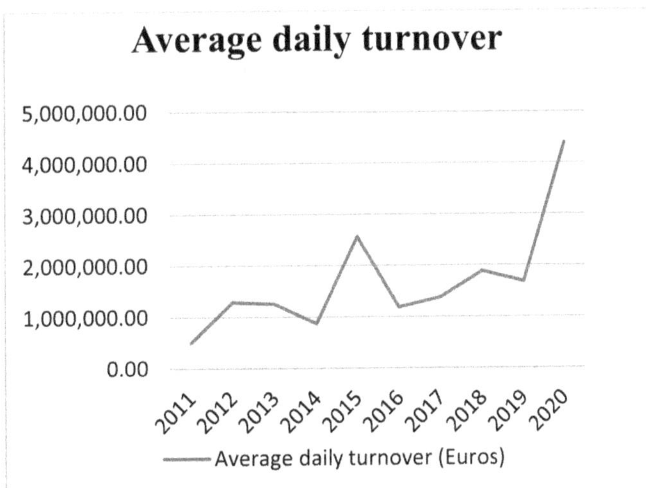

Chapter 12
Offshore Wind as a Base for a New Sustainable Business

Almudena Filgueira-Vizoso
University of A Coruña, Spain

Joaquín Enríquez-Díaz
https://orcid.org/0000-0001-8711-0795
University of A Coruña, Spain

Isabel Lamas-Galdo
University of A Coruña, Spain

Félix Puime Guillén
University of A Coruña, Spain

David Cordal-Iglesias
University of A Coruña, Spain

Begoña Álvarez García
https://orcid.org/0000-0001-7918-3986
University of A Coruña, Spain

Laura Castro-Santos
https://orcid.org/0000-0001-9284-1170
University of A Coruña, Spain

ABSTRACT

The aim of this chapter is to examine the offshore wind as a pillar for a new sustainable business. In this context, the chapter firstly analyses the significance of renewable energies. Secondly, it analyses several types of offshore renewable energies, the state of offshore wind energy in Europe, and the projections of offshore wind in the world. Thirdly, it presents an overview of the levelized cost of energy (LCOE), comparing its value for different energy technologies. Moreover, a new concept, called SCOE, is introduced to incorporates society in the LCOE equation. Finally, conclusions talk about the importance of choosing a sustainable way of generating electricity in our future.

INTRODUCTION

During the last years people and Governments are concerned about global warming and how it can affect to our life's in the future. In this context, the Paris Agreement, which has been adopted at the Paris Climate Conference (COP21) at the end of 2015, tried to limit the increase of temperature of the world up to 2ºC (United Nations Framework Convention on Climate Change, 2015).

DOI: 10.4018/978-1-7998-7634-2.ch012

Spain, as part of the European Union, is among the 190 parties to this Agreement, whose main purpose is to develop policies and climate-neutrality for the present century.

The main agreements of the Paris agreement related to the mitigation process of reducing emissions are (United Nations Framework Convention on Climate Change, 2015):

- "A long-term goal of keeping the increase in global average temperature to well below 2°C above pre-industrial levels.
- To aim to limit the increase to 1.5°C, since this would significantly reduce risks and the impacts of climate change.
- On the need for global emissions to peak as soon as possible, recognizing that this will take longer for developing countries.
- To undertake rapid reductions thereafter in accordance with the best available science, so as to achieve a balance between emissions and removals in the second half of the century".

On the other hand, the Madrid Climate Conference (COP25) has took place in Madrid on December 2019. It was carried out in support of Chile, the organizing country, which due to internal circumstances was forced to renounce the organization of acts and events just one month before it began (Madrid Climate Conference (COP25), 2020).

The agreements reached have been reflected in the document "Chile Madrid is time to act", in which the main points are (Madrid Climate Conference (COP25), 2020):

- "Calls for an increase in the ambition of the commitments in 2020, following the schedule set at the Paris summit, stressing the "urgent need" for the new commitments of the countries to bridge the existing gap from the current ones with which they would be objectives of the Paris Agreement which according to scientific reports.
- Countries should be more ambitious regarding their emission reduction commitments (NDCs) in 2020 to respond to the climate emergency."

Otherwise, during the Madrid Conference, the European Union has activated some measures to deal with the climate emergency in the New Green Deal, which main objective is to "achieve the Climate neutrality in 2050 and agreeing to turn the European Investment Bank (EIB) into a Climate Bank" (Madrid Climate Conference (COP25), 2020). In addition, the EIB announced that it will stop financing fossil energy related projects in 2021 (Madrid Climate Conference (COP25), 2020).

On the other hand, the "Directive 2009/28/EC of the European Parliament and of the Council of 23 April 2009 on the promotion of the use of energy from renewable sources and amending and subsequently repealing Directives 2001/77/EC and 2003/30/EC" (Official Journal of the European Union & EC, 2009) establishes "an overall policy for the production and promotion of energy from renewable sources in the European Union (EU)". It means that the EU achieve, at least 20% of its total energy needs with renewables by 2020. It makes that each country improve its independence of the fossil fuels in the production of electricity.

This normative has been reviewed in 2018 by the "Directive (EU) 2018/2001 of the European Parliament and of the Council on the promotion of the use of energy from renewable sources" (EU, 2018) to try to cover the emission reduction objectives achieved in the Paris Conference in 2015. This new directive "establishes a new binding renewable energy target for the EU for 2030 of at least 32%, with a clause for a possible upwards revision by 2023" (EU, 2018). Therefore, it makes more restrictive the directive of 2009, forcing the European countries to be more environmentally friendly regarding the electricity production using renewable sources.

The majority of the new components of the Directive of 2018 need to be transposed into national laws by European member states by 2021. It indicates that all the countries of the EU should adapt their electricity production to renewable energy sources.

However, nowadays the majority of the electricity using renewable sources has been produced onshore, which makes that we have a problem in order to increase the production because a great part of the onshore locations is occupied by traditional renewable energies (solar, onshore wind energy, hydropower, etc.). In this context, it is important to notice that the future of renewable energies in Europe comes from the hand of offshore renewable energies.

The objective of the present chapter is to analyse the offshore wind as a base for a new sustainable business. In this context, the chapter firstly will analyse the importance of renewable energies. Secondly, it studies the main types of offshore renewable energies, the situation of offshore wind energy in Europe and the prospects of offshore wind in the world. Thirdly, it gives an overview of the important parameter of the Levelized Cost Of Energy (LCOE), comparing its value for different energy technologies. In addition, a new concept, called SCOE is introduced to includes society in the LCOE equation. Finally, conclusions talk about the importance of selecting a sustainable way of producing electricity in our future.

BACKGROUND

Climate change has become an urgent issue and the need to accelerate adaptation to make the world more resilient is critical. In fact, without immediate action, climate impacts could push an additional 100 million people into poverty by 2030 (Word Energy Council (WEC), 2016).

The majority of the governments are using carbon pricing today in the form of carbon taxes, Emissions Trading Systems (ETSs) and offset instrument as part of broader policy packages to attack climate change (Word Energy Council (WEC), 2016). In this context, the first carbon-pricing initiatives were developed in Sweden (1991), in the Regional Greenhouse Gas Initiative (RGGI) (2009) and in the EU (2015). In the Swedish case a carbon tax of 150 $ per tonne of CO_2 reduced the emissions by 25% since it was introduced (Word Energy Council (WEC), 2016). Regarding RGGI, it improved the air quality and it saved 10 M$ of illness, hospital visits, lost workdays and premature deaths between 2009 – 2015. Finally, from 1990 to 2016, emissions intensity of the EU economy was reduced 50% and decoupling happened in all member states (Word Energy Council (WEC), 2016).

Regarding World Energy Council (WEC) (Word Energy Council (WEC), 2016), "*Electricity consumption doubles in 2040 compared to 2015, as clean heat and mobility become a priority in many geographies. Industrial production decouples from CO_2 emissions through increased energy efficiency, deployment of best available technologies and a shift to low-carbon fuels, including electricity. The buildings sector accounts for about half of the increase in electricity demand, reflecting growth in income levels and improved access to clean energy in developing economies. In the transport sector, electricity, biofuels and hydrogen account for one-quarter of the sectoral energy consumption*". In this sense, electrification and efficiency are the foreground of the decarbonization pathway, of course, considering better systems integration, smart grids and improved management. Therefore, the electricity production sector will develop a deep transformation towards low-carbon or clean sources.

Nowadays, some countries like Spain are closing their main coal power stations, for instance, the Coal Power Station of As Pontes (A Coruña) of 1,4 GW, that is the highest installation in Spain, and the Coal Power Station Litoral de Carboneras (Almería) of 1,2 GW of power. In this context, the future energy roadmap should replace its electricity production; motivated by the fact that the present energy consumption is increasing continuously due to the electric cars, the home automation devices, etc.

Therefore, renewable energies will have a great development in the future of the humanity. In this context, there are two main types of renewable energies: onshore renewable energies and offshore renewable energies. During the last thirty years onshore renewable energies, such as onshore wind, solar energy and hydro energy, had achieved a great development. It does that certain onshore areas are nowadays occupied by wind farms, for instance, some of which had been repowered in recent years. Moreover, onshore wind locations produce less electricity than the offshore ones due to their high roughness and their low wind speed. Therefore, offshore locations will represent the future of the clean energy that the society need.

OFFSHORE RENEWABLE ENERGIES

Classification

Offshore renewable energies are produced in offshore locations. There are several types of offshore renewable energies: offshore wind, wave energy, tides, currents, salinity gradient energy and ocean thermal energy. However, the state of the technology is more developed in offshore wind and wave energy.

Offshore renewable energies can be classified in several ways:

1. **Depending on their distance from the shore:**
   a. Nearshore (López, Veigas, & Iglesias, 2015): close to the shore.
   b. Farshore: far to the shore.
2. **Depending on the depth where they are installed**:
   a. Fixed (Esteban, Couñago, López-Gutiérrez, Negro, & Vellisco, 2015; Galicia Ártabra Digital, 2015): the technology is fixed to the seabed up to 50 m of depth.
   b. Floating (L. D. C. V. Castro-Santos, 2015; L. Castro-Santos, Filgueira-Vizoso, Carral-Couce, & Formoso, 2016; Fan, Mu, & Ma, 2016): the technology is floating on the sea in depths higher than 50 m.
3. **Depending on the type of source considered**:
   a. Offshore wind: it generates the electricity using the offshore wind.
   b. Wave energy (Lindroth & Leijon, 2011; Yemm, Pizer, Retzler, & Henderson, 2012): it generates the electricity using wave energy.
   c. Tidal (Zabihian & Fung, 2011): it generates the electricity using the tides and their difference on height.
   d. Salinity (Hussain, Arif, & Aslam, 2017; Zabihian & Fung, 2011): it generates the electricity considering the salinity gradients.
   e. Currents (Douglas, 2008): it generates the electricity using the currents and their speed.

The most commercially energy source developed is the offshore wind, whose impact in the economy of some countries is increasing year by year during the last decade.

Regarding offshore wind, in 2018 Europe connected 409 new offshore wind turbines to the grid, which represents 2,649 MW of net additional capacity. Europe has a total installed offshore wind capacity of 18,400 MW, representing 4,543 grid-connected wind turbines across 11 countries (Wind Europe, 2018).

The average size of newly-installed offshore wind turbines in 2018 was 6.8 MW, being the UK the country that has the largest turbine in the world connected to the grid (8.8 MW from MHI Vestas Offshore Wind) (Wind Europe, 2018). The average size of wind farms in construction in 2018 was 561 MW, being the UK where the largest wind farm in the world was installed: 1,200 MW Hornsea One project (Wind Europe, 2018). Regarding economics, investments in new offshore wind amounted to 10.3 billion of euros in 2018, a 37% increase from 2017 (Wind Europe, 2018).

Regarding offshore wind, there are two main types of technologies (Dvorak, Archer, & Jacobson, 2010): fixed (up to 50 m of depth) (monopiles and jackets) and floating (more than 50 m of depth) (semisubmersible, tensioned leg platform and spar).

Europe is the world leader in wave energy technologies. The first WECs (Wave Energy Converters) were the Pelamis structure in the UK (750 kW) and the Archimedes Wave Swing platform (2 MW) in Portugal in 2004 (International Renewable Energy Agency (IRENA), 2014). The first wave energy farm (2.25 MW) based on three Pelamis converters was tested in 2008 in Portugal. Aquamarine Power (315 kW) has been installed in 2009 in Orkney Islands. The Basque Energy Board (EVE) installed the first commercial breakwater in Mutriku with 296 kW in 2011. Three WaveRollers (110 kW) have been installed in Portugal. However, American, Canadian, Israelian, Japanese and Australian enterprises have also developed wave energy devices: Oceanlinx in South Australia, Carnegie Wave Energy (Australia, Canada, Reunion Island), Eco Wave Power (China, Mexico), Mitsui (Japan), etc. (International Renewable Energy Agency (IRENA), 2014).

Wave energy technologies are made of the following components: 1) the structure that captures the energy of the wave, 2) foundation or mooring keeping, 3) the power take-off (PTO) system by which mechanical energy is converted into electrical energy, and 4) the control systems to safeguard and optimize performance in operating conditions (International Renewable Energy Agency (IRENA), 2014). In this context, there are different types of wave energy considering the way the wave energy is converted: Oscillating Water Column (OWC), oscillating body converters and overtopping converters.

OWC are conversion systems with a semisubmerged chamber, keeping a trapped air pocket above a column of water (International Renewable Energy Agency (IRENA), 2014). Waves generate the column to act like a piston, moving up and down and thereby forcing the air out of the chamber and back into it. This continuous movement generates a reversing stream of high-velocity air, which is channelled through rotor-blades driving an air turbine-generator group to produce electricity (International Renewable Energy Agency (IRENA), 2014). Examples of OWC are: Pico (Pego, Marques, Salvador, Guedes Soares, & Monteiro, 2016; WavEC, 2012), LIMPET, Sakata, Mutriku, Ocean Energy, Sperboy (MarineEnergy, 2013), etc.

Oscillating body converters are either floating or submerged (International Renewable Energy Agency (IRENA), 2014). They exploit the more powerful wave regimes that normally occur in deep waters where the depth is greater than 40 m. There are many ways to transform the oscillating movement into electricity: hydraulic generators with linear hydraulic actuators, linear electric generators, piston pumps, etc. (International Renewable Energy Agency (IRENA), 2014). Examples of Oscillating systems are: AquaBuoy (L. Castro-Santos, Silva, Bento, Salvação, & Guedes Soares, 2018; Weinstein et al., 2003),

Wavebob (Wavebob, 2013), PowerBuoy (Drew, Plummer, & Sahinkaya, n.d.), Pelamis (Pelamis, 2012; Pizer et al., 2005), AWS (Marei, Mokhtar, & El-Sattar, 2015), WaveRoller, Oyster, etc.

Overtopping converters or terminators are based on floating or bottom fixed water reservoir structure, and also usually reflecting arms, which ensure that as waves arrive, they spill over the top of a ramp structure and are restrained in the reservoir of the device (International Renewable Energy Agency (IRENA), 2014). The potential energy, due to the height of collected water above the sea surface, is transformed into electricity using conventional low head hydro turbines (International Renewable Energy Agency (IRENA), 2014). Examples of overtopping platforms are: TAPCHAN (Aderinto & Li, 2018), SSG (Veigas, López, & Iglesias, 2014), Wave Dragon (L. Castro-Santos et al., 2018; Kofoed, Frigaard, Friis-Madsen, & Sørensen, 2006; Web page, 2016), etc.

When a renewable energy farm is planned, it is important to know the type of offshore renewable energy technology (Pérez-Collazo, Greaves, & Iglesias, 2015); the layout of the farm (Chen & Macdonald, 2014; Mittal, Mitra, & Kulkarni, 2017; Pillai, Chick, Khorasanchi, Barbouchi, & Johanning, 2017) and their influence on costs (Rezaei Mirghaed & Roshandel, 2013). However, it also is important to recognize where it can be installed because there are areas where the offshore energy resource is very good, but where the farm cannot be installed for several reasons: legal aspects, navigation areas, environmental protected regions, visual impact (Maslov, Claramunt, Wang, & Tang, 2017), etc. Therefore, the establishment of a tool that can manage these issues has a great importance.

Finally, it is important to plan where an offshore renewable farm will be located in economic terms. Therefore, the economic feasibility of the farm is as important as the technical aspects (Mytilinou & Kolios, 2019; O'Connor, Lewis, & Dalton, 2013; Pantaleo, Pellerano, Ruggiero, & Trovato, 2005).

The majority of the present installations are fixed structures on the seabed. However, the future trend of offshore wind is to install floating substructures in deep waters (more than 50 m of depth) in the Atlantic Ocean. **Figure 1** shows the building of a semisubmersible floating offshore wind platform called WindFloat for the WindFloat Atlantic project in a shipyard. It is the first floating offshore wind farm in Portugal and the second floating offshore wind farm in Europe.

Offshore Wind in Europe

Europe has a total offshore wind capacity installed of 22,072 MW. It represents 5,047 offshore grid-connected wind turbines through 12 European countries in 2019 (Wind Europe, 2020) (it includes demonstrators of single turbine or announced as demonstrator by developer):

- UK: it has 40 farms connected with a cumulative capacity of 9,945 MW.
- Germany: it has 28 farms connected with a cumulative capacity of 7,445 MW.
- Denmark: it has 14 farms connected with a cumulative capacity of 1,703 MW.
- Belgium: it has 8 farms connected with a cumulative capacity of 1,556 MW.
- Netherlands: it has 6 farms connected with a cumulative capacity of 1,118 MW.
- Sweden: it has 5 farms connected with a cumulative capacity of 192 MW.
- Finland: it has 3 farms connected with a cumulative capacity of 70.7 MW.
- Ireland: it has 1 farm connected with a cumulative capacity of 25.2 MW.
- Spain: it has 2 farms connected with a cumulative capacity of 5 MW.
- Portugal: it has 1 farm connected with a cumulative capacity of 8.4 MW.
- Norway: it has 1 farm connected with a cumulative capacity of 2.3 MW.

- France: it has 1 farm connected with a cumulative capacity of 2 MW.

Figure 1. Building the floating offshore wind platform called WindFloat for the WindFloat Atlantic project in a shipyard.
[Source: own]

The 77% (16,908 MW) of the cumulative capacity is installed in North Sea, followed by 13% (2,930 MW) of the Irish Sea, 10% (2,219 MW) of the Baltic Sea and less than 1% (15 MW) of the Atlantic Ocean (Wind Europe, 2020).

Analysing the European situation regarding offshore wind and its evolution in the last ten years numerous improvements can be highlighted. Firstly, the average capacity of wind turbines is around 8MW in 2019, being 3MW ten years earlier. Regarding the average distance to the coast, it was from 15 km in 2009 to 58 km in 2019. In this sense, the number of wind turbines at sea twenty years ago was ridiculous. Regarding the average size of the wind farms, the installed power has tripled, from 200 MW in 2009 to 600 MW in 2019. Finally, the typical depth at which these farms are being installed is an average of 33 km (Joselin Herbert, Iniyan, Sreevalsan, & Rajapandian, 2007; Wieczorek A Negro S Harmsen R Heimeriks G Luo L et. al., 2013).

All these parameters have facilitated the implementation of more offshore wind farms. It is due to the fact that the number of locations for the farms have been increased because the total MW of the offshore wind farms have been augmented. It improves their economic feasibility and, therefore, reduces their Levelized Cost Of Energy (LCOE).

Prospects of Offshore Wind in the World

Another important parameter to take into account is that the total investment in offshore wind farms was from 2018 to 2019 of 16,000 million euros (Wind Europe, n.d.). Regarding the market prospects outside of Europe, according to the IRENA report (IRENA, 2019) a large deployment is expected in Asian waters in the next 30 years, with a total capacity that will exceed 100GW in 2030 and 600GW in 2050. With these values, it is expected that China will surpass Europe in less than 20 years. On the other hand, it is also expected that in the United States, offshore wind capacity would increase more strongly (almost 23GW in 2030 and 164GW by 2050).

Therefore, the IRENA report (IRENA, 2019) shows a significant growth in offshore wind energy with a total installed capacity of 228GW in 2030 and over 1000GW in 2050, with offshore wind representing 17% of the total installed wind power capacity of 6000GW by 2050, all this with the main objective of reducing greenhouse gas emissions to zero.

This fact will increase the industry of offshore wind for shipyards, manufacturing of turbines, industrial engineering, etc. This new industry will create a great employment in several sectors, which will help the European economy to increase its independence of the external production of technology. It can help the EU to get out of the present Covid-19 crisis, promoting the sustainable economy and the reduction of gas emissions.

LEVELIZED COST OF ENERGY

Definition

The Levelized Cost Of Energy (LCOE) is an indicator to characterize the economic evaluation of the energy system cost, including all costs along the useful lifetime, initial investment, operation and maintenance, fuel, capital and other costs, including possible environmental costs. The LCOE is used to compare the generation costs of different energy resources on a consistent basis. It is useful since it is possible to compare different methods of electricity generation, renewable or non renewable, of unequal life spans, different project sizes and capital costs, and capacities. The LCOE provides a standardized indicator which allows to compare, for instance, a photovoltaic with a thermal installation. The lower LCOE indicates which installation generates cheaper energy (L. Castro-Santos, Martins, & Guedes Soares, 2016; Lerch, De-Prada-Gil, Molins, & Benveniste, 2018).

Briefly, the LCOE represents the cost of a system related to its lifetime. It is computed as the sum of costs divided by the sum of electrical energy produced over the lifetime, as indicated by Eq. (1).

$$LCOE = \frac{\sum_{t=0}^{n} \frac{I_t + M_t + D_t}{\left(1+r\right)^t}}{\sum_{t=0}^{n} \frac{E_t}{\left(1+r\right)^t}} \quad (1)$$

where:

- I_t is the investment cost in the year t.
- M_t is the operation and maintenance cost in the year t.
- D_t is the dismantling cost in the year t (some authors does not consider it).

- E_t is the electricity generating in the year *t*.
- *r* is the discount rate.
- *n* is the expected lifetime.

Regarding the limitations of the LCOE, an important handicap is that it ignores time effects associated with matching electricity production to demand. The generation cost of a power plant is different if it runs continuously at nominal load or intermittently at low load. This is too important for intermittent renewable energies. These sources may produce electricity when it is not needed, and the price of this energy may be much lower than those produced at another time [12–15](Aldersey-Williams & Rubert, 2019; Florian & Sørensen, 2017; Tegen et al., 2012).

Comparison of LCOE of Different Energy Technologies

Considering the LCOE of different energies, both renewable and non-renewable, a conclusion about the feasibility of these technologies can be established. According to the Lazard report for the year 2019 (Lazard, 2020) the comparison of renewable and non-renewable energy can be analysed (see Figure 2).

Analysing the different renewable and non-renewable energy sources, it is shown that wind energy has favourable LCOE values, being more difficult to achieve in the case of offshore wind energy due to the fact that the technology is less developed and therefore its initial investment is higher.

It is important to notice that increasing the average power of each turbine, the total power of the farms and the distances to the coast and depth at which they are installed the LCOE value decrease significantly. Wind power is the cheapest source of electricity generation in most of the world. In fact, onshore wind energy is cheaper than any other energy source, including conventional power generation sources such as coal and gas.

According to WIND EUROPE in 2017 (Wind Europe, n.d.), the share of wind energy in electricity demand in the U.S. was 29.6%, 13.2 billion euros were saved on the purchase of fossil fuels, 382 million fewer tons of greenhouse gases were emitted, 239 billion euros were invested and 569.000 jobs were created. These values are for a 323 GW installed.

On the other hand, Figure 3 analyses the evolution of the LCOE during the last 10 years (Lazard, 2020). It is important to notice that from 2009 to 2020, the LCOE fell by 70.4%, from 135$/MWh to 40$/MWh.

FUTURE RESEARCH DIRECTIONS

Discuss future and emerging trends. Provide insight about the future of the book's theme from the perspective of the chapter focus. Viability of a paradigm, model, implementation issues of proposed programs, etc., may be included in this section. If appropriate, suggest future research opportunities within the domain of the topic.

The future of the LCOE was a parameter developed by SIEMENS GAMESA (Siemens Gamesa, 2020) that is gaining more and more force. Its name is the SCOE (Samadi, 2017), this parameter broadens the scope of the calculation of the cost of electricity from the LCOE and includes society in the equation. In this sense, SCOE takes into account, in addition to the factors that the LCOE usually takes into consideration, the following:

Figure 2. LCOE range depending on the energy source for the year 2019.
Source: own elaboration based on the Lazard 2019 report (Lazard, 2020)
[2] The subsidized analysis includes sensitivities related to the TCJA and U.S. federal tax subsidies

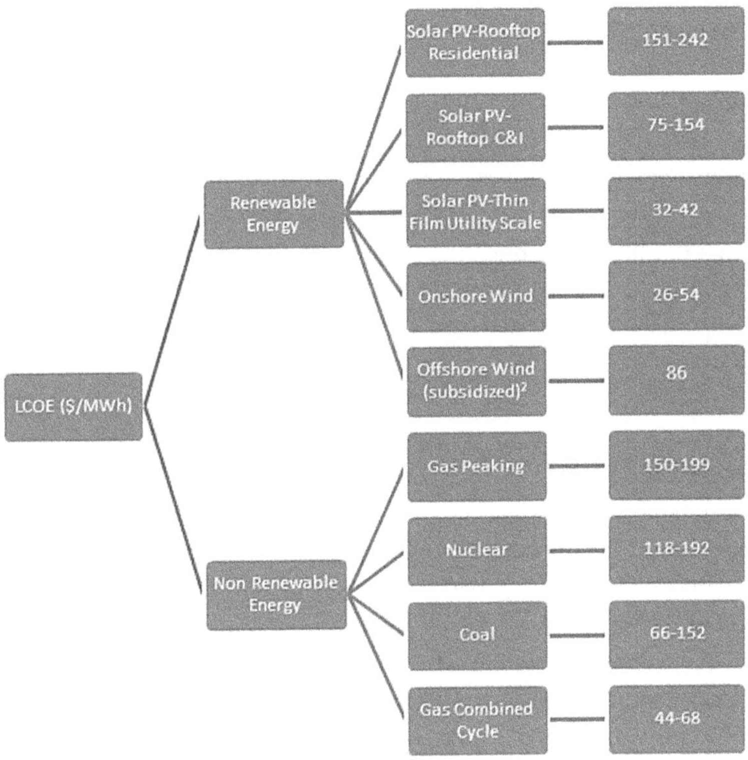

Figure 3. Evolution over time of the LCOE of wind energy and percentage of reduction with respect to the initial year (2009).
Source: own.

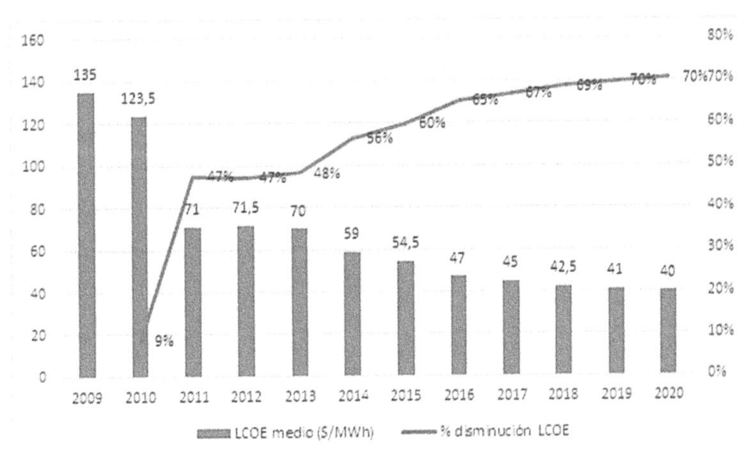

- Partially hidden subsidies, conventional energies also are subject to subsidies, but these are not reflected in the LCOE, which creates erroneous comparisons between the different energies (Niesten, Jolink, & Chappin, 2018).
- Variation in availability costs.
- Social costs of energy.
- Geopolitical impact to avoid dependence on fossil fuel imports and thus avoid price variability.
- Network access costs.
- Economic benefits (Søren Krohn; Poul-Erik Morthorst; Shimon Awerbuch, 2009).

The SCOE cost model allows to reduce the value of the LCOE and shows the benefit it will bring to new generations. This model shows that offshore wind energy is the pillar of the sustainable energy of the future generating clean and environmentally friendly electricity (Hwang, Kim, & Ryu, 2019).

CONCLUSION

This chapter has studied the offshore wind as a base for a new sustainable business. For this purpose, the chapter firstly has considered the importance of renewable energies. Secondly, it analyses the types of offshore renewable energies, the present situation of offshore wind energy in Europe and the prospects of offshore wind in the world. Thirdly, it has given an outline of the important parameter of the Levelized Cost Of Energy (LCOE), comparing its value for different energy technologies. Finally, a new concept, called SCOE was introduced to includes society in the LCOE equation.

LCOE of renewable energies, such as solar, onshore wind or offshore wind, can give better results that LCOE of traditional ways of obtaining electricity, such as coal or natural gas. It is important to consider the total life-cycle of the generation process, including dismantling of installations. Because usually dismantling process is not included in the calculation of LCOE of the conventional ways of generating electricity.

These good forecasts about renewable energies and, mainly offshore wind energy, give a little hope to the world in the sense of reactivate the world economic situation due to the SARS-CoV-2 pandemic.

In this sense, Governments and private sector should finance this type of technologies to reduce their initial investment, which will bring competitivity to these sorts of structures. It will give prosperity to all the stakeholders involved in the industrial process.

Offshore renewable energies provide an environmentally friendly new market to exploit. It will bring new buildings to the old European shipyards, new jobs to the society and a new way of generating electricity to support the future requirements of humanity (such as the electric car).

Definitely, our civilization should choose a new future path of sustainability to be in peace with our environment.

ACKNOWLEDGMENT

This research was partially funded by Project PID2019-105386RA-I00 “Design of a tool for the selection of offshore renewable energy locations and technologies: application to Spanish territorial waters (SEARENEW)", financed by Ministerio de Ciencia e Innovación – Agencia Estatal de Investigación/10.13039/501100011033

REFERENCES

Aderinto, T., & Li, H. (2018). Ocean Wave Energy Converters: Status and Challenges. *Energies*, *11*(5), 1250. doi:10.3390/en11051250

Aldersey-Williams, J., & Rubert, T. (2019). Levelised cost of energy – A theoretical justification and critical assessment. *Energy Policy*, *124*, 169–179. doi:10.1016/j.enpol.2018.10.004

Baita-Saavedra, E., Cordal-Iglesias, D., Filgueira-Vizoso, A., & Castro-Santos, L. (2019). Economic aspects of a concrete floating offshore wind platform in the Atlantic Arc of Europe. *International Journal of Environmental Research and Public Health*, *16*(21), 4122. Advance online publication. doi:10.3390/ijerph16214122 PMID:31717702

Baita-Saavedra, E., Cordal-Iglesias, D., Filgueira-Vizoso, A., Morató, À., Lamas-Galdo, I., Álvarez-Feal, C., Carral, L., & Castro-Santos, L. (2020). An Economic Analysis of An Innovative Floating Offshore Wind Platform Built with Concrete: The SATH® Platform. *Applied Sciences (Basel, Switzerland)*, *10*(11), 3678. doi:10.3390/app10113678

Castro-Santos, L., Filgueira-Vizoso, A., Carral-Couce, L., & Formoso, J. Á. F. (2016). Economic feasibility of floating offshore wind farms. *Energy*, *112*, 868–882. doi:10.1016/j.energy.2016.06.135

Castro-Santos, L., Martins, E., & Guedes Soares, C. (2016). Methodology to calculate the costs of a floating offshore renewable energy farm. *Energies*, *9*(5), 324. doi:10.3390/en9050324

Castro-Santos, L., Silva, D., Bento, A. R., Salvação, N., & Guedes Soares, C. (2018). Economic feasibility of wave energy farms in Portugal. *Energies*, *11*(11), 1–16. doi:10.3390/en11113149

Castro-Santos, L. D. C. V., & Diaz-Casas, V. (2015). Cost Comparison of Three Floating Offshore Wind Platforms. *Journal of Coastal Research*, *31*(5), 1217–1221. doi:10.2112/JCOASTRES-D-13-00134.1

Chen, L., & Macdonald, E. (2014). A system-level cost-of-energy wind farm layout optimization with landowner modeling. *Energy Conversion and Management*, *77*, 484–494. doi:10.1016/j.enconman.2013.10.003

Douglas, C. (2008). Life cycle assessment of the Seagen marine current turbine. *Proceedings of the …*, *222*, 1–12. 10.1243/14750902JEME94

Drew, B., Plummer, A. R., & Sahinkaya, M. N. (n.d.). *A review of wave energy converter technology*. doi:10.1243/09576509JPE782

Dvorak, M. J., Archer, C. L., & Jacobson, M. Z. (2010). California offshore wind energy potential. *Renewable Energy*, *35*(6), 1244–1254. doi:10.1016/j.renene.2009.11.022

Esteban, M. D., Couñago, B., López-Gutiérrez, J. S., Negro, V., & Vellisco, F. (2015). Gravity based support structures for offshore wind turbine generators: Review of the installation process. *Ocean Engineering, 110*, 281–291. doi:10.1016/j.oceaneng.2015.10.033

EU. (2018). Directive (EU) 2018/2001 of the European Parliament and of the Council on the promotion of the use of energy from renewable sources. *Official Journal of the European Union, 2018*(L 328), 82–209. Retrieved from https://eur-lex.europa.eu/legal-content/EN/TXT/PDF/?uri=CELEX:32018L2001&from=EN

Fan, Y., Mu, A., & Ma, T. (2016). Design and control of a point absorber wave energy converter with an open loop hydraulic transmission. *Energy Conversion and Management, 121*, 13–21. doi:10.1016/j.enconman.2016.04.107

Florian, M., & Sørensen, J. D. (2017). Risk-based planning of operation and maintenance for offshore wind farms. In Energy Procedia (Vol. 137). doi:10.1016/j.egypro.2017.10.349

Galicia Ártabra Digital. (2015). *Navantia finaliza el montaje de la primera jacket para Iberdrola*. Retrieved March 3, 2016, from http://www.galiciaartabradigital.com/archivos/126229

Hussain, A., Arif, S. M., & Aslam, M. (2017). Emerging renewable and sustainable energy technologies: State of the art. *Renewable & Sustainable Energy Reviews, 71*, 12–28. doi:10.1016/j.rser.2016.12.033

Hwang, S.-H., Kim, M.-K., & Ryu, H.-S. (2019). Real Levelized Cost of Energy with Indirect Costs and Market Value of Variable Renewables: A Study of the Korean Power Market. *Energies, 12*(13), 2459. doi:10.3390/en12132459

International Renewable Energy Agency (IRENA). (2014). *Wave Energy Technology Brief. Future Energy: Improved, Sustainable and Clean Options for our Planet*. doi:10.1016/B978-0-08-099424-6.00017-X

IRENA. (2019). *Future of Wind Deployment, investment, technology, grid integration and socio-economic aspects*. IRENA.

Joselin Herbert, G. M., Iniyan, S., Sreevalsan, E., & Rajapandian, S. (2007, August). A review of wind energy technologies. In *Renewable and Sustainable Energy Reviews*. Pergamon. doi:10.1016/j.rser.2005.08.004

Kofoed, J. P., Frigaard, P., Friis-Madsen, E., & Sørensen, H. C. (2006). Prototype testing of the wave energy converter wave dragon. Renewable Energy. doi:10.1016/j.renene.2005.09.005

Krohn, Morthorst, & Awerbuch. (2009). *The Economics of Wind Energy*. Academic Press.

Lazard. (2020). *Levelized Cost of Energy and Levelized Cost of Storage – 2020*. New York: Author.

Lerch, M., De-Prada-Gil, M., Molins, C., & Benveniste, G. (2018). Sensitivity analysis on the levelized cost of energy for floating offshore wind farms. *Sustainable Energy Technologies and Assessments, 30*, 77–90. Advance online publication. doi:10.1016/j.seta.2018.09.005

Lindroth, S., & Leijon, M. (2011, December 1). Offshore wave power measurements - A review. In *Renewable and Sustainable Energy Reviews*. Pergamon. doi:10.1016/j.rser.2011.07.123

López, M., Veigas, M., & Iglesias, G. (2015). On the wave energy resource of Peru. *Energy Conversion and Management, 90*, 34–40. doi:10.1016/j.enconman.2014.11.012

Madrid Climate Conference (COP25). (2020). *Madrid Climate Conference (COP25)*. Retrieved April 23, 2020, from https://www.dsn.gob.es/gl/actualidad/sala-prensa/madrid-cumbre-del-clima-cop25

Marei, M. I., Mokhtar, M., & El-Sattar, A. A. (2015). MPPT strategy based on speed control for AWS-based wave energy conversion system. *Renewable Energy, 83*, 305–317. doi:10.1016/j.renene.2015.04.039

MarineEnergy. (2013). *Sperboy Webpage*. Retrieved August 15, 2019, from https://marineenergy.biz/tag/sperboy/

Maslov, N., Claramunt, C., Wang, T., & Tang, T. (2017). Method to estimate the visual impact of an offshore wind farm. *Applied Energy, 204*, 1422–1430. doi:10.1016/j.apenergy.2017.05.053

Mittal, P., Mitra, K., & Kulkarni, K. (2017). Optimizing the number and locations of turbines in a wind farm addressing energy-noise trade-off: A hybrid approach. *Energy Conversion and Management, 132*, 147–160. doi:10.1016/j.enconman.2016.11.014

Myhr, A., Bjerkseter, C., Ågotnes, A., & Nygaard, T. A. (2014). Levelised cost of energy for offshore floating wind turbines in a life cycle perspective. *Renewable Energy, 66*, 714–728. doi:10.1016/j.renene.2014.01.017

Mytilinou, V., & Kolios, A. J. (2019). Techno-economic optimisation of offshore wind farms based on life cycle cost analysis on the UK. *Renewable Energy, 132*, 439–454. doi:10.1016/j.renene.2018.07.146

Niesten, E., Jolink, A., & Chappin, M. (2018, January). Investments in the Dutch onshore wind energy industry: A review of investor profiles and the impact of renewable energy subsidies. In *Renewable and Sustainable Energy Reviews*. Elsevier Ltd. doi:10.1016/j.rser.2017.06.056

O'Connor, M., Lewis, T., & Dalton, G. (2013). Techno-economic performance of the Pelamis P1 and Wavestar at different ratings and various locations in Europe. *Renewable Energy, 50*, 889–900. doi:10.1016/j.renene.2012.08.009

Official Journal of the European Union, & EC. Directive 2009/28/EC of the European Parliament and of the Council of 23 April 2009 on the promotion of the use of energy from renewable sources and amending and subsequently repealing Directives 2001/77/EC and 2003/30/EC (2009). Belgium: Official Journal of the European Union.

Pantaleo, A., Pellerano, A., Ruggiero, F., & Trovato, M. (2005). Feasibility study of off-shore wind farms: An application to Puglia region. *Solar Energy, 79*(3), 321–331. doi:10.1016/j.solener.2004.08.030

Pego, A., Marques, M., Salvador, R., Guedes Soares, C., & Monteiro, A. (2016). The potential offshore energy cluster in Portugal. In *Progress in Renewable Energies Offshore - Proceedings of 2nd International Conference on Renewable Energies Offshore, RENEW 2016*. 10.1201/9781315229256-102

Pelamis. (2012). *Pelamis wave power*. Retrieved from http://www.pelamiswave.com/

Pérez-Collazo, C., Greaves, D., & Iglesias, G. (2015). A review of combined wave and offshore wind energy. *Renewable & Sustainable Energy Reviews, 42*, 141–153. doi:10.1016/j.rser.2014.09.032

Pillai, A. C., Chick, J., Khorasanchi, M., Barbouchi, S., & Johanning, L. (2017). Application of an offshore wind farm layout optimization methodology at Middelgrunden wind farm. *Ocean Engineering, 139*(December), 287–297. doi:10.1016/j.oceaneng.2017.04.049

Pizer, D. J., Retzler, C., Henderson, R. M., Cowieson, F. L., Shaw, M. G., Dickens, B., & Hart, R. (2005). Pelamis WEC - Recent advances in the numerical and experimental modelling programme. *6th European Wave and Tidal Energy Conference*.

Rezaei Mirghaed, M., & Roshandel, R. (2013). Site specific optimization of wind turbines energy cost: Iterative approach. *Energy Conversion and Management, 73*, 167–175. doi:10.1016/j.enconman.2013.04.016

Samadi, S. (2017). The Social Costs of Electricity Generation—Categorising Different Types of Costs and Evaluating Their Respective Relevance. *Energies, 10*(3), 356. doi:10.3390/en10030356

Siemens Gamesa. (2020). *Costes de la energía eólica Redefinimos el precio de la electricidad*. Author.

Tegen, S., Hand, M., Maples, B., Lantz, E., Schwabe, P., & Smith, A. (2012). 2010 Cost of Wind Energy. *Contract (New York, N.Y.), 303*, 275–3000.

United Nations Framework Convention on Climate Change. (2015). *Paris Agreement*. Retrieved from https://unfccc.int/files/meetings/paris_nov_2015/application/pdf/paris_agreement_english_.pdf

Veigas, M., López, M., & Iglesias, G. (2014). Assessing the optimal location for a shoreline wave energy converter. *Applied Energy, 132*, 404–411. doi:10.1016/j.apenergy.2014.07.067

Wav, E. C. (2012). *Web Page OWC Pico Plant*. Retrieved August 14, 2019, from http://www.pico-owc.net/en/

Wavebob. (2013). *Wavebob Webpage*. Retrieved from http://www.wavebob.com

Web page. (2016). *Wave Dragon Technology*. Retrieved September 7, 2016, from http://www.wave-dragon.net

Weinstein, A., Fredrikson, G., Claeson, L., Forsberg, J., Parks, M. J., Nielsen, K., . . . Andersen, T. L. (2003). AquaBuOY-the offshore wave energy converter numerical modeling and optimization. In Oceans 2003. Celebrating the Past ... Teaming Toward the Future (IEEE Cat. No.03CH37492) (pp. 1988-1995). IEEE. doi:10.1109/OCEANS.2003.178203

Wieczorek, A., Negro, S., Harmsen, R., Heimeriks, G., Luo, L., & Hekkert, M. P. (2013). A review of the European offshore wind innovation system. *Renewable & Sustainable Energy Reviews, 26*, 294–306. doi:10.1016/j.rser.2013.05.045

Wind Europe. (2018). *Offshore wind in Europe*. doi:10.1016/S1471-0846(02)80021-X

Wind Europe. (2020). *Offshore wind in Europe. Key trends and statistics 2019*. doi:10.1016/S1471-0846(02)80021-X

Wind Europe. (n.d.). *Wind energy in Europe in 2018*. Author.

Word Energy Council (WEC). (2016). World Energy Scenarios 2016. *World Energy Council, 1*, 9–18. Retrieved from https://www.worldenergy.org/wp-content/uploads/2016/10/World-Energy-Scenarios-2016_Full-Report.pdf

Yemm, R., Pizer, D., Retzler, C., & Henderson, R. (2012). Pelamis: experience from concept to connection. *Philosophical Transactions. Series A, Mathematical, Physical, and Engineering Sciences, 370*(1959), 365–380. doi:10.1098/rsta.2011.0312

Zabihian, F., & Fung, A. S. (2011). Review of marine renewable energies: Case study of Iran. *Renewable & Sustainable Energy Reviews, 15*(5), 2461–2474. doi:10.1016/j.rser.2011.02.006

ADDITIONAL READING

Baita-Saavedra, E., Cordal-Iglesias, D., Filgueira-Vizoso, A., Morató, À., Lamas-Galdo, I., Álvarez-Feal, C., Carral, L., & Castro-Santos, L. (2020). An economic analysis of an innovative floating offshore wind platform built with concrete: The SATH® platform. *Applied Sciences (Switzerland), 10*(11), 3678. doi:10.3390/app10113678

Castro-Santos, L., & Diaz-Casas, V. (2015). Sensitivity analysis of floating offshore wind farms. *Energy Conversion and Management, 101*, 271–277. doi:10.1016/j.enconman.2015.05.032

Castro-Santos, L., & Diaz-Casas, V. (2016). *Floating offshore wind farms* (L. Castro-Santos & V. Diaz-Casas, Eds.). Springer., doi:10.1007/978-3-319-27972-5

Castro-Santos, L., Prado, G., & Diaz-Casas, V. (2013). Methodology to study the life cycle cost of floating offshore wind farms. In 10th Deep Sea Wind R&D Conference (pp. 179–186). Trondheim, Norway.

Castro-Santos, L., Silva, D., Bento, A. R., Salvação, N., & Guedes Soares, C. (2020). Economic feasibility of floating offshore wind farms in Portugal. *Ocean Engineering, 207*, 107393. Advance online publication. doi:10.1016/j.oceaneng.2020.107393

Olaofe, Z. O. (2018). Review of energy systems deployment and development of offshore wind energy resource map at the coastal regions of Africa. *Energy, 161*, 1096–1114. doi:10.1016/j.energy.2018.07.185

Wind Europe. (2017). Wind Energy in Europe: Scenarios For 2030. Retrieved from https://windeurope.org/wp-content/uploads/files/about-wind/reports/Wind-energy-in-Europe-Scenarios-for-2030.pdf%0Ahttp://www.ewea.org/fileadmin/files/library/publications/reports/EWEA-Wind-energy-scenarios-2030.pdf

Wind Europe. (2018). Financing and investment trends. Retrieved December 15, 2019, from https://windeurope.org/about-wind/reports/financing-and-investment-trends-2018/

Wind Europe. (2020). Offshore wind in Europe. Key trends and statistics 2019. doi:10.1016/S1471-0846(02)80021-X

KEY TERMS AND DEFINITIONS

Clean Technology: System that produces energy without emitting greenhouse gases.

Farshore: Far to the shore.

LCOE: Levelized cost of energy. Indicator to characterize the economic evaluation of a type of energy system.

Nearshore: Close to the shore.

Offshore Renewable Energy: Energy extracted using an offshore technology.

Offshore Wind: Wind energy extracted in offshore locations, far or closed to the shore.

SCOE: Calculation of the cost of electricity considering LCOE and society.

Compilation of References

Accenture. (2014). *Circular Advantage: Innovative Business Models and Technologies to Create Value in a World without Limits to Growth*. Retrieved from https://tinyurl.com/hdu6tff

Acs, Z., Anselin, L., & Varga, A. (2002). Patents and innovation counts as measures of regional production of new knowledge. *Research Policy*, *31*(7), 1069–1085. doi:10.1016/S0048-7333(01)00184-6

Adams, R., Jeanrenaud, S., Bessant, J., Denyer, D., & Overy, P. (2016). Sustainability-oriented innovation: A systematic review. *International Journal of Management Reviews*, *18*(2), 180–205. doi:10.1111/ijmr.12068

Aderinto, T., & Li, H. (2018). Ocean Wave Energy Converters: Status and Challenges. *Energies*, *11*(5), 1250. doi:10.3390/en11051250

Agaton, C. B., Guno, C. S., Villanueva, R. O., & Villanueva, R. O. (2020). Economic analysis of waste-to-energy investment in the Philippines: A real options approach. *Applied Energy*, *275*(May), 115265. doi:10.1016/j.apenergy.2020.115265

Agnew, S., & Harrison, N. (2015). Financial literacy and student attitudes to debt: A cross national study examining the influence of gender on personal finance concepts. *Journal of Retailing and Consumer Services*, *25*, 122–129. doi:10.1016/j.jretconser.2015.04.006

Aguadero Fernández, F. (2010). La responsabilidad social corporativa como punto de encuentro. *REDMARKA*, *21*(1), 53–70.

Ahmad, S., Zulkurnain, N. N. A., & Khairushalimi, F. I. (2016). Assessing the fitness of a measurement model using Confirmatory Factor Analysis (CFA). *International Journal of Innovation and Applied Studies*, *17*(1), 159.

AICEP. (2018). Indústria Têxtil e de Vestuário - Uma referência a nível mundial. *Revista Portugal Global*, *113*, 8–9.

Aksoylu, S., Boztosun, D., Altinişik, F., & Baraz, E. H. (2017). A Baseline Investigation of Financial Literacy Levels: The Case of Kayseri Province. *Journal of Accounting & Finance*, (75).

Aldersey-Williams, J., & Rubert, T. (2019). Levelised cost of energy – A theoretical justification and critical assessment. *Energy Policy*, *124*, 169–179. doi:10.1016/j.enpol.2018.10.004

Alegre, J. & Chiva, R. (2008). Assessing the impact of organizational learning capability on product innovation performance: an empirical test. *Technovation*, *28*(1:2), 315-326.

Aleixo, A. M., Leal, S., & Azeiteiro, U. M. (2018). Conceptualization of sustainable higher education institutions, roles, barriers, and challenges for sustainability: An exploratory study in Portugal. *Journal of Cleaner Production*, *172*, 1664–1673. doi:10.1016/j.jclepro.2016.11.010

Allwood, J. M. (2014). Squaring the Circular Economy: The Role of Recycling Within a Hierarchy of Material Management Strategies. In E. Worrel & M. A. Reuter (Eds.), *Handbook of Recycling State-of-the-art for practitioners, analysts, and scientists*. Elsevier.

Almeida, C. M. V. B., Rodrigues, A. J. M., Bonilla, S. H., & Giannetti, B. F. (2010). Emergy as a tool for Ecodesign: Evaluating materials selection for beverage packages in Brazil. *Journal of Cleaner Production*, *18*(1), 32–43. doi:10.1016/j.jclepro.2009.03.019

Alrazi, B., De Villiers, C., & Van Staden, C. J. (2016). The environmental disclosures of the electricity generation industry: A global perspective. *Accounting and Business Research*, *46*(6), 665–701. doi:10.1080/00014788.2015.1135781

AMA. (2013). *Definitions of Marketing*. https://www.ama.org/AboutAMA/Pages/Definition-of-Marketing.aspx

Amindoust, A., & Saghafinia, A. (2016). Textile supplier selection in sustainable supply chain using a modular fuzzy inference system model. *Journal of Industrial Textiles*, *108*(7), 1250–1258.

Amram, M., & Kulatilaka, N. (2000). Opciones Reales: Evaluación de inversiones en un mundo incierto. *Gestion*.

Anderson, J. C., & Gerbing, D. W. (1988). Structural equation modeling in practice: A review and recommended two-step approach. *Psychological Bulletin*, *103*(3), 411–423. doi:10.1037/0033-2909.103.3.411

Andreasen, A. R. (1994). Social marketing: Its definition and domain. *Journal of Public Policy & Marketing*, *13*(1), 108–114. doi:10.1177/074391569401300109

Andrei, J. V., Panait, M., & Voica, C. (2018). Challenges and Approaches for the Corporate Social Responsibility and Human Resource Management in the Financial Sector. *Economics, Management and Financial Markets*, *13*(3), 415–431.

Aquila, G., de Queiroz, A. R., Balestrassi, P. P., Rotella, P. Junior, Rocha, L. C. S., Pamplona, E. O., & Nakamura, W. T. (2020). Wind energy investments facing uncertainties in the Brazilian electricity spot market: A real options approach. *Sustainable Energy Technologies and Assessments*, *42*(May), 100876. doi:10.1016/j.seta.2020.100876

Arimond, A., Borth, D., Hoepner, A. G. F., Klawunn, M., & Weisheit, S. (2020). Neural networks and value at risk. *Michael J. Brennan Irish Finance Working Paper Series*, *20*(7). https://ssrn.com/abstract=3591996

Armeanu, D. S., Enciu, A., Obreja, C., & Cioacă, S. I. (2016). The Financial Crisis' Impact on the Central and Eastern Europe Capital Markets. *Revista de Management Comparat International*, *17*(5), 420.

Arribas, I., Espinós-Vañó, M. D., García, F., & Morales-Bañuelos, P. B. (2019). The inclusion of socially irresponsible companies in sustainable stock indices. *Sustainability*, *11*(7), 2047. doi:10.3390u11072047

ARUP. (2016). *The Circular Economy in the Built Environment*. Retrieved from https://tinyurl.com/gq79eno

Asaba, S., & Wada, T. (2019). The Contact-Hitting R&D Strategy of Family Firms in the Japanese Pharmaceutical Industry. *Family Business Review*.

Asparouhov, T., & Muthén, B. (2009). Exploratory structural equation modeling. *Structural Equation Modeling*, *16*(3), 397–438. doi:10.1080/10705510903008204

Ates, S. A., Ateş, M., & Yülek, M. A. (2019). Going Beyond GDP: The Role of Social Innovation in Building a Welfare State. In *Handbook of Research on Digital Marketing Innovations in Social Entrepreneurship and Solidarity Economics* (pp. 241–258). IGI Global. doi:10.4018/978-1-5225-8939-6.ch013

Atherton, A., & Giurco, D. (2011). Campus sustainability: Climate change, transport and paper reduction. *International Journal of Sustainability in Higher Education*, *12*(3), 269–279. doi:10.1108/14676371111148054

Atkin, T., Gilinsky, A., & Newton, S. K. (2011) Sustainability in the Wine Industry: Altering the Competitive Landscape? *Proceedings of the 6th AWBR International Conference*.

Atlı, D., Vidović, M., & Omazić, M. A. (2018). Communicating Corporate Social Responsibility on the Web: A Content Analysis of Sustainability Reports in World's Best Multinational Workplaces. *International Journal of Sustainable Entrepreneurship and Corporate Social Responsibility*, *3*(2), 1–17. doi:10.4018/IJSECSR.2018070101

Audretsch, D. B. (2009). The entrepreneurial society. *The Journal of Technology Transfer*, *3*(6), 245–254. doi:10.100710961-008-9101-3

Aybars, A., Ataünal, L., & Gürbüz, A. O. (2019). ESG and Financial Performance: Impact of Environmental, Social, and Governance Issues on Corporate Performance. In Handbook of Research on Managerial Thinking in Global Business Economics (pp. 520-536). IGI Global.

Badea, L., Armeanu, D. Ş., Niţescu, D. C., Murgu, V., Panait, I., & Kuzman, B. (2020). A Study of the Relative Stock Market Performance of Companies Recognized for Supporting Gender Equality Policies and Practices. *Sustainability*, *12*(9), 3558. doi:10.3390u12093558

Baita-Saavedra, E., Cordal-Iglesias, D., Filgueira-Vizoso, A., & Castro-Santos, L. (2019). Economic aspects of a concrete floating offshore wind platform in the Atlantic Arc of Europe. *International Journal of Environmental Research and Public Health*, *16*(21), 4122. Advance online publication. doi:10.3390/ijerph16214122 PMID:31717702

Baita-Saavedra, E., Cordal-Iglesias, D., Filgueira-Vizoso, A., Morató, À., Lamas-Galdo, I., Álvarez-Feal, C., Carral, L., & Castro-Santos, L. (2020). An Economic Analysis of An Innovative Floating Offshore Wind Platform Built with Concrete: The SATH® Platform. *Applied Sciences (Basel, Switzerland)*, *10*(11), 3678. doi:10.3390/app10113678

Balanay, R., & Halog, A. (2016). Charting Policy Directions for Mining's Sustainability with Circular Economy. *Recycling*, *1*(2), 219–230. doi:10.3390/recycling1020219

Baldassarre, F., & Campo, R. (2016). Sustainability as a marketing tool: To be or to appear to be? *Business Horizons*, *59*(4), 421–429. doi:10.1016/j.bushor.2016.03.005

Baldini, M., Dal Maso, L., Liberatore, G., Mazzi, F., & Terzani, S. (2018). Role of country-and firm-level determinants in environmental, social, and governance disclosure. *Journal of Business Ethics*, *150*(1), 79–98. doi:10.100710551-016-3139-1

Bank of America. (2020), https://newsroom.bankofamerica.com/system/files/2019_Environmental_Social_Governance.pdf

Banţa, V. C. (2019). Performance evaluation of the implementation of the 2013/34/EU directive in Romania on the basis of corporate social responsibility reports. *Sustainability*, *11*(9), 2531. doi:10.3390u11092531

Bao, C., Bryan, B. A., Connor, J. D., Meyer, W. S., Ostendorf, B., Regan, C. M., & Zhu, Z. (2015). Real options analysis for land use management: Methods, application, and implications for policy. *Journal of Environmental Management*, *161*, 144–152. doi:10.1016/j.jenvman.2015.07.004 PMID:26164637

Barber, N., Taylor, C., & Strick, S. (2009). Wine consumers' environmental knowledge and attitudes: Influence on willingness to purchase. *International Journal of Wine Research*, *1*, 59–72. doi:10.2147/IJWR.S4649

Barić, A., Omazić, M. A., Aleksić, A., & Pejic-Bach, M. (2020). Influence of CSR Activities on Stakeholders in Foreign Markets. In *Recent Advancements in Sustainable Entrepreneurship and Corporate Social Responsibility* (pp. 16–36). IGI Global. doi:10.4018/978-1-7998-2347-6.ch002

Barney, J. (1991). Firm Resources and Sustained Competitive Advantage. *Journal of Management*, *17*(1), 99–120. doi:10.1177/014920639101700108

Barney, J. B., Ketchen, D. J. Jr, & Wright, M. (2011). The Future of Resource-Based Theory: Revitalization or Decline? *Journal of Management*, *37*(5), 1299–1315. doi:10.1177/0149206310391805

Baron, R. M., & Kenny, D. A. (1986). The moderator–mediator variable distinction in social psychological research: Conceptual, strategic, and statistical considerations. *Journal of Personality and Social Psychology*, *51*(6), 1173–1182. doi:10.1037/0022-3514.51.6.1173 PMID:3806354

Barry, J. (2016). Citizenship and (Un)Sustainability: A Green Republican Perspective. In S. M. Gardiner & A. Thompson (Eds.), *The Oxford Handbook of Environmental Ethics*. Oxford University Press.

Bastein, T., Roelofs, E., Rietveld, E., & Hoogendoorn, A. (2013). *Opportunities for a Circular Economy in the Netherlands*. Ministry of Infrastructure and Environment.

Batista, A. A. D. S., & Francisco, A. C. D. (2018). Organizational sustainability practices: A study of the firms listed by the corporate sustainability index. *Sustainability*, *10*(1), 226. doi:10.3390u10010226

Bayar, M. Y., Sezgin, H. F., & Özttürk, O. F. (2017). Impact of Financial Literacy on Personal Savings: A Research on Usak University Staff. *Journal of Knowledge Management, Economics and Information Technology*, *7*(6), 1–19.

Becker, Y. L., Guo, L., & Nurmamatov, O. (2020), Assessing asset tail risk with artificial intelligence: The application of artificial neural network. In Advances in Pacific Basin Business, Economics and Finance (Vol. 8). Emerald Publishing Limited.

Beck, T., Demirgüç-Kunt, A., & Levine, R. (2007). Finance, inequality and the poor. *Journal of Economic Growth*, *12*(1), 27–49. doi:10.100710887-007-9010-6

Beechler, S., & Woodward, I. (2009). The global "war for talent". *Journal of International Management*, *15*(3), 273–285. doi:10.1016/j.intman.2009.01.002

Belz, F. M., & Peattie, K. (2012). *Sustainability marketing* (2nd ed.). John Wiley & Sons, Ltd.

Berglof, E. (1990). Capital Structure as a Mechanism of Control: a Comparison of Financial Systems. In A. Masahiko, B. Gustafsson, & O. E. Williamson (Eds.), *The Firm as a Nexus of Treaties* (pp. 237–262). Sage Publications.

Bešter, J. (2017). *Ekonomsko učinkovito krožno gospodarstvo*. Ljubljana: Inštitut za ekonomsko raziskovanje.

Bhattacharya, C. B., Smith, N. C., & Vogel, D. (2004). Integrating social responsibility and marketing strategy: An introduction. *California Management Review*, *47*(1), 6–8. doi:10.2307/41166283

Bianchi, M. (2018). Financial literacy and portfolio dynamics. *The Journal of Finance*, *73*(2), 831–859. doi:10.1111/jofi.12605

Bien, C., & Sassen, R. (2020). Sensemaking of a sustainability transition by higher education institution leaders. *Journal of Cleaner Production*, *256*, 120299. doi:10.1016/j.jclepro.2020.120299

Bildirici, M., & Ersin, Ö. (2014). Modeling markov switching ARMA-GARCH neural networks models and an application to forecasting stock returns. *The Scientific World Journal*, 1–21. Advance online publication. doi:10.1155/2014/497941 PMID:24977200

Bird, M. (2020). *Financial Education, Couple's Communication, and Gender Norms: Explaining the Mixed Effects of Women's Empowerment on Intra-household Bargaining*. Retrieved from https://www.bbvaedufin.com/wp-content/uploads/2020/03/Bird-2019-BBVA-draft-Financial-Education-Couple%E2%80%99s-Communication-and-Gender-Norms-2020.02.16-CLEAN.pdf

Black, F., & Scholes, M. (1973). The Pricing of Options and Corporate Liabilities. *Journal of Political Economy, 81*(3), 637–654. doi:10.1086/260062

Blomsma, F., & Brennan, G. (2017). The emergence of circular economy: A new framing around prolonging resource productivity. *Journal of Industrial Ecology, 21*(3), 603–614. doi:10.1111/jiec.12603

Bocken, N. M. P., de Pauw, I. C., Bakker, C., & van der Grinten, B. (2016). Product design and business model strategies for a circular economy. *Journal of Industrial and Production Engineering, 33*(5), 308–320. doi:10.1080/21681015.2016.1172124

Bocken, N. M. P., & Geradts, T. H. J. (2020). Barriers and drivers to sustainable business model innovation: Organization design and dynamic capabilities. *Long Range Planning, 53*(4), 101950. doi:10.1016/j.lrp.2019.101950

Boletín Oficial del Estado. (2011). *Ley 2/2011, de 4 de marzo, de Economía Sostenible.* https://www.boe.es/eli/es/l/2011/03/04/2/con

Bollani, L., Bonadonna, A., & Peira, G. (2019). The Millennials' Concept of Sustainability in the Food Sector. *Sustainability, 11*(10), 2984. doi:10.3390u11102984

Bollas-Araya, H. M., Polo-Garrido, F., & Seguí-Mas, E. (2019). Determinants of CSR reporting and assurance: An analysis of top cooperative and mutual organisations. *Australian Accounting Review, 29*(4), 692–707. doi:10.1111/auar.12244

Bollerslev, T. (1986). Generalized autoregressive conditional heteroskedasticity. *Journal of Econometrics, 31*(3), 307–327. doi:10.1016/0304-4076(86)90063-1

Boulding, K. (1966). The Economics of the Coming Spaceship Earth. In H. Jarrett (Ed.), *Environmental Quality in a Growing Economy.* Johns Hopkins University.

Bowen, H. R. (1953). *BOWEN: Social responsibilities of the businessman.* Harper & Row.

Bower, J. (1986). *When Markets Quake Cambridge.* M.A. Harvard.

Brammer, S., Hoejmose, S., & Marchant, K. (2012). Environmental management in SME s in the UK: Practices, pressures, and perceived benefits. *Business Strategy and the Environment, 21*(7), 423–434. doi:10.1002/bse.717

Brandão, L. E., Dyer, J. S., & Hahn, W. J. (2005). Using Binomial Decision Trees to Solve Real-Option Valuation Problems. *Decision Analysis, 2*(2), 69–88. doi:10.1287/deca.1050.0040

Brandstedt, E., & Emmelin, M. E. (2016) The concept of sustainable welfare. In Sustainability and the political economy of welfare. Routledge.

Branson, N., & Zuze, T. L. (2012). Education, the great equaliser: Improving access to quality education. *South African child gauge*, 69–74.

Brezoi, A. G. (2018). Ethics and Corporate Social Responsibility in the Current Geopolitical Context. *Economic Insights - Trends and Challenges, 7*, 45–52.

Bribián, I. Z., Capilla, A. V., & Usón, A. A. (2011). Life cycle assessment of building materials: Comparative analysis of energy and environmental impacts and evaluation of the eco-efficiency improvement potential. *Building and Environment, 46*(5), 1133–1140. doi:10.1016/j.buildenv.2010.12.002

Bridges, C. M., & Wilhelm, W. B. (2008). Going beyond green: The "why and how" of integrating sustainability into the marketing curriculum. *Journal of Marketing Education, 30*(1), 33–46. doi:10.1177/0273475307312196

Brønn, P. S., & Vrioni, A. B. (2001). Corporate social responsibility and cause-related marketing: An overview. *International Journal of Advertising*, *20*(2), 207–222. doi:10.1080/02650487.2001.11104887

Brooks, C. (2008). *Introductory econometrics for finance* (2nd ed.). Cambridge University Press. doi:10.1017/CBO9780511841644

Brown, G. (2010). Sustainability in higher education. *Perspectives*, *14*(4), 103–104. doi:10.1080/13603108.2010.522888

Brown, J. A., Clark, C., & Buono, A. F. (2018). The United Nations global compact: Engaging implicit and explicit CSR for global governance. *Journal of Business Ethics*, *147*(4), 721–734. doi:10.100710551-016-3382-5

Bruni, L., & Zamagni, S. (2007). *Eficiencia, equidad, felicidad pública*. Prometeo.

Brustbauer, J. (2016). Enterprise risk management in SMEs: Towards a structural model. *International Small Business Journal*, *34*(1), 70–85. doi:10.1177/0266242614542853

Bryman, A. (2008). *Social research methods*. Oxford University Press.

Bustillo-Castillejo, M. C. (2011). El marketing social es una respuesta del mundo mercantil al desarrollo sostenible 2011. *Saber. Ciencia y Libertad*, *6*(2), 169–176. doi:10.18041/2382-3240aber.2011v6n2.2504

Buzzell, D., & Wiersema, F. (1981). Modelling changes in market share: A cross-sectional analysis. *Strategic Management Journal*, *2*(1), 27–42. doi:10.1002mj.4250020104

Calcagno, R., & Monticone, C. (2015). Financial literacy and the demand for financial advice. *Journal of Banking & Finance*, *50*, 363–380. doi:10.1016/j.jbankfin.2014.03.013

Campus de Ferrol. (2017a). *Anexo 3. Objetivo 3. Sostenibilidad medioambiental- Unidad de Eficiencia energética*. https://www.udc.es/export/sites/udc/campusindustrial/_galeria_down/PDFs-Creen-Campus-Ferrol/Anexo-3.pdf_2063069239.pdf

Campus de Ferrol. (2017b). *Informe-Memoria I Plan Green Campus Ferrol 2017-2019*. https://www.udc.es/export/sites/udc/sociedade/medio_ambiente/_galeria_down/GreenCampus/FERROL-Informe_Memoria.pdf_2063069239.pdf_2063069294.pdf

Cantele, S., & Zardini, A. (2018). Is sustainability a competitive advantage for small businesses? An empirical analysis of possible mediators in the sustainability–financial performance relationship. *Journal of Cleaner Production*, *182*(1), 166–176. doi:10.1016/j.jclepro.2018.02.016

Capece, A., Pietrafesa, R., Siesto, G., Romaniello, R., Condelli, N., & Romano, P. (2019). Selected Indigenous Saccharomyces Cerevisiae Strains as Profitable Strategy to Preserve Typical Traits of Primitivo Wine. *Fermentation (Basel, Switzerland)*, *5*(4), 87. doi:10.3390/fermentation5040087

Caraça, J., Ferreira, J., & Mendonça, S. (2006). *Desenvolvimento Sustentado da Inovação Empresarial - Modelos de Inovação*. COTEC Portugal.

Cardaci, A. (2018). Inequality Household Debt and Financial Instability: An agent based perspective. *Journal of Economic Behavior & Organization*, *149*, 434–458. doi:10.1016/j.jebo.2018.01.010

Carp, M., Păvăloaia, L., Afrăsinei, M. B., & Georgescu, I. E. (2019). Is sustainability reporting a business strategy for firm's growth? Empirical study on the Romanian capital market. *Sustainability*, *11*(3), 658. doi:10.3390u11030658

Carrigan, M., & Bosangit, C. (2016). The challenges of responsible marketing and consumption. In D. Shaw, M. Carrington, & A. Chatzidakis (Eds.), *Ethics and Morality in Consumption: Interdisciplinary Perspectives* (pp. 75–96). Routledge.

Carrington, M., Zwick, D., & Neville, B. (2016). The ideology of the ethical consumption gap. *Marketing Theory*, *16*(1), 21–38. doi:10.1177/1470593115595674

Case, H. (2016). The "social question" 1820-1920. *Modern Intellectual History*, *13*(3), 747–775. doi:10.1017/S1479244315000037

Casillas, J. C., Moreno, A. M., & Barbero, J. L. (2010). A configurational approach of the relationship between entrepreneurial orientation and growth of family firms. *Family Business Review*, *13*(1), 27–44. doi:10.1177/0894486509345159

Castellacci, F., & Natera, J. M. (2013). The dynamics of national innovation systems: A panel cointegration analysis of the coevolution between innovative capability and absorptive capacity. *Research Policy*, *42*(3), 579–594. doi:10.1016/j.respol.2012.10.006

Castellucci, F. (2010). *Resolution OIV/VITI 333/2010*. OIV.

Castro-Santos, L. D. C. V., & Diaz-Casas, V. (2015). Cost Comparison of Three Floating Offshore Wind Platforms. *Journal of Coastal Research*, *31*(5), 1217–1221. doi:10.2112/JCOASTRES-D-13-00134.1

Castro-Santos, L., Filgueira-Vizoso, A., Carral-Couce, L., & Formoso, J. Á. F. (2016). Economic feasibility of floating offshore wind farms. *Energy*, *112*, 868–882. doi:10.1016/j.energy.2016.06.135

Castro-Santos, L., Martins, E., & Guedes Soares, C. (2016). Methodology to calculate the costs of a floating offshore renewable energy farm. *Energies*, *9*(5), 324. doi:10.3390/en9050324

Castro-Santos, L., Silva, D., Bento, A. R., Salvação, N., & Guedes Soares, C. (2018). Economic feasibility of wave energy farms in Portugal. *Energies*, *11*(11), 1–16. doi:10.3390/en11113149

Cerveira, A. (2009). *Empreendedorismo e inovação. O caso da Crioestaminal*. Relatório de Estágio. Faculdade de Economia da Universidade de Coimbra.

Chabowski, B. R., Mena, J. A., & Gonzalez-Padron, T. L. (2011). The structure of sustainability research in marketing, 1958–2008: A basis for future research opportunities. *Journal of the Academy of Marketing Science*, *39*(1), 55–70. doi:10.100711747-010-0212-7

Champoux, D., & Brun, J. (2003). Occupational health and safety management in small size enterprises: An overview of the situation and avenues for intervention and research. *Safety Science*, *41*(4), 301–318. doi:10.1016/S0925-7535(02)00043-7

Charter, M., Peattie, K., Ottman, J., & Polonsky, M. J. (2002). *Marketing and sustainability. Sustainable Marketing*. Knowledge Network.

Cheng, W. H., & Hung, J. C. (2011). Skewness and lep to kurtosis in GARCH-typed VaR estimation of petroleum and metal asset returns. *Journal of Empirical Finance*, *18*(1), 160–173. doi:10.1016/j.jempfin.2010.05.004

Chen, H., & Volpe, R. P. (1998). An analysis of personal financial literacy among college students. *Financial Services Review*, *7*(2), 107–128. doi:10.1016/S1057-0810(99)80006-7

Chen, L., & Macdonald, E. (2014). A system-level cost-of-energy wind farm layout optimization with landowner modeling. *Energy Conversion and Management*, *77*, 484–494. doi:10.1016/j.enconman.2013.10.003

Chen, L., Wang, L., Wu, X., & Ding, X. (2017). A process-level water conservation and pollution control performance evaluation tool of cleaner production technology in textile industry. *Journal of Cleaner Production*, *143*, 1137–1143. doi:10.1016/j.jclepro.2016.12.006

Chen, X., Lai, K. K., & Yen, J. (2009). A statistical neural network approach for value-at-risk analysis. *2009 International Joint Conference on Computational Sciences and Optimization*, 17-21. 10.1109/CSO.2009.350

Chen, Y. S., Lai, S. B., & Wen, C. T. (2006). The influence of green innovation performance on corporate advantage in Taiwan. *Journal of Business Ethics, 67*(4), 331–339. doi:10.100710551-006-9025-5

Chesbrough, H. (2003). *Open Innovation: The New Imperative for Creating and Profiting from Technology.* Harvard Business Press.

Chesbrough, H. (2012). *Inovação aberta: como criar e lucrar com a tecnologia.* Porto Alegre: Bookman.

CIRAIG. (2015). *Circular economy: a critical literature review of concepts.* Retrieved from https://www.ciraig.org/pdf/CIRAIG_Circular_Economy_Literature_Review_Oct2015.pdf

Circle Economy. (2019). *The circularity gap report 2020.* Retrieved from https://www.circularity-gap.world/2020

Cirera, X., & Muzi, S. (2020). Measuring innovation using firm-level surveys: Evidence from developing countries. *Research Policy, 49*(3), 1039122. doi:10.1016/j.respol.2019.103912

Ciutacu, C., Chivu, L., & Preda, D. (2005). The social responsibility of the company–a challenge for the contemporary world. *The Romanian Economics Magazine, 2*, 79.

Clayton, T., Borgo, M. D., Haskel, J., & Franklin, M. (2010). *Measuring Creativity and Innovation Based on Knowledge Capital Investment.* Publications Office of the EU.

Cohen, M. A. (2010). The narrow application of Rawls in business ethics: A political conception of both stakeholder theory and the morality of markets. *Journal of Business Ethics, 97*(4), 563–579. doi:10.100710551-010-0525-y

Collier, D., Mong, J., & Conlin, J. (1984), How effective is technological innovation? *Research Management, 27*(5), 11-16.

Colombelli, A., Paolucci, E., & Ughetto, E. (2019). Hierarchical and relational governance and the life cycle of entrepreneurial ecosystems. *Small Business Economics, 52*(2), 505–521. doi:10.100711187-017-9957-4

Colucci, S., & Brandolini, D. (2011). Backtesting value-at-risk: A comparison between filtered bootstrap and historical simulation. SSRN *Electronic Journal, 6*(4), 1-36. doi:10.2139srn.1965377

Comisión de las Comunidades Europeas. (2007). *Comunicación de la Comisión. La Educación Financiera.* 808 final. Retrieved from https://eur-lex.europa.eu/legal-content/ES/TXT/PDF/?uri=CELEX:52007DC0808&from=ES

Connelly, B. L., Ketchen, D. J. Jr, & Slater, S. F. (2011). Toward a "theoretical toolbox" for sustainability research in marketing. *Journal of the Academy of Marketing Science, 39*(1), 86–100. doi:10.100711747-010-0199-0

Coombs, J., & Bierly, I. I. P. (2006). Measuring technological capability and performance. *R & D Management, 36*(4), 421–438. doi:10.1111/j.1467-9310.2006.00444.x

COTEC. (2007). *Manual de Apoio ao Preenchimento do Sistema de Innovation Scoring da COTEC.* COTEC Portugal.

COTEC. (2016). *Innovation Scoring – Relatório de Avaliação do modelo.* COTEC Portugal.

Covin, J. G., & Slevin, D. P. (1986). The development and testing of an organizational-level entrepreneurship scale. *Frontiers of Entrepreneurship Research, 1*(3), 628–639.

Cox, J., Ross, S., & Rubinstein, M. (1979). Option pricing: A simplified approach. *Journal of Financial Economics, 7*(3), 229–263. doi:10.1016/0304-405X(79)90015-1

Cox, M. G., Kisbu-Sakarya, Y., Miočević, M., & MacKinnon, D. P. (2013). Sensitivity plots for confounder bias in the single mediator model. *Evaluation Review, 37*(5), 405–431. doi:10.1177/0193841X14524576 PMID:24681690

Crals, E., & Vereeck, L. (2005). The affordability of sustainable entrepreneurship certification for SMEs. *International Journal of Sustainable Development and World Ecology*, *12*(2), 173–183. doi:10.1080/13504500509469628

Culík, M. (2016). Real options valuation with changing volatility. *Perspectives in Science*, *7*, 10–18. doi:10.1016/j.pisc.2015.11.004

Cullen, J. M. (2017). Circular economy: Theoretical benchmark or perpetual motion machine? *Journal of Industrial Ecology*, *21*(3), 483–486. doi:10.1111/jiec.12599

Dahlsrud, A. (2008). How corporate social responsibility is defined: An analysis of 37 definitions. *Corporate Social Responsibility and Environmental Management*, *15*(1), 1–13. doi:10.1002/csr.132

Dangelico, R. M., & Vocalelli, D. (2017). "Green Marketing": An analysis of definitions, strategy steps, and tools through a systematic review of the literature. *Journal of Cleaner Production*, *165*(1), 1263–1279. doi:10.1016/j.jclepro.2017.07.184

Davila, T., Epstein, M., & Shelton, R. (2012). *Making innovation work: How to manage it, measure it, and profit from it*. FT Press.

De Graaf, J., Wann, D., & Naylor, T. H. (2005). *Affluenza: The All-Consuming Epidemic* (2nd ed.). Berrett-Koehler.

de Jong, M. D., & van der Meer, M. (2017). How does it fit? Exploring the congruence between organizations and their corporate social responsibility (CSR) activities. *Journal of Business Ethics*, *143*(1), 71–83. doi:10.100710551-015-2782-2

De Massis, A., Frattini, F., Pizzurno, E., & Cassia, L. (2015). Product innovation in family versus nonfamily firms: An exploratory analysis. *Journal of Small Business Management*, *53*(1), 1–36. doi:10.1111/jsbm.12068

De Mendonca, T., & Zhou, Y. (2019). What does targeting ecological sustainability mean for company financial performance? *Business Strategy and the Environment*, *28*(8), 1583–1593. doi:10.1002/bse.2334

De Villiers, C., & Marques, A. (2016). Corporate social responsibility, country-level predispositions, and the consequences of choosing a level of disclosure. *Accounting and Business Research*, *46*(2), 167–195. doi:10.1080/00014788.2015.1039476

Deigh, L., Farquhar, J., Palazzo, M., & Siano, A. (2016). Corporate social responsibility: Engaging the community. *Qualitative Market Research*, *19*(2), 225–240. doi:10.1108/QMR-02-2016-0010

Delavande, A., Rohwedder, S., & Willis, R. J. (2008, September). *Preparation for retirement, financial literacy and cognitive resources* (Working Paper No.2008-190). Retrieved from https://mrdrc.isr.umich.edu/publications/Papers/pdf/wp190.pdf

Delmas, M. A., & Burbano, V. C. (2011). The drivers of greenwashing. *California Management Review*, *54*(1), 64–87. doi:10.1525/cmr.2011.54.1.64

Deloitte. (2020). https://www2.deloitte.com/us/en/insights/industry/financial-services/esg-investing-performance.html

Deschryver, P., & De Mariz, F. (2020). What Future for the Green Bond Market? How Can Policymakers, Companies, and Investors Unlock the Potential of the Green Bond Market? *Journal of Risk and Financial Management*, *13*(3), 61. doi:10.3390/jrfm13030061

Dess, G., & Lumpkin, G. T. (2005). Entrepreneurial orientation as a source of innovative strategy. *Innovating Strategy Process*, *1*, 3–9.

Días, R. (2008, June). Marketing ecológico y turismo. *Estudios y Perspectivas en Turismo*, *17*(2), 140–155.

Dickey, D. A., & Fuller, W. A. (1979). Distribution of the estimators for autoregressive time series with a unit root. *Journal of the American Statistical Association*, *74*(366a), 427–431.

Diéguez-Soto, J., Duréndez, A., García-Pérez-de-Lema, D., & Ruiz-Palomo, D. (2016). Technological, management, and persistent innovation in small and medium family firms: The influence of professionalism. *Canadian Journal of Administrative Sciences*, *33*(4), 332–346. doi:10.1002/cjas.1404

Diéguez-Soto, J., & López-Delgado, P. (2019). Does Family and Lone Founder Involvement Lead to Similar Indebtedness? *Journal of Small Business Management*, *57*(4), 1531–1558. doi:10.1111/jsbm.12422

Dillard, J. F., Rigsby, J. T., & Goodman, C. (2004). The making and remaking of organization context. *Accounting, Auditing & Accountability Journal*, *17*(4), 506–542. doi:10.1108/09513570410554542

DiMaggio, P. J., & Powell, W. W. (1983). The iron cage revisited: Institutional isomorphism and collective rationality in organizational fields. *American Sociological Review*, *48*(2), 147–160. doi:10.2307/2095101

Dobre, E., Stanila, G. O., & Brad, L. (2015). The influence of environmental and social performance on financial performance: Evidence from Romania's listed entities. *Sustainability*, *7*(3), 2513–2553. doi:10.3390u7032513

Dordi, T., & Weber, O. (2019). The impact of divestment announcements on the share price of fossil fuel stocks. *Sustainability*, *11*(11), 3122. doi:10.3390u11113122

Douglas, C. (2008). Life cycle assessment of the Seagen marine current turbine. *Proceedings of the ...*, *222*, 1–12. 10.1243/14750902JEME94

Dowd, K. (2005). *Measuring market risk* (2nd ed.). John Wiley & Sons Ltd. doi:10.1002/9781118673485

Dragoi, M. C., Popescu, M. F., Andrei, J. V., & Mieila, M. (2018). Developments of the Circular Economy in Romania under the New Sustainability Paradigm. *Economic Computation and Economic Cybernetics Studies and Research*, *52*(2), 125–138.

Drew, B., Plummer, A. R., & Sahinkaya, M. N. (n.d.). *A review of wave energy converter technology*. doi:10.1243/09576509JPE782

Drucker, P. (1985). Opportunities to innovate: the seven sources. Innovation and Entrepreneurship. Butterworth Heinemann.

Duca, I., & Gherghina, R. (2018). Corporate Social Responsibility and Sustainable Business. *International Journal of Innovation in the Digital Economy*, *9*(2), 26–39. doi:10.4018/IJIDE.2018040103

Dupont, G., Ojo, M., & Rossi, J. (2016). Corporate Social Responsibility and Financial Development: Promoting Global Economic Development. In Analyzing the Relationship between Corporate Social Responsibility and Foreign Direct Investment (pp. 115-126). IGI Global.

Dvorak, M. J., Archer, C. L., & Jacobson, M. Z. (2010). California offshore wind energy potential. *Renewable Energy*, *35*(6), 1244–1254. doi:10.1016/j.renene.2009.11.022

EASAC. (2016). Indicators for a circular economy. Halle: European Academies' Science Advisory Council.

EC. European Commission. (2014a). T*owards a circular economy: A zero waste programme for Europe, COM/2014/0398 final/2*. Retrieved from https://eur-lex.europa.eu/legal-content/EN/TXT/?uri=CELEX:52014DC0398R%2801%29

EC. European Commission. (2014b). *Legislative proposal to review recycling and other waste-related targets in the EU*. Retrieved from https://ec.europa.eu/environment/waste/pdf/Legal%20proposal%20review%20targets.pdf

EC. European Commission. (2014c). *Ex-post evaluation of Five Waste Streams Directives, SWD/2014/0209 final*. Retrieved from https://eur-lex.europa.eu/legal-content/EN/TXT/?uri=CELEX:52014SC0209

EC. European Commission. (2015). *Closing the loop – An EU action plan for the Circular Economy, COM/2015/0614 final*. Retrieved from https://eur-lex.europa.eu/legal-content/EN/TXT/?uri=CELEX:52015DC0614

EC. European Commission. (2016). *EU Energy in Figures - Statistical Pocketbook 2016*. Retrieved from https://publications.europa.eu/en/publication-detail/-/publication/c3d179b2-9a82-11e6-9bca-01aa75ed71a1

EC. European Commission. (2018). *Communication on a monitoring framework for the circular economy, COM/2018/029 final*. Retrieved from https://eur-lex.europa.eu/legal-content/EN/TXT/?qid=1516265440535&uri=COM:2018:29:FIN

EC. European Commission. (2020a). *Circular Economy*. Retrieved from https://ec.europa.eu/environment/circular-economy/index_en.htm

EC. European Commission. (2020b). *A new Circular Economy Action Plan For a cleaner and more competitive Europe, COM/2020/98 final*. Retrieved from https://eur-lex.europa.eu/legal-content/EN/TXT/?qid=1583933814386&uri=COM:2020:98:FIN

EEA. European Environment Agency. (2014). Resource-efficient Green Economy and EU policies. Luxembourg: Publications Office of the European Union.

EEA. European Environment Agency. (2016). *Circular Economy in Europe - Developing the knowledge base. EEA Report No. 2/2016*. Luxembourg: European Environment Agency.

Eilert, M., & Nappier Cherup, A. (2020). The Activist Company: Examining a Company's Pursuit of Societal Change Through Corporate Activism Using an Institutional Theoretical Lens. *Journal of Public Policy & Marketing*, *39*(4), 461–476. doi:10.1177/0743915620947408

ElAlfy, A., Palaschuk, N., El-Bassiouny, D., Wilson, J., & Weber, O. (2020). Scoping the Evolution of Corporate Social Responsibility (CSR) Research in the Sustainable Development Goals (SDGs) Era. *Sustainability*, *12*(14), 5544. doi:10.3390u12145544

Elan, S. (2011). *Financial literacy among retail investors in the United States*. Report prepared by the Federal Research Division, Library of Congress under an Interagency Agreement with the Securities and Exchange Commission, Washington, DC. Retrieved from https://www.loc.gov/rr/frd/pdf-files/Investor_Literacy_Report.pdf

Elia, V., Gnoni, M. G., & Tornese, F. (2017). Measuring circular economy strategies through index methods: A critical analysis. *Journal of Cleaner Production*, *142*(4), 2741–2751. doi:10.1016/j.jclepro.2016.10.196

Elkington, J. (1998). Partnerships from cannibals with forks: The triple bottom line of 21st-century business. *Environmental Quality Management*, *8*(1), 37–51. doi:10.1002/tqem.3310080106

EMF. Ellen MacArthur Foundation. (2013). T*owards the Circular Economy. Economic and business rationale for an accelerated transition*. Cowes: Ellen MacArthur Foundation.

EMF. Ellen MacArthur Foundation. (2015a). *Towards the Circular Economy. Business rationale for an accelerated transition*. Cowes: Ellen MacArthur Foundation.

EMF. Ellen MacArthur Foundation. (2015b). *Delivering the Circular Economy – A Toolkit for Policymakers*. Retrieved from https://www.ellenmacarthurfoundation.org/assets/downloads/government/Delivering_the_circular_economy_A_toolkit_for_policymakers.pdf

Ene, C. (2017). Current Issues Regarding The Protection Of Retail Investors On The Capital Market Within The European Union. *The USV Annals of Economics and Public Administration, 17*(1 (25)), 35–44.

Ene, C., & Panait, M. (2017). The financial education-Part of corporate social responsibility for employees and customers. *Revista Romana de Economie, 44*(1), 145–154.

Engel, K., Dirlea, V., Dyer, S., & Graff, J. (2015). *Strategy & Leadership.* Newcastle University. Emerald Insight.

Eniola, A. A., & Entebang, H. (2015). Financial literacy and SME firm performance. *International Journal of Research Studies in Management, 5*(1), 31–43. doi:10.5861/ijrsm.2015.1304

Ernest & Young LLP. (2016). R&D *investment execution.* Author.

Erokhin, V., & Ivolga, A. (2012). How to Ensure Sustainable Development of Agribusiness in the Conditions of Trade Integration: Russian Approach. *International Journal of Sustainable Economies Management, 1*(2), 12–23. doi:10.4018/ijsem.2012040102

Escobar Moreno, N. R. (2012). Las Comunicaciones Integradas de Marketing (CIM) como pilar de la estrategia de marketing verde y sus implicaciones en la gestión ambiental. *Revista Facultad De Ciencias Económicas, 20*(2), 69–79. doi:10.18359/rfce.2165

Espejel, J., & Fandos, C. (2009). Wine marketing strategies in Spain: A structural equation approach to consumer response to protected designations of origin (PDOs). *International Journal of Wine Business Research, 21*(3), 267–288. doi:10.1108/17511060910985980

Esteban, M. D., Couñago, B., López-Gutiérrez, J. S., Negro, V., & Vellisco, F. (2015). Gravity based support structures for offshore wind turbine generators: Review of the installation process. *Ocean Engineering, 110*, 281–291. doi:10.1016/j.oceaneng.2015.10.033

EU. (2018). Directive (EU) 2018/2001 of the European Parliament and of the Council on the promotion of the use of energy from renewable sources. *Official Journal of the European Union, 2018*(L 328), 82–209. Retrieved from https://eur-lex.europa.eu/legal-content/EN/TXT/PDF/?uri=CELEX:32018L2001&from=EN

EU. (2020a). *Circular Economy Action Plan.* Retrieved from https://ec.europa.eu/environment/circulareconomy/pdf/new_circular_economy_action_plan.pdf

EU. (2020b). *Circular economy indicators.* Retrieved from https://ec.europa.eu/eurostat/cache/scoreboards/CE/index.html

Euroflash Barometer. (2018). *SMEs, resource efficiency and green markets.* Retrieved from https://ec.europa.eu/commfrontoffice/publicopinion/index.cfm/survey/getsurveydetail/instruments/flash/surveyky/2151

European Comission. (2013). *Sustainability of textiles.* Retail Forum for Sustainability. Paper nº 11, August 2013.

European Commission. (2003). *Green paper entrepreneurship in Europe.* Retrieved from https://web.archive.org/web/20040611050753/http://www.europa.eu.int:80/comm/enterprise/entrepreneurship/green_paper/index.htm

European Commission. (2016). *Open Innovation Open Science Open to the World - a vision for Europe.* European Commission, Directorate-General for Research and Innovation.

Evci, S., & Kandır, S. Y. (2015). Altın piyasasında piyasa riskinin ölçülmesi: Riske maruz değer (VaR) yöntemi ile bir uygulama. *Bankacılar Dergisi, 26*(92), 5–104.

Facultade de Ciencias da Educación, UDC. (2017). *Informe-Memoria Plan Green Campus 2017-2019.* https://www.udc.es/export/sites/udc/sociedade/medio_ambiente/_galeria_down/GreenCampus/Ciencias-da-Educacion-Memoria-2017-2019.pdf_2063069294.pdf

Famularo, B., Bruwer, J., & Li, E. (2010). Region of origin as a choice factor: Wine knowledge and wine tourism involvement influence. *International Journal of Wine Business Research, 22*(4), 362–385. doi:10.1108/17511061011092410

Fan, H., Jiang, M., Xu, L., Zhu, H., Cheng, J., & Jiang, J. (2020). Comparison of Long Short Term Memory Networks and the Hydrological Model in Runoff Simulation. *Water (Basel), 12*(1), 175. doi:10.3390/w12010175

Fan, Y., Mu, A., & Ma, T. (2016). Design and control of a point absorber wave energy converter with an open loop hydraulic transmission. *Energy Conversion and Management, 121*, 13–21. doi:10.1016/j.enconman.2016.04.107

Faria, A. (2008). *Redes de conhecimento e inovação.* Rede 2020.

Fashion For Good. (2019). *Investing in Textile Innovation. The opportunities for investors in the textile and apparel innovation ecosystem.* Author.

Fassin, Y. (2008). SMEs and the fallacy of formalizing. *CSR. Business Ethics (Oxford, England), 17*(4), 364–378. doi:10.1111/j.1467-8608.2008.00540.x

Feldman, M., Siegel, D. S., & Wright, M. (2019). New developments in innovation and entrepreneurial ecosystems. *Industrial and Corporate Change, 28*(4), 817–826. doi:10.1093/icc/dtz031

Feng, H., Morgan, N. A., & Rego, L. L. (2017). Firm capabilities and growth: The moderating role of market conditions. *Journal of the Academy of Marketing Science, 45*(1), 76–92. doi:10.100711747-016-0472-y

Fernandez, V. P. (2005). The international CAPM and a wavelet-based decomposition of value at risk. *Studies in Nonlinear Dynamics and Econometrics, 9*(4).

Field, A. (2013). *Discovering Statistics Using IBM SPSS Statistics* (4th ed.). SAGE Publication Ltd.

Financial Times. (2020a). https://www.ft.com/content/7a893f6d-08c9-426c-8f19-aa19d434b018

Financial Times. (2020b). https://www.ft.com/content/27025f35-283f-4956-b6a0-0adbfd4c7a0e

Fink, A. (2013). *Conducting research literature reviews: from the Internet to paper.* Sage Publications.

Fischer, D., Jenssen, S., & Tappeser, V. (2015). Getting an empirical hold of the sustainable university: A comparative analysis of evaluation frameworks across 12 contemporary sustainability assessment tools. *Assessment & Evaluation in Higher Education, 40*(6), 785–800. doi:10.1080/02602938.2015.1043234

Fisk, G. (1974). *Marketing and the ecological crisis.* Harper & Row.

Florian, M., & Sørensen, J. D. (2017). Risk-based planning of operation and maintenance for offshore wind farms. In Energy Procedia (Vol. 137). doi:10.1016/j.egypro.2017.10.349

Fluch, M. (2007). Selected central banks' economic and financial literacy programs. *Monetary Policy & the Economy Q, 3*, 85–103.

Forbes, S. L., Cohen, D. A., Cullen, R., Wratten, S. D., & Fountain, J. (2009). Consumer attitudes regarding environmentally sustainable wine: An exploratory study of the New Zealand marketplace. *Journal of Cleaner Production, 17*(13), 1195–1199. doi:10.1016/j.jclepro.2009.04.008

Fornell, C., & Larcker, D. F. (1981). Evaluating structural equation models with unobservable variables and measurement error. *JMR, Journal of Marketing Research, 18*(1), 39–50. doi:10.1177/002224378101800104

Fredyna, T., Ruiz-Palomo, D., & Diéguez-Soto, J. (2019). Entrepreneurial orientation and product innovation. The moderating role of family involvement in management. *European Journal of Family Business, 9*(2), 128–145. doi:10.24310/ejfbejfb.v9i2.5392

Freeman, C. (1982). *The economics of industrial revolution*. MIT Press.

Friedman, M. (1970). A Friedman doctrine: The social responsibility of business is to increase its profits. *The New York Times Magazine*, *13*(1970), 32-33.

Friedman, M. (1970). The social responsibility of business is to maximise its profits. *New York Times Magazine*, *13*, 33.

Friedman, M. (2018). *A theory of the consumption function*. Princeton University Press. doi:10.2307/j.ctv39x7zh

Fukuda-Parr, S. (2003). The human development paradigm: Operationalizing Sen's ideas on capabilities. *Feminist Economics*, *9*(2-3), 301–317. doi:10.1080/1354570022000077980

Gabzdylova, B., Raffensperger, J. F., & Castka, P. (2009). Sustainability in the New Zealand wine industry: Drivers, stakeholders and practices. *Journal of Cleaner Production*, *17*(11), 992–998. doi:10.1016/j.jclepro.2009.02.015

Galicia Ártabra Digital. (2015). *Navantia finaliza el montaje de la primera jacket para Iberdrola*. Retrieved March 3, 2016, from http://www.galiciaartabradigital.com/archivos/126229

Gali, J. M. (2013). *Marketing de sostenibilidad*. Profit Editorial.

Gallén, M. L., & Peraita, C. (2018). The effects of national culture on corporate social responsibility disclosure: A cross-country comparison. *Applied Economics*, *50*(27), 2967–2979. doi:10.1080/00036846.2017.1412082

Galli, F., Prosperi, P., Favilli, E., D'Amico, S., Bartolini, F., & Brunori, G. (2020). How can policy processes remove barriers to sustainable food systems in Europe? Contributing to a policy framework for agri-food transitions. *Food Policy*, *96*, 101871. doi:10.1016/j.foodpol.2020.101871

Garanti, Z., & Berberoglu, A. (2018). Cultural perspective of traditional cheese consumption practices and its sustainability among post-millennial consumers. *Sustainability*, *10*(9), 3183. doi:10.3390u10093183

García-Granero, A., Llopis, O., Fernández-Mesa, A., & Alegre, J. (2015). Unravelling the link between managerial risk-taking and innovation: The mediating role of a risk-taking climate. *Journal of Business Research*, *68*(5), 1094–1104. doi:10.1016/j.jbusres.2014.10.012

Garcia-Johnson, R. (2000). *Exporting Environmentalism: US Multinational Chemical Corporations in Brazil and Mexico*. MIT Press. doi:10.7551/mitpress/2941.001.0001

Garcia-Sanchez, I., Ferrero, J., & Azevedo, T. (2019). Does Capital Market Distrust CSR Reporting?: Economic Benefits in Presence of Complementary Monitoring Mechanism. *Economic Benefits in Presence of Complementary Monitoring Mechanism*.

Garcia-Sanchez, I. M., Cuadrado-Ballesteros, B., & Frias-Aceituno, J. V. (2016). Impact of the institutional macro context on the voluntary disclosure of CSR information. *Long Range Planning*, *49*(1), 15–35. doi:10.1016/j.lrp.2015.02.004

Garriga, E., & Melé, D. (2004). Corporate social responsibility theories: Mapping the territory. *Journal of Business Ethics*, *53*(1-2), 51–71. doi:10.1023/B:BUSI.0000039399.90587.34

Gast, J., Gundolf, K., & Cesinger, B. (2017). Doing business in a Green way: A systematic review of the ecological sustainability entrepreneurship literature and future research directions. *Journal of Cleaner Production*, *147*, 44–56. doi:10.1016/j.jclepro.2017.01.065

Gergaud, O., & Ginsburgh, V. (2010). Natural Endowments, Production Technologies and the Quality of Wines in Bordeaux. Does Terroir Matter? *Journal of Wine Economics*, *5*(1), 3–21. doi:10.1017/S1931436100001346

Ghisellini, P., Cialani, C., & Ulgiati, S. (2016). A review on circular economy: The expected transition to a balanced interplay of environmental and economic systems. *Journal of Cleaner Production*, *114*, 11–32. doi:10.1016/j.jclepro.2015.09.007

Gilinsky, A. Jr, Newton, S. K., & Vega, R. V. (2016). Sustainability in the Global Wine Industry: Concepts and Cases. *Agriculture and Agricultural Science Procedia*, *8*, 37–49. doi:10.1016/j.aaspro.2016.02.006

Global Footprint Network. (2020). Retrieved from http://data.footprintnetwork.org/?_ga=2.85860889.1426762603.1589453027-229816858.1589453027#/abouttheData

Global Reporting Initiative (GRI). (2020a). *GRI's History*. Retrieved from https://www.globalreporting.org/information/about-gri/gri-history/Pages/GRI's%20history.aspx

Global Reporting Initiative (GRI). (2020b). *Sustainability Disclosure Database Data Legend*. Retrieved from https://www.globalreporting.org/SiteCollectionDocuments/GRI-Data-Legend-Sustainability-Disclosure-Database-Profiling.pdf

Globerman, S., & Shapiro, D. (2003). Governance infrastructure and US foreign direct investment. *Journal of International Business Studies*, *34*(1), 19–39. doi:10.1057/palgrave.jibs.8400001

Glosten, L. R., Jagannathan, R., & Runkle, D. E. (1993). On the relation between the expected value and the volatility of the nominal excess return on stocks. *The Journal of Finance*, *48*(5), 1779–1801. doi:10.1111/j.1540-6261.1993.tb05128.x

Go Fossil free. (n.d.). https://gofossilfree.org/divestment/commitments/

Godinho, M. (2003). Inovação: conceitos e perspectivas fundamentais. In M. J. Rodrigues, A. Neves, & M. M. Godinho (Eds.), Para uma política de inovação em Portugal. Lisboa: Publicações Dom Quixote, Lda.

González-Fernández, M., & González-Velasco, C. (2018). Innovation and Corporate Performance in the Spanish Regions. *Journal of Policy Modelin.*

Goodman, J., Korsunova, A., & Halme, M. (2017). Our collaborative future: Activities and roles of stakeholders in sustainability-oriented innovation. *Business Strategy and the Environment*, *26*(6), 731–753. doi:10.1002/bse.1941

Gordon, L. A., Loeb, M. P., & Tseng, C. Y. (2009). Enterprise risk management and firm performance: A contingency perspective. *Journal of Accounting and Public Policy*, *28*(4), 301–327. doi:10.1016/j.jaccpubpol.2009.06.006

Gordon, R., Carrigan, M., & Hastings, G. (2011). A framework for sustainable marketing. *Marketing Theory*, *11*(2), 143–163. doi:10.1177/1470593111403218

Görg, H., & Hanley, A. (2017). Firms' global engagement and management practices. *Economics Letters*, *155*, 80–83. doi:10.1016/j.econlet.2017.03.026

Grable, J. E. (2000). Financial risk tolerance and additional factors that affect risk taking in everyday money matters. *Journal of Business and Psychology*, *14*(4), 625–630. doi:10.1023/A:1022994314982

Grauel, J., & Gotthardt, D. (2016). The relevance of national contexts for carbon disclosure decisions of stock-listed companies: A multilevel analysis. *Journal of Cleaner Production*, *133*, 1204–1217. doi:10.1016/j.jclepro.2016.05.182

Green Office Movement. (2019). *What is a sustainable university?* https://www.greenofficemovement.org/sustainable-university/

Greenfield, W. M. (2004). In the name of corporate social responsibility. *Business Horizons*, *47*(1), 19–28. doi:10.1016/j.bushor.2003.11.004

Greenspan, A. (2002). Economic volatility. Remarks at a symposium sponsored by the Federal Reserve Bank of Kansas City.

Grigorescu, A., & Saseanu, A. (2010). The social responsibility influence of corporations on sustainable development, published in: Analele Universităţii Ovidius Constanţa. *Seria: Ştiinţe Economice,* (1), 1049–1054.

Groening, C., Sarkis, J., & Zhu, Q. (2018). Green marketing consumer-level theory review: A compendium of applied theories and further research directions. *Journal of Cleaner Production, 172*, 1848–1866. doi:10.1016/j.jclepro.2017.12.002

Grohmann, A., Klühs, T., & Menkhoff, L. (2018). Does financial literacy improve financial inclusion? Cross country evidence. *World Development, 111*, 84–96. doi:10.1016/j.worlddev.2018.06.020

Güneri Tosunoğlu, N., & Keskin Benli, Y. (2012). Forecasting of Morgan Stanley Capital International Turkey Index with artifcial neural networks. *Ege Academic Review, 12*(4), 541–547.

Gupta, P. (2008). *Inovação empresarial no século xxi.* G. E. Económica.

Gupta, S., Rudd, J., & Lee, N. (2014). Special Issue on Integrating marketing and operations for business sustainability. *Industrial Marketing Management, 43*(1), 1–176. doi:10.1016/j.indmarman.2013.10.004

Gurtu, A. (Ed.). (2020). *Recent Advancements in Sustainable Entrepreneurship and Corporate Social Responsibility.* IGI Global. doi:10.4018/978-1-7998-2347-6

Haffar, M., & Searcy, C. (2018). The use of context-based environmental indicators in corporate reporting. *Journal of Cleaner Production, 192*, 496–513. doi:10.1016/j.jclepro.2018.04.202

Halicki, M., & Kwater, T. (2014). Application of artificial neural network supporting the process of portfolio management in terms of time investment on the Warsaw stock exchange. *MetodyIlościowe w BadaniachEkonomicznych, 15*(2), 307–316.

Hall, B. H. (1996). The Private and Social Returns to Research and Development. In B. L. R. Smith & C. E. Barfield (Eds.), *Technology, R&D, and the Economy* (pp. 140–183). Brookings Institution and American Enterprise Institute.

Hall, J., & Wagner, M. (2012). Integrating Sustainability into Firms' Processes: Performance Effects and the Moderating Role of Business Models and Innovation. *Business Strategy and the Environment, 21*(3), 183–196. doi:10.1002/bse.728

Hansen, E. G., Grosse-Dunker, F., & Reichwald, R. (2009). Sustainability Innovation Cube – A Framework to Evaluate Sustainability-Oriented Innovations. *International Journal of Innovation Management, 13*(4), 683–713. doi:10.1142/S1363919609002479

Hansen, P. R., & Lunde, A. (2005). A forecast comparison of volatility models: Does anything beat a GARCH (1, 1)? *Journal of Applied Econometrics, 20*(7), 873–889. doi:10.1002/jae.800

Hastings, J. S., & Tejeda-Ashton, L. (2008). *Financial literacy, information, and demand elasticity: Survey and experimental evidence from Mexico* (Working Paper No. w14538). National Bureau of Economic Research. Retrieved from https://www.nber.org/system/files/working_papers/w14538/w14538.pdf

Hau, H., Massa, M., & Peress, J. (2010). Do demand curves for currencies lope down? Evidence from the MSCI global index change. *Review of Financial Studies, 23*(10), 1681–1717. doi:10.1093/rfs/hhp095

Heim, L. (2018). Killing Sustainability: Blunt Truths about Corporate Sustainability/Social Responsibility Failures and How to Avoid Them. Academic Press.

Hekkert, M. P., Suurs, R. R. A., Negro, S. A., Kuhlmann, S., & Smitsa, R. E. (2007). Functions of innovation systems: A new approach for analysing technological change. *Technological Forecasting and Social Change, 74*(4), 413–432. doi:10.1016/j.techfore.2006.03.002

Henchen, A. V., Moura-Leite, R., & Lopes, J. C. J. (2019). Sustainability and Management of Higher Education Institutions: Scientific Production Analysis. *Revista De Gestão Ambiental e Sustentabilidade*, *8*(1), 38–61. doi:10.5585/geas.v8i1.13763

Henderson, R. & Clark, K. (1990). Architectural Innovation: The reconfiguring of existing product, technologies and the failure of established firms. *Administrative Science Quaterly*, 9-30.

Henion, K. E., & Kinnear, T. C. (1976). *A guide to ecological marketing. Ecological Marketing*. American Marketing Association.

Henseler, J., Hubona, G., & Ray, P. A. (2016). Using PLS path modeling in new technology research: Updated guidelines. *Industrial Management & Data Systems*, *116*(1), 2–20. doi:10.1108/IMDS-09-2015-0382

Hernández, M. T. B. (2015). La importancia de la educación financiera y su influencia en los futuros estudiantes de Administración y Dirección de Empresas. *Anuario jurídico y económico escurialense*, *48*, 381–400.

Hernandez, E. A., Mun, J., & Rocco, C. M. (2017). Active management in state-owned energy companies: Integrating a real options approach into multicriteria analysis to make companies sustainable. *Applied Energy*, *195*, 487–502. doi:10.1016/j.apenergy.2017.03.068

Herzig, C., & Schaltegger, S. (2006). Corporate Sustainability Reporting. An Overview. In S. Schaltegger, M. Bennett, & R. Burritt (Eds.), *Sustainability Accounting and Reporting* (pp. 301–304). Springer. doi:10.1007/978-1-4020-4974-3_13

Hicks, R., & Tingley, D. (2011). Causal mediation analysis. *The Stata Journal*, *11*(4), 605–619. doi:10.1177/1536867X1201100407

Higher Education and Research for Sustainable Development. (1991). *Halifax Declaration*. https://www.iau-hesd.net/en/documentation/30-halifax-declaration.html

Higher Education and Research for Sustainable Development. (1993). *Swansea Declaration*. https://www.iau-hesd.net/sites/default/files/documents/the_swansea_declaration.pdf

Higher Education and Research for Sustainable Development. (2009). *Abuja Declaration on Sustainable Development in Africa: The Role of Higher Education*. https://www.iau-hesd.net/sites/default/files/documents/abuja_declaration_rev_20aug.pdf

Hilgert, M. A., Hogarth, J. M., & Beverly, S. G. (2003). Household financial management: The connection between knowledge and behavior. *Federal Reserve Bulletin*, *89*, 309–322.

Hinson, R., Boateng, R., & Madichie, N. (2010). Corporate social responsibility activity reportage on bank websites in Ghana. *International Journal of Bank Marketing*, *28*(7), 498–518. doi:10.1108/02652321011085176

Hochreiter, S., & Schmidhuber, J. (1997). Long short-term memory. *Neural Computation*, *9*(8), 1735–1780. doi:10.1162/neco.1997.9.8.1735 PMID:9377276

Hoefnagels, H. (1962). *La sociologie face aux "problèmes sociaux". Textes et études philosophiques*. Éditions Desclée de Brouwer, Bruge.

Ho, F. N., Wang, H. M. D., & Vitell, S. J. (2012). A global analysis of corporate social performance: The effects of cultural and geographic environments. *Journal of Business Ethics*, *107*(4), 423–433. doi:10.100710551-011-1047-y

Hofstede, G. (1980). *Cultures Consequences: International Differences in Work-Related Values*. Sage Publications.

Hofstede, G. (2001). *Culture's Consequences: Comparing Values, Behaviors, Institutions, and Organizations across Nations*. Sage Publications.

Hofstede, G. H., Hofstede, G. J., & Minkov, M. (2010). *Cultures and organizations: Software of the Mind.* McGraw-Hill.

Hoi, C. K., Wu, Q., & Zhang, H. (2013). Is corporate social responsibility (CSR) associated with tax avoidance? Evidence from irresponsible CSR activities. *The Accounting Review, 88*(6), 2025–2059. doi:10.2308/accr-50544

Homes, S., & Smart, P. (2009). Exploring open innovation practice in firm-nonprofit engagement: A corporate social responsability perspective. *Research for Development, 39*(4), 394–409.

Homrich, A. S., Galvão, G., Abadia, L. G., & Carvalho, M. M. (2018). The circular economy umbrella: Trends and gaps on integrating pathways. *Journal of Cleaner Production, 175*, 525–543. doi:10.1016/j.jclepro.2017.11.064

Hsiao, Y. J., & Tsai, W. C. (2018). Financial literacy and participation in the derivatives markets. *Journal of Banking & Finance, 88*, 15–29. doi:10.1016/j.jbankfin.2017.11.006

Hsu, J. W. (2016). Aging and strategic learning: The impact of spousal incentives on financial literacy. *The Journal of Human Resources, 51*(4), 1036–1067. doi:10.3368/jhr.51.4.1014-6712R PMID:28148971

Huang, H. C., Su, Y. C., & Tsui, J. T. (2015). Asymmetric GARCH value-at-risk over MSCI in financial crisis. *International Journal of Economicsand Financial Issues, 5*(2), 390–398.

Hughes, A. (2001). Innovation and business performance: Small entrepreneurial firms in the UK and the EU. *New Economy, 8*(3), 157–163. doi:10.1111/1468-0041.00208

Hussain, A., Arif, S. M., & Aslam, M. (2017). Emerging renewable and sustainable energy technologies: State of the art. *Renewable & Sustainable Energy Reviews, 71*, 12–28. doi:10.1016/j.rser.2016.12.033

Huston, S. J. (2010). Measuring Financial Literacy. *The Journal of Consumer Affairs, 44*(2), 296–316. doi:10.1111/j.1745-6606.2010.01170.x

Hu, V. I., & Scholtens, B. (2014). Corporate social responsibility policies of commercial banks in developing countries. *Sustainable Development, 22*(4), 276–288. doi:10.1002d.1551

Hwang, S.-H., Kim, M.-K., & Ryu, H.-S. (2019). Real Levelized Cost of Energy with Indirect Costs and Market Value of Variable Renewables: A Study of the Korean Power Market. *Energies, 12*(13), 2459. doi:10.3390/en12132459

Hysa, E., Kruja, A., Rehman, N. U., & Laurenti, R. (2020). Circular Economy Innovation and Environmental Sustainability Impact on Economic Growth: An Integrated Model for Sustainable Development. *Sustainability, 12*(12), 4831. doi:10.3390u12124831

Iacovoiu, V. B. (2018). An Empirical Analysis of Some Factors Influencing Financial Literacy. *Economic Insights - Trends and Challenges, 70*(2).

Ibrahim, D. I. D., Harun, R., & Isa, Z. M. (2010). A study on financial literacy of Malaysian degree students. *Cross-Cultural Communication, 5*(4), 51–59.

Imai, K., Keele, L., & Yamamoto, T. (2010). Identification, Inference, and Sensitivity Analysis for Causal Mediation Effects. *Statistical Science, 25*(1), 51–71. doi:10.1214/10-STS321 PMID:20954780

Indústria Têxtil e do Vestuário. (2012). *Roadmap para a Inovação 2012>>2020.* Academic Press.

Ingersoll, J. E. Jr, & Ross, S. A. (1992). Waiting to invest: Investment and uncertainty. *The Journal of Business, 65*(1), 1–29. doi:10.1086/296555

Inigo, E. A., & Albareda, I. (2019). Sustainability oriented innovation dynamics: Levels of dynamic capabilities and their path-dependent and self-reinforcing logics. *Technological Forecasting and Social Change*, *139*, 334–351. doi:10.1016/j.techfore.2018.11.023

International Association of Universities. (1993). *Kyoto Declaration on Sustainable Development.* https://iau-aiu.net/IMG/pdf/sustainable_development_policy_statement.pdf

International Monetary Fund (IMF). (2019). *Financial Development Index Database*. Retrieved from https://data.imf.org/?sk=F8032E80-B36C-43B1-AC26-493C5B1CD33B

International Renewable Energy Agency (IRENA). (2014). *Wave Energy Technology Brief. Future Energy: Improved, Sustainable and Clean Options for our Planet*. doi:10.1016/B978-0-08-099424-6.00017-X

Ioana-Maria, D., & Adriana, T. T. (2012). The impact of the business and organizational size of a company along with GRI and CSR adoption on integrating sustainability reporting practices. *The Annals of the University of Oradea*, 910.

Ioannou, I., & Serafeim, G. (2012). What drives corporate social performance? The role of nation-level institutions. *Journal of International Business Studies*, *43*(9), 834–864. doi:10.1057/jibs.2012.26

Ionescu, G. G. (2006). Misiunea si responsabilitatea sociala a organizatiei de afaceri. *Management & Marketing-Bucharest*, (2), 53–72.

Ionescu, R. (2019). Corporate Social Responsibility Programs of the Bucharest Stock Exchange. *Economic Insights - Trends and Challenges.*

Ionescu, R., & Rădulescu, I. D. (2019). Behavioral Finance and the Fast Evolving World of Fintech. *Economic Insights - Trends and Challenges.*

IRENA. (2019). *Future of Wind Deployment, investment, technology, grid integration and socio-economic aspects*. IRENA.

Isenberg, D. (2011). The entrepreneurship ecosystem strategy as a new paradigm for economy policy: principles for cultivating entrepreneurship. Babson Entrepreneurship Ecosystem Project, Babson College.

Isenberg, D. J. (2010). How to start an entrepreneurial revolution. *Harvard Business Review*, *88*(6), 40–50.

Jamali, D., & Mirshak, R. (2007). Corporate social responsibility (CSR): Theory and practice in a developing country context. *Journal of Business Ethics*, *72*(3), 243–262. doi:10.100710551-006-9168-4

Janeiro, P. (2009). *Barreiras à Inovação*. Editora de Negócios.

Jang, J. S. R., Sun, C. T., & Mizutani, E. (1997). *Neuro-fuzzy and soft computing: A computational approach to learning and machine intelligence*. PrinceHall.

Jappelli, T., & Padula, M. (2013). Investment in Financial Literacy and Saving Decisions. *Journal of Banking & Finance*, *37*(8), 2779–2792. doi:10.1016/j.jbankfin.2013.03.019

Jarque, C. M., & Bera, A. K. (1987). A test for normality of observations and regression residuals. *International Statistical Review/Revue Internationale de Statistique*, 163-172.

Jensen, P., & Webster, E. (2009). Another Look at the Relationship between Innovation Proxies. *Australian Economic Papers*, *48*(3), 252–269. doi:10.1111/j.1467-8454.2009.00374.x

Jia, J., & Li, Z. (2020). Does external uncertainty matter in corporate sustainability performance? *Journal of Corporate Finance*, *65*(July), 101743. doi:10.1016/j.jcorpfin.2020.101743

Jones, D. P., & Johnstone, S. M. (2016). Responding to the Challenge of Sustainability. *Change: The Magazine of Higher Learning*, *48*(4), 27–33. doi:10.1080/00091383.2016.1198171

Jones, G. V., & Alves, F. (2012). Impact of climate change on wine production: A global overview and regional assessment in the Douro Valley of Portugal. *International Journal of Global Warming*, *4*(3-4), 383–406. doi:10.1504/IJGW.2012.049448

Jorge, E., Lopez-Valeiras, E., & Gonzalez-Sanchez, M. B. (2020). The importance given to food naturalness attributes by millennial university students. *Sustainability*, *12*(2), 728. doi:10.3390u12020728

Jorion, P. (2001). *Value at risk, the new benchmark for managing financial risk* (2nd ed.). McGraw-Hill.

Joselin Herbert, G. M., Iniyan, S., Sreevalsan, E., & Rajapandian, S. (2007, August). A review of wind energy technologies. In *Renewable and Sustainable Energy Reviews*. Pergamon. doi:10.1016/j.rser.2005.08.004

JRC. (2016). *Scoping the Sharing Economy: Origins, Definitions, Impact and Regulatory Issues*. Retrieved from https://ec.europa.eu/jrc/sites/jrcsh/files/JRC100369.pdf

Kalantaridis, C., & Pheby, J. (1999). Processes of Innovation Among Manufacturing SMEs: The Experience of Bedfordshire. *Entrepreneurship and Regional Development*, *11*(1), 57–78. doi:10.1080/089856299283290

Karaman, A. S., Kilic, M., & Uyar, A. (2018). Sustainability reporting in the aviation industry: Worldwide evidence. *Sustainability Accounting. Management and Policy Journal*, *9*(4), 362–391.

Karaman, A. S., Kilic, M., & Uyar, A. (2020). Green logistics performance and sustainability reporting practices of the logistics sector: The moderating effect of corporate governance. *Journal of Cleaner Production*, *258*, 120718. doi:10.1016/j.jclepro.2020.120718

Katrandjiev, H. (2016). Ecological marketing, green marketing, sustainable marketing: Synonyms or an evolution of ideas. *Economic Alternatives*, *1*(7), 71–82.

Kemper, J. A., & Ballantine, P. W. (2019). What do we mean by sustainability marketing? *Journal of Marketing Management*, *35*(3-4), 277–309. doi:10.1080/0267257X.2019.1573845

Khan, S. A. R., Yu, Z., Golpîra, H., & Sharif, A. (2019). The nexus between corporate social responsibility and corporate performance: An empirical evidence. *LogForum*, *15*.

Khan, S. S., & Khan, S. A. (2020). Construction of New Circulation Model for Green Supply Chain of Agricultural Products in China. In S. A. Khan (Ed.), *Global Perspectives on Green Business Administration and Sustainable Supply Chain Management* (pp. 220–230). IGI Global. doi:10.4018/978-1-7998-2173-1.ch014

Kilbourne, W. E., & Beckmann, S. C. (1998). Review and critical assessment of research on marketing and the environment. *Journal of Marketing Management*, *14*(6), 513–532. doi:10.1362/026725798784867716

Kılıç, M., Uyar, A., & Karaman, A. S. (2019). What impacts sustainability reporting in the global aviation industry? An institutional perspective. *Transport Policy*, *79*, 54–65. doi:10.1016/j.tranpol.2019.04.017

Kim, R. C. (2018). Can creating shared value (CSV) and the United Nations Sustainable Development Goals (UN SDGs) collaborate for a better world? Insights from East Asia. *Sustainability*, *10*(11), 4128. doi:10.3390u10114128

Kim, S., & Lee, J. (2020). Accounting Treatment of R&D for Environmentally Responsible Firms: Evidence from South Korea. *Sustainability*, *12*(8), 3418. doi:10.3390u12083418

King, G., Tomz, M., & Wittenberg, J. (2000). Making the Most of Statistical Analyses: Improving Interpretation and Presentation. *American Journal of Political Science*, *44*(2), 341–355. doi:10.2307/2669316

Kingma & Ba. (2014). *Adam: A method for stochastic optimization.* arXiv preprint arXiv:1412.6980.

Kingma, D. P., & Ba, J. (2014). *Adam: A Method for Stochastic Optimization.* arXiv:1412.6980.

Klewitz, J., & Hansen, E. G. (2014, February). Sustainability-oriented innovation of SMEs: A systematic review. *Journal of Cleaner Production, 65*(15), 57–75. doi:10.1016/j.jclepro.2013.07.017

Knight, F. H. (1921). *Risk, Uncertainty and Profit.* Houghton Mifflin.

Knight, G. A., & Cavusgil, S. T. (2004). Innovation, organizational capabilities, and the born-global firm. *Journal of International Business Studies, 35*(2), 124–141. doi:10.1057/palgrave.jibs.8400071

Kofoed, J. P., Frigaard, P., Friis-Madsen, E., & Sørensen, H. C. (2006). Prototype testing of the wave energy converter wave dragon. Renewable Energy. doi:10.1016/j.renene.2005.09.005

Kolk, A. (2016). The social responsibility of international business: From ethics and the environment to CSR and sustainable development. *Journal of World Business, 51*(1), 23–34. doi:10.1016/j.jwb.2015.08.010

Kolk, A., & Perego, P. (2010). Determinants of the adoption of sustainability assurance statements: An international investigation. *Business Strategy and the Environment, 19*(3), 182–198.

Kotler, P., & Zaltman, G. (1971). Social marketing: An approach to planned social change. *Journal of Marketing, 35*(3), 3–12. doi:10.1177/002224297103500302 PMID:12276120

Kotzé, L., & Smit, A. (2008). Personal financial literacy and personal debt management: The potential relationship with new venture creation. *The Southern African Journal of Entrepreneurship and Small Business Management, 1*(1), 35–50. doi:10.4102ajesbm.v1i1.11

KPMG. I. (2017). *The KPMG Survey of Corporate Responsibility Reporting 2017.* Retrieved from https://assets.kpmg/content/dam/kpmg/xx/pdf/2017/10/kpmg-survey-of-corporate-responsibility-reporting-2017.pdf

Kralikova, R., & Sobotova, L. (2019). Environmental Management System- A Way to Sustainable Development in Universities. *Acta Technica Corviniensis-Bulletin of Engineering, 12*(1), 69–72. http://acta.fih.upt.ro/pdf/2019-1/ACTA-2019-1-13.pdf

Krohn, Morthorst, & Awerbuch. (2009). *The Economics of Wind Energy.* Academic Press.

Kuckertz, A. (2019). Let's take the entrepreneurial ecosystem metaphor seriously! *Journal of Business Venturing Insights, 11*(e00124), 1–7. doi:10.1016/j.jbvi.2019.e00124

Kühn, A. L., Stiglbauer, M., & Fifka, M. S. (2018). Contents and determinants of corporate social responsibility website reporting in Sub-Saharan Africa: A seven-country study. *Business & Society, 57*(3), 437–480. doi:10.1177/0007650315614234

Kumar, A., Moktadir, A., Liman, Z. R., Gunasekaran, A., Hegemann, K., & Khan, S. A. R. (2020). Evaluating sustainable drivers for social responsibility in the context of ready-made garments supply chain. *Journal of Cleaner Production, 248*, 119231. doi:10.1016/j.jclepro.2019.119231

Kumar, V., Rahman, Z., & Kazmi, A. A. (2013). Sustainability marketing strategy: An analysis of recent literature. *Global Business Review, 14*(4), 601–625. doi:10.1177/0972150913501598

Kumar, V., Rahman, Z., Kazmi, A. A., & Goyal, P. (2012). Evolution of sustainability as marketing strategy: Beginning of new era. *Procedia: Social and Behavioral Sciences, 37*, 482–489. doi:10.1016/j.sbspro.2012.03.313

Kupiec, P. (1995). Techniques for verifying the accuracy of risk management models. *Journal of Derivatives, 3*(2), 73–84. doi:10.3905/jod.1995.407942

Kuzey, C., & Uyar, A. (2017). Determinants of sustainability reporting and its impact on firm value: Evidence from the emerging market of Turkey. *Journal of Cleaner Production, 143*, 27–39. doi:10.1016/j.jclepro.2016.12.153

Kwaitkowski, D., Phillips, P. C. B., Schmidt, P., & Shin, Y. (1992). Testing the null hypothesis of stationarity against the alternative of a unit root. *Journal of Econometrics, 54*(1-3), 159–178. doi:10.1016/0304-4076(92)90104-Y

Lambin, J. J. (1986). *Le marketing stratégique: fondements, méthodes et applications*. McGraw-Hill.

Lambin, J. J. (2016). *Market-driven management: marketing strategico e operativo*. McGraw-Hill Education.

Lamothe, P., & Méndez, M. (2013). *Opciones Reales: métodos de simulación y valoración*. Ecobook.

Larose, D. T. (2005). *Discovering knowledge in data: An introduction to data mining*. Press, Hoes Lane.

Latham, S. F., & Braun, M. (2009). Managerial risk, innovation, and organizational decline. *Journal of Management, 35*(2), 258–281. doi:10.1177/0149206308321549

Lazard. (2020). *Levelized Cost of Energy and Levelized Cost of Storage – 2020*. New York: Author.

Leal Filho, W., Will, M., Salvia, A. L., Adomssent, M., Grahl, A., & Spira, F. (2019). The role of green and Sustainability Offices in fostering sustainability efforts at higher education institutions. *Journal of Cleaner Production, 232*, 1394–1401. doi:10.1016/j.jclepro.2019.05.273

Lebelle, M., Lajili Jarjir, S., & Sassi, S. (2020). Corporate Green Bond Issuances: An International Evidence. *Journal of Risk and Financial Management, 13*(2), 25. doi:10.3390/jrfm13020025

Lechner, C., & Gudmundsson, S. V. (2014). Entrepreneurial orientation, firm strategy and small firm performance. *International Small Business Journal, 32*(1), 36–60. doi:10.1177/0266242612455034

Lee, J., & Kim, E. (2020). The Influence of Corporate Environmental Responsibility on Overinvestment Behavior: Evidence from South Korea. *Sustainability, 12*(5), 1901. doi:10.3390u12051901

Lee, N., Kotler, P., & Roberto, N. (2002). *Social marketing improving the quality of life*. Sage Publications.

Leonidou, C. N., Katsikeas, C. S., & Morgan, N. A. (2013). Greening the marketing mix: Do firms do it and does it pay off? *Journal of the Academy of Marketing Science, 41*(2), 151–170. doi:10.100711747-012-0317-2

Lerch, M., De-Prada-Gil, M., Molins, C., & Benveniste, G. (2018). Sensitivity analysis on the levelized cost of energy for floating offshore wind farms. *Sustainable Energy Technologies and Assessments, 30*, 77–90. Advance online publication. doi:10.1016/j.seta.2018.09.005

Lettice, F., & Parekh, M. (2010). The social innovation process: Themes, challenges and implications for practice. *International Journal of Technology Management, 51*(1), 139–158. doi:10.1504/IJTM.2010.033133

Lewandovski, M. (2016). Designing the Business Models for Circular Economy–Towards the Conceptual Framework. *Sustainability, 8*(43), 1–28. doi:10.3390u8010043

Liaw, K. T. (2020). Survey of Green Bond Pricing and Investment Performance. *Journal of Risk and Financial Management, 13*(9), 193. doi:10.3390/jrfm13090193

Li, J., & Zhou, S. (2019). Can executives' financial literacy affect the financial exclusion of enterprises? Based on the perspective of financial exclusion of small and medium enterprises. *Journal Central University Finance Economic, 5*, 19–32.

Lim, A., & Tsutsui, K. (2012). Globalization and commitment in corporate social responsibility: Cross-national analyses of institutional and political-economy effects. *American Sociological Review, 77*(1), 69–98. doi:10.1177/0003122411432701

Lim, W. M. (2016). A blueprint for sustainability marketing: Defining its conceptual boundaries for progress. *Marketing Theory*, *16*(2), 232–249. doi:10.1177/1470593115609796

Lindroth, S., & Leijon, M. (2011, December 1). Offshore wave power measurements - A review. In *Renewable and Sustainable Energy Reviews*. Pergamon. doi:10.1016/j.rser.2011.07.123

Ling, Y. A. N., Simsek, Z., Lubatkin, M. H., & Veiga, J. F. (2008). Transformational leadership's role in promoting corporate entrepreneurship: Examining the CEO-TMT interface. *Academy of Management Journal*, *51*(3), 557–576. doi:10.5465/amj.2008.32626023

Linsmeier, T. J., & Pearson, N. D. (2000). Value at risk. *Financial Analysts Journal*, *56*(2), 47–67. doi:10.2469/faj.v56.n2.2343

Liu, B., Wang, J., Chan, K. C., & Fung, A. (2020). The impact of entrepreneurs's financial literacy on innovation within small and medium-sized enterprises. *International Small Business Journal*, *0266242620959073*, 1–19. doi:10.1177/0266242620959073

Locarek-Junge, H., & Prinzler, R. (1998). Estimating value-at-risk using neural networks. In C. Weinhardt, H. M. Selhausen, & M. Morlock (Eds.), *Informations systeme in der Finanzwirtschaft*. Springer. doi:10.1007/978-3-642-60327-3_28

Lodh, S., Nandy, M., & Chen, J. (2014). Innovation and family ownership: Empirical evidence from India. *Corporate Governance*, *22*(1), 4–23. doi:10.1111/corg.12034

Loncar, D., Milovanovic, I., Rakic, B., & Radjenovic, T. (2017). Compound real options valuation of renewable energy projects: The case of a wind farm in Serbia. *Renewable & Sustainable Energy Reviews*, *75*, 354–367. doi:10.1016/j.rser.2016.11.001

López-Bayón, S., González-Díaz, M., Solís-Rodríguez, V., & Fernández-Barcala, M. (2018). Governance decisions in the supply chain and quality performance: The synergistic effect of geographical indications and ownership structure. *International Journal of Production Economics*, *197*, 1–12. doi:10.1016/j.ijpe.2017.12.022

López, I., Arriaga, A., & Pardo, M. (2018). La dimensión social del concepto de desarrollo sostenible: ¿La eternal olvidada? *Revista Española de Sociología*, *27*(1), 25–41. doi:10.22325/fes/res.2018.2

López, M., Veigas, M., & Iglesias, G. (2015). On the wave energy resource of Peru. *Energy Conversion and Management*, *90*, 34–40. doi:10.1016/j.enconman.2014.11.012

Lozano, J. M. (2009). *La empresa ciudadana como empresa responsable y sostenible*. Ed Trotta.

Lu, S. (2019). *FASH455 Global Apparel & Textile Trade and Sourcing*. WTO Reports World Textile and Apparel Trade in 2018.

Lupu, I., Bobirca, A. B., Miclăuş, P. G., & Ciumara, T. (2020). Risk management of companies included in the Euro stoxx sustainability index. An investors' perception. *Amfiteatru Economic*, *22*(55), 707–725. doi:10.24818/EA/2020/55/707

Lusardi, A., & Scheresberg, C. D. B. (2013). *Financial literacy and high-cost borrowing in the United States*. Working Paper (No. w18969). National Bureau of Economic Research.

Lusardi, A., & Mitchell, O. (2014). The economic importance of financial literacy: Theory and Evidence. *Journal of Economic Literature*, *52*(1), 5–44. doi:10.1257/jel.52.1.5 PMID:28579637

Lusardi, A., & Mitchell, O. S. (2007). Baby Boomer Retirement Security: The Role of Planning, Financial Literacy, and Housing Wealth. *Journal of Monetary Economics*, *54*(1), 205–224. doi:10.1016/j.jmoneco.2006.12.001

Lusardi, A., & Mitchell, O. S. (2011). Financial literacy and planning: implications for retirement wellbeing. In A. Lusardi & O. Mitchell (Eds.), *Financial Literacy. Implications for Retirement Security and the Financial Marketplace* (pp. 17–39). Oxford University Press. doi:10.1093/acprof:oso/9780199696819.003.0002

Lusardi, A., & Mitchell, O. S. (2017). How Ordinary Consumers Make Complex Economic Decisions: Financial Literacy and Retirement Readiness. *The Quarterly Journal of Finance*, *7*(3), 1–31. doi:10.1142/S2010139217500082

Lusardi, A., Mitchell, O. S., & Curto, V. (2010). Financial literacy among the young. *The Journal of Consumer Affairs*, *44*(2), 358–380. doi:10.1111/j.1745-6606.2010.01173.x

Lusardi, A., & Tufano, P. (2009). Teach workers about the perils of debt. *Harvard Business Review*, *87*(11), 22–24.

Lusardi, A., & Tufano, P. (2015). Debt literacy, financial experiences, and overindebtedness. *Journal of Pension Economics and Finance*, *14*(4), 332–368. doi:10.1017/S1474747215000232

M'Gonigle, M., & Starke, J. C. (2006). Minding place: Towards a (rational) political ecology of the sustainable university. *Environment and Planning. D, Society & Space*, *24*(3), 325–348. doi:10.1068/d3104

MacKinnon, J. G. (1996). Numerical distribution functions for unit root and cointegration tests. *Journal of Applied Econometrics*, *11*(6), 601–618. doi:10.1002/(SICI)1099-1255(199611)11:6<601::AID-JAE417>3.0.CO;2-T

Macko, A., & Tyszka, T. (2009). Entrepreneurship and risk taking. *Applied Psychology*, *58*(3), 469–487. doi:10.1111/j.1464-0597.2009.00402.x

Madrid Climate Conference (COP25). (2020). *Madrid Climate Conference (COP25).* Retrieved April 23, 2020, from https://www.dsn.gob.es/gl/actualidad/sala-prensa/madrid-cumbre-del-clima-cop25

Mafudi, M., & Suyono, E. (2018). Firm specific attributes and corporate social responsibility disclosure in manufacturing and mining companies: Evidence from Indonesia. *Journal of Economics & Management Perspective*, *12*(4), 14–27.

Malerba, F., & Adams, P. (2014). Sectorial Systems of Innovation. In M. Dodson, D. M. Gann, & N. Phillips (Eds.), The Oxford Handbook of Innovation Management (pp. 183-203). Oxford, UK: University Press.

Mallikarjuna, M., & Rao, R. P. (2019). Evaluation of forecasting methods from selected stock market returns. *Financial Innovation*, *5*(1), 40. doi:10.118640854-019-0157-x

Mancebón, M. J., Ximénez-de-Embún, D. P., Mediavilla, M., & Gómez-Sancho, J. M. (2019). Factors that influence the financial literacy of young Spanish consumers. *International Journal of Consumer Studies*, *43*(2), 227–235. doi:10.1111/ijcs.12502

Mangematin, V., & Nesta, L. (1999). What kind of knowledge can a firm absorb? *International Journal of Technology Management*, *18*(3/4), 149–172. doi:10.1504/IJTM.1999.002771

Manne, H. G. (2006). Milton Friedman Was Right. "Corporate social responsibility" is bunk. *Wall Street Journal, 24.*

Manoochehri, G. (2010). Measuring Innovation: Challenges and Best Practices. California. *Journal of Operations Management*, *8*(1).

March, J. G. (1987). Ambiguity and accounting: The elusive link between information and decision making. *Accounting, Organizations and Society*, *12*(2), 153–168. doi:10.1016/0361-3682(87)90004-3

March, J. G., & Shapira, Z. (1987). Managerial perspectives on risk and risk taking. *Management Science*, *33*(11), 1404–1418. doi:10.1287/mnsc.33.11.1404

Marei, M. I., Mokhtar, M., & El-Sattar, A. A. (2015). MPPT strategy based on speed control for AWS-based wave energy conversion system. *Renewable Energy, 83*, 305–317. doi:10.1016/j.renene.2015.04.039

Marimon, F., del Mar Alonso-Almeida, M., del Pilar Rodríguez, M., & Alejandro, K. A. C. (2012). The worldwide diffusion of the global reporting initiative: What is the point? *Journal of Cleaner Production, 33*, 132–144. doi:10.1016/j.jclepro.2012.04.017

MarineEnergy. (2013). *Sperboy Webpage*. Retrieved August 15, 2019, from https://marineenergy.biz/tag/sperboy/

Maroufkhani, P., Wagner, R., & Ismail, W. K. W. (2018). Entrepreneurial ecosystems: A systematic review. *Journal of Enterprising Communities: People and Places in the Global Economy, 12*(4), 545–564. doi:10.1108/JEC-03-2017-0025

Marriott, D. N., & Mellett, H. (1996). Health care managers' financial skills: Measurement, analysis and implications. *Accounting Education, 5*(1), 61–74. doi:10.1080/09639289600000006

Martinez, R. J., & Dacin, M. T. (1999). Efficiency Motives and Normative Forces: Combining Transactions Costs and Institutional Logic. *Journal of Management, 25*(1), 75–96. doi:10.1177/014920639902500104

Mascareñas, J. (2007). *Opciones reales en la valoración de proyectos de inversión*. Documento de trabajo, Universidad Complutense de Madrid.

Maslov, N., Claramunt, C., Wang, T., & Tang, T. (2017). Method to estimate the visual impact of an offshore wind farm. *Applied Energy, 204*, 1422–1430. doi:10.1016/j.apenergy.2017.05.053

Mason, C., & Brown, R. (2014). Entrepreneurial ecosystems and growth oriented entrepreneurship. *Final report to OECD, 30*(1), 77-102.

Matei, M. (2013). *Responsabilitatea socială a corporaţiilor şi instituţiilor şi dezvoltarea durabilă a României*. Expert Publishing House.

Matei, M., & Voica, M. C. (2013). Social Responsibility in the Financial and Banking Sector. *Economic Insights - Trends and Challenges, 65*(1).

Matten, D., & Moon, J. (2008). "Implicit" and "explicit" CSR: A conceptual framework for a comparative understanding of corporate social responsibility. *Academy of Management Review, 33*(2), 404–424. doi:10.5465/amr.2008.31193458

Matuszak, Ł., & Różańska, E. (2017). CSR disclosure in Polish-listed companies in the light of Directive 2014/95/EU requirements: Empirical evidence. *Sustainability, 9*(12), 2304. doi:10.3390u9122304

Mayring, P. (2015). Qualitative Content Analysis: Theoretical Background and Procedures. In A. Bikner-Ahsbahs, C. Knipping, & N. Presmeg (Eds.), *Approaches to Qualitative Research in Mathematics Education. Advances in Mathematics Education*. Springer. doi:10.1007/978-94-017-9181-6_13

Mazzarol, T. (2014). *Growing and sustaining entrepreneurial ecosystems: what they are and the role of government policy*. White Paper WP01-2014. Small Enterprise Association of Australia and New Zealand (SEAANZ). Retrieved from https://www.iicie.com/uploads/White-Paper/1463661660SEAANZ_WP_01_2014_Mazzarol.pdf

McDonagh, P., & Prothero, A. (2014). Sustainability marketing research: Past, present and future. *Journal of Marketing Management, 30*(11-12), 1186–1219. doi:10.1080/0267257X.2014.943263

McManus, P. (1996). Contested terrains: Politics, stories and discourses of sustainability. *Environmental Politics, 1996*(5), 48–73. doi:10.1080/09644019608414247

Méndez-Suárez, M., Monfort, A., & Gallardo, F. (2020). Sustainable Banking: New Forms of Investing under the Umbrella of the 2030 Agenda. *Sustainability, 12*(5), 2096. doi:10.3390u12052096

Menon, A., & Menon, A. (1997). Enviropreneurial marketing strategy: The emergence of corporate environmentalism as market strategy. *Journal of Marketing*, *61*(1), 51–67. doi:10.1177/002224299706100105

Metaxas, T., & Tsavdaridou, M. (2010). Corporate social responsibility in europe: Denmark, Hungary and Greece. *Journal of Contemporary European Studies*, *18*(1), 25–46. doi:10.1080/14782801003638679

Mieila, M. (Ed.). (2017). *Measuring Sustainable Development and Green Investments in Contemporary Economies*. IGI Global. doi:10.4018/978-1-5225-2081-8

Mihalcova, B., Gallo, P., & Lukac, J. (2020). Management of Innovations in Finance Education: Cluster Analysis for OECD Countries. *Marketing and Management of Innovations*, *1*, 235–244. doi:10.21272/mmi.2020.1-19

Miles, M. P., & Covin, J. G. (2000). Environmental marketing: A source of reputational, competitive, and financial advantage. *Journal of Business Ethics*, *23*(3), 299–311. doi:10.1023/A:1006214509281

Miletic, S., Korenak, B., & Ivanis, I. (2013). Performance of MSCI World Index during the global financial crisis: Value-at-risk approach. *Employment, Education and Entrepreneurship (EEE 2013) Conference Belgrade-Serbia*, 419-436.

Ministerio de educación, cultura y deporte. (2017). *Pisa 2015. Programa para la evaluación internacional de los alumnos. Competencia financiera.* Informe español. Retrieved from https://www.educacionyfp.gob.es/inee/dam/jcr:e9052910-6614-4cd8-8969-02d20ad42c7e/Competencia%20financiera_Inf%20espa%C3%B1ol.pdf

Ministerio de Educación. (2011). *La responsabilidad social de la universidad y el desarrollo sostenible.* https://sede.educacion.gob.es/publiventa/detalle.action?cod=14925

Minton, E., Lee, C., Orth, U., Kim, C. H., & Kahle, L. (2012). Sustainable marketing and social media: A cross-country analysis of motives for sustainable behaviors. *Journal of Advertising*, *41*(4), 69–84. doi:10.1080/00913367.2012.10672458

Missiacos Cárdenas, S. (2016). ¿Por qué necesitamos construir una universidad sustentable? *UC Maule*, (51), 9.

Mitchell, P. (2015). *Employment and the circular economy - Job Creation through resource efficiency in London*. London Sustainable Development Commission, the London Waste and Recycling Board and the Greater London Authority.

Mittal, P., Mitra, K., & Kulkarni, K. (2017). Optimizing the number and locations of turbines in a wind farm addressing energy-noise trade-off: A hybrid approach. *Energy Conversion and Management*, *132*, 147–160. doi:10.1016/j.enconman.2016.11.014

Modigliani, F., & Brumberg, R. H. (1954). Utility Analysis and the Consumption Function: An Interpretation of Cross-Section Data. In K. K. Kurihara (Ed.), *Post-Keynesian Economics* (pp. 388–436). Rutgers University Press.

Molina-García, A., Florido-Ruiz, B., Campos-Valenzuela, M., & Diéguez-Soto, J. (2020). The effect of family ownership and generation on financial literacy. *Small Business International Review*, *4*(1), 1–15. doi:10.26784bir.v4i1.236

Monteiro, S., Ribeiro, V., & Lemos, K. (2020). Linking Corporate Social Responsibility Reporting With the UN Sustainable Development Goals: Evidence From the Portuguese Stock Market. In Conceptual and Theoretical Approaches to Corporate Social Responsibility, Entrepreneurial Orientation, and Financial Performance (pp. 134-151). IGI Global.

Monteiro, T. A., Giuliani, A. C., Antonio, C., Cavazos-Arrollo, J., & Kassouf Pizzinato, N. (2015). Mezcla el marketing verde: Una perspectiva Teórica. *Cuadernos del Cimbage*, *17*, 103–126.

Moraga, G., Huysveld, S., Mathieux, F., Blengini, G. A., Alaerts, L., Van Acker, K., de Meester, S., & Dewulf, J. (2019). Circular economy indicators: What do they measure? *Resources, Conservation and Recycling*, *146*, 452–461. doi:10.1016/j.resconrec.2019.03.045 PMID:31274959

Moravcikova, D., Krizanova, A., Kliestikova, J., & Rypakova, M. (2017). Green Marketing as the Source of the Competitive Advantage of the Business. *Sustainability*, *9*(12), 2218. doi:10.3390u9122218

Moreiras, M. A. N., López, S. F., & Búa, M. V. (2019). El Efecto de la Innovación en el Empleo: Análisis de las Empresas Cotizadas Españolas. *European Journal of Applied Business and Management*, *5*(1).

Moreno, D., & Olmeda, I. (2007). Is the predictability of emerging and developed stock markets really exploitable? *European Journal of Operational Research*, *182*(1), 436–454. doi:10.1016/j.ejor.2006.07.032

Morris, M. H., Webb, J. W., Fu, J., & Singhal, S. (2013). A Competency-Based Perspective on Entrepreneurship Education: Conceptual and Empirical Insights. *Journal of Small Business Management*, *51*(3), 352–369. doi:10.1111/jsbm.12023

MSCI. (2020). *MSCI Emerging Markets Index*. https://www.msci.com/emerging-markets

Mwangi, W. P., & Cheluget, J. (2018). Role of Financial Literacy, Financial Innovation, Financial Inclusion on SME Access to Credit in Kenya: A Case of Kumisa SACCO. *Journal of Finance and Accounting*, *2*(2), 1–18.

Myers, S. & Marquis, D.G. (1969). *Successful industrial innovations. A study of factors Underlying Innovation in Selected Firms*. Academic Press.

Myers, S. (1977). Determinants of Corporate Borrowing. *Journal of Financial Economics*, *5*(2), 147–175. doi:10.1016/0304-405X(77)90015-0

Myhr, A., Bjerkseter, C., Ågotnes, A., & Nygaard, T. A. (2014). Levelised cost of energy for offshore floating wind turbines in a life cycle perspective. *Renewable Energy*, *66*, 714–728. doi:10.1016/j.renene.2014.01.017

Mytilinou, V., & Kolios, A. J. (2019). Techno-economic optimisation of offshore wind farms based on life cycle cost analysis on the UK. *Renewable Energy*, *132*, 439–454. doi:10.1016/j.renene.2018.07.146

Nelson, B. D. (1991). Conditional heteroskedasticity in asset returns: A new approach. *Econometrica*, *59*(2), 347–370. doi:10.2307/2938260

Niesten, E., Jolink, A., & Chappin, M. (2018, January). Investments in the Dutch onshore wind energy industry: A review of investor profiles and the impact of renewable energy subsidies. In *Renewable and Sustainable Energy Reviews*. Elsevier Ltd. doi:10.1016/j.rser.2017.06.056

Nilsson, L., Persson, P. O., Rydén, L., Darozhka, S., & Zaliauskiene, A. (2007). *Cleaner Production: Technologies and Tools for Resource Efficient Production*. Baltic University Press.

Nour, A. I., Sharabati, A. A. A., & Hammad, K. M. (2020). Corporate Governance and Corporate Social Responsibility Disclosure. *International Journal of Sustainable Entrepreneurship and Corporate Social Responsibility*, *5*(1), 20–41. doi:10.4018/IJSECSR.2020010102

Nti, I. K., Adekoya, A. F., & Weyori, B. A. (2020). A systematic review of fundamental and technical analysis of stock market predictions. *Artificial Intelligence Review*, *53*(4), 3007–3057. doi:10.100710462-019-09754-z

Nunes, M., Oliveira, E., Mello, V. E., Áquila, G., Souza, L. C., & Rotela, P. (2017). Oil price volatility: A real option valuation approach in an African oil field. *Journal of Petroleum Science Engineering*, *150*, 297–304. doi:10.1016/j.petrol.2016.12.024

Nunnally, J. C. (1978). *Psychometric theory*. McGraw-Hill., doi:10.2307/1161962

O'Connor, M., Lewis, T., & Dalton, G. (2013). Techno-economic performance of the Pelamis P1 and Wavestar at different ratings and various locations in Europe. *Renewable Energy*, *50*, 889–900. doi:10.1016/j.renene.2012.08.009

OCDE. (2005). *Manual de Oslo: Diretrizes para a recolha e interpretação de dados sobre a inovação* (3rd ed.). Paris: Author.

OECD (2014). *PISA 2012 Results: Students and Money: Financial Literacy Skills for the 21st Century (Volume 6)*. OECD Publishing. doi:10.1787/9789264208094-en

OECD. (2002). *Towards Sustainable Household Consumption? Trends and Policies in OECD Countries*. OECD.

OECD. (2005). *Oslo Manual. Guidelines for collecting and interpreting innovation data*. OECD Publishing.

OECD. (2005). *Recommendation on principles and good practices for financial education and awareness*. Retrieved from https://www.oecd.org/finance/financial-education/35108560.pdf

OECD. (2010). *PISA 2012 Financial literacy framework*. OECD Publishing.

OECD. (2012). *Gender Equality in Education, Employment and Entrepreneurship: Final Report to the MCM 2012*. Retrieved from https://www.oecd.org/employment/50423364.pdf

OEDE. (2014). *PISA 2012 Results: Students and Money. Financial Literacy Skills for the 21st Century, 6*. OECD Publishing.

Official Journal of the European Union, & EC. Directive 2009/28/EC of the European Parliament and of the Council of 23 April 2009 on the promotion of the use of energy from renewable sources and amending and subsequently repealing Directives 2001/77/EC and 2003/30/EC (2009). Belgium: Official Journal of the European Union.

OIV. (2004). Resolution OIV/CST 1/2004. Definition of Sustainable Vitiviniculture. Paris: OIV.

Opon, J., & Henry, M. (2020). A multicriteria analytical framework for sustainability evaluation under methodological uncertainties. *Environmental Impact Assessment Review*, *83*(April), 106403. doi:10.1016/j.eiar.2020.106403

Orazalin, N., & Mahmood, M. (2018). Economic, environmental, and social performance indicators of sustainability reporting: Evidence from the Russian oil and gas industry. *Energy Policy*, *121*, 70–79. doi:10.1016/j.enpol.2018.06.015

Ortas, E., Álvarez, I., & Garayar, A. (2015). The environmental, social, governance, and financial performance effects on companies that adopt the United Nations Global Compact. *Sustainability*, *7*(2), 1932–1956. doi:10.3390u7021932

Ortiz Nicolas, P. (2007). *Las cuatro llaves: marketing de cambio social*. Ed Signo.

OskayB.LinssenT.Van VlietT.BoumanB.PasmaN. (2017). Advancing financial risk estimates by incorporating GARCH into Value at risk. doi:10.2139srn.3137587

Ottman, J. A., Stafford, E. R., & Hartman, C. L. (2006). Avoiding green marketing myopia: Ways to improve consumer appeal for environmentally preferable products. *Environment*, *48*(5), 22–36. doi:10.3200/ENVT.48.5.22-36

Oyewole, P. (2001). Social costs of environmental justice associated with the practice of green marketing. *Journal of Business Ethics*, *29*(3), 239–251. doi:10.1023/A:1026592805470

Özçalışıcı, M. (2016). Yapay sinir ağları ile çok aşamalı fiyat tahmini: BIST30 senetleri üzerine bir araştırma. *Dokuz Eylül Üniversitesi İktisadi ve İdari Bilimler Fakültesi Dergisi*, *31*(2), 209–227. doi:10.24988/deuiibf.2016312517

Palazzo, M., Vollero, A. & Siano, A. (2020). From strategic corporate social responsibility to value creation: an analysis of corporate website communication in the banking sector. *International Journal of Bank Marketing*. doi:10.1108/IJBM-04-2020-0168

Panait, M., Radulescu, I., & Brezoi, A. (2020). Financial Markets–Under the Sign of CSR. Some Evidences Regarding Financial Education. *LUMEN Proceedings, 11*, 96-106.

Panait, M., Voica, M. C., & Radulescu, I. (2014). The activity of capital market actors: Under the sign of social responsibility. *Procedia Economics and Finance*, *8*, 522–528. doi:10.1016/S2212-5671(14)00123-3

Pankov, S., Velamuri, V. K., & Schneckenberg, D. (2019). Towards sustainable entrepreneurial ecosystems: Examining the effect of contextual factors on sustainable entrepreneurial activities in the sharing economy. *Small Business Economics*. Advance online publication. doi:10.100711187-019-00255-5

Pantaleo, A., Pellerano, A., Ruggiero, F., & Trovato, M. (2005). Feasibility study of off-shore wind farms: An application to Puglia region. *Solar Energy*, *79*(3), 321–331. doi:10.1016/j.solener.2004.08.030

Papadas, K. K., Avlonitis, G. J., & Carrigan, M. (2017). Green marketing orientation: Conceptualization, scale development and validation. *Journal of Business Research*, *80*, 236–246. doi:10.1016/j.jbusres.2017.05.024

Páramo Morales, D. (2016). Una Aproximación al marketing social. *Pensamiento & Gestión.*, *41*, 7–12.

Patton, J. (2007). Metrics for Knowledge-based project organizations. *Advanced Management Journal*, *71*(1).

Pauliuk, S. (2018). Critical appraisal of the circular economy standard BS8001:2017 and a dashboard of quantitative system indicators for its implementation in organizations. *Resources, Conservation and Recycling*, *129*, 81–92. doi:10.1016/j.resconrec.2017.10.019

Peattie, K. (2015). Sustainability marketing. In Handbook of research on sustainable consumption. Edward Elgar Publishing. doi:10.4337/9781783471270.00014

Peattie, K., & Charter, M. (2003). Green marketing. In The Marketing Book. Academic Press.

Peattie, K. (2001). Towards sustainability: The third age of green marketing. *The Marketing Review*, *2*(2), 129–146. doi:10.1362/1469347012569869

Peattie, K., & Belz, F. M. (2010). Sustainability marketing—An innovative conception of marketing. *Marketing Review St. Gallen*, *27*(5), 8–15. doi:10.100711621-010-0085-7

Peattie, K., & Crane, A. (2005). Green marketing: Legend, myth, farce or prophesy. *Qualitative Market Research*, *8*(4), 357–370. doi:10.1108/13522750510619733

Pego, A., Marques, M., Salvador, R., Guedes Soares, C., & Monteiro, A. (2016). The potential offshore energy cluster in Portugal. In *Progress in Renewable Energies Offshore - Proceedings of 2nd International Conference on Renewable Energies Offshore, RENEW 2016*. 10.1201/9781315229256-102

Pejić Bach, M., Starešinić, B., Omazić, M. A., Aleksić, A., & Seljan, S. (2020). m-Banking Quality and Bank Reputation. *Sustainability*, *12*(10), 4315. doi:10.3390u12104315

Pelamis. (2012). *Pelamis wave power*. Retrieved from http://www.pelamiswave.com/

Peng, M. W., Wang, D. Y., & Jiang, Y. (2008). An institution-based view of international business strategy: A focus on emerging economies. *Journal of International Business Studies*, *39*(5), 920–936. doi:10.1057/palgrave.jibs.8400377

Pérez, A., López-Gutiérrez, C., & García de los Salmones, M. M. (2019). Do all CSR news affect market value equally? *Social Responsibility Journal*, *16*(8), 1107–1123. doi:10.1108/SRJ-03-2019-0116

Perez-Batres, L. A., Miller, V. V., & Pisani, M. J. (2011). Institutionalizing sustainability: An empirical study of corporate registration and commitment to the United Nations global compact guidelines. *Journal of Cleaner Production*, *19*(8), 843–851. doi:10.1016/j.jclepro.2010.06.003

Pérez-Collazo, C., Greaves, D., & Iglesias, G. (2015). A review of combined wave and offshore wind energy. *Renewable & Sustainable Energy Reviews*, *42*, 141–153. doi:10.1016/j.rser.2014.09.032

Petrescu, A. G., Bîlcan, F. R., Petrescu, M., Holban Oncioiu, I., Türkeş, M. C., & Căpuşneanu, S. (2020). Assessing the Benefits of the Sustainability Reporting Practices in the Top Romanian Companies. *Sustainability*, *12*(8), 3470. doi:10.3390u12083470

Phillips, P. C., & Perron, P. (1988). Testing for a unit root in time series regression. *Biometrika*, *75*(2), 335–346. doi:10.1093/biomet/75.2.335

Pici, E., Pasmaciu, J., Hysa, E., Hoxhaj, J., & Hodo, M. (2014). Evaluation of millennium development goals process: Case of Albania. *Mediterranean Journal of Social Sciences*, *5*(14), 33. doi:10.5901/mjss.2014.v5n14p33

Piciocchi, P., Vollero, A., & Palazzo, M. (2009). Towards the integration between corporate community relations and CSR communication strategies. The ENEL case study. *Esperienze d'Impresa*, *17*(2).

Pillai, A. C., Chick, J., Khorasanchi, M., Barbouchi, S., & Johanning, L. (2017). Application of an offshore wind farm layout optimization methodology at Middelgrunden wind farm. *Ocean Engineering*, *139*(December), 287–297. doi:10.1016/j.oceaneng.2017.04.049

Pinto, H. (2012). *Inovação estratégica na indústria têxtil e do vestuário nacional: estudo de caso.* Dissertação de Mestrado. Universidade do Minho.

Pizer, D. J., Retzler, C., Henderson, R. M., Cowieson, F. L., Shaw, M. G., Dickens, B., & Hart, R. (2005). Pelamis WEC - Recent advances in the numerical and experimental modelling programme. *6th European Wave and Tidal Energy Conference.*

Poças, A. (2015). *O contributo da inovação para a competitividade das organizações Estudo de caso.* Instituto Politécnico de Viana do Castelo.

Polèse, M., & Stren, R. E. (2000). *The Social Sustainability of Cities: Diversity and the Management of Change.* University of Toronto Press. doi:10.3138/9781442682399

Popescu, C. R. G., & Popescu, G. N. (2019). An exploratory study based on a questionnaire concerning green and sustainable finance, corporate social responsibility, and performance: Evidence from the Romanian business environment. *Journal of Risk and Financial Management*, *12*(4), 162. doi:10.3390/jrfm12040162

Porter, M. E., & Kramer, M. R. (2002). The competitive advantage of corporate philanthropy. *Harvard Business Review*, *80*(12), 56–68. PMID:12510538

Porter, M. E., & Kramer, M. R. (2006). Strategy and society: The link between competitive advantage and corporate social responsibility. *Harvard Business Review*, *84*(12), 78–88. PMID:17183795

Potting, J., Hekkert, M., Worrell, E., & Hanemaaijer, A. (2017). *Circular economy: measuring innovation in the product chain. Policy report.* PBL Netherlands Environmental Assessment Agency.

Prendeville, S., & Bocken, N. (2017). Design for Remanufacturing and Circular Business Models. In M. Matsumoto, K. Masui, S. Fukushige, & S. Kondoh (Eds.), *Sustainability Through Innovation in Product Life Cycle Design. EcoProduction (Environmental Issues in Logistics and Manufacturing).* Springer. doi:10.1007/978-981-10-0471-1_18

Preston, F. (2012). *A Global Redesign? Shaping the Circular Economy. Briefing Paper.* Chatham House.

Pringles, R., Olsina, F., & Penizzotto, F. (2020). Valuation of defer and relocation options in photovoltaic generation investments by a stochastic simulation-based method. *Renewable Energy*, *151*, 846–864. doi:10.1016/j.renene.2019.11.082

Prothero, A., McDonagh, P., & Dobscha, S. (2010). Is green the new black? Reflections on a green commodity discourse. *Journal of Macromarketing*, *30*(2), 147–159. doi:10.1177/0276146710361922

Pucheta-Martínez, M. C., & Gallego-Álvarez, I. (2018). Environmental reporting policy and corporate structures: An international analysis. *Corporate Social Responsibility and Environmental Management*, *25*(5), 788–798. doi:10.1002/csr.1494

Purani, K., Sahadev, S., & Kumar, D. S. (2014). Globalization and academic research: The case of sustainability marketing. *IIM Kozhikode Society & Management Review*, *3*(1), 93–99. doi:10.1177/2277975214520910

Purvis, B., Mao, Y., & Robinson, D. (2019). Three pillars of sustainability: In search of conceptual origins. *Sustainability Science*, *14*(3), 681–695. doi:10.100711625-018-0627-5

Quoquab, F., Mohamed Sadom, N. Z., & Mohammad, J. (2020). *Sustainable Marketing*. The Palgrave Handbook of Corporate Social Responsibility.

Rahman, I., Park, J., & Chi, C. G. Q. (2015). Consequences of "greenwashing": Consumers' reactions to hotels' green initiatives. *International Journal of Contemporary Hospitality Management*, *27*(6), 1054–1081. doi:10.1108/IJCHM-04-2014-0202

Raimi, L., Akhuemonkhan, I., & Ogunjirin, O. D. (2015). Corporate Social Responsibility and Entrepreneurship (CSRE): Antidotes to poverty, insecurity and underdevelopment in Nigeria. *Social Responsibility Journal*, *11*(1), 56–81. doi:10.1108/SRJ-11-2012-0138

Raimi, L., Fadipe, A. O., & Shokunbi, M. O. (2020). Responsible Investment (RI): An Alternative Funding Option for Roads-Bridges Management in Nigeria Under the Public-Private Partnership Framework. *International Journal of Economic Behavior*, *5*(1), 43–57.

Rakic, B., & Rakic, M. (2015). Holistic management of marketing sustainability in the process of sustainable development. *Environmental Engineering and Management Journal*, *14*(4), 887–900. doi:10.30638/eemj.2015.100

Ramasastry, A. (2015). Corporate social responsibility versus business and human rights: Bridging the gap between responsibility and accountability. *Journal of Human Rights*, *14*(2), 237–259. doi:10.1080/14754835.2015.1037953

Ramesh, B., Dieguez, T., Ferreira, L. P., & Silva, F. J. G. (2018). A Strategy to Reinforce the Textile and Clothing Sector Cluster in Portugal. *Transdisciplinary Engineering Methods for Social Innovation of Industry 4.0: Proceedings of the 25th ISPE.*

Ramísio, P., Pinto, L. M. C., Gouveia, N., Costa, H., & Arezes, D. (2019). Sustainability Strategy in Higher Education Institutions: Lessons learned from a nine-year case study. *Journal of Cleaner Production*, *222*, 300–309. doi:10.1016/j.jclepro.2019.02.257

Rauch, A., Wiklund, J., Lumpkin, G. T., & Frese, M. (2009). Entrepreneurial orientation and business performance: An assessment of past research and suggestions for the future. *Entrepreneurship Theory and Practice*, *33*(3), 761–787. doi:10.1111/j.1540-6520.2009.00308.x

Raworth, K. (2017). *Doughnut Economics. Seven Ways to Think Like a 21st-Century Economist*. Random House Business.

Rebelo, J., & Caldas, J. (2013). The Douro wine region: A cluster approach. *Journal of Wine Research*, *24*(1), 19–37. doi:10.1080/09571264.2012.717220

Rech, S. R. (2006). *Cadeia produtiva da moda: um modelo conceitual de análise da competitividade no elo confecção*. Tese (Doutorado em Engenharia de Produção). Universidade Federal de Santa Catarina – Programa de Pós-Graduação em Engenharia de Produção.

Redding, G. (2005). The thick description and comparison of societal systems of capitalism. *Journal of International Business Studies, 36*(2), 123–155. doi:10.1057/palgrave.jibs.8400129

Rezaei Mirghaed, M., & Roshandel, R. (2013). Site specific optimization of wind turbines energy cost: Iterative approach. *Energy Conversion and Management, 73*, 167–175. doi:10.1016/j.enconman.2013.04.016

Richtnér, A. (2017). *Creating Better Innovation Measurement Practices*. Academic Press.

Ringov, D., & Zollo, M. (2007). Corporate responsibility from a socio-institutional perspective. The impact of national culture on corporate social performance. *Corporate Governance, 7*(4), 476–485. doi:10.1108/14720700710820551

Ripoll, F. S., & Hervás-Oliver, J. L. (2011). ¿Qué explica la innovación en PyMEs? *Dirección y Organización*, (43), 5–15.

Ritala, P., & Almpanopoulou, A. (2017). In defense of 'eco' in innovation ecosystem. *Technovation, 60–61*, 39–42. doi:10.1016/j.technovation.2017.01.004

Rivera-Hernández, J. E., Alcántara-Salinas, G., Blanco-Orozco, N. V., & Houbron, E. P. (2017). ¿Desarrollo sostenible o sustentable? La controversia de un concepto. *Revista Posgrado y Sociedad, 15*(1), 57–67. doi:10.22458/rpys.v15i1.1825

Rizos, V., Tuokko, K., & Behrens, A. (2017). *The Circular Economy: A review of definitions, processes and impacts*. CEPS Research Report No 2017/8, April 2017.

Rodríguez Rad, C. J., Sánchez del Rio Vásquez, M. E., Navarro García, A., Rondan Cataluña, F. J., & Pérez Méndez, M. B. (2018). Adaptación de la distribución minorista al consumidor ecológico: el caso de España y Alemania. In J. A. Trespalacios Gutiérrez, R. Vázquez Casielles, E. Estrada Alonso, & C. González Mieres (Eds.), *Nuevos horizontes del marketing y de la distribución comercial* (pp. 355–376). Cátedra Fundación Ramón Areces de Distribución Comercial.

Rogers, J. (2002). *Strategy*. Value and Risk – The Real Options Approach.

Rosário, I. (2011). *Gestão de Inovação numa empresa de serviços de engenharia civil*. Dissertação de Mestrado da Faculdade de Engenharia da Universidade do Porto, Mestrado em Engenharia Civil – Especialização em Construções.

Rosenbusch, N., Brinckmann, J., & Bausch, A. (2011). Is innovation always beneficial? A meta-analysis of the relationship between innovation and performance in SMEs. *Journal of Business Venturing, 26*(4), 441–457. doi:10.1016/j.jbusvent.2009.12.002

Ross, S., Westerfield, R., & Jordan, B. (2010). *Fundamentos de Finanzas Corporativas*. McGraw-Hill.

Rubiano, D. (2011). *Risco, Incerteza e aversão à inovação: o Setor de Automação Industrial e a Demanda Tecnológica da Indústria de Petróleo e Gás Natural no Brasil*. Dissertação de Mestrado do Instituto de Economia da Universidade Federal do Rio de Janeiro, Mestrado em Ciências Económicas.

Ruiz-Corbella, M., & Bautista-Cerro, M. J. (2016). La responsabilidad social en la universidad española. *Teoría De La Educación. Revista Interuniversitaria, 28*(1, 1 (en-jun)), 159–188. doi:10.14201/teoredu2016281159188

Sahay, A. (2011). Philanthropy, CSR and sustainability. In Green Technologies: Concepts, Methodologies, Tools and Applications (pp. 1281-1304). IGI Global.

Sak, H., Senior, A., & Beaufays, F. (2014). *Long Short-Term Memory Based Recurrent Neural Network Architectures for Large Vocabulary Speech Recognition*. arXiv:1402.1128.

Samadi, S. (2017). The Social Costs of Electricity Generation—Categorising Different Types of Costs and Evaluating Their Respective Relevance. *Energies, 10*(3), 356. doi:10.3390/en10030356

Sannino, G., Lucchese, M., Zampone, G., & Lombardi, R. (2020). Cultural dimensions, Global Reporting Initiatives commitment, and corporate social responsibility issues: New evidence from Organisation for Economic Co-operation and Development banks. *Corporate Social Responsibility and Environmental Management*, *27*(4), 1–11. doi:10.1002/csr.1914

Santillo, D. (2007). Reclaiming the definition of sustainability. *Environmental Science and Pollution Research International*, *14*(1), 60–66. doi:10.1065/espr2007.01.375 PMID:17352129

Santos, G., Braga, A., Lima, V., Teixeira, P., & Sá, J. (2018). Value creation through quality and innovation - a case study on Portugal. *The TQM Journal*.

San, V., Spoann, V., & Schmidt, J. (2018). Industrial pollution load assessment in Phonm Penh, Cambodia using an industrial pollution projection system. *The Science of the Total Environment*, *615*, 990–999. doi:10.1016/j.scitotenv.2017.10.006 PMID:29751449

Sarkar, C., & Kotler, P. (2018). *Brand Activism: From Purpose to Action*. Idea Bite Press.

Sauvé, S., Bernard, S., & Sloan, P. (2016). Environmental sciences, sustainable development and circular economy: Alternative concepts for trans-disciplinary research. *Environmental Development*, *17*, 48–56. doi:10.1016/j.envdev.2015.09.002

Savlovschi, L. I., & Robu, N. R. (2011). The role of SMEs in modern economy. *Economia. Seria Management*, *14*(1), 277–281.

Scaringella, L., & Radziwon, A. (2018). Innovation, entrepreneurial, knowledge, and business ecosystems: Old wine in new bottles? *Technological Forecasting and Social Change*, *136*, 59–87. doi:10.1016/j.techfore.2017.09.023

Schaltegger, S., Lüdeke-Freund, F., & Hansen, E. (2016). Business models for sustainability: A co-evolutionary analysis of sustainable entrepreneurship, innovation, and transformation. *Organization & Environment*, *29*(3), 264–289. doi:10.1177/1086026616633272

Schumpeter, A. J. (1934). *The Theory of Economic Development: An Inquiry into Profits, Capital, Credit, Interest, and the Business Cycle*. Harvard Economic Studies.

Schumpeter, A. J. (1939). *Business Cycle: A Theoretical, Historical, and Statistical Analysis of the Capitalist Process*. McGraw-Hill.

SDSN. (2020). *Accelerating Education for the SDGS in Universities. A Guide for Universities, Colleges, and Tertiary and Higher Education Institutions*. New York: Sustainable Development Solutions Network (SDSN). https://irp-cdn.multiscreensite.com/be6d1d56/files/uploaded/accelerating-education-for-the-sdgs-in-unis-web.pdf

Seguin, G., & Leeuwen, C. V. (2006). The Concept of Terroir in Viticulture. *Journal of Wine Research*, *17*(1), 1–10. doi:10.1080/09571260600633135

Sehovac, L., & Grolinger, K. (2020). Deep Learning for Load Forecasting: Sequence to Sequence Recurrent Neural Networks with Attention. *IEEE Access: Practical Innovations, Open Solutions*, *8*, 36411–36426. doi:10.1109/ACCESS.2020.2975738

Sellers-Rubio, R., & Nicolau-Gonzalbez, J. L. (2016). Estimating the willingness to pay for a sustainable wine using a Heckit Model. *Wine Economics and Policy*, *5*(2), 96–104. doi:10.1016/j.wep.2016.09.002

Sen, A. (1993). Capability and well-being. In M. Nussbaum & A. Sen (Eds.), *The quality of life* (pp. 30–53). Clarendon Press. doi:10.1093/0198287976.003.0003

Sen, A. (1997). Maximization and the Act of Choice. *Econometrica*, *65*(4), 745–779. doi:10.2307/2171939

Sen, A. (2004). Capabilities, lists, and public reason. *Feminist Economics*, *10*(3), 77–80. doi:10.1080/1354570042000315163

Sen, A. (2013). The ends and means of sustainability. *Journal of Human Development, 14*(1), 6–20.

Shen, C. H., Lin, S. J., Tang, D. P., & Hsiao, Y. J. (2016). Self-control, financial literacy and harmful consumer credit behavior in Taiwan market. *Academia Economic Papers, 44*(2), 251–294.

Sheth, J., & Sisodia, R. (2005). A Dangerous Divergence: Marketing and Society. *Journal of Public Policy & Marketing, 24*(1), 160–162. doi:10.1509/jppm.24.1.160.63896

Shwetzer, C., Maritz, A., & Nguyen, Q. (2019). Entrepreneurial ecosystems: A holistic and dynamic approach. *Journal of Industry-University Collaboration, 1*(2), 79–95. doi:10.1108/JIUC-03-2019-0007

Sichigea, M., Siminica, M. I., Circiumaru, D., Carstina, S., & Caraba-Meita, N. L. (2020). A Comparative Approach of the Environmental Performance between Periods with Positive and Negative Accounting Returns of EEA Companies. *Sustainability, 12*(18), 7382. doi:10.3390u12187382

Siemens Gamesa. (2020). *Costes de la energía eólica Redefinimos el precio de la electricidad.* Author.

Sierra-Garcia, L., Garcia-Benau, M. A., & Bollas-Araya, H. M. (2018). Empirical analysis of non-financial reporting by Spanish companies. *Administrative Sciences, 8*(3), 29. doi:10.3390/admsci8030029

Silva, C. (2018). *Os desperdícios da Indústria Têxtil.* Dissertação de Mestrado. Instituto Politécnico do Cávado e do Ave.

Siminica, M., Ionascu, C., & Sichigea, M. (2019). Corporate Social Performance versus Financial Performance of the Romanian Firms. *Prague Economic Papers, 28*(1), 49–69. doi:10.18267/j.pep.687

Siminica, M., & Sichigea, M. (2018). Corporate Social Responsibility as a Voluntary Initiative but a Mandatory Non-financial Reporting Link Between the Social and Financial Performance of Romanian Companies. In *Current Issues in Corporate Social Responsibility* (pp. 77–96). Springer. doi:10.1007/978-3-319-70449-4_6

Simionescu, L. N., & Dumitrescu, D. (2018). Empirical study towards corporate social responsibility practices and company financial performance. Evidence for companies listed on the Bucharest Stock Exchange. *Sustainability, 10*(9), 3141. doi:10.3390u10093141

Simões, V. C. (2015). *Gestão da Inovação.* Apontamentos do Mestrado em Gestão e Estratégia Industrial. Instituo Superior de Economia e Gestão.

Singh, I., & Evans, J. (2010). Natural resource-based sustainable development using a cluster approach. In J. Richards (Ed.), *Mining, Society, and a Sustainable World* (pp. 183–201). Springer.

Sistema Universitario de Galicia. (2016). *Plan galego de financiamento universitario 2016-2020.* https://www.udc.es/export/sites/udc/goberno/_galeria_down/vepes/documentos/planfinanciamento20162020.pdf_2063069294.pdf

Sivam, A., Dieguez, T., Ferreira, L., & Silva, F. (2019). Key settings for successful Open Innovation Arena. *Journal of Computational Design and Engineering, 6*(4), 507–515. doi:10.1016/j.jcde.2019.03.005

Smith, M. (1993). *Neural networks for statistical modeling.* Van Nostrand Reinhold.

Snijkers, G., & Willimack, D. (2011). The missing link: from concepts to questions ineconomic surveys. *Proceedings of the 2nd European Establishment StatisticsWorkshop (EESW11).*

Spigel, B. (2017). The relational organization of entrepreneurial ecosystems. *Entrepreneurship Theory and Practice, 41*(1), 49–72. doi:10.1111/etap.12167

Spinelli, S., Timmons, J. A., & Adams, R. J. (2011). *New venture creation: Entrepreneurship for the 21st century* (9th ed.). McGraw-Hill Education.

SSE. (2020). *Sustainable Stock Exchanges.* https://sseinitiative.org/

Stam, E. (2015). Entrepreneurial ecosystems and regional policy: A sympathetic critique. *European Planning Studies, 23*(9), 1759–1769. doi:10.1080/09654313.2015.1061484

Stam, E. (2018). Measuring Entrepreneurial Ecosystems. In A. O'Connor, E. Stam, F. Sussan, & D. Audretsch (Eds.), *Entrepreneurial Ecosystems. Place-Based Transformations and Transitions* (pp. 173–196). Springer.

Stam, E., & van de Ven, A. (2019). Entrepreneurial ecosystem elements. *Small Business Economics*, 1–24.

Stango, V., & Zinman, J. (2007). *Fuzzy math and red ink: When the opportunity cost of consumption is not what it seems* (Working Paper). Retrieved from http://legacy.iza.org/en/papers/Zinman12072007.pdf

Stango, V., & Zinman, J. (2009). Exponential growth bias and household finance. *The Journal of Finance, 64*(6), 2807–2849. doi:10.1111/j.1540-6261.2009.01518.x

Starček, S., & Trunk, A. (2013). The meaning and concept of financial education in the society of economic changes. *International Conference Active Citizenship by Knowledge Management & Innovation.*

Stellner, C., Klein, C., & Zwergel, B. (2015). Corporate social responsibility and Eurozone corporate bonds: The moderating role of country sustainability. *Journal of Banking & Finance, 59*, 538–549. doi:10.1016/j.jbankfin.2015.04.032

Su, B., Heshmati, A., Geng, Y., & Yu, X. (2013). A review of the circular economy in China: Moving from rhetoric to implementation. *Journal of Cleaner Production, 42*, 215–227. doi:10.1016/j.jclepro.2012.11.020

Su, J., Watchravesringkan, K., Zhou, J., & Gil, M. (2019). Sustainable clothing: Perspectives from US and Chinese young Millennials. *International Journal of Retail & Distribution Management, 47*(11), 1141–1162. doi:10.1108/IJRDM-09-2017-0184

Sulaiman, N. (2016). *The Impact of Financial Knowledge and Capabilities on SME Firm Performance in Australia.* RMIT University.

Sung, S. Y., & Choi, J. N. (2018). Effects of training and development on employee outcomes and firm innovative performance: Moderating roles of voluntary participation and evaluation. *Human Resource Management, 57*(6), 1339–1353. doi:10.1002/hrm.21909

Sun, Y., Kim, K. H., & Kim, J. (2014). Examining relationships among sustainable orientation, perceived sustainable marketing performance, and customer equity in the fast fashion industry. *Journal of Global Fashion Marketing, 5*(1), 74–86. doi:10.1080/20932685.2013.866319

Sustainability Campus Webpage. (n.d.). https://www.udc.es/es/campus_sustentabilidade/

Szadziewska, A., Spigarska, E., & Majerowska, E. (2018). The disclosure of non-financial information by stock-exchange-listed companies in Poland, in the light of the changes introduced by the Directive 2014/95/EU. *Zeszyty Teoretyczne Rachunkowości, 2018*(99), 65–95. doi:10.5604/01.3001.0012.2933

Szirmai, A., Naudé, W., & Goedhuys, M. (2011). *Entrepreneurship, innovation, and economic development.* Oxford University Press. doi:10.1093/acprof:oso/9780199596515.001.0001

Tait, P., Saunders, C., Dalziel, P., Rutherford, P., Driver, T., & Guenther, M. (2019). Estimating wine consumer preferences for sustainability attributes: A discrete choice experiment of Californian Sauvignon blanc purchasers. *Journal of Cleaner Production, 233*, 412–420. doi:10.1016/j.jclepro.2019.06.076

Taques, F.H., López, M.G., Basso, L.F. & Areal, N. (2020). Indicators used to measure service innovation and manufacturing innovation. *Journal of Innovation & Knowledge.* . doi:10.1016/j.jik.2019.12.001

Teece, D. J. (2018). Business models and dynamic capabilities. *Long Range Planning, 51*(1), 40–49. doi:10.1016/j.lrp.2017.06.007

Tegen, S., Hand, M., Maples, B., Lantz, E., Schwabe, P., & Smith, A. (2012). 2010 Cost of Wind Energy. *Contract (New York, N.Y.), 303*, 275–3000.

Thakur, B. P. S., & Kannadhasan, M. (2019). Corruption and cash holdings: Evidence from emerging market economies. *Emerging Markets Review, 38*, 1–17. doi:10.1016/j.ememar.2018.11.008

Thogersen, J. (2010). Country Differences in Sustainable Consumption: The Case of Organic Food. *Journal of Macromarketing, 30*(2), 171–185. doi:10.1177/0276146710361926

Thomas, N. J. (2018). Sustainability marketing. The need for a realistic whole systems approach. *Journal of Marketing Management, 34*(17-18), 1530–1556. doi:10.1080/0267257X.2018.1547782

Tian, G., Zhou, S., & Hsu, S. (2020). Executive financial literacy and firm innovation in China. *Pacific-Basin Finance Journal, 62*, 101348. doi:10.1016/j.pacfin.2020.101348

Tidd, J., & Bessant, J. (2009). *Managing Innovation - Integrating Technological, Market and Organizational Change*. John Wiley & Sons.

Timbate, L., & Park, C. K. (2018). CSR performance, financial reporting, and investors' perception on financial reporting. *Sustainability, 10*(2), 522. doi:10.3390u10020522

Tiwari, A. K., Shahbaz, M., & Islam, F. (2013). Does financial development increase rural-urban income inequality? *International Journal of Social Economics, 40*(2), 151–168. doi:10.1108/03068291311283616

Tiwari, S., Tripathi, D. M., Srivastava, U., & Yadav, P. K. (2011). Green marketing-emerging dimensions. *Journal of Business Excellence, 2*(1), 18.

Tollin, K., Christensen, L. B., & Wilke, R. (2017). Sustainability in business from a marketing perspective. *Journal of Strategic Marketing, 23*(6), 471–496. doi:10.1080/0965254X.2014.991348

Trencher, G., Yarime, M., McCormick, K. B., Doll, C. N., & Kraines, S. B. (2014). Beyond the third mission: Exploring the emerging university function of co-creation for sustainability. *Science & Public Policy, 41*(2), 151–179. doi:10.1093cipolct044

Trianni, A., Cagno, E., & Neri, A. (2017). Modeling barriers to the adoption of industrial sustainability measures. *Journal of Cleaner Production, 168*, 1482–1504. doi:10.1016/j.jclepro.2017.07.244

Trigeorgis, L. (1996). *Real Options: Managerial Flexibility and Strategy in Resource Allocation*. MIT Press.

Trippi, R. R. (1995). *Artificial intelligence in finance and investing: state-of-the-art Technologies for securities selection and portfolio management* (1st ed.). McGraw-Hill, Inc.

Tsay, R. (2010). *Analysis of financial time series* (3rd ed.). John Wiley & Sons. doi:10.1002/9780470644560

Tsujimoto, M., Kajikawa, Y., Tomita, J., & Matsumoto, Y. (2018). A review of the ecosystem concept – Towards coherent ecosystem design. *Technological Forecasting and Social Change, 136*, 49–58. doi:10.1016/j.techfore.2017.06.032

Tukker, A. (2004). Eight types of product–service system: Eight ways to sustainability? Experiences from SusProNet. *Business Strategy and the Environment, 13*(4), 246–260. doi:10.1002/bse.414

Tukker, A. (2015). Product services for a resource-efficient and circular economy - A review. *Journal of Cleaner Production, 97*, 76–91. doi:10.1016/j.jclepro.2013.11.049

Turan, F., Cetinkaya, S., & Ustun, C. (2016). A methodological framework to analyze stakeholder preferences and propose strategic pathways for a sustainable university. *Higher Education*, *72*(6), 743–760. doi:10.100710734-015-9973-8

Uğuz, S. (2019). *Makine öğrenmesi teorik yönleri ve python uygulamaları ile bir yapay zeka ekolü*. Nobel Akademik Yayıncılık Eğitim Danışmanlık Tic. Ltd. Şti. ANKARA.

ULSF. (1990). *Talloires Declaration*. http://ulsf.org/talloires-declaration/

ULSF. (2001). *Global Higher Education for Sustainability Partnership (GHESP) is Launched in December 2000*. https://ulsf.org/global-higher-education-for-sustainability-partnership-ghesp-is-launched-in-december-2000/

UNEP & Sida. (2006). Applying Cleaner Production to MEAs – Global Status Report. United Nations Environment Programme, Division of Technology, Industry and Economics.

UNESCO. (2005). *United Nations Decade of Education for Sustainable Development (2005-2014): International Implementation Scheme*. https://unesdoc.unesco.org/ark:/48223/pf0000148654

United Nations Development Programme (UNDP). (2020). Retrieved from http://hdr.undp.org/en/content/human-development-index-hdi

United Nations Framework Convention on Climate Change. (2015). *Paris Agreement*. Retrieved from https://unfccc.int/files/meetings/paris_nov_2015/application/pdf/paris_agreement_english_.pdf

United Nations, European Commission, International Monetary Fund, Organisation for Economic Cooperation and Development, & World Bank. (2003). Handbook of National Accounting: Integrated Environmental and Economic Accounting 2003. United Nations.

United Nations. (2015, October). *Resolution adopted by the General Assembly on 25 September 2015*. Retrieved 28/02/2018, from General Assembly: http://www.un.org/ga/search/view_doc.asp?symbol=A/RES/70/1&Lang=E

Universidade da Coruña. (2013). *Plan Estratéxico UDC 2020*. https://www.udc.es/export/sites/udc/goberno/_galeria_down/vepes/documentos/PLAN1320.pdf_2063069294.pdf

Universidade da Coruña. (n.d.a). *Informes Green Campus Centros UDC 2019*. https://www.udc.es/es/sociedade/medio_ambiente/GreenCampus/

Universidade da Coruña. (n.d.b). *Organigrama*. https://www.udc.es/es/transparencia/egoberno/organigrama/

Universidade de Santiago de Compostela. (n.d.a). *Desarrollo sostenible*. https://www.usc.gal/es/usc/institucional/desarrollo-sostenible

Universidade de Santiago de Compostela. (n.d.b). *Mecenazgo*. https://www.usc.gal/es/usc/mecenazgo

Universidade de Vigo. (n.d.a). *Cátedras*. https://www.uvigo.gal/es/universidad/contratar-colaborar-universidad/proyectos-abiertos-colaboracion/catedras

Universidade de Vigo. (n.d.b). *Green Campus*. https://www.uvigo.gal/campus/pontevedra-campus-crea/green-campus

Universidade de Vigo. (n.d.c). *Responsabilidad social y Agenda 2030*. https://www.uvigo.gal/es/universidad/conocenos/responsabilidad-social-agenda-2030

Universidade de Vigo. (n.d.d). *Sostibilidade-OMA*. http://oma.webs.uvigo.es/Sostibilidade/Inicio.php

Uyar, A., Karaman, A. S., & Kilic, M. (2019). Institutional drivers of sustainability reporting in the global tourism industry. *Tourism Economics*, 1–24. doi:10.1177/1354816619886250

Uysal, T. U., Kurt, G., & Karabulut, A. N. (2019). Are Social Marketing Investments Used as a Tool for Voluntary Reporting or Disclosure? In *Advanced Methodologies and Technologies in Digital Marketing and Entrepreneurship* (pp. 597–609). IGI Global.

Van Dam, Y. K., & Apeldoorn, P. A. (1996). Sustainable marketing. *Journal of Macromarketing*, *16*(2), 45–56. doi:10.1177/027614679601600204

van der Borgh, M., Cloodt, M., & Romme, A. G. L. (2012). *Value creation by knowledge-based Business Ecosystems*. Harper Business.

Van Rooij, M., Lusardi, A., & Alessie, R. (2011). Financial literacy and stock market participation. *Journal of Financial Economics*, *101*(2), 449–472. doi:10.1016/j.jfineco.2011.03.006

Van Weelden, E., Mugge, R., & Bakker, C. (2016). Paving the way towards circular consumption: WBCSD. *Circular Metrics: Landscape Analysis*. Retrieved from https://www.wbcsd.org/Programs/Circular-Economy/Factor-10/Metrics-Measurement/Resources/Landscape-analysis

Varey, R. J. (2010). Marketing means and ends for a sustainable society: A welfare agenda for transformative change. *Journal of Macromarketing*, *30*(2), 112–126. doi:10.1177/0276146710361931

Varey, R. J. (2011). A sustainable society logic for marketing. *Social Business*, *1*(1), 69–83. doi:10.1362/204440811X570563

Vaz, N., Fernandez-Feijoo, B., & Ruiz, S. (2016). Integrated reporting: An international overview. *Business Ethics (Oxford, England)*, *25*(4), 577–591. doi:10.1111/beer.12125

Veigas, M., López, M., & Iglesias, G. (2014). Assessing the optimal location for a shoreline wave energy converter. *Applied Energy*, *132*, 404–411. doi:10.1016/j.apenergy.2014.07.067

Velt, H., Torkkeli, L., & Laine, I. (2020). Entrepreneurial Ecosystem Research: Bibliometric Mapping of the Domain. *Journal of Business Ecosystems*, *1*(2), 43–83. doi:10.4018/JBE.20200701.oa1

Verbano, C., & Venturini, K. (2013). Managing risks in SMEs: A literature review and research agenda. *Journal of Technology Management & Innovation*, *8*(3), 186–197. doi:10.4067/S0718-27242013000400017

Vergamini, D., Bartolini, F., Prosperi, P., & Brunori, G. (2019). Explaining regional dynamics of marketing strategies: The experience of the Tuscan wine producers. *Journal of Rural Studies*, *72*, 136–152. doi:10.1016/j.jrurstud.2019.10.006

Vieira, F. (2007). *Distritos industriais e inovação: o setor dos moldes em Portugal*. Tese de Doutoramento. Universidade do Minho.

Vinetur. (2018). *Ribeira Sacra celebrará en octubre el III desafío Vía Romana*. Retrieved from https://www.vinetur.com/2018042246919/ribeira-sacra-celebrara-en-octubre-el-iii-desafio-via-romana.html

Voica, C., & Panait, M. (2017). Foreign Banks' Activity in Romania - Under the Sign of Ethics and CSR or Under the Profit's Sign? *Journal of Financial and Monetary Economics*, *4*, 439–447.

Voica, M. C. (2017). Financial inclusion as a tool for sustainable development. *Romanian Journal of Economics*, *44*(1), 121–129.

Voinea, C. L., Logger, M., Rauf, F., & Roijakkers, N. (2019). Drivers for Sustainable Business Models in Start-Ups: Multiple Case Studies. *Sustainability*, *11*(24), 6884. doi:10.3390u11246884

Vollero, A., Palazzo, M., Siano, A., & Elving, W. J. (2016). Avoiding the greenwashing trap: Between CSR communication and stakeholder engagement. *International Journal of Innovation and Sustainable Development*, *10*(2), 120–140. doi:10.1504/IJISD.2016.075542

Volosevici, D. (2013). Corporations—between Governance and Social Responsibility: The European Commission Approach. *Economic Insights - Trends and Challenges, 65*(2).

Von Gaudecker, H. (2015). How does household portfolio diversification vary with financial literacy and financial advice? *The Journal of Finance, 70*(2), 489–507. doi:10.1111/jofi.12231

Vukić, N. M., Omazić, M. A., Pejic-Bach, M., Aleksić, A., & Zoroja, J. (2020). Leadership for Sustainability: Connecting Corporate Responsibility Reporting and Strategy. In Leadership Styles, Innovation, and Social Entrepreneurship in the Era of Digitalization (pp. 44-72). IGI Global.

Walczak, S. (2004). Forecasting emerging market indexes with neural networks. In Neural Networks in Business Forecasting. Idea Group Publishing.

Wang, H., Liang, P., Li, H., & Yang, R. (2016). Financing Sources, R&D Investment and Enterprise Risk. *Procedia Computer Science, 91*, 122–130. doi:10.1016/j.procs.2016.07.049

Wang, Y., & Poutziouris, P. (2010). Entrepreneurial risk taking: Empirical evidence from UK family firms. *International Journal of Entrepreneurial Behaviour & Research, 16*(5), 370–388. doi:10.1108/13552551011071841

Wärneryd, K. E. (1988). The psychology of innovative entrepreneurship. doi:10.1007/978-94-015-7791-5_11

Wav, E. C. (2012). *Web Page OWC Pico Plant*. Retrieved August 14, 2019, from http://www.pico-owc.net/en/

Wavebob. (2013). *Wavebob Webpage*. Retrieved from http://www.wavebob.com

WCED. (1987). *Report of the World Commission on Environment and Development: Our Common Future*. Retrieved from https://sustainabledevelopment.un.org/content/documents/5987our-common-future.pdf

Web page. (2016). *Wave Dragon Technology*. Retrieved September 7, 2016, from http://www.wavedragon.net

Weinstein, A., Fredrikson, G., Claeson, L., Forsberg, J., Parks, M. J., Nielsen, K., . . . Andersen, T. L. (2003). AquaBuOY-the offshore wave energy converter numerical modeling and optimization. In Oceans 2003. Celebrating the Past ... Teaming Toward the Future (IEEE Cat. No.03CH37492) (pp. 1988-1995). IEEE. doi:10.1109/OCEANS.2003.178203

Wettstein, F. (2012). CSR and the debate on business and human rights: Bridging the great divide. *Business Ethics Quarterly*, •••, 739–770.

Whitehead, B., Andrews, D., Shah, A., & Maidment, G. (2014). Assessing the environmental impact of data centres part 1: Background, energy use and metrics. *Building and Environment, 82*, 151–159. doi:10.1016/j.buildenv.2014.08.021

Widdowson, D., & Hailwood, K. (2007). Financial literacy and its role in promoting a sound financial system. *Reserve Bank of New Zealand Bulletin, 70*(2).

Wieczorek, A., Negro, S., Harmsen, R., Heimeriks, G., Luo, L., & Hekkert, M. P. (2013). A review of the European offshore wind innovation system. *Renewable & Sustainable Energy Reviews, 26*, 294–306. doi:10.1016/j.rser.2013.05.045

Wiklund, J., & Shepherd, D. (2005). Entrepreneurial orientation and small business performance: A configurational approach. *Journal of Business Venturing, 20*(1), 71–91. doi:10.1016/j.jbusvent.2004.01.001

Willer, H., & Lernoud, J. (2018). *The World of Organic Agriculture: Statistics and Emerging Trends 2018*. Frick: Research Institute of Organic Agriculture (FiBL).

Wind Europe. (2018). *Offshore wind in Europe*. doi:10.1016/S1471-0846(02)80021-X

Wind Europe. (n.d.). *Wind energy in Europe in 2018*. Author.

Witjes, S., & Lozano, R. (2016). Towards a more Circular Economy: Proposing a framework linking sustainable public procurement and sustainable business models. *Resources, Conservation and Recycling, 112*, 37–44. doi:10.1016/j.resconrec.2016.04.015

Woolley, J. (2017). *Infrastructure for entrepreneurship*. Oxford Research Encyclopedia of Business and Management. Retrieved and printed from business.oxfordre.com

Word Energy Council (WEC). (2016). World Energy Scenarios 2016. *World Energy Council, 1*, 9–18. Retrieved from https://www.worldenergy.org/wp-content/uploads/2016/10/World-Energy-Scenarios-2016_Full-Report.pdf

World Bank. (2020). *Worldwide Governance Indicators*. Retrieved from https://info.worldbank.org/governance/wgi/

World Business Council for Sustainable Development (WBCSD). (2002). *Sustainable development reporting: Striking the balance*. Retrieved from http://docs.wbcsd.org/2002/12/SustainableDevReporting-StrikingTheBalance.pdf

World Economic Forum. (2013). *Young Global Leaders: Circular Economy Innovation & New Business Models Dialogue*. Retrieved from http://www3.weforum.org/docs/WEF_YGL_CircularEconomyInnovation_PositionPaper_2013.pdf

World Voices Nexus. (n.d.). *Own-Income Generation: A Pillar of Financial Sustainability in Institutions of Higher Learning*. https://www.worldcces.org/58/post/2019/11/own-income-generation-a-pillar-of-financial-sustainability-in-institutions-of-higher-learning.html

Wörsdörfer, D., Lier, S., & Crasselt, N. (2017). Real options-based evaluation model for transformable plant designs in the process industry. *Journal of Manufacturing Systems, 42*, 29–43. doi:10.1016/j.jmsy.2016.11.001

Xiao, C., Wang, Q., van der Vaart, T., & van Donk, D. P. (2018). When does corporate sustainability performance pay off? The impact of country-level sustainability performance. *Ecological Economics, 146*, 325–333. doi:10.1016/j.ecolecon.2017.11.025

Yang, Q. Z., Zhou, J., & Xu, K. (2014). A 3R Implementation Framework to Enable Circular Consumption in Community. *International Journal of Environmental Sciences and Development, 5*(2), 217–222. doi:10.7763/IJESD.2014.V5.481

Ye, J., & Kulathunga, K. M. M. C. B. (2019). How does financial literacy promote sustainability in SMEs? A developing country perspective. *Sustainability, 11*(10), 2990. doi:10.3390u11102990

Yemm, R., Pizer, D., Retzler, C., & Henderson, R. (2012). Pelamis: experience from concept to connection. *Philosophical Transactions. Series A, Mathematical, Physical, and Engineering Sciences, 370*(1959), 365–380. doi:10.1098/rsta.2011.0312

Yılmaz, A. (2020). *Yapay Zeka*. Kodlab Yayın Dağıtım Yazılım ve Eğitim Hizmetleri San. ve Tic. Ltd. Şti.

Ylitalo, P. (2017). *Value creation metrics in systematic idea generation*. Tese Doutoral de Tecnologia e Ciências Naturais da Universidade de Oulu, Linnanmaa.

Yüksel, R., & Akkoç, S. (2016). Altın fiyatlarının yapay sinirağları ile tahmini bir uygulama. *Doğuş Üniversitesi Dergisi, 1*(17), 39–50. doi:10.31671/dogus.2018.41

Zabihian, F., & Fung, A. S. (2011). Review of marine renewable energies: Case study of Iran. *Renewable & Sustainable Energy Reviews, 15*(5), 2461–2474. doi:10.1016/j.rser.2011.02.006

Zahra, S. A. (2005). Entrepreneurial risk taking in family firms. *Family Business Review, 18*(1), 23–40. doi:10.1111/j.1741-6248.2005.00028.x

Zakoian, J. M. (1994). Threshold heteroskedastic models. *Journal of Economic Dynamics & Control, 18*(5), 931–955. doi:10.1016/0165-1889(94)90039-6

Zaman, G., Panait, M. C., Voica, M. C., & Ene, C. (2020). Corporate Social Responsibility in the Agri-Food Sector. Recent Advancements in Sustainable. doi:10.4018/978-1-7998-2347-6.ch003

Zamfir, A. M., Mocanu, C., & Grigorescu, A. (2017). Circular economy and decision models among European SMEs. *Sustainability*, *9*(9), 1507. doi:10.3390u9091507

Zhao, Y., & Thompson, P. (2019). Investments in managerial human capital: Explanations form prospect and regulatory focus theories. *International Small Business Journal*, *37*(4), 365–394. doi:10.1177/0266242619828264

Zucca, G., Smith, D. E., & Mitry, D. J. (2009). Sustainable viticulture and winery practices in California: What is it, and do customers care? *International Journal of Wine Research*, 189-194.

About the Contributors

Joaquín Enríquez-Díaz is a full time assistant professor in the Department of Business of the Universidade da Coruña. He is a BSc in Economics and MSc in Banking and Finance. Joaquín is currently a PhD student at the Universidade da Coruña. His research interests include: Economic and financial analysis of innovation barriers and drivers, financial economic education and teaching Innovation. Author of scientific publications of international impact in these topics. He also obtained a predoctoral research support from the Galician Plan for Research, Innovation and Growth of the Consellería de Cultura.

Laura Castro-Santos is an Industrial Engineer by the University of A Coruña. Her PhD in Industrial Engineering was obtained in 2013 at the University of A Coruña. She has collaborated in several national and international research projects in the field of offshore renewable energies, some of them in several research stays in Portugal. She has published lots of papers related to offshore renewable energies (offshore wind and waves) in international journals and she assisted to international conferences in this field. Nowadays, she is Lecturer and teach several subjects at the Naval and Industrial Engineering Department at the University of A Coruña.

Felix Puime Guillén has a degree in C.C. Economic and Business Administration from the University of Santiago de Compostela. Doctor in Business Administration and Management from the University of Vigo. Professor Doctor of the Department of Business of the University of A Coruña. Regular professor of Business Schools in Spain, Europe and Latin America. Author of numerous publications in specialized financial journals Speaker at national and international scientific conferences. He has more than 32 years of experience in the business world in the field of corporate finance, both nationally and internationally.

* * *

Begoña Alvarez García is a Lecturer in the Department of Business at the Universidade da Coruña (Spain). She has also been a lecturer at the University of Paris IX-Dauphine (France) and the Coordinator of the Master in Banking and Finance at the Universidade da Coruña. She holds a PhD degree in Economy and Management from the Universidade da Coruña and she was given an Extraordinary Doctorate Award. She has completed several research stages in the Universities of Paris-Dauphine and the Massachusetts Institute of Technology (MIT). She has participated in several European and national research projects and she has published several books related to financial topics.

Sinem Ates has a PhD degree in Business Administration from Galatasaray University. She has been working in Yalova University and teaching accounting courses such as Introduction to Accounting, Financial Accounting, New Concepts in Accounting and Finance, Computer-Based Accounting Practices. Her main research interests include IFRS, value relevance, sustainability accounting, and accounting education.

Barbara Bradač Hojnik is an Associate Professor of Entrepreneurship at the Faculty of Economics and Business, University of Maribor, and is teaching entrepreneurship at the Faculty. In the last years she participates in almost twenty national and international research projects. She is a member of Slovenian Entrepreneurship Observatory research team, of Global Entrepreneurship Monitor Slovenia team, and of the research programme Entrepreneurship for Innovative Society. She participated in numerous international scientific conferences and is the author or co-author of several scientific articles, books and chapters in scientific monographs. Her research focuses primarily on entrepreneurship in general, corporate entrepreneurship, social, environmental and sustainable entrepreneurship, entrepreneurship policy, entrepreneurship ecosystem, and SMEs.

Marta Campos Valenzuela is a Financial Literacy and Corporate Social Responsibility researcher at the University of Malaga, belonging to the Department of Finance and Accounting (Faculty of Economic and Business Sciences) and part of the Chair of Business Viability at the University of Malaga. She has a double degree in Law and Business Administration and Management, as well as a Master's Degree in Legal Practice at the Center for Financial Studies (Madrid). One year of the degree completed in Strasbourg (France) and stays in Canada and at the Britany of France. Applied in financial literacy and CSR in small and medium enterprises and family businesses. Currently a PhD student in Economics and Business. She has experience in the development of different activities aimed at business ethics and the promotion of innovative and entrepreneurial activities, such as the Family Business Seminar, aimed at developing tasks to improve the decisions of family businesses. He has also coordinated various conferences on family business and Financial Education such as the XX International AECA Congress or the XXXVI EBEN Spain Congress (European Business Ethics Network).

Emre Çevik has completed her BA degree in Econometrics Department, Faculty of Economics and Administrative Sciences, Dokuz Eylül University. Dr. Çevik has completed her MA and PhD degree in Econometrics Department, Institute of Social Sciences, Marmara University. Dr. Çevik, who has been working as Research Assistant in Econometrics Department, Faculty of Economics and Administrative Sciences in Kırklareli University. He is interested in non-linear time series analysis, macro economics, and financial market.

David Cordal-Iglesias has a higher technical certificate in computer application development and a higher technical certificate in computer systems from Rodolfo Ucha Piñeiro, Ferrol. Research support assistant at the University of A Coruña in the SEARENEW research project. Previously, he was working in the European Interreg research project Arcwind, where he is studying the floating offshore wind platforms built using concrete. Author of several research papers.

Teresa Dieguez is a Doctor on Economics, MBA on Prospective and Organizational Strategy, Master on Innovation and Technological Transfer, Specialist on Strategy and Entrepreneurship, Phd Student on Social Development and Sustainability.

Julio Diéguez-Soto is an Associate Professor of Finance and Accounting at the University of Málaga (Spain). He is the Director of the Finance and Accounting Department and the Academic Director of Firm Feasibility Chair. His main research interests include Performance, Capital Structure, Innovation, Professionalization and MCS in Family Firms. He has published his latest research findings in International journals such as Small Business Economics, Journal of Small Business Management, Family Business Review, Journal of Family Business Strategy, Business Research Quarterly, Review of Managerial Science, Canadian Journal of Administrative Sciences, Innovation: Organization and Management, Journal of Scientific and Industrial Research, and Review of Business Management, among others.

Almudena Filgueira Vizoso obtained her PhD at the University of A Coruña in 2012. She currently has a position as associate professor since 2013 and develop her research and her classes at the Higher Polytechnic School of the University of A Coruña. She has a research six-year term complement (sexenio), she has directed two PhD (one in 2017 and one in 2019; mark: cum laude). She has participated in several research projects and she has published papers in recognized research journals.

Carmen Gago-Cortés has a PhD in Economics by the University of A Coruna (UDC), Spain, from 2017. Assistant Professor in the Business Department of the Faculty of Economics and Business (UDC) from 2015. She emphasizes her research in the field of sustainable development. She is the author of scientific publications of international impact in this area. This positioning has seen recognized with the obtaining of different awards, as the Outstanding Paper in the 2016 Emerald Literati Network Awards for Excellence. In 2018, she was given an Extraordinary Doctorate Award. At labor level, she has been the coordinator of different types of Rental Housing Programs of the regional government of Galicia (Spain) from 2006 to 2012.

Raquel González Castro is assistant research in the Department of Business of the Universidade da Coruña, Spain. She is BSc in Business Administration and Management. Her research interests include management, finance, sustainability, and subjects related to the interactions between social and economic issues. Currently she works as a financial consultant for OVB Allfinanz.

Sandra Hernández Zelaya is an assistant professor of the Faculty of Communication in the Pontifical University of Salamanca, where she teaches various subjects related with marketing areas. She has a doctorate in Human and Social Sciences from Pontifical University of Salamanca. She has academic experience as a professor and researcher in national and foreign universities. Currently she continues her research work and is part of the research team of the faculty of communication at Pontifical University of Salamanca, whose name is innovation and entrepreneurial creativity. As part of the dissemination activities of her research, she has participated in different national and international congresses. In the same line, she has participated as a reviewer of academic journals and has different publications focused on marketing and communications.

Carlos Hervés-Beloso is a full professor at Vigo University. He has a long experience as a teacher and researcher in several universities, in Spain and abroad. Carlos Hervés-Beloso is the head of RGEAF, a research group of ECOBAS (Economics and Business Administration for Society) founded by Xunta de Galicia.

Razvan Ionescu is entrepreneur in the IT industry since 2010. Holds a bachelor's degree in Public Administration from the Dimitrie Cantemir Christian University in Bucharest as well as a master's degree in Economics from the Petroleum-Gas University of Ploiesti. His research interests include Financial Markets, Behavioral Finance, Corporate Governance and Corporate Social Responsibility, Financial Technology.

Radulescu Irina is member of Faculty of Economic Sciences from Petroleum-Gas University of Ploiesti since 2004. Between 2016-2020 she was the head of Business Administration Department and now she is the dean of the faculty. She has experience in coordinating international projects being involved in Phare projects or European funded projects related to development of innovative skills. The main research interests are international trade, the dark side of global economy (the phenomenon of corruption, arms trade, shadow economy etc.), digital economy.

Eloi Jorge has over 10 years of experience in the wine sector, with a rollout in several areas such as TV show co-producer; business plans development and international and domestic events participation. This experience, allowed him to has the necessary bases to embrace a new cycle with an approach to the wine sector from an academic perspective, starting with the MSc in Entrepreneurship and Internationalization and the Ph.D. in Economic Analysis and Business Strategy. Elói Jorge collaborates on the date with the research group ECOBAS - RGEAF.

Suzan Kantarcı Savaş has completed her BA degree in Statistics Department, Faculty of Science, Ege University. Dr. Kantarcı-Savaş has completed her MA and PhD degree in Statistics Field, Graduate School of Natural and Applied Sciences, Dokuz Eylül University. Dr. Kantarcı-Savaş, who has been working as Research Assistant Dr. in Econometrics Department, Faculty of Economics and Administrative Sciences in Kırklareli University. She is interested in applied statistics, multivariate statistics, machine learning, fuzzy logic, and optimization.

Isabel Lamas-Galdo has a PhD in Industrial Engineering. Since 2008 she is an associate professor at University of Coruña, degrees of Industrial Engineering, Mechanical Engineering and Naval Engineering. She has written 5 books and several papers in scientific journals. Besides, she has participated in several national and international congresses. She also has professional experience in engineering projects.

Angeles Longarela-Ares is a researcher on finance, sustainability, energy efficiency investments and economics of education. Author of scientific publications of international impact in those areas. Assistant professor in the Business Department of the Faculty of Economics and Business (UDC) from 2015. She obtained research support from the Galician Plan for Research, Innovation and Growth 2011-2015 (I2C Plan) of the Consellería de Cultura, Educación y Ordenación Universitaria of the Xunta de Galicia from 2015 to 2018.

Sofía Louise Martínez-Martínez is an Entrepreneurship and Innovation researcher at the University of Málaga, belonging to the Vice-Rectorate of Social Innovation and Entrepreneurship (Link by UMA-Atech) and part of the Chair of Sustainable Entrepreneurship. She has a university degree in Business Management and a university degree in Law and has developed International Management studies at the Technische Hochschule Nürnberg Georg Simon Ohm (Germany) in 2015, and at the Pontifical Catholic University of Lima (Perú) in 2017. Master in Applied Sociology focused on research methods and techniques in Social Science and currently PhD student in Business and Economics. She has experience in developing different activities for promoting entrepreneurship spirit, as the University-Business Ecosystem Forum, that encourage the transfer of research results and the creation of technology-based companies. She has been coordinator in Málaga of the International Entrepreneurship program Explorer, created by CISE (Santander International Entrepreneurship Center) in collaboration with Link By UMA-Atech (University of Málaga) and the Technology Park of Andalusia. She is also part of the GEM (Global Entrepreneurship Monitor) researching group of Spain. She develops research in the fields of Entrepreneurial University, finance of academic spinoff, entrepreneurial competences and innovation.

Estefanía Mourelle is a researcher on macroeconomics and econometrics, specially international economics and nonlinear models; also, introduction to economics of education. Senior lecturer in the Economics Department of the Faculty of Economics and Business (UDC).

António Monteiro de Oliveira is researcher at the Centre for Intercultural Studies (CEI) and senior lecture at ISCAP (P.Porto). Phd in Economic Analysis and Business Strategy, MSc in Entrepreneurship and Internationalization, founding member of Entrepreneurs Academy – National Portuguese Young Entrepreneur Association and a member of the Mentors Portuguese National Network, as well as of the Portuguese Guilds of Certified Accountants and Economists. He was secretary in the Portuguese National Evaluation Committee of Private Higher Education and in the Portuguese National Evaluation Committee of Higher Education. He is also involved in various national and international projects related with Entrepreneurship promotion.

Mirela Panait currently holds the position of PhD Associate Professor at Faculty of Economic Sciences, Petroleum-Gas University of Ploiesti (Romania). She is also scientific researcher at Institute of National Economy from Romanian Academy. Her work experience derives from and includes: teaching courses and seminaries; research activities; participating in scientific conferences; reviewer for several international scientific journals and conferences. Regarding research activities, these are represented by publishing seven books and over 100 scientific papers in the field of interest: foreign investment, capital market, corporate social responsibility and sustainable development. She has published articles in leading international journals, including Land Use Policy, Energies, Sustainability and PlosOne. She is reviewer for journals and conferences like Sustainability, Energies, Journal of Risk and Financial Management. She is also guest editor or associate editor for prestigious journals from MDPI group or IGI Global publishing house.

Raisa Pérez-Vas is PhD student at the Faculty of Economics and Business at University of Vigo (Spain). She collaborates in the M.A. Finance at the University of Vigo. Her research interest include real options and valuation of investment projects.

Fernando Reyes Reina is currently affiliated as Adjunct Professor to the faculty of Communications of the Pontifical University of Salamanca and to the Faculty of Economics and Business of the University of Salamanca. He is also currently Associate Editor of Business Ethics, the Environment & Responsibility. He has participated in several national and international conferences and received several awards for his research.

Husam Rjoub is currently an Assistant Professor in the Faculty of Economics and Administrative Sciences, Cyprus International University. He received his MA and Ph.D. (Banking and Finance) from Near East University in 2007 and 2013 respectively. Both MA and Ph.D. dissertations focused on determinants of bank profitability. He has teaching experience of more than 10 years in the areas of Banking, Finance, Economics, and Management. Currently, he is the coordinator of the Doctorate of Business Administration (DBA) at Cyprus International University. His main research interests are Asset Pricing (CAPM, APT, F&F) and International Finance (FDI). He has presented many research papers at international and national conferences. His publications appear in many prestigious international refereed journals indexed in the web of science and Scopus. He serves as Editorial Board and referee for a list of prestigious international journals. Also, he joined a conference program committee (IBIMA).

María Elena Rodríguez Benito is a assistant professor in the areas of marketing and communications at Universidad Pontificia de Salamanca (UPSA). Her research areas are marketing ethics, sustanaibility and social innovation. She is a member of the research team of innovations and business creativity in the Faculty of communications at Universidad Pontificia de Salamanca.

Esin Cumhur Yalçın has completed her BA degree in Econometrics Department, Faculty of Economics and Administrative Sciences, Dokuz Eylül University. Dr. Yalçın has completed her MA and PhD degree in Econometrics Department, Institute of Social Sciences, Dokuz Eylül University. Dr. Yalçın, who has been working as Assist. Prof. Dr. in Econometrics Department, Faculty of Economics and Administrative Sciences, in Kırklareli University. She is interested in applied statistics, multivariate statistics, time series analysis and structural equation modelling.

Index

F

G

H

I

L

M

N

O

P

R

S

T

U

V

W

www.ingramcontent.com/pod-product-compliance
Lightning Source LLC
LaVergne TN
LVHW062141300926
849161LV00010B/2596

* 9 7 8 1 7 9 9 8 7 6 3 4 2 *